THE
CAMBRIDGE EDITION OF
THE WORKS OF
JOSEPH CONRAD

THE WORKS OF JOSEPH CONRAD

A PERSONAL RECORD

MR. JOSEPH CONRAD.

JOSEPH CONRAD

A PERSONAL RECORD

EDITED BY
ZDZISŁAW NAJDER
AND
J. H. STAPE

CAMBRIDGE
UNIVERSITY PRESS

CAMBRIDGE UNIVERSITY PRESS
Cambridge, New York, Melbourne, Madrid, Cape Town, Singapore, São Paulo, Delhi

Cambridge University Press
The Edinburgh Building, Cambridge CB2 8RU, UK

Published in the United States of America by
Cambridge University Press, New York

www.cambridge.org
Information on this title: www.cambridge.org/9780521861762

First published 2008

Printed in the United Kingdom at the University Press, Cambridge

A catalogue record for this publication is available from the British Library

ISBN   978-0-521-86176-2 hardback

Published in association with

Center for Conrad Studies
Institute for Bibliography and Editing
Kent State University

Preparation of this volume has been supported by

Research and Graduate Studies, Kent State University
The Kent State University Foundation

CONTENTS

ILLUSTRATIONS

Photograph of Joseph Conrad by C. G. Beresford (1904),
frontispiece to Nelson 1916 edition of *A Personal Record*   *frontispiece*

Figures

Maps

PREFACE

JOSEPH CONRAD'S place in twentieth-century literature is now firmly established. His novels, stories, and other writings have become integral to modern thought and culture. Yet the need for an accurate and authoritative edition of these works remains. Owing to successive rounds of authorial revision, transmissional errors, and deliberate editorial intervention, Conrad's texts exist in various unsatisfactory and sometimes confused forms. In his last years he attempted to have his works published in a uniform edition that would fix and preserve them for posterity. But though trusted by scholars, students, and general readers alike, the received texts in the British and American collected editions published since 1921 have proved to be at least as defective as their predecessors. The Cambridge Edition, grounded in thorough research on the original documents, is designed to reverse this trend by presenting Conrad's novels, stories, and other prose in texts that are as trustworthy as modern scholarship can make them.

The present volume contains critical texts of *A Personal Record* and its two prefatory statements, 'A Familiar Preface' and the 'Author's Note'. The Cambridge text of *A Personal Record* is based on the serial text with the following exceptions: Chapter 1 is based on the surviving revised serial proofs; the conclusion of Chapter 3 is based on the proof state recoverable in a published facsimile; a brief passage in chapter 6 is based on the sole surviving manuscript leaf. These texts incorporate readings drawn from later authoritative documents as well as editorial emendations as does the text of 'A Familiar Preface' (based on the holograph manuscript) and the 'Author's Note' (based on the revised state of the first typescript).

The 'Introduction' provides a literary history of the work focussed on its genesis, development, and reception and its place in Conrad's life and art. The essay on 'The Texts' traces its textual history, examining the sources of the texts and explaining the policies followed in editing them. The apparatus records basic textual evidence, documenting the discussion of genealogy and authority in 'The Texts' as well as other editorial decisions, while the 'Notes' comment on specific readings that require glosses or involve special textual problems. Although they may interest the great variety of readers, the 'Introduction' and 'Notes' are written primarily for an audience of non-specialists, whereas the textual essay and apparatus are intended for the scholar and specialist.

This volume follows certain policies and conventions observed throughout the Cambridge Edition. The pages of the text contain line numbers in their margins to facilitate reference to the Notes and other editorial matter. References to Conrad's other works cite volumes of the Cambridge Edition already published, or else the Doubleday collected edition in its Sun-Dial printing (1921) in the Dent printings (1923 and subsequently). Superior letters (e.g., 'Mʳ') in the original documents have been lowered (i.e., to 'Mr'). The beginnings of paragraphs are represented by standard modern indentation regardless of the various conventions of these documents, and Conrad's '_ "' is reduced to simple inverted commas. Dashes of variable lengths are normally printed as one-em dashes. Other typographical elements in the texts and titles of the original documents (e.g., display capitals, chapter heads, running titles) have been standardized.

The texts and apparatus in this volume were prepared by computer. Those interested in data and documentation not published here should contact the Chief Executive Editor.

In addition to those named in the Acknowledgements, the editors wish to thank the Trustees and beneficiaries of the Estate of Joseph Conrad and Doubleday and Company and J. M. Dent and Company for permission to publish these new texts of Conrad's works. The support of the institutions and individuals listed on p. vii has been essential to the success of the series and is gratefully acknowledged.

CHIEF EXECUTIVE EDITOR

ACKNOWLEDGEMENTS

THANKS are due to the following institutions and individuals for facilitating access to manuscripts and unpublished materials: the Berg Collection, the New York Public Library, Astor, Lenox, and Tilden Foundations, and Philip Milito; George Arents Library for Special Collections, Syracuse University; Firestone Library, Princeton University, and Margaret Sherry; the Harry Ransom Humanities Research Center, University of Texas at Austin; and the Lilly Library, Indiana University.

A number of individuals kindly supplied information or otherwise shared their expertise, and we would especially like to thank: Andrzej Busza, Keith Carabine, Mario Curelli, Gail Fraser, the late Raymond Gauthier, Owen Knowles, Eugenia Maresch, Gene M. Moore, Ludwik Przyłuski, Max Saunders, Allan H. Simmons, and Robert W. Trogdon. We are also indebted to the work of the late Hans van Marle.

For assistance with the on-site verification of texts, gratitude is expressed to Robert W. Trogdon, and for assistance with support tasks, to Catherine Tisch and Gale Graham.

J. H. Stape is grateful to The Joseph Conrad Society (UK) for a research travel grant from the Juliet and Mac McLauchlan Bequest.

For their support of the Edition we also wish to express gratitude to present and former administrators of Kent State University, including, in alphabetical order, Rudolph O. Buttlar, Carol A. Cartwright, Cheryl A. Casper, Ronald J. Corthell, Joseph H. Danks, Susanna G. Fein, Paul L. Gaston, Alex Gildzen, Charlee Heimlich, Dean H. Keller, Sanford E. Marovitz, Thomas D. Moore, Terry P. Roark, Michael Schwartz, F. S. Schwarzbach, Carol M. Toncar, and Eugene P. Wenninger. Acknowledgement of special support goes to the staffs of Kent State University's Libraries and Media Services and Don L. Tolliver, Jeanne M. Somers, and Mark W. Weber and the Systems staff, including Thomas E. Klinger, Todd M. Ryan, and Richard A. Wiggins.

The facsimiles that accompany the text are reproduced by courtesy of the Berg Collection, the New York Public Library; the Frank and Nelson Doubleday Collection, Manuscripts Division, Department of Rare Books and Special Collections, Princeton University Library; the George Arents Rare Book Library, Syracuse University; and the Harry Ransom Humanities Research Center, University of Texas at Austin.

CHRONOLOGY

JOSEPH CONRAD'S life may be seen as having several distinct stages: in Poland and in Russian exile before his father's death (1857–69); in Poland and the south of France under the care of his maternal uncle (1870–78); in the British merchant marine, mainly as junior officer sailing in the Far East (1879 – early 1890s); after a transitional period (early 1890s), as writer of critical esteem (1895–1914); as acclaimed writer, though perhaps with his greatest work achieved (1914–24). After 1895 the history of his life is essentially the history of his works. Publication dates given below are those of the London editions, except for those of the present volume.

1857 December 3	Józef Teodor Konrad Korzeniowski (Nałęcz coat-of-arms) born in Berdyczów (officially, Berdychir) in the Ukraine to Apollo Korzeniowski and Ewelina (or Ewa), née Bobrowska, Korzeniowska
1862 May	Korzeniowski, his wife, and son forced into exile in Russia
1865 April	Ewa Korzeniowska dies
1868	Korzeniowski permitted to leave Russia
1869 February	Korzeniowski and Conrad move to Cracow
May	Korzeniowski dies
1870	Conrad, under care of uncle Tadeusz Bobrowski, begins study with tutor, Adam Pulman
1873 May	Visits Vienna, Switzerland, and northern Italy; first view of the sea
1874 October	Takes position in Marseilles with Delestang et Fils, bankers and shippers
1875	Apprentice in *Mont-Blanc*
1876–7	In *Saint-Antoine*
1878 February or March	Attempts suicide
April	Leaves Marseilles in British steamer *Mavis*

1878 June	Lands at Lowestoft, Suffolk; first time in England
July–September	Sails as ordinary seaman in *Skimmer of the Sea* (coastal waters of England)
1878–80	In *Duke of Sutherland, Europa*
1880	Meets G. F. W. Hope, Adolf Krieger
June	Passes examination for second mate
1880–1	Third mate in *Loch Etive*
1881–4	Second mate in *Palestine, Riversdale, Narcissus*
1884 December	Passes examination for first mate
1885–6	Second mate in *Tilkhurst*
1886	Submits perhaps his first story, 'The Black Mate', to *Tit-Bits* competition
August	Becomes a British subject
November	Passes examination for master; receives 'Certificate of Competency as Master'
1886–7	Second mate in *Falconhurst*
1887–8	First mate in *Highland Forest*, in *Vidar*
1888–9	Captain of barque *Otago*
1889 Autumn	Begins *Almayer's Folly* in London
1890 February–April	In Poland and Ukraine for first time since 1874
May–December	To the Congo as second-in-command, then temporarily as captain, of *Roi des Belges*
1891	Manages warehouse of Barr, Moering, London
1891–3	First mate in *Torrens*
1893	Meets John Galsworthy, Edward L. Sanderson
August–October	Visits Bobrowski in Polish Ukraine, briefly passing through Poland
November	Signs on as second mate in *Adowa*, which never makes voyage
1894	Meets Edward Garnett, Jessie George
January	Ends career as seaman
February	Bobrowski dies
1895 April	*Almayer's Folly*

1896 March	*An Outcast of the Islands.* Marries Jessie George; honeymoon in Brittany; settles in Stanford-le-Hope, Essex
1897	Begins friendship with R. B. Cunninghame Graham; meets Henry James, Stephen Crane
December	*The Nigger of the 'Narcissus'*
1898	Meets Ford Madox (Hueffer) Ford, H. G. Wells
January	Alfred Borys Conrad born
April	*Tales of Unrest*
October	Moves to Pent Farm, Nr Hythe, Kent, sub-let from Ford
1900	Begins association with J. B. Pinker
October	*Lord Jim*
1901 June	*The Inheritors* (with Ford)
1902 November	*Youth: A Narrative and Two Other Stories*
1903 April	*Typhoon and Other Stories*
October	*Romance* (with Ford)
1904 October	*Nostromo*
1905 June	*One Day More* staged in London
1906	Meets Arthur Marwood
August	John Alexander Conrad born
October	*The Mirror of the Sea*
1907 September	*The Secret Agent.* Moves to Someries, Luton, Bedfordshire
December	Begins 'Razumov' (later *Under Western Eyes*)
1908 August	*A Set of Six*
September–December	Composes first four instalments of 'Some Reminiscences' (later *A Personal Record*) for Ford's *English Review*. Works on 'Razumov' intermittently
October–November	Possibly drafts 'Prince Roman', apparently first seen as part of 'Some Reminiscences'
November 25	First instalment of 'Some Reminiscences' and review of Anatole France's *L'île des Pingouins* in the December issue of the *English Review*

1909 January	Recommences 'Razumov', making progress throughout spring
February?–May	Composes three further instalments of 'Some Reminiscences'
February 14	Moves to Aldington, Kent
April–May	*The Nature of a Crime*, collaboration with Ford, appears along with 'Some Reminiscences' in *English Review*
May 25	Final instalment of 'Some Reminiscences' in June number of *English Review*
June 23	Ends 'Some Reminiscences', following breach with Ford, although contemplating continuing them
June 29	Writes to Bliss Carman about a possible 'autobiographical sea-paper' for *Gentleman's Journal*
1910	Moves to Capel House, Orlestone, Kent
September	Completes 'Prince Roman'
December	*Under Western Eyes* begins appearing in *English Review* and *North American Review*
1911 July 27	Signs Memorandum of Agreement with Nash for book edition of *Some Reminiscences*
August–September	Writes ' A Familiar Preface' for *Some Reminiscences*
October	*Under Western Eyes*. Reads proofs for English edition of *Some Reminiscences*
1912 January 3	*A Personal Record* in America; as *Some Reminiscences* in England (*ca.* 22 January)
April	Nash issues second impression of *Some Reminiscences*
October	*'Twixt Land and Sea*
1913 September	*Chance*, with 'main' publication date of January 1914
1914 July–November	Visits Poland and Ukraine with family; delayed by outbreak of First World War; returns via Austria and Italy
1915 February	*Within the Tides*
September	*Victory*
1916	Second English edition of *Some Reminiscences* under title *A Personal Record*

1917	Second American edition of *A Personal Record*
March	*The Shadow-Line*
1919 March	Moves to Spring Grove, near Wye, Kent
August	*The Arrow of Gold*
September	Writes 'Author's Note' for Dent's new edition of *A Personal Record*
October	Moves to Oswalds, Bishopsbourne, near Canterbury, Kent
November	Third English edition of *A Personal Record*, with first appearance of 'Author's Note'
1920 June	*The Rescue*
1921 January	Visits Corsica (until April). Collected Editions begin publication in England (Heinemann) and in America (Doubleday)
February	*Notes on Life and Letters*
1922 November	*The Secret Agent* staged in London
1923 May–June	Visits America, guest of F. N. Doubleday
December	*The Rover*
1924 May	Declines knighthood
August 3	Dies at Oswalds (Roman Catholic burial, Canterbury)
September	*The Nature of a Crime* (with Ford)
October	*The Shorter Tales*
1925 January	*Tales of Hearsay*
September	*Suspense*
1926 March	*Last Essays*
1928 June	*The Sisters*

ABBREVIATIONS

[London is the place of publication unless otherwise indicated.]

Carabine	Keith Carabine, *The Life and the Art: A Study of Conrad's 'Under Western Eyes'*. Amsterdam: Rodopi, 1996
CEW	Norman Sherry, *Conrad's Eastern World*. Cambridge University Press, 1966
CH	*Conrad: The Critical Heritage*, ed. Norman Sherry. Routledge & Kegan Paul, 1973
Chronology	Owen Knowles, *A Conrad Chronology*. Macmillan, 1990
Enc. Brit.	*Encyclopaedia Britannica*. 11th edn. Cambridge University Press, 1910–11
Hervouet	Yves Hervouet, *The French Face of Joseph Conrad*. Cambridge University Press, 1990
Letters	*The Collected Letters of Joseph Conrad*, ed. Frederick R. Karl, Laurence Davies, *et al.* 9 vols. Cambridge University Press, 1983–2007
Ludwig	*Letters of Ford Madox Ford*, ed. Richard M. Ludwig. Princeton University Press, 1965
Monod	Sylvère Monod, 'Notes', *Conrad: Œuvres: Souvenirs personnels*. Bibliothèque de la Pléiade. Paris: Gallimard, 1987
Najder	Zdzisław Najder, *Joseph Conrad: A Chronicle*. Trans. Halina Carroll-Najder. New Brunswick, NJ: Rutgers University Press, 1983
Najder, 1997	Zdzisław Najder, *Conrad in Perspective: Essays on Art and Fidelity*. Cambridge University Press, 1997
Najder, *Conrad*	*Conrad Under Familial Eyes*, ed. Zdzisław Najder. Trans. Halina Carroll-Najder. Cambridge University Press, 1983
Najder, *Letters*	*Conrad's Polish Background: Letters to and from Polish Friends*, ed. Zdzisław Najder. Oxford University Press, 1964

Pamiętnik	Tadeusz Bobrowski, *Pamiętnik mojego życia. O sprawach i ludziach mego czasu* [*Memoirs of My Life: On the Affairs and Men of My Time*]. 2 vols. (1900). Ed. Stefan Kieniewicz. Warsaw: Państwowy Instytut Wydawniczy, 1979
Saunders	Max Saunders, *Ford Madox Ford: A Dual Life.* 2 vols. Oxford University Press, 1996–7

Locations of Unpublished Documents

Berg	Berg Collection, The New York Public Library, Astor, Lenox and Tilden Foundations
BL	British Library
Colgate	Everett Needham Case Library, Colgate University
HRHRC	Harry Ransom Humanities Research Center, University of Texas at Austin
Indiana	Lilly Library, Indiana University at Bloomington
Princeton	Firestone Library, Princeton University
Syracuse	George Arents Research Library for Special Collections, Syracuse University
Yale	Beinecke Rare Book and Manuscript Library, Yale University

INTRODUCTION

SERIALIZED IN 1908–9 in the *English Review* under the title 'Some Reminiscences' and first published in book form in early 1912, *A Personal Record* is Conrad's only sustained piece of autobiographical writing.[1] Reminiscences are scattered throughout *The Mirror of the Sea* (1906), and the essay 'Poland Revisited' (1915) focusses on his ill-fated journey to Poland during the summer and autumn of 1914. The former, however, is principally concerned with presenting a kaleidoscopic view of life at sea, celebrating maritime traditions, and affirming the sea's centrality to the English imagination. The latter deals with a few months of Conrad's life, while offering backward glances at his childhood and his early experience in the British Merchant Service. Despite Conrad's claim that *The Shadow-Line: A Confession* (1917) was a 'sort of autobiography' (*Letters*, V, 543), it is patently a work of fiction. The very uniqueness, then, of *A Personal Record* gives it a special attraction and importance. During Conrad's lifetime, the book proved popular. On its original publication in 1912, it quickly went into a second printing. It was published in separate editions in 1916 and 1919 in England and in 1918 went into a second edition in America before appearing in the collected English and American editions of 1921.

This slim volume – unintentionally slim, as Conrad's work on the series broke off by force of circumstance – is Conrad's major public statement about the events of his life. As his fame grew, and particularly from 1912 onwards, he was from time to time involved in the advertising schemes of his American publishers, especially Doubleday.[2] These advertising efforts required him to reveal, even in a sense to 'market', aspects of his personal life, but they were not initiated by him, and his involvement was sometimes against the grain. Nonetheless, there

---

[1] The several titles and forms under which this work appeared require distinctions in terminology. *A Personal Record* refers throughout to the final work and, where context makes clear, to the first American edition, which appeared under this title. 'Some Reminiscences' refers to the serial version and, when italicized, to the first English edition. 'Instalment' refers to the texts as serialized in the *English Review*; for the sake of convenience the word 'chapters' is used for their book form, although this designation does not appear in the book editions.

[2] See, for example, 'The "Knopf Document": Transcriptions and Commentary', ed. J. H. Stape, in *Conrad between the Lines: Documents in a Life*, ed. Gene M. Moore, Allan H. Simmons, and J. H. Stape (2000), pp. 57–86.

is ample evidence that he wished to add to the 'record' as he had left it in June 1909, when the last of his reminiscences appeared in the *English Review*. When looking for a publisher for the book form in the spring of 1911, he already mentioned that 'Later on another personal vol. of that sort could be added,'[1] and not long after *A Personal Record* appeared, he told Austin Harrison, the new editor of the *English Review*, that he was thinking of a 'suite' to his reminiscences 'under the general title Some Portraits family and others – my uncle the conspirator, two marriages, episodes of the liberation of the peasants and of the '63 rising and so on.'[2] He returned to his idea a year later, mentioning to Harrison the possibility of writing '3 Rem[iniscen]ces papers of about 5000 w[ords] each' (*Letters*, v, 161).

Nothing came of these projects. But even late in his career, Conrad and his literary agent, J. B. Pinker, mooted the topic. Referring to an idea previously discussed, Conrad wrote: 'I note what you say about any eventual Reminiscences. I must tell you however that as long as the "novel" vein lasts I would not take up deliberately the other thing.'[3] Jessie Conrad gives flesh to the bare bones here, recounting that:

> *A Personal Record* would have had a successor if Conrad had lived only a few more years. Much of the material for it we had discussed only a few days before his death. "Prince Roman" was to be included,[4] as being in every way personal. He had the intention of including some of his very early experiences before he left Poland.
>
> (*Joseph Conrad as I Knew Him* (1926), pp. 138–9)

By force of circumstances, then, *A Personal Record* remains Conrad's most concerted attempt to discern a pattern in his life, or perhaps to impose one *a posteriori*. It is thus a double document: of presenting the gist of his life to the public and exposing its internal sense to himself – of publicity and self-reflection. Despite its title's claim, it is less a 'record' – dates and a conventional narrative line are eschewed for a more free-flowing structure – than an artful construction of selected fragments of memory. An exercise in self-expression might be expected from this kind of excursion into the past, but the contrary

---

[1] Conrad to Unwin, 17 May 1911 (*Letters*, IV, 441).
[2] Conrad to Austin Harrison, [15 February 1912] (*Letters*, v, 20–21). The transcription 'his[?] peasants' in *Letters* is rejected on the basis of our reading of the original (Berg).
[3] Conrad to Pinker, 24 January 1922 (*Letters*, VII, 409).
[4] 'Prince Roman' was partly drafted in October–November 1908, apparently to form part of 'Some Reminiscences'. It was completed on 24 September 1910. For a discussion of its composition, see '*Twixt Land and Sea*, ed. J. A. Berthoud, Laura L. Davis, and S. W. Reid (2007), p. lxiii.

is closer to the truth: the volume takes issue with direct confessions of the kind made by the *philosophe* Jean-Jacques Rousseau, Conrad's anti-hero. On the one hand, Conrad stresses his individuality and even exceptionality, as grounded in his origins and the unusual shape of his career; on the other, he firmly declares that he wants to be judged as a seaman and as a writer according to the general criteria of those professions. He describes his singularity but declines to use it as a plea.

Origins

IN THE EARLY Autumn of 1908, Conrad had several reasons for exploring the subject of his past, his career at sea, and his Polish origins. His finances were in disarray and a chance for additional income offered itself; he had reached mid-life, a time when many people take stock of their successes and failures; and, lastly, a specific provocation may have urged him to public revelation. On 10 August 1908, only a few weeks before he began writing his reminiscences, the well-known critic Robert Lynd commented in his review of *A Set of Six* in the *Daily News*:

Mr Conrad, as everybody knows, is a Pole, who writes in English by choice, as it were, rather than by nature. To some of us . . . it seems a very regrettable thing, even from the point of view of English literature. A writer who ceases to see the world coloured by his own language – for language gives colour to thoughts and things in a way that few people understand – is apt to lose the concentration and intensity of vision without which the greatest literature cannot be made. Mr Conrad, without either country or language, may be thought to have found a new patriotism for himself in the sea. His vision of men, however, is the vision of a cosmopolitan, of a homeless person. (*CH*, pp. 210–12)

Conrad's initial reaction was one of utter dejection. On 21 August, he complained to Edward Garnett, the friend who, fourteen years earlier, had recommended publishing his first novel: 'It is like abusing a tongue-tied man. For what can one say. The statement is simple and brutal; and any answer would involve too many feelings of one's inner life, stir too much secret bitterness and complex loyalty to be even attempted with any hope of being understood' (*Letters*, IV, 107–8). Two days later Conrad repeated his thoughts to John Galsworthy, at the time one of his closest confidants, adding 'I don't know why I am telling You all this. My heart has been like a stone and my hand wore lead all day – and I don't know why I should inflict this mood on You.

It's indecent. And yet to hold one's tongue is too difficult, at times.'[1] But then he decided to do precisely what he had seemingly ruled out: to deal in print with his 'complex' feelings and loyalties. In one sense, 'Some Reminiscences' became his considered reply.

On 18 September 1908, Conrad announced to his agent a new project: of writing memoirs for serialization in the new and ambitious literary monthly, the *English Review*, edited by his friend and sometime collaborator Ford Madox (Hueffer) Ford.[2] Conrad claimed to have already finished 'one and a half' sections (*Letters*, IV, 126) during a stay with the Fords at Aldington, Kent.[3] The long and dramatic letter telling Pinker about his plans has a number of threads. Conrad requested his agent, to whom he was deeply in debt, to accept a new, comprehensive financial arrangement. The Conrads badly wanted to move from the cottage at Someries, near Luton, Bedfordshire, that they had been renting since September 1907. They had disliked the place almost from the first but could not leave without paying off local debts and obtaining money for a new rental arrangement. Above all, however, Conrad was desperate to ensure that regular coverage of his expenses – which he estimated at £500 per year[4] – was not dependent on supplying new copy. The fees promised by Ford, apparently £20 per instalment (see below), were to provide extra money for immediate disbursements and lessen, if only minimally, Conrad's dependence on his agent.

In announcing his new venture, Conrad doubtless considered it more politic to ascribe the whole idea of writing his reminiscences to Ford: 'Hueffer suggested them to me and offered to take me down from dictation.'[5] Conrad assured Pinker that he could 'guarantee (*if needed*) 1.500 to 2000 words of *Remin^{ces}* per week – that is if some really important advantage for both of us should depend on it' (*Letters*, IV, 139). Apart from serializing his recollections in England, Conrad also

[1] Conrad to Galsworthy, Sunday [23 August 1908] (*Letters*, IV, 110).

[2] Here and throughout referred to as Ford, although Hueffer formally changed his surname only in 1919.

[3] The Conrads arrived at Aldington on 29 August and returned to Someries on 21 September (*Letters*, IV, 114, 127). The arrival date suggests that Conrad probably began work on the first instalment after the turn of the month.

[4] To put this figure into perspective, the average annual earned income shortly after the turn of the century was £90 per annum; by 1924, the year of Conrad's death, it had risen to £210. See Najder, pp. 276–7, and Arthur L. Bowley and Sir Josiah Stamp, *The National Income, 1924: A Comparative Study of the Income in the United Kingdom in 1911 and 1924* (1927).

[5] Conrad to Pinker, 18 September [1908] (*Letters*, IV, 125).

optimistically hoped to sell the American serial rights and encouraged his agent to approach American magazines with the prospect of at least six instalments, which 'must be treated as a very special thing and made much of. I believe there is a good deal of curiosity as to my personality in the US and, if I am to believe several competent opinions, in this country as well.'[1] But Pinker was waiting for the delayed text of 'Razumov', as *Under Western Eyes* was then called, and undoubtedly feared that other writing would be at its expense. He remained cool to the whole idea. Moreover, this was not the first time that Conrad had tried to persuade him to embrace unwanted work that was intended to augment his client's income while he neglected work already commisioned. The short stories Conrad wrote when struggling with *Nostromo* (1904–6) are a case in point.

Pinker may also have been sceptical about the marketability of 'auto-biographical things', that would be 'concerned with Polish life and life at sea'. Conrad was later to flesh out his intentions in the following terms: 'To make Polish life enter English literature is no small ambition – to begin with. But I think it can be done. To reveal a very particular state of society, bring forward individuals with very special traditions and touch in a personal way upon such events for instance as the liberation of the serfs.'[2] This emphasis upon Polish history and culture was thus central to his initial plans. By tackling a Polish subject, and one located in the territory of the Russian Empire, he would also be wading into some of the same political and moral thickets that he was attempting to present in 'Razumov', a novel that deals with 'the real problems of the political life and death of a huge empire, on whose fate also depended the fate of Poland' (Najder, p. 358). If there are few tangible connections between the two books Conrad worked on alternately for a period of almost nine months, an underlying emotional link exists between them. In the finished work, however, the ambition 'to make Polish life enter English literature' is fulfilled only to a limited degree: scattered memories of his family's experience in the Polish Ukraine – such as the extended fragment about his great-uncle's stepfather – lack an evident connection to Conrad's life and contain little of inherent interest to his English and American audiences. As actual work on them got underway, the 'Reminiscences' moved in different directions from those Conrad originally announced.

---

[1] Ibid.   [2] Conrad to Pinker, Wednesday, [7] October 1908 (*Letters*, IV, 138).

THE GROWTH OF THE TEXT

THE SCARCITY OF pre-print material for *A Personal Record* and the disappearance of the *English Review*'s files means that the genesis and transmission of the work must be reconstructed almost exclusively from Conrad's surviving letters to Ford and to Pinker. Endorsed cheques from Ford help fill in the history of composition. Although the manuscript of 'A Familiar Preface' survives, it is undated and little mentioned in the surviving correspondence. The composition of the 'Author's Note' is, by contrast, well documented.

1908–1909

Conrad wrote his 'Reminiscences' in two stages as he intermittently worked on 'Razumov'.[1] The autumn and early winter of 1908 saw the composition of the first four instalments for Ford's *English Review*,[2] as Conrad managed to add about 6,500 words to 'Razumov'. He wrote three further instalments of the 'Reminiscences' between about mid-February and mid- or late-April 1909, as work on the novel began to pick up pace. From Pinker's standpoint, or indeed anyone's concerned primarily with the writing of *Under Western Eyes*, the 'Reminiscences' and later 'The Secret Sharer' would appear to be like a distraction that impeded the novel's progress, but from Conrad's, and perhaps Ford's, and from a more distant perspective, their writing could be regarded as a practical, if not psychological, necessity issuing in important original works that complement the novel and have stood the test of time. Pinker's hostility to the new project seems, in fact, to have been short-sighted: 'Razumov' progressed fitfully both before and after Conrad composed his recollections, and at this period he may have apparently reached an impasse with it. Thus, rather than impeding the novel's composition, the writing of these memoirs may have helped Conrad to regain focus on what was, nominally at least, his major project.

Aware when he became involved in the venture that Ford had financial backing for only four numbers of the *English Review*, Conrad informed his agent that four instalments would be 'ready by Dec' 1908, a prediction that, in the event, proved accurate. Conrad's plans of mid-October to dictate 'more Rem^ces a paper or two anyhow'[3] to

---

[1] See 'The Texts', pp. 140–41. For a history of the novel's composition, see Carabine.

[2] For a history of the *English Review*, see Saunders, I, 242–52. Douglas Goldring's *South Lodge* (1943), pp. 14–30, provides a vivid account of the editing of the first issue.

[3] Conrad to Pinker, 13 October 1908 (*Letters*, IV, 145).

his secretary, L. M. Hallowes, bore fruit, and dictation was the main method of composition for the three remaining papers of the first series.[1] Indeed, Ford's later claims that he took down *A Personal Record* from Conrad's dictation can largely be dismissed by establishing the circumstances and chronology of the work's production: only the first instalment could have been produced in this way.[2]

On 4 October 1908, Conrad dispatched corrected proofs of the first instalment to Pinker, estimating it as about 7,500 words.[3] (The final version is closer to 7,200.) He suggested that a 'clean' typed copy be made from the 'scored proof' to circulate in the American market. He also informed his agent that the second instalment was 'nearly ready', and on the 8th told him of its completion (*Letters*, IV, 141). Apologetic about its length (6,000 words), Conrad forwarded a copy to Ford on the 10th, and on the 12th sent another to Pinker for forwarding to America (*Letters*, IV, 142, 144). The existence of multiple copies indicates that ribbon-copy typescript and a carbon copy (rather than manuscript) were at issue. Cheques from Ford for £20 and £10, dated 17 and 20 October, represent payment for completed work.[4] Conrad told Ford that he had made a fresh start and omitted from the second instalment 'the few words which you were good enough to let me dictate to you when last here' (12 October 1908, *Letters*, IV, 144).[5] In a word, the dictated text that Ford took down was jettisoned. The

[1] Conrad to Pinker, 30 September 1908 and [21 or 28 October] 1908 (*Letters*, IV, 133, 146).
[2] Ford's claims are made in his *Return to Yesterday* (1931), pp. 190–91, and Ford to George T. Keating, [December 1936], Ludwig, pp. 267–8. For a detailed discussion of these topics, see 'The Texts', pp. 133–5, 137–9.
[3] *Letters*, IV, 135. For a discussion of the revisions in this proof, see 'The Texts', pp. 135–7.
[4] Conrad apparently received £20 for each of the first four instalments. The following cancelled cheques drawn on the London City & Midland Bank, Limited, Shepherd's Bush, signed by Ford and endorsed by Conrad survive (Berg): 17 October 1908 for £20, paid out on the 20th; 20 October for £10, paid out on the 24th; 27 October for £10, paid out on 3 November; 8 December for £10, paid out on the 14th; 11 December for £10, paid out on the 18th. The total of £60 roughly accords with the £2 per 1,000 words that Ford offered to Edward Garnett on 17 October 1908 (Ludwig, pp. 27–8); however, Conrad twice mentions having received £80 from Ford (to Ford and to Pinker, 17 December 1908), a figure he recommended that Norman Douglas stipulate for his articles (*Letters*, IV, 166, 168, 197). Another cheque for £25 (filed in Ezra Pound Collection, Box 12, Folder 1, HRHRC) drawn on the same bank, dated 17 April 1909, and paid out on the 22nd, is either payment for Conrad's reminiscences in the May issue (to be published on or about 25 April) or for his contribution to *The Nature of a Crime* in the same issue. If the former, Ford paid a higher fee for the April–June instalments of the reminiscences.
[5] Conrad's two preceding letters to Ford of Tuesday [29 September or 6 October] and 10 October (*Letters*, IV, 142), the latter accompanying the text of the second instalment, make clear that it was not dictated to Ford.

third instalment was composed between the beginning of October and the 17th, when Miss Hallowes was at Someries for a fortnight's work on 'Razumov,'[1] or when she arrived back 'for another week' of work on the novel late that month (*Letters*, IV, 145). A cheque for £10, dated 27 October, tends to favour the later time. In any case, a *terminus ad quem* for the instalment's completion is certain: by 23 November, a copy was in the hands of Paul R. Reynolds in New York,[2] the agent Pinker dealt with to place his clients' work in America.

On 25 November, Conrad was at work on the fourth and last of the originally planned instalments, but a 'horrid lingering attack of gout' slightly delayed its completion:[3] he sent sixteen revised typescript pages to Pinker; eleven more were, he said, ready for revision and to be posted later. Ford was to receive Conrad's typed copy from Pinker.[4] On 9 December, Conrad forwarded the conclusion to his agent, pressing for its speedy typing and dispatch to Ford (*Letters*, IV, 159). As this instalment was scheduled to appear in the *English Review*'s March 1909 issue, the haste was undoubtedly motivated by an actual or perceived need for cash rather than an immediate deadline. Two cheques for £10, dated 8 and 11 December, indicate that Ford received copy in a timely fashion.

When forwarding the typescript of the fourth instalment to Pinker, Conrad informed him that 'This is the end of Reminis[es] for the present. I will do no more especially as you are not calling for america [*sic*]'. He then thought the existing text amounted to 'half a vol.' (*Letters*, IV, 159). As Ford foraged for funding, writing came to a halt,[5] and Conrad became fully engaged again with his 'confoundedly difficult' novel (*Letters*, IV, 175). He had, moreover, no immediate need to commit himself to continuing his memoirs, although Ford had early on spoken of as many as twelve instalments 'or whatever number is necessary.'[6] Further writing, however, depended on the *English Review*'s continued existence: 'we shall see how the R[eview] goes. Ford . . . hopes that he

[1] Conrad to Galsworthy, [29 September or 6 October 1908], and Conrad to Pinker, 14 October 1908 (*Letters*, IV, 132, 145).

[2] Paul R. Reynolds to J. B. Pinker, 23 November 1908 (Berg).

[3] Conrad to Pinker, 25 November [1908], and Conrad to Elsie Hueffer, 12 December 1908 (*Letters*, IV, 153, 161).

[4] Conrad to Ford and to Pinker, [7 December 1908] (*Letters*, IV, 157, 158).

[5] Conrad to Ford, 17 [December] 1908 and to Pinker, 17 December 1908 (*Letters*, IV, 165–7, 168).

[6] Conrad to Pinker, 18 September [1908] (*Letters*, IV, 126).

may go on for a year; in which case he wants after an interval of four months another set of four reminiscence papers.'[1]

Be that as it may, thoughts of a book had been stimulated. Conrad spoke of a volume of 80,000 words, and then possibly another, but seemed, at least when writing to Pinker, to make his plans dependent upon receiving an additional 'offer for a series', that is, apart from what Ford proposed.[2] Such an offer never materialized. In January 1909, Conrad again mentioned to his agent the prospect of 'one or two vols of Reminiscences', but in the context of making an offer to Heinemann (and thus easing his indebtedness to Pinker), not of any plans for actual writing.[3]

Once the survival of the *English Review* had become certain after the turn of the year, Conrad resolved to write further reminiscences. Composition of the first instalment of this second series began in February and was apparently little impeded by the Conrads' move from Someries to Aldington on the 14th. However, its composition became troubled as Conrad suffered from a cold and grappled with depression. He reported to Galsworthy on 6 March that he had completed it with 'the greatest difficulty'.[4] The second shortest in the series (about 5,000 words), the instalment deals passingly with the writing of *Nostromo* and glances back on Conrad's friendship with the American novelist Stephen Crane. Its generalized discussion of authorship strikes a different note from what had previously appeared. Conrad possibly dictated this and the seventh instalment to his wife, Jessie, Miss Hallowes not being available, or perhaps these two instalments, like the sixth, were written out by hand. On balance, and given Conrad's statement in late 1911 to John Quinn, the wealthy American lawyer interested in collecting his manuscripts, that 'All the text almost was dictated and then worked upon in typed copy,'[5] dictation seems more likely. (Some of the looseness of the prose may also be attributed to it.)

Composition of the sixth 'paper' – destined for the May 1909 issue – can be confidently placed between about 6 March, the date by which Conrad had finished the fifth instalment, and mid- to late April. A cheque for £25, dated 17 April (HRHRC), either testifies

---

[1] Conrad to Pinker, 21 December 1908 (*Letters*, IX, 130).

[2] Conrad to Pinker, 25 November 1908 (*Letters*, IV, 153).

[3] Conrad to Pinker, Thursday [21 January 1909] (*Letters*, IV, 189).

[4] Conrad to Galsworthy, 6 March 1909; see also Conrad to Stephen Reynolds, 6 March 1909 (*Letters*, IV, 198, 199).

[5] Conrad to Quinn, 30 September [= November] 1911 (*Letters*, IV, 514–15).

to completion or is an advance on work almost finished.[1] A surviving holograph sheet from this instalment[2] indicates that the whole of it may have been written out in longhand and presents further evidence against 'collaboration' with Ford, even though the Conrads were now established near him in Aldington. (Ford frequently stayed in London and was experiencing marital difficulties that explain his absences in town.)

In late April, Conrad declared to Galsworthy that he was planning to 'write enough to complete a vol: of Reminiscences' despite the fact that Pinker did 'not think much of them'.[3] The seventh instalment, in the June issue, however, was the last published. Conrad's promise to Ford on 20 May to return proofs the next day (*Letters*, IV, 237) and his brusque enquiry whether he would be paid for his work is the only mention of it in surviving correspondence.

Conrad claimed to have made a stab at writing the instalment due for July (*Letters*, IV, 254), but, as the publication deadline loomed, he found he was unable to write anything and abandoned his attempt. Later, he pleaded illness as the reason. But, indeed, the last two instalments were written against the backdrop of a rapidly deteriorating relationship with Ford.[4] Symptoms of discord are discernible in March – 'The fact is that H[ueffer] loves to manage people' he resentfully wrote to Norman Douglas – and by mid-May the conflict raged.[5] Whether Conrad's painful clash with a man considered an intimate friend a few months earlier or 'a damnable go of gout' (*Letters*, IV, 258) at the beginning of June made him miss the July instalment's deadline is impossible to say. A notoriously psychosomatic affliction, the gout may have been triggered by the quarrel with Ford. Naturally it was easier and more convenient for Conrad to blame his body than his mental state.

On 13 July 1909, he summed up his situation in a letter to Galsworthy: 'it was simply impossible to write anything – even a letter' (*Letters*, IV, 254). By then Ford's dramatically phrased note in the July number had made Conrad cross:[6] '*We regret that owing to the serious*

---

[1] Assuming that this was not payment for Conrad's contribution to *The Nature of a Crime*, the second part of which appeared in May. See p. xxvii, n. 4 above.

[2] See Fig. 1, p. 122.

[3] Conrad to Galsworthy, 30 April 1909 (*Letters*, IV, 224); see also Conrad to H. M. Capes, 13 May 1909 (*Letters*, IV, 233).

[4] For the full story, see Najder, pp. 347–51.

[5] Conrad to Douglas, Sunday [14 March 1909] (*Letters*, IV, 205); see also Conrad to Ford, 20 May 1909 (*Letters*, IV, 235–7).

[6] 'I was vexed by that silly editorial note': Conrad to Garnett, 19 July 1909 (*Letters*, IV, 258).

illness of Mr. Joseph Conrad we are compelled to postpone the publication of the next instalment of his Reminiscences.[1] Probably Conrad discerned in these words a mixture of reprobation and pressure to continue. In any event, on 23 June he wrote to E. V. Lucas that his 'reminiscences have come to an end now' (*Letters*, IV, 247). He would later link their termination with his decision to break off his connection with the *English Review*, which had changed owners. For his part, Ford complained about the 'ragged' condition of the suddenly broken off memoirs.[2]

Conrad, however, not only stuck to his guns, refusing to continue them, but also asserted to Ford that the '*whole* of the contribution to the *ER* as it stands now without the addition of a single word shall form the Part First' and that 'the very phrase ending the 7th instalment is to my mind an excellent terminal . . . It is another instalment which would make the thing ragged.'[3] Upon the book's appearance in early 1912 he repeated this claim to Edward Garnett.[4] In December 1909, aware that in book form the *English Review* text was rather short, he wrote to one of his French translators that he had had 'a notion of writing 30,000 words more' to make up a volume (*Letters*, IV, 308). Even then, while defending the artistic completeness of what he had written, he kept thinking about a continuation, and, in June 1909, sought out Lucas's advice about developing his reminiscences in the form 'of a volume (or even two short vols of say 65,000 words each).'[5]

ADDITIONS: 1911 AND 1919

WHATEVER Conrad's defence to Ford of his work in its serial form, he nonetheless felt the need to write a longish preface, titled 'A Familiar Preface', for Nash's edition of *Some Reminiscences*. Composed during August–September 1911, this preface introduces the volume to a new audience and attempts to justify the work's shape. Not incidentally, it added bulk to what remained a slim volume.

The preface intertwines two strands of thought. Conrad stresses a distrust of emotional display in stating his allegiances, a strand that culminates in the oft-quoted declaration that 'the temporal world . . . rests notably, among others, on the idea of Fidelity' (15.14–17). The

---

[1] *English Review*, July 1909, p. 824.   [2] Conrad to Ford, 31 July 1909 (*Letters*, IV, 263–4).
[3] Ibid.   [4] Conrad to Edward Garnett, 27 January 1912 (*Letters*, V, 12).
[5] Conrad to Lucas, 23 June 1909 (*Letters*, IV, 247).

other, more elaborated strand sets forth the way this work ought to be understood as the result of 'friendly pressure' (11.4) and as presenting a double opposition to the author's life as a writer: first of leaving Poland, then of spending a number of years at sea in the French and the British Merchant Services. In introducing his volume of personal prose, Conrad takes special care to present himself, on the one hand, as 'not sufficiently literary' for a professional writer (13.7), and, on the other, as a man of action viewing literature from a distance. This pose suits a number of aims, serving in part to justify the seemingly casual structure of the recollections. 'A Familiar Preface' also responds to the reception of the reminiscences as they were published in the *English Review*. Conrad could particularly have had in mind the reservations about the first instalment's development expressed by his friend Sidney Colvin, an art historian and critic.[1] Pinker had also raised objections, and Conrad was possibly anticipating potential criticism by reviewers even before they made it.

With this preface added, and as book publication approached, the question of a title became pressing. His earliest versions, 'The Art and the Life' or 'The Pages and the Years – Reminiscences', both mentioned to Pinker in October 1908 (*Letters*, IV, 139) were not surprisingly abandoned as the work took form. In May 1911, when Conrad mentioned book publication to Unwin, he indicated that he was thinking of 'some such title as *The Double Call: An Intimate Note*'.[2] Four months later this somewhat elusive title was transformed into '*A Personal Note* or something of that kind'.[3] According to Conrad, Nash had insisted on something conventional: 'My suggestion to Nash was "A Personal Record", but Nash looked so frightened at such an eccentricity that I hastened to assure him that he could call it anything he jolly well liked.'[4] In the event, the serial title 'Some Reminiscences', which underscored the work's open and casual structure and had the advantage of consistency for a work already in print, suited the firm's autobiography list, the titles of which included 'Memoirs', 'Reminiscences', and 'Recollections'.

Conrad's American publisher proved less squeamish than Nash: Harpers' edition published in New York in January 1912 bore the title *A Personal Record*, one that put a seal of artistic completeness on its

---

[1] See Conrad to Colvin, 28 December 1908 (*Letters*, IV, 175).
[2] Conrad to Unwin, 17 May 1911 (*Letters*, IV, 441).
[3] Conrad to Pinker, 13 September 1911 (*Letters*, IV, 477).
[4] Conrad to J. M. Dent, 20 March 1919 (*Letters*, VI, 390).

form. This was adopted for the second English edition, published by
Thomas Nelson & Sons in 1916, and for all later English and American
editions. Thus the title evolved from being off-handedly descriptive,
with its meaning '*some* aspects of what I could recollect of my life', to
becoming the formal declaration: 'This is what I wish to present to the
public as a report of my activities, of the leading facts of and factors
in my life, as an account of doings by which I wish to be remembered
and assessed.'

Provided with a preface and lightly revised for book publication,
Conrad's reminiscences had seemingly achieved final form on their
publication in America and England in January 1912, but a new edition
to appear under the imprint of J. M. Dent & Sons in November 1919
called for yet another preface and offered an opportunity to clarify
certain things about himself and his family heritage. Like 'A Familiar
Preface', the 'Author's Note' was concerned with presenting a general
image of himself as a writer and suggesting how his work should be
interpreted. It also added an extended fragment devoted to Conrad's
father, Apollo Korzeniowski – the only discussion of him in the volume
that is more than a passing allusion – and a moving, if brief, portrait
of his mother.

Here he also raises three polemical points. First, he eloquently
denies having made a choice between French and English as his writing language. In so doing, he specifically answers Sir Hugh Clifford,
who made this claim in 1904,[1] but more immediately takes issue with
Hugh Walpole, who repeated Clifford's assertion in a book published
in June 1916. He also crosses swords with H. L. Mencken, whose recent
A Book of Prefaces (1917) reiterated Clifford's statement.[2] Secondly, in
response to an unnamed American critic – also Mencken, who, in fact,
keenly admired his work – he firmly rejects the classification of himself
as representative of 'Sclavonism' and stresses Poland's links with Western European traditions and ideas. The third, most complicated, point
concerns the epithet 'Revolutionist' applied to his father. Conrad not
surprisingly declines to identify Tadeusz Nalepiński, the 'sympathetic'
critic (6.14) whose remark appeared in a Warsaw daily in late March
1912.[3] A precocious and versatile writer who was to die shortly after

[1] See 'Notes' for details.
[2] Conrad to Walpole of 7 June 1918 (*Letters*, VI, 227–8). Preoccupied by the war, Conrad only
   read Walpole's book in the late spring of 1918. See also Conrad to Mencken, 11 November
   1918 (*Letters*, VI, 144).
[3] See 6.14–16n for details.

the Great War, Nalepiński did not attempt, as Conrad claims he did, 'to account for certain characteristics' of his work by the fact of his being 'the son of a Revolutionist' (6.14–16). Coming from Nalepiński, who was soon to join Józef Piłsudski's Legions in fighting for an independent and democratic Poland, the epithet would, in any case, have been anything but negative.[1] Conrad, however, uses the opportunity to vent his antagonism towards all revolutions – as he does in a somewhat different context in 'A Familiar Preface' – no doubt having in mind, above all, the Bolshevik Revolution of November 1917.

SOURCES, INFLUENCES, STRUCTURE

Sources

THE main source material for *A Personal Record* is, of course, Conrad's own life, or, rather, carefully selected episodes from it that he wished to reveal to his readers. Several 'recollections', however, are based on, and at times more or less direct translations of, *Pamiętnik* (1900), the posthumously published memoirs of his uncle and guardian Tadeusz Bobrowski. These deal with family history as seen through Bobrowski's eyes. As Paul Kirschner and Yves Hervouet have painstakingly shown,[2] Conrad encrusted his texts with phrases and even whole fragments borrowed from other writers. (Whether he did so consciously or not is beside the point here.) In this case, however, Conrad openly points at his source by placing in inverted commas the story of his uncle's sisters – his own mother and aunt – as told by his uncle,[3] an acknowledgement unique in the whole of his canon. Several other fragments are not marked off as quoted, but are nevertheless easily recognizable when placed side-by-side with *Pamiętnik*.[4]

Conrad's use of his uncle's *Memoirs* as a source in the first four instalments of the reminiscences may suggest that they are a potential mine

---

[1] Piłsudski was himself a 'revolutionist' in 1905–6 as the leader of the 'Revolutionary Faction' of the underground Polish Socialist Party, active in attacks on Russian police.

[2] Kirschner, *Conrad: The Psychologist as Artist* (1968), and Hervouet, *The French Face of Joseph Conrad* (1990).

[3] See pp. 38.22–40.28.

[4] See 'Appendix'. For a discussion, see 'Joseph Conrad and Tadeusz Bobrowski', Najder, 1997, pp. 44–67. After Conrad's death, Jessie Conrad donated Conrad's copy of Bobrowski's memoirs (*Pamiętnik*, ed. J. N. Niewiarowski, 2 vols., Lwów, 1900), with his scribblings in the margins, to the Polish Legation, London. It was preserved in the library of the former Polish Embassy in Pond Street and passed to the Polish Library in King's Road, London. At present, it remains unlocated.

of literary material, but this is true to a limited degree only. Bobrowski's book is full of gossip, often of a malicious kind, and was bought up and destroyed by members of families mentioned in it. It is also an important historical source for the history of Poles in the Ukraine in the second half of the nineteenth century, but is nonetheless themat-ically highly circumscribed and politically biased despite its pretences of impartiality. Written in a rather bland style, it tends to pedantry rather than clarity. Sarcasm is common, irony rare. One would look in vain for descriptions of the landscape or of everyday life. In fact, it barely mentions most of the country's inhabitants – Ukrainians in the villages, Jews in the towns. The fragment in the third instalment of the reminiscences about 'X', Conrad's maternal grandmother's sec-ond husband, is typical of scandalous content but differs in tone from the terse way in which Bobrowski usually recounts gossip.

Conrad used his uncle's *Memoirs* not only as a source of translated fragments but also to prod his own recollections of stories heard in childhood. In this way, he could insert other people's reminiscences into 'his'. Having recourse to materials from outside his own psyche appears to have facilitated composition. As he wove his seemingly art-less, but intricate, narrative, veering into associative excursions and then returning to the motif of the manuscript of *Almayer's Folly*, he had at his disposal a fairly solid block of 'hard facts' as evoked or reported by his uncle. These are set off against his own less structured, more fluid experience. From the fourth instalment onwards, the external foil of facts disappears, with its role, to some extent, taken over by a recollection of Conrad's father from a period when Conrad himself was yet unable to make decisions about his future and thus from a time of his life not requiring explanatory and justifying interpretation.

Although his memories as well as Bobrowski's form the volume's principal sources, the reminiscences cannot themselves be treated as a repository of the facts of Conrad's life. The differences between the description of his consecutive examinations for his maritime certifi-cates and their documented results are a signal example of suppres-sion, artistic transformation, and shaping of the raw materials of his life for the public persona of author.[1] That he omits to mention two failed examinations on his path to his Master's certificate is a deliberate

---

[1] See Hans van Marle, 'Plucked and Passed on Tower Hill: Conrad's Examination Ordeals', *Conradiana*, 8 (1976), 99–109, and Najder, pp. 83–4, 90–91.

choice motivated less, it can be argued, to conceal an unflattering reality than to give a dramatically satisfying shape to 'memory'.

Placing some of the details Conrad presents against documented fact reveals casual lapses of memory or outright mistakes based on insufficient knowledge. For example, he misremembered that W. H. Jacques, the first reader of *Almayer's Folly* or, indeed, of his fiction, had not died in Australia but in England; he placed his mother's visit to her family at Nowochwastów in 1864, whereas it occurred in 1863; he forgot that Adam Pulman, his tutor, studied not philosophy but medicine at university and mis-remembered where he had learnt of his death; he made W. W. Jacobs markedly younger than himself, whereas they were born only six years apart. There are other minor errors. The name of Emma Bovary's father in Flaubert's famous novel is given inaccurately, and a statue by Michelangelo misidentified. None of this is particularly important for the general reader; however, anyone interested in the relation between Conrad's fictions and fact should be aware that the distance between the two is sometimes considerable. Factual precision was evidently not a primary aim of these reminiscences.

It is unclear what sources Conrad intended to draw on in his original plan for writing about 'the liberation of the serfs' (an action his father advocated). Bobrowski contains nothing about the actual event, and Conrad was aware that the peasants in Russia's westernmost provinces, and notably in the so-called 'Kingdom of Poland', were not serfs.[1] Most probably he knew as well that in these ethnically Polish provinces the legal and economic ramifications of the land reform proclaimed in 1864 by Tsar Alexander II were, for political reasons, different and more advantageous to the peasantry than in Russia proper. Ludwik Krżyanowski's meticulous study of 'fact and fiction' in 'Prince Roman,'[2] which was to have formed part of *A Personal Record* (or a sequel perhaps), does not help answer the question of how much and from what sources Conrad knew about the history of his homeland in the nineteenth century.

Influences

STRUCTURALLY, the four first sections of the reminiscences follow the same pattern: a series of loose associations is artfully linked

---

[1] *Pamiętnik*, p. 438, n. 6.
[2] 'Joseph Conrad's "Prince Roman": Fact and Fiction,' in *Joseph Conrad: Centennial Essays*, ed. Ludwik Krżyanowski (1960), pp. 27–72.

together by returns to the topic of Conrad's first novel, *Almayer's Folly* (more precisely, of its manuscript), and interspersed with 'learned' digressions. Whether Conrad was consciously following a demonstrably Sternian mode cannot be proved but seems likely. He may even have done so without thinking about *Tristram Shandy* (1760–7) and *A Sentimental Journey* (1768) and by relying on memories of his early reading. Laurence Sterne's work had been translated and travestied in Poland since the late eighteenth century,[1] and it had several enthusiastic and skilful followers in the first half of the nineteenth whose works Conrad would certainly have read.[2] His reference in *Chance* to 'A sort of anti-sentimental journey' suggests, however, a knowledge of Sterne's original.[3]

Under Sterne's influence a whole Polish literary genre, the *gawęda*, developed, a genre that influences the structure and method of *A Personal Record*. A tale told by a clearly individualized narrator, the *gawęda* has a seemingly loose structure and aspires to give an impression of a carefree stream of recollection. In reality, however, the form is subject to clearly defined conventions: the narrator relates events from his personal experience and assumes a specific audience composed of his own milieu and social class (usually the landed gentry). The *gawęda* existed in a domesticated cultural environment and presented no challenges to its rules. The narrator felt entirely at home with his listeners, habitually winking to them to confirm mutual understanding.

In composing *A Personal Record*, Conrad, like authors in the *gawęda* tradition, feigns the randomness of associative discourse. In fact, however, he subjects his seemingly free play of reminiscence to self-confessed programmatic limitations and to formal constraints (the latter signalled, for example, by direct appeals to the reader). He uses this familiar Polish convention in a completely different context to communicate not with an audience culturally like himself but, contrariwise, to explain his particularity and difference to readers from milieux other than his own. Thus this semi-Sternian form is used not to domesticate a subject but to place a filter, in the shape of a personalized narrator, between the writer and the story he narrates. This offers

---

[1] In addition to translations from the English original, there were Polish translations from French versions.

[2] See Najder, *Letters*, p. 16; Wit Tarnawski, *Conrad the Man, the Writer, the Pole*, trans. Rosamond Batchelor (1984), pp. 104–10; and Najder 1997, p. 105. An earlier version of Tarnawski's reflections on the volume appeared as 'Conrad's *A Personal Record*', *Conradiana*, 12 (1969), 55–8.

[3] P. 150.

enormous artistic possibilities, as 'Youth' and 'Heart of Darkness' – both influenced by the *gawęda* – demonstrate. However, the form also requires concentrated effort of a kind that Conrad was not always able to muster when he was writing his reminiscences.

Structure

THE first part, with its motif of the growth of *Almayer's Folly* serving as the warp, is the most suggestive of purposeful design. The Sternian element, whether premeditated or not, was immediately noticed by reviewers but, with the exception of Polish scholars, later forgotten by critics. It becomes diluted in the final three chapters, which are less tightly constructed than the first four, though they have writing and the sea alternately in focus: Chapter 5 takes up the writing of fiction; Chapter 6 discusses the author as writer-and-seaman in one person; and Chapter 7 is a meditation on Conrad's early experiences in the South of France and his apprenticeship in the Mediterranean. The tone remains discursive and digressions continue to abound, but instead of a recurrent motif, strings of associations pursue relatively clear thematic lines.

Conrad's narrative method, ostensibly the same as in the earlier chapters, is in fact looser and less structured. These chapters lack a pivot: there are neither recurrent motifs nor the foil of a body of facts bound up with the lives of people other than Conrad himself – his uncle, parents, other members of his family. The whole patterning of the text is at the mercy of the narrator's own associations, without any other self-imposed artistic rigour. This renders the text both more spontaneous and more arbitrary. The Sternian model may be still recognizable, but in the vestigial form of a game of associations and witticisms, played with a feel for atmosphere, not with an intention to tell a rounded story.

RECEPTION

THE RECEPTION of autobiographical writing presents peculiar problems both for the writer and for his critics. The latter tend to read the life history through the prism of the author's works – in the case of *A Personal Record*, Conrad's novels and tales published up to 1912. The author wants not only to monitor the new book's critical reception but also to keep an eye on how the act of self-exposure affects his public image and influences the reading of his other works. For Conrad another aspect was also important. *A Personal Record* was a piece of self-justification, both cultural – involving his status as a 'foreigner' in England – and personal, as a man with an unusual biography.

Conrad's mixed feelings about publishing the work as he had left it in 1909 proved prescient: reviewers of *Some Reminiscences* immediately reacted with respectful curiosity, mingled with outright bafflement, to the book's narrative method and structure. Conrad's fiction, his treatment of his maritime career in *The Mirror of the Sea*, and rumours about his Polish origins had roused vivid interest in his autobiography, but reviewers, in the end, found this interest largely unsatisfied.

The warning implicit in the casual, even cautious, title – that only 'some' aspects of Conrad's past would be on display – went unheeded. The review in the *Outlook* represented the general tenor of critical reactions: *Some Reminiscences* was 'quite unlike any biography that ever was written. Its discursiveness, the chronological chaos of it, are hardly to be described' (17 February 1912, p. 253). W. L. Courtney, a veteran reviewer generally unsympathetic to Conrad's work, again grumbled, criticizing the book's 'fragmentary and inchoate' character (*Daily Telegraph*, 31 January 1912, p. 16). The poet and novelist Andrew Lang went even further, calling the book 'disappointing' as an autobiography (*Morning Post*, 22 February 1912, p. 2). The review in the *Evening Standard and St James Gazette* said that in the 'whole gallery of portraits, all clear, careful, and distinct', the portrait of the author himself was lacking – 'the one we came to see' (2 February 1912, p. 5). And a notice in the *English Review*, possibly by Ford Madox Ford, rightly warned that 'These reminiscences will not be of much use to chroniclers' (April 1912, 158). Other critics more gently couched their reactions by pointing at Conrad's 'reticence' in not providing hard data about his past or at the 'elusiveness' of his personality (*Glasgow News*, 8 February 1912, p. 10). The reviewer for *T. P.'s Weekly* explained Conrad's reserve by reference to his cultural and linguistic situation: 'I have a theory that when a man is not writing in his native language a certain reticence is his heritage. Conrad is a Pole. Like Pierre Loti, he has been a sailor. But unlike Loti he learned English well enough to serve as a model to those who value a sensitive touch' (12 April 1912, p. 457).

If the content of Conrad's ostensible autobiography was often perceived as baffling, its form was frequently found bewildering. The *Nation* complained that the volume was 'wild in its disorder', belying the author's references to 'his quarter-deck discipline' (24 February

1912, p. 857). Too much tacking (as in sailing), too little straight course was the way *Public Opinion* put it (1 March 1912, p. 205). Other verdicts used the words 'haphazardness' (*Sunday Times*, 28 January 1912, p. 7), 'hotch-potch', and 'chaotic' (*Outlook*, 17 February 1912, p. 253), and 'fitful' and 'desultory' (Desmond O'Brien, *Truth*, 13 March 1912, p. 662). The *Times Literary Supplement* judged the book 'as wilfully constructed as his novels' (25 January 1912, p. 34). Richard Curle, a journalist and short-story writer soon to become a close friend of Conrad's, considered that 'the author seems to wander along the fringe of an invoked past, picking out a remembrance here and there, without any particular purpose of enlightenment or sequence' (2 February 1912, p. 4). Fifteen years later another friend, Sir Hugh Clifford, seemed to echo these complaints, writing that *A Personal Record* is 'perhaps the most disjointed piece of autobiography that has ever been written, and it presents a curious instance of Conrad's predilection for assailing the narrative which he sets out to attack from all manner of unexpected angles'.[1]

The brief notice in the *English Review*, significantly, defended Conrad against the charge of formlessness. The anonymous critic of the *Athenæum* as well as Andrew Lang noted an analogy with Sterne. The former wrote that Conrad's 'self-portraiture is at once characteristic and unforgettable, a thing of significant glimpses and sayings, wilfully discursive – indeed, reminding us of Sterne in its indifference to the claims of mere narrative and the subtlety of its touches' (3 February 1912, p. 124). The latter adduced the Sternian resemblance not as an explanation but as a shrug: 'The narrative of Tristram Shandy, indeed, is not more discursive and erratic than these reminiscences' (*Morning Post*, 22 February 1912, p. 2). A few years later Hugh Walpole, a popular novelist who was later to become Conrad's friend, added, appreciatively, that *Some Reminiscences* had only *Tristram Shandy* for its rival 'in the business of getting everything done without moving a step forward'.[2]

Although registering their puzzlement and objections, most reviewers expressed an appreciation of a 'curious beauty of style and feeling' (*Birmingham Daily Post*, 2 February 1912, p. 4) and of 'the beautiful veil of fiction' that 'hangs between author and reader' (*Westminster Gazette*, 3 February 1912, p. 4). F. G. Bettany in the *Sunday Times* declared the

---

[1] *A Talk on Joseph Conrad and His Work.* English Association, Ceylon Branch (Colombo, 1927), p. 10.

[2] *Joseph Conrad* [1916], p. 22.

volume 'finely written' (28 January 1912, p. 7), and the *Observer* even called it 'a masterpiece' (28 January 1912, p. 5), commenting that it was 'built to music' and possessed 'a haunting quality'. *Public Opinion* reminded its readers that 'Mr Conrad is a Pole, he is a master of the English language' (1 March 1912, p. 205); 'And how finely he writes the English language', exclaimed the *Daily News* (26 January 1912, p. 3). The stress was placed on Conrad's prodigiousness.

Indeed, most reviewers unreservedly praised the volume's language. The *Daily Chronicle* (29 January 1912, p. 6) admired the flowing rhythms of Conrad's prose. The *Standard* estimated that there were 'few living novelists writing in English with more distinction' (6 February 1912, p. 5), and the *Glasgow News* went further in calling Conrad 'perhaps the greatest living writer of English prose' (8 February 1912, p. 10). On the other hand, the *Spectator*, quoting specific examples, remarked that Conrad was 'still writing in a foreign language' with persistent but sometimes lapsing vigilance (13 July 1912, p. 60), and the *Nation* likewise judged that Conrad wrote 'excellent, but always foreign, English' (24 February 1912, p. 857).

All in all, Conrad's cultural identity remained a problem for his critics. Although most mentioned his non-English point of view, the *Outlook*'s reviewer found Conrad's humour 'peculiarly English' (17 February 1912, p. 253). Richard Curle, to the contrary, ascribed the 'fatalistic melancholy' of the fiction to Conrad's Polish background (*Manchester Guardian*, 2 February 1912, p. 4). The *Glasgow News* considered Conrad 'a pessimist' saved from despair by his pride, or rather his dignity, and also ascribed these qualities of mind to his Polishness (8 February 1912, p. 10). The *Spectator* wrote of Conrad's intense seriousness, a sustained intensity, a 'dull beat in his irony' and a 'dogged brilliance' due apparently to his Polish roots, and it praised the book for doing much 'to make intelligible a personality which to the English mind must always have appeared something remote and mysterious' (13 July 1912, pp. 61, 60).

British reviewers were divided as to whether Conrad's hope, declared in the final sentences of 'A Familiar Preface', was justified: that a 'coherent justifiable personality' (18.19–20) would emerge from his reminiscences. F. G. Bettany found it 'not quite fulfilled' because of the chosen method of self-presentation: 'Of himself, as apart from his external circumstances and the sensations they produced at the moment, he does not tell us so much as he seems to imagine and he passes from one phase of himself to another so rapidly as to confuse our impressions.

This is one of the disadvantages of his casual method' (*Sunday Times*, 28 January 1912, p. 7). The *Nation* deemed the personality 'elusive' (24 February 1912, p. 857), and another critic judged that, though *Some Reminiscences* was a better book than *Almayer's Folly*, no image of the writer emerged:

> he reminisces; he does not confess. He tells us a lot about his early years, and how he came to go to sea, and how he came to leave it. But intentionally or not, he does not lay bare his soul, and in these 'Reminiscences,' as in the novels, anything we want to know concerning Mr. Conrad we have to find out for ourselves.
>
> (*Evening Standard and St James Gazette*, 2 February 1912, p. 5)

Yet these were minority voices. Most reviewers considered the book to show 'a powerful man, living his life vehemently, intensely'; 'Not a man of letters' but 'a man of life'; that 'we have to do with a rare mind, great artist, undimmed eye and steeled heart'; with a very much needed 'radiant and humane intelligence'; that the personality of 'one of the greatest novelists' was evident in the text.[1] The *World* fully responded to Conrad's hope, assessing that the reader obtained from the volume 'a vivid and coherent . . . impression of personality' (13 February 1912, p. 244).

British reviewers found themselves reviewed by an anonymous Polish critic, who berated their lack of understanding of the book's form and contents. For him, the work's obvious goal was to make palpable and comprehensible the author's national background and his astonishing evolution into 'one of the best' English novelists (*Czas*, 17 February 1912, afternoon edn, pp. 4–5). Another Pole, Józef Retinger, a writer and political activist who was soon to become close to Conrad, barely mentioned the volume's Polish elements, presenting it in poetic terms as answering the question of how one becomes an artist (*Museion*, June [1912], 105–7). The third, and most interesting, Polish reaction was that of Tadeusz Nalepiński, who was staying in London when the book appeared. (A close friend of the distinguished anthropologist Bronisław Malinowski, he possibly met Conrad.) Nalepiński's article is less a review than a compendium of general information about Conrad for a Polish audience.[2] He also perceptively noticed the similarity between the book's narrative construction and the traditional Polish *gawęda*,

[1] *The Daily News*, 26 January 1912, p. 3; *Daily Mail*, 9 February 1912, p. 8; [H. H. Child], *Times Literary Supplement*, 25 January 1912, p. 34; Perceval Gibbon, *Bookman*, April 1912, 26; *Birmingham Daily Post*, 2 February 1912, p. 4.

[2] *Kurier Warszawski*, 24 March 1912, pp. 7–8.

an oral tale whose written and more sophisticated nineteenth-century exemplars owed much to Sterne.

Fewer and less elaborate than British reviews, the North American ones differed little in tone. Although known in America, Conrad was yet to have the large following there that he was soon to win with *Chance* (1913); he could nonetheless report to his agent the view of the American critic James Huneker, who called on him at Capel House, that 'the Rems had a wonderful *press*-success in the States and that this reception will have an extremely favourable influence on the future of my work'.[1] As in Britain, there were muted complaints about the 'haphazard fashion' of the writing (*Dial*, 1 March 1912, p. 172) and 'a fashion fragmentary and careless of chronology' (*New York Times Book Review*, 18 February 1912, pp. 77–8). The reviewer of the *Nation* found Conrad's strenuous attempts at establishing conversational contact with his reader unsuccessful, and authorial reserve was also noted: the *North American Review* characterized the reminiscences as 'impersonal' (April 1912, pp. 569–70).

The 'oddity' of Conrad's English was also commented upon, with the *Dial* giving specific examples of his abuse of participial constructions in place of infinitives. The essayist and short-story writer Christopher Morley in an otherwise favourable commentary would later write that 'Conrad's prose . . . seems always like some notable translation from the French'.[2] The reviewer of the *Canadian Magazine* set the record for inattentive, if enthusiastic, reading: 'Joseph Conrad . . . though a Russian, is the first of living English authors' (July 1912, pp. 289–90). The *Catholic World* even complained that the book was too short (May 1912, pp. 254–6). H. L. Mencken in *Smart Set* praised Conrad for liberating himself from sentimentality, and opined that he was 'not only a great artist, but also a great artistic revolutionist' (October 1912, pp. 149–50). Intentionally or not, this remark formed a paradoxical rejoinder to Conrad's own claim in 'A Familiar Preface': 'I have not been revolutionary in my writings' (17.18–19).

The first scholarly commentary on *A Personal Record*, in a study by Wacław Borowy (1924), noted compositional analogies with *Trzy po trzy* [Tittle-Tattle Talk] (1877) by Aleksander Fredro (1791?–1873),[3] the leading Polish writer of comedies. It identifies their origins in both

---

[1] Conrad to Pinker, [12 October 1912] (*Letters*, v, 115).
[2] *Shandygaff: A Number of Most Agreeable Inquirendoes upon Life and Letters* (1918), p. 243.
[3] The memoir was written prior to 1848.

writers' conscious recourse to and modelling on Sterne.[1] Later, the volume suffered a general critical neglect, although it was long an object of interest to Conrad's biographers. However, the first of these, Conrad's friend G. Jean-Aubry, barely mentioned it in his *Joseph Conrad: Life and Letters* (1927).[2] Jocelyn Baines, in his biography (1960), chiefly used it as a source of illustrative quotation and analysed it as an *apologia pro vita sua*. Baines's summing-up – 'And it is Conrad's public face which is displayed; there is no analysis, no probing below the surface' – exposes the book's internal paradox as an apology by a man who ardently wishes to remain discreetly in the shade.[3]

In his introduction to the Anchor Books edition of *The Mirror of the Sea and A Personal Record* (1960), Morton Dauwen Zabel, an influential champion of Conrad's work in America in the 1940s and 1950s, was the first scholar writing in English to devote more than a few sentences to the volume. He concentrated on the psychological function of the text for Conrad himself: 'like most of his self-confessing confrères he used his self and his personal history more for purposes of self-projection, apology, or mystification than for those of personal chronicle or intimacy'. Commenting on Conrad's idea concerning the projected 'vision of personality', he points out that 'Such a "vision" is bound to be something radically different from an objective or literal record of experience' (pp. xi–xv). And he went even further in his biographical criticism, saying that 'The professed ideals of Conrad's ethic are those of sobriety, fidelity, duty, responsible purpose, and honor. . . . But the actual bent of his temper and emotion was unquestionably at continuous odds with them' (pp. xxii–xxviii).

Zdzisław Najder was the first to analyse Conrad's use of his uncle Tadeusz Bobrowski's memoirs as a source for some parts of the work.[4] Wit Tarnawski in his *Conrad człowiek, pisarz, Polak* [Conrad the Man, The Writer, and The Pole] (1972) saw in *A Personal Record* an attempt to justify the author's 'twofold desertion of his country' – by going to sea and writing in English. Tarnawski found that for Conrad the book had a cathartic function and constituted the 'settlement of an outstanding debt to his native country'.[5] He was thus typical of those

---

[1] 'Fredro i Conrad. Z tajników sztuki pisarskiej' [Fredro and Conrad: From the Secrets of Literary Art], *Tygodnik Wileński*, 16 (1925), 1–2.

[2] See I, 74, and II, 146, 149, 204.   [3] *Joseph Conrad: A Critical Biography*, p. 354.

[4] 'Joseph Conrad i Tadeusz Bobrowski', *Przegld Humanistyczny*, 5 (1964), 13–24. This study was only made available in English in Najder, 1997, pp. 44–67.

[5] Tarnawski, pp. 104–10.

Polish critics who, encouraged by the psychoanalytical speculations of the Jungian analyst Gustav Morf,[1] tended to sniff out symptoms of a guilt complex in *A Personal Record*, one supposedly partly engendered by Eliza Orzeszkowa's bitter attack on Conrad in 1899 for 'deserting' his homeland.[2] (The charge is remarkably ill-informed: Orzeszkowa characterized Conrad as a popular and well-paid author – hardly his position in the 1890s.)

J. M. Kertzer (1975) approached *A Personal Record* as a piece of fiction, 'an artful examination of a set of personal experiences which correspond to experiences portrayed in the novels.'[3] He argued for a cohesion of its thematic content and claimed that the book 'provides the clearest example of one of Conrad's major themes: the efforts of an individual to establish a moral pattern in his life.' Conrad tries to discover this moral pattern by looking back at his past decisions; however, Kertzer found that he 'treats himself more leniently than he does his fictional characters who face similar problems but find them less easily resolved.' Although following a very different line of enquiry, Hans van Marle's meticulous research into Conrad's maritime career (1976) supported a view of the work as shaped by artistic and moral impulses, with facts being either suppressed or highlighted for narrative and dramatic effect.[4]

In the mid-1970s as well, David Thorburn pointed out the distance between Conrad's initial synopsis of the planned content of *A Personal Record* and the actual book, and later analysed Conrad's narrative strategies, linking them with impressionism.[5] Frederick R. Karl in his 1979 biography of Conrad likewise connected the volume's narrative techniques with Conrad's theory of literary impressionism and with the associative methods of Marcel Proust.[6] Zdzisław Najder (1983) hypothesizes that Conrad wrote *A Personal Record* prompted by Robert Lynd's review of *A Set of Six*; he also questioned Ford's alleged role in writing the book from Conrad's dictation and identified the objective of its

---

[1] *The Polish Heritage of Joseph Conrad* (1930).   [2] See Najder, *Conrad*, pp. xix–xx, 182–92.

[3] 'Conrad's Personal Record', *University of Toronto Quarterly*, 44 (1975), 290–303.

[4] 'Plucked and Passed', and 'An Ambassador of Conrad's Future: The *James Mason* in Marseilles, 1874', *L'Époque Conradienne*, 14 (1988), 63–7.

[5] *Conrad's Romanticism* (1974), pp. 61–3, and 'Evasion and Candor in *A Personal Record*', in Claude Thomas, ed., *Studies in Joseph Conrad*. Cahiers d'Études et de Recherches Victoriennes et Édouardiennes, 2 (Montpellier: Centre d'études de recherches Victoriennes et Édouardiennes, Université Paul-Valéry, 1975), pp. 223–38.

[6] *Joseph Conrad: The Three Lives* (1979), pp. 661, 671.

thematic arrangement as the creation of a personal mythology.[1] Brian
Finney in his synthetic study of British literary autobiography considered *A Personal Record* 'an extreme example of the use of inner form'
(that is, form dictated by the 'shape or meaning to the life' described,
as seen by the author). In other words, he took the text and structure
of *A Personal Record* as an expression of Conrad's antecedent vision
of his own life.[2] Juliet McLauchlan (1984) analysed the implications
of Conrad's repeated use of the term 'piety',[3] and Jean M. Szczypien
has commented on Conrad's presentation of his family history and
heritage.[4]

In *The Invention of the West* (1995), Christopher GoGwilt has argued
that *A Personal Record* plays 'a major role in sustaining the coherence of
Conrad's œuvre'. Conrad copes there with the problems of his uncertain cultural identity and of his escape from his native community.
According to GoGwilt, in writing *A Personal Record* Conrad had discovered an 'absence of Polish identity', any reconstruction of which 'can
only be a fabrication'.[5] In a more recent study, Keith Carabine (1996)
discerned thematic congruences in *A Personal Record* and *Under Western
Eyes* and encouraged reading them in a complementary fashion.[6]

Christine de Vinne analyses *A Personal Record* (2002) as a 'confessional narrative', referring directly to the term's religious meaning.
Her analysis intertwines two planes of argument: structural, in which
she shows Conrad's links to the traditions of confessional literature, grounded in a narrator–narratee (= confessant–confessor)
relationship; and psychological, in which she claims that *A Personal
Record* served Conrad for a double purpose of self-definition and excul-
pation, achieved by transferring responsibility (and guilt) to the 'confessor', that is, the reader.[7]

Critics and scholars have thus far mainly treated the volume as a
source of information about its author's psychology, opinions and

---

[1] Najder, pp. 340–1, 343.

[2] *The Inner I: British Literary Autobiography of the Twentieth Century* (1985), pp. 73–9.

[3] 'Piety in Joseph Conrad's *A Personal Record*', *Polish Review*, 19.3 (1984), 11–23.

[4] See 'Conrad's '*A Personal Record*: Composition, Intention, Design: Polonism', *Journal of Modern Literature*, 16.1 (1989), 3–30; 'The Historical Background for Joseph Conrad's *A Personal
Record*', *The Conradian*, 15.2 (1991), 12–32; 'Echoes from *Konrad Wallenrod* in *Almayer's Folly*
and *A Personal Record*', *Nineteenth-Century Literature*, 53.1 (1998), 91–110.

[5] Christopher GoGwilt, *The Invention of the West: Joseph Conrad and the Double-Mapping of Europe
and Empire* (1995), pp. 109–58.

[6] See Carabine.

[7] Christine de Vinne, 'Begging the Question of Confession: Joseph Conrad's *A Personal Record*',
Prose Studies 25.3 (December 2002), 82–99.

the facts of his life. There has been a trend leading from acceptance (that is, taking Conrad's reminiscences as close to reality or at least illustrative of it) to revision (that is, investigating the discrepancies between the author's own version of events and surviving documents). Thus from seeing *A Personal Record* as a 'record' of Conrad's life as lived, critics have increasingly recognized it as a fable about how he wanted it to have been lived and how he wanted it to be publicly understood. Kertzer's attempt to consider it a piece of self-sustained fiction, however, remains isolated. Paradoxically, Polish scholars, who display an inclination to consider *A Personal Record* as a psychological document of self-atonement, have also devoted much attention to its formal structure. However this may be, both the sweep of the critical literature and the volume's appearance in French, German, Italian, and Polish translations testify to Conrad's position as a major world writer and to the centrality of *A Personal Record* for understanding the shape and dynamics of his early literary career.[1]

Conrad's subtle adaptation and colouring of his prose to explore the facts of his life and the values that sustained it also makes the volume an important stylistic achievement. The seemingly debonair narrative tone, with here and there harder glimmers of wry humour and sarcasm, forms a screen tinged with self-irony through which the reader perceives subjects that are personal, intimate, puzzling – even embarrassing – and sometimes intensely emotional. These include Conrad's memories of his parents; his departure from a country with a singularly demanding patriotic heritage; his writing in an adopted language; his desire to go to sea; and his transformation into a professional writer in a language learned as an adult. However, as several early commentators noted, there is little direct intimacy in all this. The volume's a-chronological structure, which is in part due to an insistence not on the subject's development but rather on the continuity of a multi-faceted personality through experiences widely separate in time and place, cannily fends off identification with the narrating voice.

The associative method not only allows Conrad to pass easily from the particular subject at hand to general issues but also enables him

---

[1] The first annotated edition, accompanying Renato Prinzhofer's translation, appeared in 1982 in *Tutte le opere di Joseph Conrad*, supervised by Ugo Mursia. The volume also appeared in G. Jean-Aubry's 1924 translation, revised by Roger Hibon, in 1987 in the Pléiade edition, *Conrad: Œuvres*, under the general editorship of Sylvère Monod, with notes and a commentary by Monod. Two annotated editions have appeared in English: Zdzisław Najder's in the Oxford World's Classics series (1988) and Mara Kalnins' in Penguin's Twentieth-Century Classics series (1998).

to conceal himself. The events of his life are shown in sudden flashes of reflection, sometimes beguilingly playful and evasive, more often serious and precise. His views on the role of the imagination, which for Conrad is basically re-constructive – it is re-imagination, in fact – in art and on the art of prose fiction develop ideas formulated in 1896 in his celebrated preface to *The Nigger of the 'Narcissus'*.

The feeling of distance that Conrad maintains between himself and his subjects, and thus also between himself and his readers, is intensified by the fact that some of the stories told here are indebted to Bobrowski's memoirs, with Conrad re-ordering his uncle's words in new linguistic and emotional contexts. Professing that there were no 'draperies of fiction' or 'veils' separating the novelist from his reader (12.35–7), Conrad wove a very different fabric, less conventional but not less artful – at once protective, decorative, and decorous. The resulting narrative structure exhibits the unity of artistic and psychological principles on which the book is constructed and enables Conrad to create a private mythology – an artefact of his life, as it were – without blatantly distorting the facts.

This way of telling, indeed, blunts and obfuscates 'hard facts', and much of Conrad's life alluded to, or reflected on, in these pages has only been fully exposed by patient and inquisitive research. The distortions are of scant importance to appreciating *A Personal Record*, but they are significant in pointing to the book's fundamental idea of presenting 'a coherent, justifiable personality both in its origin and in its action' (18.19–20). The departures from reality are explainable by reference to this basic idea and that underlying need: to impress coherence on his life, with all its anomalous passages, unusual decisions, and sudden changes, and with all its uncertainties, typical of a man prone to depression. The search for consistency and the real need for it are indicated in two ways: by omitting events that would put it into question, and by adducing imagined events. But this search is most visible in avoiding the suggestion – typical of autobiographies of writers temperamentally close to Romanticism – of internal tensions, of the Faustian 'two souls in one breast', of hesitancy, and of conflicting desires and aspirations. Somewhat past the mid-point of his life when he turned to these recollections, Conrad desired and managed to present himself as being of a piece.

To call this fictional, 'created' Conrad 'public' as opposed to 'private' (that is, 'real') would be singularly misleading. The private and public faces are not in question, but rather the actual Conrad and

Conrad as he wished to be. Writing about himself was a way of dealing with his readers, but, it was, first of all, a way of coming to terms and dealing with himself. He wanted to be, not only to be seen to be, like that.

As he looked back on his life, a few especially sensitive and painful issues loomed, 'pressing questions' that, as he had written a few years earlier in *The Mirror of the Sea*, 'have remained unanswered to this day' (p. 155). Leaving Poland had evidently impressed itself upon his conscience as an act to be explained and somehow justified, particularly in light of his parents' 'sacrifice' for their country. He declares his own 'fidelity to a special tradition' (44.12–13) and even 'love' for Poland's memory here, and, although he repeatedly stresses the hopelessness of Polish national aspirations, he shows his compatriots in a nimbus of romantic heroism. While preserving his natural pride, he could thus portray his expatriation as combined with an awareness of continuing his ancestors' tragically futile exertions. And the images of his native land are like memories of a long-submerged Atlantis, as if his leaving her meant that she had ceased to exist.

Conrad presents his resolve to go to sea as unswerving, wilful, and absurdly unusual: it was, in fact, none of these. His joining the British Merchant Service was a matter of accident, not of design. He quite rightly claims that he did not 'choose' English as the language of his literary work; writing in that language was for him pre-eminently not a consequence of inherent determinism but a result of the force of events. Similarly, he adjusts many other, less essential, elements and aspects of his life. The final sentence in which the Mediterranean landscape and seascape appear as grey, livid, and drab in contrast to the brightness of the Red Ensign, the symbol of the British Merchant Service, is perhaps the most striking example of his wizardry.

It is precisely this wizardry that makes *A Personal Record* so captivating and moving a book, one that tells us certain things about Conrad's actual past, about his family background and national heritage, and more about his persistent quest to impose a meaning on his life, one consistent with the stern demands of the moral principles that he formulated and in which he believed.

A PERSONAL RECORD

AUTHOR'S NOTE

THE RE-ISSUE OF THIS book in a new form does not strictly speaking require another Preface. But since this is distinctly a place for personal remarks I take the opportunity to refer in this Author's Note to two points arising from certain statements about myself I have noticed of late in the press.

One of them bears upon the question of language. I have always felt myself looked upon somewhat in the light of a phenomenon, a position which outside the circus world cannot be regarded as desirable. It needs a special temperament for one to derive much gratification from the fact of being able to do freakish things intentionally, and, as it were, from mere vanity.

The fact of my not writing in my native language has been of course commented upon frequently in reviews and notices of my various works and in the more extended critical articles. I suppose that was unavoidable; and indeed those comments were of the most flattering kind to one's vanity. But in that matter I have no vanity that could be flattered. I could not have it. The first object of this note is to disclaim any merit there might have been in an act of deliberate volition.

The impression of my having exercised a choice between the two languages, French and English, both foreign to me, has got abroad somehow. That impression is erroneous. It originated, I believe, in an article written by Sir Hugh Clifford and published in the year '98, I think, of the last century. Some time before, Sir Hugh Clifford came to see me. He is, if not the first, then, one of the two first friends I made for myself by my work; the other being Mr Cunninghame Graham, who, characteristically enough, had been captivated by my story, "An Outpost of Progress." These friendships which have endured to this day I count amongst my precious possessions.

Mr Hugh Clifford (he was not decorated then) had just published his first volume of Malay sketches. I was naturally delighted to see him and infinitely gratified by the kind things he found to say

about my first books and some of my early short stories, the action of which is placed in the Malay Archipelago. I remember that after saying many things which ought to have made me blush to the roots of my hair with outraged modesty he ended by telling me
5 with the uncompromising yet kindly firmness of a man accustomed to speak unpalatable truths even to Oriental potentates (for their own good of course) that as a matter of fact I didn't know anything about Malays. I was perfectly aware of this. I have never pretended to any such knowledge, and I was moved – I wonder to this day at my
10 impertinence – to retort: "Of course I don't know anything about Malays. If I knew only one hundredth part of what you and Frank Swettenham know of Malays I would make everybody sit up." He went on looking kindly (but firmly) at me and then we both burst out laughing. In the course of that most welcome visit twenty years
15 ago, which I remember so well, we talked of many things, the characteristics of various languages was one of them, and it is on that day that my new friend carried away with him the impression that I had exercised a deliberate choice between French and English. Later when moved by his friendship (no empty word to him) to
20 write a study in the *North American Review* on Joseph Conrad he conveyed that impression to the public.

This misapprehension, for it is nothing else, was no doubt my fault. I must have expressed myself badly in the course of a friendly and intimate talk when one doesn't watch one's phrases carefully.
25 My recollection of what I meant to say is: that *had I been under the necessity* of making a choice between the two, and though I knew French fairly well and was familiar with it from infancy, I would have been afraid to attempt expression in a language so perfectly "crystallized." This I believe, was the word I used. And
30 then we passed to other matters. I told him a little about myself; and what he had to tell me of his work in the East, his own particular East of which I had but the mistiest, short glimpse, was of the most absorbing interest. The present Governor of Nigeria may not remember that conversation as well as I do but I am sure
35 that he will not mind this, what in diplomatic language is called, "rectification" of a statement made to him by an obscure writer his generous sympathy had prompted him to seek out and make his friend.

The truth of the matter is that my faculty to write in English is as
40 natural as any other aptitude with which I might have been born.

I have a strange and overpowering feeling that it had always been an inherent part of myself. English was for me neither a matter of choice nor adoption. The merest idea of choice had never entered my head. And as to adoption – well, yes, there was adoption; but it was I who was adopted by the genius of the language, which directly I came out of the stammering stage made me its own so completely that its very idioms I truly believe had a direct action on my temperament and fashioned my still plastic character.

It was a very intimate action and for that very reason it is too mysterious to explain. The task would be as impossible as trying to explain love at first sight. There was something in this conjunction of exulting, almost physical recognition, the same sort of emotional surrender and the same pride of possession, all united in the wonder of a great discovery; but there was on it none of that shadow of dreadful doubt that falls on the very flame of our perishable passions. One knew very well that this was for ever!

A matter of discovery and not of inheritance, that very inferiority of the title makes the faculty still more precious, lays the possessor under a life-long obligation to remain worthy of his great fortune. But it seems to me that all this sounds as if I were trying to explain – a task which I have just pronounced to be impossible. If in action we may admit with awe that the Impossible recedes before men's indomitable spirit, the Impossible in matters of analysis will always make a stand at some point or other.

All I can claim after all those years of devoted practice, with the accumulated anguish of its doubts, imperfections and falterings in my heart, is the right to be believed when I say that if I had not written in English I would not have written at all.

The other remark which I wish to make here is also a rectification but of a less direct kind. It has nothing to do with the medium of expression. It bears on the matter of my authorship in another way. It is not for me to criticise my judges, the more so because I always felt that I was receiving more than justice at their hands. But it seems to me that their unfailingly interested sympathy has ascribed to racial and historical influences much of what I believe appertains simply to the individual. Nothing is more foreign than what in the literary world is called Sclavonism to the Polish temperament with its tradition of self-government, its chivalrous view of moral restraints and an exaggerated respect for individual rights: not to mention the important fact that the whole

Polish mentality, Western in complexion, had received its training from Italy and France and, historically, had always remained, even in religious matters, in sympathy with the most liberal currents of European thought. An impartial view of humanity in all its degrees of splendour and misery together with a special regard for the rights of the unprivileged of this earth, not on any mystic grounds but on the grounds of simple fellowship and honourable reciprocity of services, was the dominant characteristic of the mental and moral atmosphere of the houses which sheltered my hazardous childhood: – matters of calm and deep conviction both lasting and consistent, and removed as far as possible from that humanitarianism that seems to be merely a matter of crazy nerves or a morbid conscience.

One of the most sympathetic of my critics tried to account for certain characteristics of my work by the fact of my being, in his own words, the son of a Revolutionist. No epithet could be less applicable to a man with such a strong sense of responsibility in the region of ideas and action and so indifferent to the promptings of personal ambition as my father. Why the description "revolutionary" should have been applied all through Europe to the Polish risings of 1831 and 1863 I really cannot understand. Those risings were purely revolts against foreign domination. The Russians themselves called them "rebellions" which, from their point of view was the exact truth. Amongst the men concerned in the preliminaries of the 1863 movement my father was no more revolutionary than the others, in the sense of working for the subversion of any social or political scheme of existence. He was simply a patriot in the sense of a man who believing in the spirituality of a national existence could not bear to see that spirit enslaved.

Called out publicly in a kindly attempt to justify the work of the son that figure of my past cannot be dismissed without a few more words. As a child of course I knew very little of my father's activities, for I was not quite twelve when he died. What I saw with my own eyes was the public funeral, the cleared streets, the hushed crowds; but I understood perfectly well that this was a manifestation of the national spirit seizing a worthy occasion. That bare-headed mass of work people, youths of the University, women at the windows, school-boys on the pavement, could have known nothing positive about him except the fame of his fidelity to the one guiding emotion in their hearts. I had nothing but that knowledge myself; and this great silent demonstration seemed to me the most natural tribute in the world – not to the man but to the Idea.

What had impressed me much more intimately was the burning of his manuscripts a fortnight or so before his death. It was done under his own superintendence. I happened to go into his room 5 a little earlier than usual that evening, and remaining unnoticed stayed to watch the nursing-sister feeding the blaze in the fire-place. My father sat in a deep arm-chair propped up with pillows. This is the last time I saw him out of bed. His aspect was to me not so much that of a man desperately ill as mortally weary – a 10 vanquished man. That act of destruction affected me profoundly by its air of surrender. Not before death however. To a man of such strong faith death could not have been an enemy.

For many years I believed that every scrap of his writings had been burnt, but in July of 1914 the Librarian of the University of 15 Cracow calling on me during our short visit to Poland mentioned the existence of a few manuscripts of my father and especially of a series of letters written before and during his exile to his most intimate friend who had sent them to the University for preser-vation. I went to the library at once but had only time then for a 20 mere glance. I intended to come back next day and arrange for copies being made of the whole correspondence. But next day there was war. So perhaps I shall never know now what he wrote to his most intimate friend in the time of his domestic happiness, of his new paternity, of his strong hopes – and later, in the hours 25 of disillusion, bereavement and gloom.

I had also imagined him to be completely forgotten forty-five years after his death. But this was not the case. Some young men of letters had discovered him, mostly as a remarkable translator of Shakespeare, Victor Hugo and Alfred de Vigny, to whose drama 30 *Chatterton* translated by himself he had written an eloquent pref-ace, defending the poet's deep humanity and his ideal of noble stoicism. The political side of his life was being recalled too; for some men of his time, his co-workers in the task of keeping the national spirit firm in the hope of an independent future, had 35 been in their old age publishing their memoirs where the part he played was for the first time publicly disclosed to the world. I learned then of things in his life I never knew before, things which outside the group of the initiated could have been known to no living being except my mother. It was thus that from a volume 40

of posthumous Memoirs dealing with those bitter years I learned
the fact that the first inception of the secret National Committee
intended primarily to organise moral resistance to the augmented
pressure of Russianism, arose on my father's initiative and that
5 its first meetings were held in our Warsaw house, of which all I
remember distinctly is one room, white and crimson, probably
the drawing-room. In one of its walls there was the loftiest of all
archways. Where it led to remains a mystery; but to this day I cannot get rid of the belief that all this was of enormous proportions
10 and that the people appearing and disappearing in that immense
space were beyond the usual stature of mankind as I got to know it
in later life. Amongst them I remember my mother, a more familiar figure than the others, dressed in the black of the national
mourning worn in defiance of ferocious police regulations. I have
15 also preserved from that particular time the awe of her mysterious
gravity which, indeed, was by no means smileless. For I remember
her smiles too. Perhaps for me she could always find a smile. She
was young then, certainly not thirty yet. She died four years later
in exile.

20   In the pages which follow I mention her visit to her brother's
house about a year before her death. I also speak a little of my
father as I remember him in the years following what was for him
the deadly blow of her loss. And now, having been again evoked
in answer to the words of a friendly critic, these Shades may be
25 allowed to return to their place of rest where their forms in life
linger yet, dim but poignant, and awaiting the moment when their
haunting reality, their last trace on earth, shall pass forever with
me out of the world.

J. C.

30   1919.

A PERSONAL RECORD

A FAMILIAR PREFACE

A S A GENERAL RULE WE do not want much encouragement
to talk about ourselves; yet this little book is the result of
a friendly suggestion and even of a little friendly pressure. I
defended myself with some spirit; but, with characteristic tenacity, 5
the friendly voice insisted.

"You know, you really must." It was not an argument, but I submitted at once. If one must! . . .

You perceive the force of a word. He who wants to persuade
should put his trust not in the right argument but in the right 10
word. The power of sound has been always greater than the power
of sense. I don't say this by way of disparagement. It is better for
mankind to be impressionable than reflective. Nothing humanely
great – great, I mean, as affecting a whole mass of lives – had
come from reflexion. On the other hand, you cannot fail to see 15
the power of mere words, such words as Glory, for instance, or
Pity. I won't mention any more. They are not far to seek. Shouted
with perseverance, with ardour, with conviction these two by their
sound alone have set whole nations in motion and upheaved the
dry, hard ground on which rests our whole social fabric. There's 20
"virtue" for you if you like! . . . Of course the accent must be
attended to. The right accent. That's very important. The capa-
cious lung, the thundering or the tender vocal chords. Don't talk
to me of your Archimedes' lever. He was an absent-minded person
with a mathematical imagination. Mathematics command all my 25
respect, but I have no use for engines. Give me the right word and
the right accent and I will move the world.

What a dream – for a writer! Because written words have their
accent too. Yes! Let me only find the right word! Surely it must
be lying somewhere amongst the wreckage of all the plaints and 30
all the exultations poured out aloud since the first day when
hope, the undying, came down on earth. It may be there close by,
disregarded, invisible, quite at hand. But it's no good. I believe

11

there are men who can lay hold of a needle in a pottle of hay at the first try. For myself, I have never had such luck.

And then there is that accent. Another difficulty. For who is going to tell whether the accent is right or wrong till the word is shouted, and fails to be heard, perhaps, and goes down wind leaving the world unmoved. Once upon a time there lived an Emperor who was a sage and something of a literary man. He jotted down on ivory tablets thoughts maxims, reflexions which chance has preserved for the edification of posterity. Amongst other weighty sayings – I am quoting from memory – I remember this solemn admonition: "Let all thy words have the accent of heroic truth." The accent of heroic truth! This is very fine, but I am thinking that it is an easy matter for an austere Emperor to jot down grandiose advice. Most of the working truths on this earth are humble, not heroic: and there have been times in the history of mankind when the accents of heroic truth have moved it to nothing but derision.

Nobody will expect to find between the covers of this little book words of extraordinary potency or accents of irresistible heroism. However humiliating for my self-esteem, I must confess that the counsels of Marcus Aurelius are not for me. They are more fit for a moralist than for an artist. Truth of a modest sort I can promise you and also sincerity, that complete, praiseworthy sincerity which while it delivers one into the hands of one's enemies is as likely as not to embroil one with one's friends.

"Embroil" is perhaps too strong an expression. I can't imagine either amongst my enemies or my friends a being so hard up for something to do as to quarrel with me. "To disappoint one's friends" would be nearer the mark. Almost all friendships of the writing period of my life have come to me through my books and I know that a novelist lives in his work. He stands there the only reality in an invented world amongst imaginary things, happenings and people. Writing about them he is only writing about himself. But the disclosure is not complete. He remains to a certain extent a figure behind the veil, a suspected rather than a seen presence – a movement and a voice behind the draperies of fiction. In these personal notes there is no such veil. And I can not help thinking of a passage in the "Imitation of Christ" where the ascetic author who knew life so profoundly says that "there are persons esteemed on their reputation who by showing themselves

destroy the opinion one had of them." This is the danger incurred
by an author of fiction who sets out to talk about himself without
disguise.

While these reminiscent pages were appearing serially I was
remonstrated with for bad economy, as if such writing were a   5
form of self-indulgence wasting the substance of future volumes. It
seems that I am not sufficiently literary. Indeed, a man who never
wrote a line for print till he was thirty-six cannot bring himself
to look upon his existence and his experience, upon the sum of
his thoughts, sensations and emotions, upon his memories and   10
his regrets, and the whole possession of his past as only so much
material for his hands. Once before some three years ago when I
published "The Mirror of the Sea," a volume of Impressions and
Memories, the same remarks were made to me. Practical remarks.
But truth to say I have never understood the kind of thrift they   15
recommended. I wanted to pay my tribute to the sea, its ships and
its men to whom I remain indebted for so much which has gone to
make me what I am. That seemed to me the only shape in which
I could offer it to their shades. There could not be a question
in my mind of anything else. It is quite possible that I am a bad   20
economist; but it is certain that I am incorrigible.

Having matured in the surroundings and under the special conditions of sea-life I have a special piety towards that form of my past;
for its impressions were vivid, its appeal direct, its demands such
as could be responded to with the natural elation of youth and   25
strength equal to the call. There was nothing in them to perplex a
young conscience. Having broken away from my origins under a
storm of blame from every quarter which had the merest shadow
of right to voice an opinion, removed by great distances from such
natural affections as were still left to me and even estranged in a   30
measure from them by the totally unintelligible character of the
life which had seduced me so mysteriously from my allegiance I
may safely say that through the blind force of circumstances the
sea was to be all my world and the Merchant Service my only
home for a long succession of years. No wonder then that in my   35
two exclusively sea-books "The Nigger of the Narcissus" and "The
Mirror of the Sea" (and in the few short sea-stories like "Youth"
and "Typhoon") I have tried with an almost filial regard to render
the vibration of life in the great world of waters, in the hearts of the
simple men who have for ages traversed its solitudes and also that   40

something sentient which seems to dwell in ships – the creatures of their hands and the objects of their care.

One's literary life must turn frequently for sustenance to memories and seek discourse with the shades; unless one has made up one's mind to write only in order to reprove mankind for what it is or praise it for what it is not or – generally – to teach it how to behave. Being neither quarrelsome, nor a flatterer, nor a sage I have done none of these things; and I am prepared to put up serenely with the insignificance which attaches to persons who are not meddlesome in some way or other. But resignation is not indifference. I would not like to be left standing as a mere spectator on the bank of the great stream carrying onwards so many lives. I would fain claim for myself the faculty of a little insight expressed in a voice of sympathy and compassion.

It seems to me that in one at least authoritative quarter of criticism I am suspected of a certain unemotional acceptance of facts, of what the French would call a "sécheresse du cœur." Fifteen years of unbroken silence before praise or blame testify sufficiently to my respect for criticism, that fine flower of personal expression in the garden of letters. But this is more of a personal matter, reaching the man behind the work and therefore it may be alluded to in a volume which is a personal note in the margin of the public page. Not that I feel hurt in the least. The charge – if it amounted to a charge at all – was made in the most considerate terms, in a tone of regret.

My answer is that if it be true that every novel contains an element of autobiography – and this can hardly be denied since the creator can only express himself in his creation – then there are some of us to whom an open display of sentiment is repugnant. I would not unduly praise the virtue of restraint. It is often merely temperamental. But it is not always a sign of coldness. It may be pride. There can be nothing more humiliating than to see the shaft of one's emotion miss the mark either of laughter or tears. Nothing more humiliating! And this for the reason that should the mark be missed, should the open display of emotion fail to move then it must perish unavoidably in disgust or contempt.

No artist can be reproached for shrinking from a risk which only fools run to meet and only genius dare confront with impunity. In a task which mainly consists in laying one's soul more or less bare to the world a regard for decency even at the cost of success is but

the regard for one's own dignity which is inseparably united with
the dignity of one's work.

And then – it is very difficult to be wholly joyous or wholly sad
on this earth. The comic, when it is human, soon takes upon itself
a face of pain; and some of our griefs (some only, not all, for it is 5
the capacity for suffering which makes man august in the eyes of
men) have their source in weaknesses which must be recognised
with smiling compassion as the common inheritance of us all.
Joy and sorrow in this world pass into each other, mingling their
forms and their murmurs in the twilight of life as mysterious as an 10
overshadowed ocean, while the dazzling brightness of supreme
hopes lies far off, fascinating and still, on the distant edge of the
unattainable horizon.

Yes! I too would like to hold the magic wand giving that command over laughter and tears which is declared to be the highest 15
achievement of imaginative literature. Only, to be a great magician one must surrender oneself to occult and irresponsible powers, either outside or within one's own breast. We have all heard of
simple men selling their souls for love or power to some grotesque
devil. The most ordinary intelligence can perceive without much 20
reflexion that anything of the sort is bound to be a fool's bargain. I
don't lay claim to particular wisdom because of my dislike and distrust of such a transaction. It may be my sea-training acting upon
a natural disposition to keep good hold on the one thing really
mine, but the fact is that I have a positive horror of losing even 25
for one moving moment that full possession of myself which is the
first condition of good service. And I have carried my notion of
good service from my earlier into my later existence. I, who have
never sought in the written word anything else but a form of the
Beautiful, I have carried over that article of creed from the decks 30
of ships to the more circumscribed space of my desk, and by that
act, I suppose, I have become permanently imperfect in the eyes
of the ineffable company of pure esthetes.

As in political so in literary action a man wins friends for himself mostly by the passion of his prejudices and by the consistent 35
narrowness of his outlook. But I have never been able to love what
was not lovable or hate what was not hateful out of deference for
some general principle. Whether there be any courage in making
this admission I know not. After the middle turn of life's way we
consider dangers and joys with a tranquil mind. So I proceed in 40

peace to declare that I have always suspected in the effort to bring
into play the extremities of emotions the debasing touch of insin-
cerity. In order to move others deeply we must deliberately allow
ourselves to be carried away beyond the bounds of our normal
5 sensibility – innocently enough perhaps and of necessity, like an
actor who raises his voice on the stage above the pitch of natural
conversation – but still we have to do that. And surely this is no
great sin. But the danger lies in the writer becoming the victim of
his own exaggeration, losing the exact notion of sincerity and in
10 the end coming to despise truth itself as something too cold, too
blunt for his purpose – as in fact not good enough for his insistent
emotion. From laughter and tears the descent is easy to snivelling
and giggles.

These may seem selfish considerations; but you can't in sound
15 morals condemn a man for taking care of his own integrity. It is
his clear duty. And least of all you can condemn an artist pursuing
however humbly and imperfectly a creative aim. In that interior
world where his thought and his emotions go seeking for the experience of imagined adventures there are no policemen, no law, no
20 pressure of circumstance or dread of opinion to keep him within
bounds. Who then is going to say Nay to his temptations if not his
conscience?

And besides – this, remember, is the place and the moment
of perfectly open talk – I think that all ambitions are lawful
25 except those that climb upwards on the miseries or credulities of
mankind. All intellectual and artistic ambitions are permissible,
up to and even beyond the limit of prudent sanity. They can
hurt no one. If they are mad then so much the worse for the
artist. Indeed, as virtue is said to be, such ambitions are their own
30 reward. Is it such a mad presumption to believe in the sovereign
power of one's art, to try for other means, for other ways of affirming this belief in the deeper appeal of one's work? To try to go
deeper is not to be insensible. A historian of hearts is not a historian of emotions, yet he penetrates further, restrained as he may
35 be, since his aim is to reach the very fount of laughter and tears.
The sight of human affairs deserves admiration and pity; they are
worthy of respect too, and he is not insensible who pays them the
undemonstrative tribute of a sigh which is not a sob, and of a
smile which is not a grin. Resignation, not mystic, not detached,
40 but resignation open eyed, conscious and informed by love is the

only one of our feelings for which it is impossible to become a sham.

Not that I think resignation the last word of wisdom. I am too much the creature of my time for that. But I think that the proper wisdom is to will what the gods will without perhaps being certain what their will is – or even if they have a will of their own. And in this matter of life and art it is not the Why that matters so much to our happiness as the How. As the Frenchman said: "Il y a toujours la manière." Very true. Yes. There is the manner. The manner in laughter, in tears, in irony, in indignations and enthusiasms, in judgements – and even in love. The manner in which as in the features and character of a human face the inner truth is foreshadowed for those who know how to look at their kind.

Those who read me know my conviction that the world, the temporal world, rests on a few very simple ideas, so simple that they must be as old as the hills. It rests notably, amongst others, on the idea of Fidelity. At a time when nothing which is not revolutionary in some way or other can expect to attract much attention I have not been revolutionary in my writings. The revolutionary spirit is mighty convenient in this, that it frees one from all scruples as regards ideas. Its hard, absolute optimism is repulsive to my mind by the menace of fanaticism and intolerance it contains. No doubt one should smile at these things; but imperfect Esthete I am no better Philosopher. All claim to special righteousness awakens in me that scorn and anger from which a philosophical mind should be free . . .

I fear that trying to be conversational I have only managed to be unduly discursive. I have never been very well acquainted with the art of conversation – that art which, I understand, is supposed to be lost now. My young days, the days when one's habits and character are formed, have been rather familiar with long silences. Such voices as broke into them were anything but conversational. No. I haven't got the habit. Yet this discursiveness is not so irrelevant to the handful of pages which follow. They, too, have been charged with discursiveness, with disregard of chronological order (which is in itself a crime), with unconventionality of form (which is an impropriety): I was told severely that the public would view with displeasure the informal character of my recollections.

"Alas," I protested mildly. "Could I begin with the sacramental words 'I was born on such a date in such a place?' The remoteness of the locality would have robbed the statement of all interest. I haven't lived through wonderful adventures to be related seriatim. I haven't known distinguished men on whom I could pass fatuous remarks; I haven't been mixed up with great or scandalous affairs. This is but a bit of psychological document and even so I haven't written it with a view to put forward any conclusion of my own."

But my objector was not placated. Those were good reasons for not writing at all – not a defence of what stood written already, he said.

I admit that almost anything, anything in the world, would serve as a good reason for not writing at all. But since I have written them, all I want to say in their defence is that these memories put down without any regard for established conventions have not been thrown off without system and purpose. They have their hope and their aim. The hope that from the reading of these pages there may emerge at last the vision of a personality, the man behind the books so fundamentally dissimilar as, for instance "Almayer's Folly" and "The Secret Agent" – and yet a coherent justifiable personality both in its origin and in its action. This is the hope. The immediate aim closely associated with the hope is to give the record of personal memories by presenting faithfully the feelings and sensations connected with the writing of my first book and with my first contact with the sea.

In the purposely mingled resonance of this double strain a friend here and there will perhaps detect a subtle accord.

J. C. K.

A PERSONAL RECORD

I

Books may be written in all sorts of places. Verbal inspiration may enter the berth of a mariner on board a ship frozen fast in a river in the middle of a town; and since saints are supposed to look benignantly on humble believers, I indulge in the pleasant fancy that the shade of old Flaubert – who imagined himself to be (amongst other things) a descendant of Vikings – might have hovered with amused interest over the decks of a 2000-ton steamer called the *Adowa*, on board of which, gripped by the inclement winter alongside a quay in Rouen, the tenth chapter of "Almayer's Folly" was begun. With interest, I say, for was not the kind Norman giant with enormous moustaches and a thundering voice the last of the Romantics? Was he not, in his unworldly, almost ascetic, devotion to his art a sort of literary, saint-like hermit?

" *'It has set at last,' said Nina to her mother, pointing to the hills behind which the sun had sunk.* . . ." These words of Almayer's romantic daughter I remember tracing on the grey paper of a pad which rested on the blanket of my bed-place. They referred to a sunset in Malayan Isles and shaped themselves in my mind, in a hallucinated vision of forests and rivers and seas, far removed from a commercial and yet romantic town of the northern hemisphere. But at that moment the mood of visions and words was cut short by the third officer, a cheerful and casual youth, coming in with a bang of the door and the exclamation: "You've made it jolly warm in here."

It was warm. I had turned on the steam-heater after placing a tin under the leaky water-cock – for perhaps you do not know that water will leak where steam will not. I am not aware of what my young friend had been doing on deck all that morning, but the hands he rubbed together vigorously were very red and imparted to me a chilly feeling by their mere aspect. He has remained the only banjoist of my acquaintance, and being also a younger son of

a retired colonel the poem of Mr. Kipling, by a strange aberration
of associated ideas, always seems to me to have been written with
an exclusive view to his person. When he did not play the banjo
he loved to sit and look at it. He proceeded to this sentimental
5 inspection and after meditating a while over the strings under my
silent scrutiny inquired airily:

"What are you always scribbling there, if it's fair to ask?"

It was a fair enough question, but I did not answer him, and simply turned the pad over with a movement of instinctive secrecy:
10 I could not have told him he had put to flight the psychology of
Nina Almayer, her opening speech of the tenth chapter and the
words of Mrs. Almayer's wisdom which were to follow in the omi-
nous oncoming of a tropical night. I could not have told him that
Nina had said: "It has set at last." He would have been extremely
15 surprised and perhaps have dropped his precious banjo. Neither
could I have told him that the sun of my sea-going was setting too,
even as I wrote the words expressing the impatience of passionate
youth bent on its desire. I did not know this myself, and it is safe
to say he would not have cared, though he was an excellent young
20 fellow and treated me with more deference than, in our relative
positions, I was strictly entitled to.

He lowered a tender gaze on his banjo and I went on looking
through the port-hole. The round opening framed in its brass
rim a fragment of the quays, with a row of casks ranged on the
25 frozen ground and the tail-end of a great cart. A red-nosed carter
in a blouse and a woollen night-cap leaned against the wheel.
An idle, strolling custom-house guard, belted over his blue *capote*,
had the air of being depressed by exposure to the weather and the
monotony of official existence. The background of grimy houses
30 found a place in the picture framed by my port-hole, across a wide
stretch of paved quay brown with frozen mud. The colouring was
sombre, and the most conspicuous feature was a little *café* with
curtained windows and a shabby front of white woodwork, corresponding with the squalor of these poorer quarters bordering
35 the river. We had been shifted down there from another berth in
the neighbourhood of the Opera House, where that same port-
hole gave me a view of quite another sort of *café* – the best in the
town, I believe, and the very one where the worthy Bovary and
his wife, the romantic daughter of old Père Renault, had some
40 refreshment after the memorable performance of an opera which

was the tragic story of Lucia di Lammermoor in a setting of light music.

I could recall no more the hallucination of the Eastern Archipelago which I certainly hoped to see again. The story of "Almayer's Folly" got put away under the pillow for that day. I do 5 not know that I had any occupation to keep me away from it; the truth of the matter is that on board that ship we were leading just then a contemplative life. I will not say anything of my privileged position. I was there "just to oblige," as an actor of standing may take a small part in the benefit performance of a friend. 10

As far as my feelings were concerned I did not wish to be in that steamer at that time and in those circumstances. And perhaps I was not even wanted there in the usual sense in which a ship "wants" an officer. It was the first and last instance in my sea life when I served ship-owners who have remained completely 15 shadowy to my apprehension. I do not mean this for the well-known firm of London ship-brokers which had chartered the ship to the, I will not say, short-lived, but ephemeral Franco-Canadian Transport Company. A death leaves something behind, but there was never anything tangible left from the F. C. T. C. It flourished 20 no longer than roses live, and unlike the roses it blossomed in the dead of winter, emitted a sort of faint perfume of adventure and died before spring set in. But indubitably it was a company, it had even a house-flag, all white with the letters F. C. T. C. art-fully tangled up in a complicated monogram. We flew it at our 25 main-mast head, and now I have come to the conclusion that it was the only flag of its kind in existence. All the same we on board, for many days, had the impression of being a unit of a large fleet with fortnightly departures for Montreal and Quebec as advertised in pamphlets and prospectuses which came aboard 30 in a large package in Victoria Dock, London, just before we started for Rouen, France. And in the shadowy life of the F. C. T. C. lies the secret of that, my last employment in my calling, which in a remote sense interrupted the rhythmical development of Nina Almayer's story. 35

The then secretary of the London Shipmasters' Society with its modest rooms in Fenchurch Street was a man of indefatigable activity and the greatest devotion to his task. He is responsible for what was my last association with a ship. I call it that because it can hardly be called a sea-going experience. Dear Captain Froud – it is 40 impossible not to pay him the tribute of affectionate familiarity at this distance of years – had very sound views as to the advancement of knowledge and status for the whole body of the officers of the mercantile marine. He organised for us courses of professional lectures, St. John ambulance classes, corresponded industriously with public bodies and members of Parliament on subjects touching the interests of the service; and as to the oncoming of some inquiry or commission relating to matters of the sea and to the work of seamen, it was a perfect Godsend to his need of exerting himself on our corporate behalf. Together with this high sense of his official duties he had in him a vein of personal kindness, a strong disposition to do what good he could to the individual members of that craft of which in his time he had been a very excellent master. And what greater kindness can one do to a seaman than to put him in the way of employment. Captain Froud did not see why the Shipmasters' Society, besides its general guardianship of our interests, should not be unofficially an employment agency of the very highest class.

"I am trying to persuade all our great ship-owning firms to come to us for their men. There is nothing of a trade union spirit about our society, and I really don't see why they should not," he said once to me. "I am always telling the captains, too, that all things being equal they ought to give preference to the members of the society. In my position I can generally find for them what they want amongst our members or our associate members."

In my wanderings about London from West to East and back again (I was very idle then) the two little rooms in Fenchurch Street were a sort of resting-place where my spirit, hankering after the sea, could feel itself nearer to the ships, the men and the life of its choice – nearer there than on any other spot of the solid earth. This resting-place used to be, at about five o'clock in the afternoon, full of men and tobacco smoke, but Captain Froud had the smaller room to himself and there he granted private interviews, whose principal motive was to render service. Thus, one murky November afternoon he beckoned me in with a crooked finger and that peculiar glance above his spectacles which is perhaps my strongest physical recollection of the man.

"I have had in here a shipmaster, this morning," he said, getting back to his desk and motioning me to a chair, "who is in want of an officer. It's for a steamship. You know, nothing pleases me more than to be asked but unfortunately I do not quite see to my way . . ."

As the outer room was full of men I cast a wondering glance at the closed door but he shook his head:

"Oh, yes, I should be only too glad to get that berth for one of them. But the fact of the matter is, the captain of that ship wants an officer who can speak French fluently, and that's not so easy to find. I do not know anybody myself but you. It's a second officer's berth and, of course, you would not care . . . would you now? I know that it isn't what you are looking for."

It was not. I had given myself up to the idleness of a haunted man who looks for nothing but words wherein to capture his visions. But I admit that outwardly I resembled sufficiently a man who could make a second officer for a steamer chartered by a French company. I showed no sign of being haunted by the fate of Nina and by the murmurs of tropical forests; and even my intimate intercourse with Almayer (a person of weak character) had not put a visible mark upon my features. For many years he and the world of his story had been the companions of my imagination without, I hope, impairing my ability to deal with the realities of sea life. I had had the man and his surroundings with me ever since my return from the eastern waters, some four years before the day of which I speak.

It was in the front sitting-room of furnished apartments in a Pimlico square that they first began to live again with a vividness and poignancy quite foreign to our former real intercourse. I had been treating myself to a long stay on shore, and in the necessity of occupying my mornings, Almayer (that old acquaintance) came nobly to the rescue. Before long, as was only proper, his wife and daughter joined him round my table and then the rest of that Pantai band came full of words and gestures. Unknown to my respectable landlady, it was my practice directly after my breakfast to hold animated receptions of Malays, Arabs and half-castes. They did not clamour aloud for my attention. They came with a silent and irresistible appeal – and the appeal, I affirm here, was not to my self-love or my vanity. It seems now to have had a moral character, for why should the memory of these beings seen, in their obscure sun-bathed existence, demand to express itself in the shape of a novel, except on the ground of that mysterious fellowship which unites in a community of hopes and fears all the dwellers on this earth?

I did not receive my visitors with boisterous rapture as the bearers of any gifts of profit or fame. There was no vision of a printed book before me as I sat writing at that table, situated in a decayed part of Belgravia. After all these years, each leaving its evidence of slowly blackened pages, I can honestly say that it is a sentiment akin to piety which has prompted me to render in words assembled with conscientious care the memory of things far distant and of men who had lived.

But, coming back to Captain Froud and his fixed idea of never disappointing shipowners or ship-captains, it was not likely that I should fail him in his ambition – to satisfy at a few hours' notice the unusual demand for a French-speaking officer. He explained to me that the ship was chartered by a French company intending to establish a regular monthly line of sailings from Rouen, for the transport of French emigrants to Canada. But, frankly, this sort of thing did not interest me very much. I said gravely that if it were really a matter of keeping up the reputation of the Shipmasters' Society, I would consider it. But the consideration was just for form's sake. The next day I interviewed the Captain, and I believe we were impressed favourably with each other. He explained that his chief mate was an excellent man in every respect and that he could not think of dismissing him so as to give me the higher position; but that if I consented to come as second officer I would be given certain special advantages – and so on.

I told him that if I came at all the rank really did not matter.

"I am sure," he insisted, "you will get on first rate with Mr. Paramor."

I promised faithfully to stay for two trips at least, and it was in those circumstances that what was to be my last connection with a ship began. And after all there was not even one single trip. It may be that it was simply the fulfilment of a fate, of that written word on my forehead which apparently forbade me, through all my sea wanderings, ever to achieve the crossing of the Western Ocean – using the words in that special sense in which sailors speak of Western Ocean trade, of Western Ocean packets, of Western Ocean hard cases. The new life attended closely upon the old and the nine chapters of "Almayer's Folly" went with me to the Victoria Dock, whence in a few days we started for Rouen. I won't go so far as

saying that the engaging of a man fated never to cross the Western
Ocean was the absolute cause of the Franco-Canadian Transport
Company's failure to achieve even a single passage. It might have
been that, of course; but the obvious, gross obstacle was clearly
the want of money. Four hundred and sixty bunks for emigrants   5
were put together in the 'tween decks by industrious carpenters
while we lay in the Victoria Dock, but never an emigrant turned up
in Rouen – of which, being a humane person, I confess I was glad.
Some gentlemen from Paris – I think there were three of them,
and one was said to be the Chairman – turned up indeed and went   10
from end to end of the ship, knocking their silk hats cruelly against
the deck-beams. I attended them personally, and I can vouch for
it that the interest they took in things was intelligent enough,
though, obviously, they had never seen anything of the sort before.
Their faces as they went ashore wore a cheerfully inconclusive   15
expression. Notwithstanding that this inspecting ceremony was
supposed to be a preliminary to immediate sailing, it was then, as
they filed down our gangway, that I received the inward monition
that no sailing within the meaning of our charter-party would ever
take place.   20

It must be said that in less than three weeks a move took place.
When we first arrived we had been taken up with much ceremony
well towards the centre of the town, and, all the street corners
being placarded with the tricolour posters announcing the birth
of our company, the *petit bourgeois* with his wife and family made a   25
Sunday holiday from the inspection of the ship. I was always in evidence in my best uniform to give information as though I had been
a Cook's tourists' interpreter, while our quarter-masters reaped a
harvest of small change from personally conducted parties. But
when the move was made – that move which carried us some mile   30
and a half down the stream to be tied up to an altogether mud-
dier and shabbier quay – then indeed the desolation of solitude
became our lot. It was a complete and soundless stagnation for, as
we had the ship ready for sea to the smallest detail, as the frost was
hard and the days short, we were absolutely idle – idle to the point   35
of blushing with shame when the thought struck us that all the
time our salaries went on. Young Cole was aggrieved because, as
he said, we could not enjoy any sort of fun in the evening after loaf-
ing like this all day: even the banjo lost its charm since there was
nothing to prevent his strumming on it all the time between the   40

meals. The good Paramor – he was really a most excellent fellow – became unhappy as far as was possible to his cheery nature, till one dreary day I suggested, out of sheer mischief, that he should employ the dormant energies of the crew in hauling both cables
5   up on deck and turning them end for end.

For a moment Mr. Paramor was radiant. "Excellent idea!" but directly his face fell. "Why . . . Yes! But we can't make that job last more than three days," he muttered discontentedly. I don't know how long he expected us to be stuck on the river-side out-
10 skirts of Rouen, but I know that the cables got hauled up and turned end for end according to my satanic suggestion, put down again and their very existence utterly forgotten, I believe, before a French river pilot came on board to take our ship down, empty as she came, into the Havre roads. You may think that this state of
15 forced idleness favoured some advance in the fortunes of Almayer and his daughter. Yet it was not so. As if it were some sort of evil spell, my banjoist cabin-mate's interruption, as related above, had arrested them short at the point of that fateful sunset for many weeks together. It was always thus with this book, begun in '89
20 and finished in '94 – with that shortest of all the novels which it was to be my lot to write. Between its opening exclamation call-ing Almayer to his dinner in his wife's voice and Abdullah's (his enemy) mental reference to the God of Islam – "The Merciful, the Compassionate" – which closes the book, there were to come
25 several long sea passages, a visit (to use the elevated phraseology suitable to the occasion) to the scenes (some of them) of my child-hood and the realisation of childhood's vain words, expressing a light-hearted and romantic whim.

It was in 1868, when nine years old or thereabouts, that while
30 looking at a map of Africa of the time and putting my finger on the blank space then representing the unsolved mystery of that continent, I said to myself with absolute assurance and an amazing audacity which are no longer in my character now:

"When I grow up I will go *there*."
35   And of course I thought no more about it till after a quarter of a century or so an opportunity offered to go there – as if the sin of childish audacity were to be visited on my mature head. Yes. I did go there: *There* being the region of Stanley Falls which in '68 was the blankest of blank spaces on the earth's figured surface.
40 And the MS. of "Almayer's Folly," carried about me as it were a

talisman or a treasure, went *There* too. That it ever came out of
There seems a special dispensation of Providence; because a good
many of my other properties, infinitely more valuable and useful
to me, remained behind through unfortunate accidents of trans-
portation. I call to mind, for instance, a specially awkward turn   5
of the Congo between Kinchassa and Leopoldsville – more particularly when one had to take it at night in a big canoe with only
half the proper number of paddlers. I failed in being the second
white man on record drowned at that interesting spot through the
upsetting of a canoe. The first was a young Belgian officer, but the   10
accident happened some months before my time, and he, too, I
believe, was going home; not perhaps quite so ill as myself – but
still he was going home. I got round the turn more or less alive,
though I was too sick to care whether I did or not, and, always with
"Almayer's Folly" amongst my diminishing baggage, I arrived at   15
that delectable capital Boma, where before the departure of the
steamer that was to take me home I had the time to wish myself
dead over and over again with perfect sincerity. At that date there
were in existence only seven chapters of "Almayer's Folly," but the
chapter in my history which followed was that of a long, long ill-   20
ness and very dismal convalescence. Geneva, or more precisely
the hydropathic establishment of Champel, is rendered for ever
famous by the termination of the eighth chapter in the history of
Almayer's decline and fall. The events of the ninth are inextricably
mixed up with the details of proper management of a waterside   25
warehouse owned by a certain city firm whose name does not matter. But that work, undertaken to accustom myself again to the
activities of a healthy existence, soon came to an end. The earth
had nothing to hold me with for very long. And then that memorable story, like a cask of choice madeira, got carried for three   30
years to and fro upon the sea. Whether this treatment improved
its flavour or not, of course I would not like to say. As far as appearance is concerned it certainly did nothing of the kind. The whole
MS. acquired a faded look and an ancient, yellowish complexion.
It became at last unreasonable to suppose that anything in the   35
world would ever happen to Almayer and Nina. And yet something most unlikely to happen on the high seas was to wake them
up from their state of suspended animation.

What is it that Novalis says: "It is certain my conviction gains
infinitely the moment another soul will believe in it." And what is   40

a novel if not a conviction of our fellow men's existence, strong enough to take upon itself a form of imagined life clearer than reality and whose accumulated verisimilitude of selected episodes puts to shame the pride of documentary history? Providence which
5 saved my MS. from the Congo rapids brought it to the knowledge of a helpful soul far out on the open sea. It would be on my part the greatest ingratitude ever to forget the sallow, sunken face and the deep-set, dark eyes of the young Cambridge man (he was a "passenger for his health" on board the good ship *Torrens* outward
10 bound to Australia) who was the first reader of "Almayer's Folly" – the very first reader I ever had. "Would it bore you very much reading a MS. in a handwriting like mine?" I had asked him one evening on a sudden impulse at the end of a longish conversation, whose subject was Gibbon's "History." Jacques (that was his name)
15 was sitting in my cabin one stormy dog-watch below, after bringing me a book to read from his own travelling store.

"Not at all," he answered with his courteous intonation and a faint smile. As I pulled a drawer open, his suddenly aroused curiosity gave him a watchful expression. I wonder what he expected
20 to see. A poem, may be. All that's beyond guessing now. He was not a cold but a calm man, still more subdued by disease – a man of few words and of an unassuming modesty in general intercourse, but with something uncommon in the whole of his person which set him apart from the undistinguished lot of our sixty
25 passengers. His eyes had a thoughtful, introspective look. In his attractive, reserved manner, and in a veiled, sympathetic voice, he asked:

"What is this?" "It is a sort of tale," I answered with an effort. "It is not even finished yet. Nevertheless I would like to know what
30 you think of it." He put the MS. in the breast-pocket of his jacket; I remember perfectly his thin, brown fingers folding it lengthwise. "I will read it to-morrow," he remarked seizing the door-handle, and then, watching the roll of the ship for a propitious moment, he opened the door and was gone. In the moment of his exit I
35 heard the sustained booming of the wind, the swish of the water on the decks of the *Torrens* and the subdued, as if distant, roar of the rising sea. I noted the growing disquiet in the great restlessness of the ocean, and responded professionally to it with the thought that at eight o'clock, in another half-hour or so at the farthest, the
40 top-gallant sails would have to come off the ship.

Next day, but this time in the first dog-watch, Jacques entered my cabin. He had a thick, woollen muffler round his throat and the MS. was in his hand. He tendered it to me with a steady look but without a word. I took it in silence. He sat down on the couch and still said nothing. I opened and shut a drawer under my desk, on which a filled-up log-slate lay wide open in its wooden frame waiting to be copied neatly into the sort of book I was accustomed to write with care, the ship's log-book. I turned my back squarely on the desk. And even then Jacques never offered a word. "Well, what do you say?" I asked at last. "Is it worth finishing?" This question expressed exactly the whole of my thoughts.

"Distinctly," he answered in his sedate, veiled voice and then coughed a little.

"Were you interested?" I inquired further almost in a whisper.

"Very much!"

In a pause I went on meeting instinctively the heavy rolling of the ship, and Jacques put his feet on the couch. The curtain of my bed-place swung to and fro as it were a punkah, the bulkhead lamp circled in its gimbals and now and then the cabin door rattled slightly in the gusts of wind. It was in latitude 40 south, and nearly in the longitude of Greenwich, as far as I can remember, that these quiet rites of Almayer's and Nina's resurrection were taking place. In the prolonged silence it occurred to me that there was a good deal of retrospective writing in the story as far as it went. Was it intelligible in its action, I asked myself, as if already the story-teller were being born into the body of a seaman. But I heard on deck the whistle of the officer of the watch and remained on the alert to catch the order that was to follow this call to attention. It reached me as a faint, fierce shout to "Square the yards." "Aha!" I thought to myself, "a westerly blow coming on." Then I turned to my very first reader who, alas!, was not to live long enough to know the end of the tale.

"Now let me ask you one more thing: is the story quite clear to you as it stands?"

He raised his dark, gentle eyes to my face and seemed surprised.
"Yes! Perfectly."

This was all I was to hear from his lips concerning the merits of "Almayer's Folly." We never spoke together of the book again. A long period of bad weather set in and I had no thoughts left but for my duties, whilst poor Jacques caught a fatal cold and had to keep

close in his cabin. When we arrived in Adelaide the first reader of my prose went at once up-country, and died rather suddenly in the end either in Australia or it may be on the passage while going home through the Suez Canal. I am not sure which it was now, and I
5 do not think I ever heard precisely; though I made inquiries about him from some of our return passengers who, wandering about to "see the country" during the ship's stay in port, had come upon him here and there. At last we sailed, homeward bound, and still not one line was added to the careless scrawl of the many pages
10 which poor Jacques had had the patience to read with the very shadows of Eternity gathering already in the hollows of his kind, steadfast eyes.

The purpose instilled into me by his simple and final "Distinctly" remained dormant, yet alive to await its opportunity. I daresay I am
15 compelled, unconsciously compelled, now to write volume after volume, as in past years I had been compelled to go to sea voyage after voyage. Leaves must follow upon each other as leagues used to follow in the days gone by, on and on to the appointed end, which, being Truth itself, is One – one for all men and for all
20 occupations.

I do not know which of the two impulses has appeared more mysterious and more wonderful to me. Still, in writing, as in going to sea, I had to wait my opportunity. Let me confess here that I was never one of those wonderful fellows that would go afloat in a
25 wash-tub for the sake of the fun, and if I may pride myself upon my consistency, it was ever just the same with my writing. Some men, I have heard, write in railway carriages, and could do it, perhaps, sitting cross-legged on a clothes-line; but I must confess that my sybaritic disposition will not consent to write without something
30 at least resembling a chair. Line by line, rather than page by page, was the growth of "Almayer's Folly."

And so it happened that I very nearly lost the MS., advanced now to the first words of the ninth chapter, in the Friedrichstrasse railway station (that's in Berlin, you know), on my way to Poland, or
35 more precisely to Ukraine. On an early, sleepy morning changing trains in a hurry I left my Gladstone bag in a refreshment room. A worthy and intelligent *Kofferträger* rescued it. Yet in my anxiety I was not thinking of the MS. but of all the other things that were packed in the bag.

In Warsaw, where I spent two days, those wandering pages were never exposed to the light, except once to candle-light, while the bag lay open on a chair. I was dressing hurriedly to dine at a sporting club. A friend of my childhood (he had been in the Diplomatic Service, but had turned to growing wheat on paternal acres, and we had not seen each other for over twenty years) was sitting on the hotel sofa waiting to carry me off there.

"You might tell me something of your life while you are dressing," he suggested kindly.

I do not think I told him much of my life-story either then or later. The talk of the select little party with which he made me dine was extremely animated and embraced most subjects under heaven, from big-game shooting in Africa to the last poem published in a very modernist review, edited by the very young and patronised by the highest society. But it never touched upon "Almayer's Folly," and next morning, in uninterrupted obscurity, this inseparable companion went on rolling with me in the south-east direction towards the Government of Kiev.

At that time there was an eight-hours' drive, if not more, from the railway station to the country house which was my destination.

"Dear boy" (these words were always written in English), so ran the last letter received from that house in London, – "Get yourself driven to the only inn in the place, dine as well as you can and some time in the evening my own confidential servant, factotum and majordomo, a Mr. V. S. (I warn you he is of noble extraction), will present himself before you, reporting the arrival of the small sledge which will take you here on the next day. I send with him my heaviest fur, which I suppose with such overcoats as you may have with you will keep you from freezing on the road."

Sure enough, as I was dining, served by a Hebrew waiter, in an enormous barn-like bedroom with a freshly painted floor, the door opened and, in travelling costume of long boots, big sheep-skin cap and a short coat girt with a leather belt, the Mr. V. S. (of noble extraction), a man of about thirty-five, appeared with an air of perplexity on his open and moustachioed countenance. I got up from the table and greeted him in Polish, with, I hope, the right shade of consideration demanded by his noble blood and his confidential position. His face cleared up in a wonderful way. It appeared that, notwithstanding my uncle's earnest assurances, the good fellow had remained in doubt of our understanding each other. He imagined I would talk to him in some foreign language. I was told that his last words on getting into the sledge to come to meet me shaped an anxious exclamation:

"Well! Well! Here I am going, but God only knows how I am to make myself understood to our Master's nephew."

We understood each other very well from the first. He took charge of me as if I were not quite of age yet. I had a delightful boyish feeling of coming home from school when he muffled me up next morning in an enormous bear-skin travelling-coat and took his seat protectively by my side. The sledge was a very small one and it looked utterly insignificant, almost like a toy behind the four big bays harnessed two and two. We three, counting the coachman, filled it completely. He was a young fellow with clear blue eyes; the high collar of his livery fur coat framed his cheery countenance and stood all round level with the top of his head.

"Now, Joseph," my companion addressed him, "do you think we will manage to get home before six?" His answer was that we would surely, with God's help, and providing there were no heavy drifts in the long stretch between certain villages whose names came with an extremely familiar sound to my ears. He turned out an excellent coachman with an instinct for keeping the road amongst the snow-covered fields and a natural gift of getting the best out of the horses.

"He is the son of that Joseph that I suppose the Captain remembers. He who used to drive the Captain's late grandmother of holy memory," remarked V. S. busy tucking fur rugs about my feet.

I remembered perfectly the trusty Joseph who used to drive my grandmother. Why! he it was who let me hold the reins for the first time in my life and allowed me to play with the great four-in-hand whip outside the doors of the coach-house.

"What became of him?" I asked. "He is no longer serving, I suppose."

"He served our master," was the reply. "But he died of cholera ten years ago now – that great epidemic we had. And his wife died at the same time – the whole houseful of them, and this is the only boy that was left."

The MS. of "Almayer's Folly" was reposing in the bag under our feet.

I saw again the sun setting on the plains as I saw it in the travels of my childhood. It set, clear and red, dipping into the snow in full view as if it were setting on the sea. It was twenty-three years since I had seen the sun set over that land; and we drove on in the darkness that fell swiftly upon the livid expanse of snows till, out of the waste of a white earth joining a bestarred sky, surged up black shapes, the clumps of trees about a village of the Ukrainian plain. A cottage or two glided by, a low interminable wall and then, glimmering and winking through a screen of fir-trees, the lights of the master's house.

That very evening the wandering MS. of "Almayer's Folly" was unpacked and unostentatiously laid on the writing-table in my room, the guest-room which had been, I was informed in an affect-edly careless tone, awaiting me for some fifteen years or so. It attracted no attention from the affectionate presence hovering round the son of the favourite sister.

"You won't have many hours to yourself while you are staying with me, brother," he said – this form of address borrowed from the speech of our peasants being the usual expression of the highest good humour in a moment of affectionate elation. "I shall be always coming in for a chat."

As a matter of fact we had the whole house to chat in, and were everlastingly intruding upon each other. I invaded the retirement of his study where the principal feature was a colossal silver ink-stand presented to him on his fiftieth year by a subscription of all his wards then living. He had been guardian of many orphans of land-owning families from the three southern provinces – ever since the year 1860. Some of them had been my schoolfellows and playmates, but not one of them, girls or boys, that I know of has ever written a novel. One or two were older than myself – considerably older, too. One of them, a visitor I remember in my early years, was the man who first put me on horseback, and his four-horse bachelor turn-out, his perfect horsemanship and gen-eral skill in manly exercises was one of my earliest admirations. I seem to remember my mother looking on from a colonnade in front of the dining-room windows as I was lifted upon the pony, held, for all I know, by the very Joseph – the groom attached spe-cially to my grandmother's service – who died of cholera. It was certainly a young man in a dark blue, tail-less coat and huge Cos-sack trousers, that being the livery of the men about the stables.

It must have been in 1864, but reckoning by another mode of calculating time, it was certainly in the year in which my mother obtained permission to travel south and visit her family, from the exile into which she had followed my father. For that, too, she had
5 had to ask permission, and I know that one of the conditions of that favour was that she should be treated exactly as a condemned exile herself. Yet a couple of years later, in memory of her eldest brother who had served in the Guards and dying early left hosts of friends and a loved memory in the great world of St. Petersburg,
10 some influential personages procured for her this permission – it was officially called the "Highest Grace" – of a three months' leave from exile.

This is also the year in which I first begin to remember my mother with more distinctness than a mere loving, wide-browed,
15 silent, protecting presence, whose eyes had a sort of commanding sweetness; and I also remember the great gathering of all the relations from near and far, and the grey heads of the family friends paying her the homage of respect and love in the house of her favourite brother who, a few years later was to take the place for
20 me of both my parents.

I did not understand the tragic significance of it all at the time, though indeed I remember that doctors also came. There were no signs of invalidism about her – but I think that already they had pronounced her doom unless perhaps the change to a southern
25 climate could re-establish her declining strength. For me it seems the very happiest period of my existence. There was my cousin, a delightful quick tempered little girl, some months younger than myself, whose life, lovingly watched over, as if she were a royal princess, came to an end with her fifteenth year. There were other
30 children, too, many of whom are dead now, and not a few whose very names I have forgotten. Over all this hung the oppressive shadow of the great Russian Empire – the shadow lowering with the darkness of a new-born national hatred fostered by the Moscow school of journalists against the Poles after the ill-omened rising
35 of 1863.

This is a far cry back from the MS. of "Almayer's Folly," but the public record of these formative impressions is not the whim of an uneasy egotism. These, too, are things human, already distant in their appeal. It is meet that something more should be left
40 for the novelist's children than the colours and figures of his own

hard-won creation. That which in their grown-up years may appear to the world about them as the most enigmatic side of their natures and perhaps must remain for ever obscure even to themselves, will be their unconscious response to the still voice of that inexorable past from which his work of fiction and their personalities are 5 remotely derived.

Only in men's imagination does every truth find an effective and undeniable existence. Imagination, not invention, is the supreme master of art as of life. An imaginative and exact rendering of authentic memories may serve worthily that spirit of piety towards 10 all things human which sanctions the conceptions of a writer of tales, and the emotions of the man reviewing his own experience.

II

As I HAVE SAID, I was unpacking my luggage after a journey from London into Ukraine. The MS. of "Almayer's Folly" – my companion already for some three years or more, and then in the ninth chapter of its age – was deposited unostentatiously on the writing-table placed between two windows. It didn't occur to me to put it away in the drawer the table was fitted with, but my eye was attracted by the good form of the same drawer's brass handles. Two candelabra with four candles each lighted up festally the room which had waited so many years for the wandering nephew. The blinds were down.

Within five hundred yards of the chair on which I sat stood the first peasant hut of the village – part of my maternal grandfather's estate, the only part remaining in the possession of a member of the family; and beyond the village in the limitless blackness of a winter's night there lay the great unfenced fields – not a flat and severe plain, but a kindly bread-giving land of low rounded ridges, all white now, with the black patches of timber nestling in the hollows. The road by which I had come ran through the village with a turn just outside the gates closing the short drive. Somebody was abroad on the deep snow-track; a quick tinkle of bells stole gradually into the stillness of the room like a tuneful whisper.

My unpacking had been watched over by the servant who had come to help me, and, for the most part, had been standing attentive but unnecessary at the door of the room. I did not want him in the least, but I did not like to tell him to go away. He was a young fellow, certainly more than ten years younger than myself; I had not been – I won't say in that place but within sixty miles of it ever since the year '67; yet his guileless physiognomy of the open peasant type seemed strangely familiar. It was quite possible that he might have been a descendant, a son or even a grandson,

of the servants whose friendly faces had been familiar to me in
my early childhood. As a matter of fact he had no such claim on
my consideration. He was the product of some village near by and
was there on his promotion, having learned the service in one or
5   two houses as pantry-boy. I know this because I asked the worthy
V– next day. I might well have spared the question. I discovered
before long that all the faces about the house and all the faces in
the village, the grave faces with long moustaches of the heads of
families, the downy faces of the young men, the faces of the little
10   fair-haired children, the handsome, tanned, wide-browed faces of
the mothers seen at the doors of the huts were as familiar to me as
though I had known them all from childhood, and my childhood
were a matter of the day before yesterday.

The tinkle of the traveller's bells, after growing louder, had
15   faded away quickly, and the tumult of barking dogs in the village
had calmed down at last. My uncle, lounging in the corner of a
small couch, smoked his long Turkish *chibouk* in silence.

"This is an extremely nice writing-table you have got for my
room," I remarked.

20   "It is really your property," he said, keeping his eyes on me, with
an interested and wistful expression as he had done ever since
I had entered the house. "Forty years ago your mother used to
write at this very table. In our house in Oratow it stood in the little
sitting-room which, by a tacit arrangement, was given up to the
25   girls – I mean to your mother and her sister who died so young.
It was a present to them jointly from our Uncle Nicholas B. when
your mother was seventeen and your aunt two years younger. She
was a very dear, delightful girl, that aunt of yours, of whom I suppose you know nothing more than the name. She did not shine
30   so much by personal beauty and a cultivated mind, in which your
mother was far superior. It was her good sense, the admirable
sweetness of her nature, her exceptional facility and ease in daily
relations that endeared her to everybody. Her death was a terrible
grief and a serious moral loss for us all. Had she lived she would
35   have brought the greatest blessings to the house it would have
been her lot to enter, as wife, mother and mistress of a household. She would have created round herself an atmosphere of
peace and content which only those who can love unselfishly are
able to evoke. Your mother – of far greater beauty, exceptionally
40   distinguished in person, manner and intellect – had a less easy

disposition. Being more brilliantly gifted she also expected more from life. At that trying time especially, we were greatly concerned about her state. Suffering in her health from the shock of her father's death (she was alone in the house with him when he died suddenly), she was torn by the inward struggle between her love for the man whom she was to marry in the end and her knowledge of her dead father's declared objection to that match. Unable to bring herself to disregard that cherished memory and that judgment she had always respected and trusted, and, on the other hand, feeling the impossibility to resist a sentiment so deep and so true, she could not have been expected to preserve her mental and moral balance. At war with herself, she could not give to others that feeling of peace which was not her own. It was only later, when united at last with the man of her choice that she developed those uncommon gifts of mind and heart which compelled the respect and admiration even of our foes. Meeting with calm fortitude the cruel trials of a life reflecting all the national and social misfortunes of the community, she realised the highest conceptions of duty as a wife, a mother and a patriot, sharing the exile of her husband and representing nobly the ideal of Polish womanhood. Our Uncle Nicholas was not a man very accessible to feelings of affection. Apart from his worship for Napoleon the Great, he loved really, I believe, only three people in the world: his mother – your great-grandmother, whom you have seen but cannot possibly remember; his brother, our father, in whose house he lived for so many years; and of all of us, his nephews and nieces grown up round him, your mother alone. The modest, lovable qualities of the youngest sister he did not seem able to see. It was I who felt most profoundly this unexpected stroke of death falling upon the family less than a year after I had become its head. It was terribly unexpected. Driving home one wintry afternoon to keep me company in our empty house, where I had to remain permanently administering the estate and attending to the complicated affairs – (the girls took it in turn week and week about) – driving, as I said, from the house of the Countess Tekla Potocka, where our invalid mother was staying then to be near a doctor, they lost the road and got stuck in a snowdrift. She was alone with the coachman and old Valery, the personal servant of our late father. Impatient of delay while they were trying to dig themselves out, she jumped out of the sledge and went to look for the road herself. All this

happened in '51, not ten miles from the house in which we are
sitting now. The road was soon found but snow had begun to fall
thickly again and they were four more hours getting home. Both
men took off their sheepskin-lined great-coats and used all their
own rugs to wrap her up against the cold, notwithstanding her
protests, positive orders and even struggles, as Valery afterwards
related to me. 'How could I,' he remonstrated with her, 'go to meet
the blessed soul of my late master if I let any harm come to you
while there's a spark of life left in my body?' When they reached
home at last the poor old man was stiff and speechless from exposure, and the coachman was in not much better plight, though
he had the strength to drive round to the stables himself. To my
reproaches for venturing out at all in such weather, she answered
characteristically that she could not bear the thought of abandoning me to my cheerless solitude. It is incomprehensible how it was
that she was allowed to start. I suppose it had to be! She made
light of the cough which came on next day, but shortly afterwards
inflammation of the lungs set in, and in three weeks she was no
more! She was the first to be taken away of the young generation
under my care. Behold the vanity of all hopes and fears! I was the
most frail at birth of all the children. For years I remained so delicate that my parents had but little hope of bringing me up; and
yet I have survived five brothers and two sisters, and many of my
contemporaries; I have outlived my wife and daughter too – and
from all those who have had some knowledge at least of these old
times you alone are left. It has been my lot to lay in an early grave
many honest hearts, many brilliant promises, many hopes full of
life."

He got up brusquely, sighed and left me, saying: "We will dine
in half an hour." Without moving I listened to his quick steps
resounding on the waxed floor of the next room, traversing the
ante-room lined with bookshelves, where he paused to put his
chibouk in the pipe-stand before passing into the drawing-room
(these were all *en suite*), where he became inaudible on the thick
carpet. But I heard the door of his study-bedroom close. He was
then sixty-two years old and had been for a quarter of a century
the wisest, the firmest, the most indulgent of guardians, extending
over me a paternal care and affection, a moral support which I
seemed to feel always near me in the most distant parts of the
earth.

As to Mr. Nicholas B., sub-lieutenant of 1808, lieutenant of 1813 in the French Army and for a short time *Officier d'Ordonnance* of Marshal Marmont; afterwards Captain in the 2nd Regiment of Mounted Rifles in the Polish Army – such as it existed up to 1830 in the reduced kingdom established by the Congress of Vienna – I must say that from all that more distant past, known to me traditionally and a little *de visu,* and called out by the words of the man just gone away, he remains the most incomplete figure. It is obvious that I must have seen him in '64, for it is certain that he would not have missed the opportunity of seeing my mother for what he must have known would be the last time. From my early boyhood to this day, if I try to call up his image, a sort of mist rises before my eyes, a mist in which I perceive vaguely only a neatly brushed head of white hair (which is exceptional in the case of the B. family, where it is the rule for men to go bald in a becoming manner, before thirty) and a thin, curved, dignified nose, a feature in strict accordance with the physical tradition of the B. family. But it is not by these fragmentary remains of perishable mortality that he lives in my memory. I knew, at a very early age, that my grand-uncle Nicholas B. was a Knight of the Legion of Honour and that he had also the Polish Cross for valour *Virtuti Militari.* The knowledge of these glorious facts inspired in me an admiring veneration; yet it is not that sentiment, strong as it was, which resumes for me the force and the significance of his personality. It is overborne by another and complex impression of awe, compassion and horror. Mr. Nicholas B. remains for me the unfortunate and miserable (but heroic) being who once upon a time had eaten a dog.

It is a good forty years since I heard the tale, and the effect has not worn off yet. I believe this is the very first, say, realistic, story I heard in my life; but all the same I don't know why I should have been so frightfully impressed. Of course I know what our village dogs look like – but still. . . . No! At this very day, recalling the horror and compassion of my childhood, I ask myself whether I am right in disclosing to a cold and fastidious world that awful episode in the family history. I ask myself – is it right? – especially as the B. family had always been honourably known in a wide country-side for the delicacy of their tastes in the matter of eating and drinking. But upon the whole, and considering that this gastronomical degradation overtaking a gallant young officer lies really at the

door of the Great Napoleon, I think that to cover it up by silence
would be an exaggeration of literary restraint. Let the truth stand
here. The responsibility rests with the Man of St. Helena in view of
his deplorable levity in the conduct of the Russian campaign. It was
5   during the memorable retreat from Moscow that Mr. Nicholas B.,
in company of two brother officers – as to whose morality and natural refinement I know nothing – bagged a dog on the outskirts of
a village and subsequently devoured him. As far as I can remember
the weapon used was a cavalry sabre, and the issue of the sport-
10 ing episode was rather more of a matter of life and death than if
it had been an encounter with a tiger. A picket of Cossacks was
sleeping in that village lost in the depths of the great Lithuanian
forest. The three sportsmen had observed them from a hiding-
place making themselves very much at home amongst the huts
15 just before the early winter darkness set in at four o'clock. They
had observed them with disgust and perhaps with despair. Late
in the night the rash counsels of hunger overcame the dictates of
prudence. Crawling through the snow they crept up to the fence
of dry branches which generally encloses a village in that part of
20 Lithuania. What they expected to get and in what manner, and
whether this expectation was worth the risk, goodness only knows.
However, these Cossack parties, in most cases wandering without
an officer, were known to guard themselves badly and often not at
all. In addition, the village lying at a great distance from the line
25 of French retreat, they could not suspect the presence of strag-
glers from the Grand Army. The three officers had strayed away
in a blizzard from the main column and had been lost for days in
the woods, which explains sufficiently the terrible straits to which
they were reduced. Their plan was to try and attract the attention
30 of the peasants in that one of the huts which was nearest to the
enclosure; but as they were preparing to venture into the very jaws
of the lion, so to speak, a dog (it is mighty strange that there was
but one), a creature quite as formidable under the circumstances
as a lion, began to bark on the other side of the fence . . .

35   At this stage of the narrative, which I heard many times (by
request) from the lips of Captain Nicholas B.'s sister-in-law, my
grandmother, I used to tremble with excitement.

        The dog barked. And if he had done no more than bark three
officers of the Great Napoleon's army would have perished hon-
40 ourably on the points of Cossacks' lances, or perchance escaping

the chase would have died decently of starvation. But before they had time to think of running away, that fatal and revolting dog, being carried away by the excess of his zeal, dashed out through a gap in the fence. He dashed out and died. His head, I understand, was severed at one blow from his body. I understand also that later on, within the gloomy solitudes of the snow-laden woods, when, in a sheltering hollow, a fire had been lit by the party, the condition of the quarry was discovered to be distinctly unsatisfactory. It was not thin – on the contrary, it seemed unhealthily obese; its skin showed bare patches of an unpleasant character. However, they had not killed that dog for the sake of the pelt. He was large. . . . He was eaten. . . . The rest is silence. . . .

A silence in which a small boy shudders and says firmly–

"I could not have eaten that dog."

And his grandmother remarks with a smile:

"Perhaps you don't know what it is to be hungry."

I have learned something of it since. Not that I have been reduced to eat dog. I have fed on the emblematical animal, which, in the language of the volatile Gauls, is called *la vache enragée*; I have lived on ancient salt junk, I know the taste of shark, of trepang, of snake, of nondescript dishes containing things without a name – but of the Lithuanian village dog – never! I wish it to be distinctly understood that it is not I but my grand-uncle Nicholas, of the Polish landed gentry, *Chevalier de la Légion d'Honneur*, &c. &c., who, in his young days, had eaten the Lithuanian dog.

I wish he had not. The childish horror of the deed clings absurdly to the grizzled man. I am perfectly helpless against it. Still if he really had to, let us charitably remember that he had eaten him on active service, while bearing up bravely against the greatest military disaster of modern history, and, in a manner, for the sake of his country. He had eaten him to appease his hunger no doubt, but also for the sake of an unappeasable and patriotic desire, in the glow of a great faith that lives still, and in the pursuit of a great illusion kindled like a false beacon by a great man to lead astray the effort of a brave nation.

Pro patria!

Looked at in that light it appears a sweet and decorous meal.

And looked at in the same light my own diet of *la vache enragée* appears a fatuous and extravagant form of self-indulgence; for why should I, the son of a land which such men as these have turned up

with their ploughshares and bedewed with their blood, undertake
the pursuit of fantastic meals of salt junk and hard tack upon the
wide seas? On the kindest view it seems an unanswerable question.
Alas! I have the conviction that there are men of unstained recti-
5　tude who are ready to murmur scornfully the word desertion. Thus
the taste of innocent adventure may be made bitter to the palate.
The part of the inexplicable should be allowed for in appraising
the conduct of men in a world where no explanation is final. No
charge of faithlessness ought to be lightly uttered. The appear-
10　ances of this perishable life are deceptive like everything that falls
under the judgment of our imperfect senses. The inner voice may
remain true enough in its secret counsel. The fidelity to a special
tradition may last through the events of an unrelated existence,
following faithfully too the traced way of an inexplicable impulse.
15　　It would take too long to explain the intimate alliance of contradictions in human nature which makes love itself wear at times
the desperate shape of betrayal. And perhaps there is no possible
explanation. Indulgence – as somebody said – is the most intelligent of all the virtues. I venture to think that it is one of the least
20　common, if not the most uncommon of all. I would not imply by
this that men are foolish – or even most men. Far from it. The
barber and the priest, backed by the whole opinion of the village,
condemned justly the conduct of the ingenious hidalgo who, sal-
lying forth from his native place, broke the head of the muleteer,
25　put to death a flock of inoffensive sheep and went through very
doleful experiences in a certain stable. God forbid that an unworthy churl should escape merited censure by hanging on to the
stirrup-leather of the sublime *caballero*. His was a very noble, a very
unselfish fantasy, fit for nothing except to raise the envy of baser
30　mortals. But there is more than one aspect to the charm of that
exalted and dangerous figure. He, too, had his frailties. After reading so many romances he desired naively to escape with his very
body from the intolerable reality of things. He wished to meet
eye to eye the valorous giant Brandabarbaran, Lord of Arabia,
35　whose armour is made of the skin of a dragon, and whose shield,
strapped to his arm, is the gate of a fortified city. O amiable and
natural weakness! O blessed simplicity of a gentle heart without
guile! Who would not succumb to such a consoling temptation?
Nevertheless it was a form of self-indulgence, and the ingenious
40　hidalgo of La Mancha was not a good citizen. The priest and the

barber were not unreasonable in their strictures. Without going so far as the old King Louis-Philippe, who used to say in his exile, "The people are never in fault" – one may admit that there must be some righteousness in the assent of a whole village. Mad! Mad! He who kept in pious meditation the ritual vigil-of-arms by the well of an inn and knelt reverently to be knighted at daybreak by the fat, sly rogue of a landlord, has come very near perfection. He rides forth, his head encircled by a halo – the patron saint of all lives spoiled or saved by the irresistible grace of imagination. But he was not a good citizen.

Perhaps that and nothing else was meant by the well-remembered exclamation of my tutor.

It was in the jolly year 1873, the very last year in which I have had a jolly holiday. There have been idle years afterwards, jolly enough in a way and not altogether without their lesson, but this year of which I speak was the year of my last school-boy holiday. There are other reasons why I should remember that year, but they are too long to state formally in this place. Moreover, they have nothing to do with that holiday. What has to do with the holiday is that before the day on which the remark was made we had seen Vienna, the Upper Danube, Munich, the Falls of the Rhine, the Lake of Constance – in fact it was a memorable holiday of travel. Of late we had been tramping slowly up the Valley of the Reuss. It was a delightful time. It was much more like a stroll than a tramp. Landing from a Lake of Lucerne steamer in Fluellen, we found ourselves at the end of the second day, with the dusk overtaking our leisurely footsteps, a little way beyond Hospenthal. This is not the day on which the remark was made: in the shadows of the deep valley and with the habitations of men left some way behind, our thoughts ran not upon the ethics of conduct but upon the simpler human problem of shelter and food. There did not seem anything of the kind in sight and we were thinking of turning back when suddenly at a bend of the road we came upon a building, ghostly in the twilight.

At that time the work on the St. Gothard Tunnel was going on, and that magnificent enterprise of burrowing was directly responsible for the unexpected building, standing all alone upon the very roots of the mountains. It was long though not big at all; it was low; it was built of boards, without ornamentation, in barrack-hut style, with the white window-frames quite flush with the yellow face of its plain front. And yet it was a hotel; it had even a name which I have forgotten. But there was no gold-laced door-keeper at its humble door. A plain but vigorous servant-girl answered our inquiries, then a man and woman who owned the place appeared.

5 It was clear that no travellers were expected, or perhaps even desired, in this strange hostelry, which in its severe style resembled the house which surmounts the unseaworthy-looking hulls of the toy Noah's Arks, the universal possession of European childhood. However, its roof was not hinged and it was not full to the

10 brim of slabsided and painted animals of wood. Even the live tourist animal was nowhere in evidence. We had something to eat in a long, narrow room at one end of a long, narrow table, which, to my tired perception and to my sleepy eyes, seemed as if it would tilt up like a see-saw plank, since there was no one at the

15 other end to balance it against our two dusty and travel-stained figures. Then we hastened upstairs to bed in a room smelling of pine planks, and I was fast asleep before my head touched the pillow.

In the morning my tutor (he was a student of the Cracow University)

20 sity) woke me up early, and as we were dressing remarked: "There seems to be a lot of people staying in this hotel. I have heard a noise of talking up till 11 o'clock." This statement surprised me; I had heard no noise whatever, having slept like a top.

We went downstairs into the long and narrow dining-room with

25 its long and narrow table. There were two rows of plates on it. At one of the many uncurtained windows stood a tall bony man with a bald head set off by a bunch of black hair above each ear and with a long black beard. He glanced up from the paper he was reading and seemed genuinely astonished at our intrusion. By-and-by more

30 men came in. Not one of them looked like a tourist. Not a single woman appeared. These men seemed to know each other with some intimacy, but I cannot say they were a very talkative lot. The bald-headed man sat down gravely at the head of the table. It all had the air of a family party. By-and-by, from one of the vigorous

35 servant-girls in national costume, we discovered that the place was really a boarding-house for some English engineers engaged at the works of the St. Gothard Tunnel; and I could listen my fill to the sounds of the English language, as far as it is used at a breakfast-table by men who do not believe in wasting many words on the

40 mere amenities of life.

This was my first contact with British mankind apart from the tourist kind seen in the hotels of Zurich and Lucerne – the kind which has no real existence in a workaday world. I know now that the bald-headed man spoke with a strong Scotch accent. I have met many of his kind since, both ashore and afloat. The second 5 engineer of the steamer *Mavis*, for instance, ought to have been his twin brother. I cannot help thinking that he really was, though for some reasons of his own he assured me that he never had a twin brother. Anyway the deliberate bald-headed Scot with the coal-black beard appeared to my boyish eyes a very romantic and 10 mysterious person.

We slipped out unnoticed. Our mapped out route led over the Furka Pass towards the Rhône Glacier, with the further intention of following down the trend of the Häsli Valley. The sun was already declining when we found ourselves on the top of the pass, and the 15 remark alluded to was presently uttered.

We sat down by the side of the road to continue the argument begun half a mile or so before. I am certain it was an argument because I remember perfectly how my tutor argued and how without the power of reply I listened with my eyes fixed obstinately 20 on the ground. A stir on the road made me look up – and then I saw my unforgettable Englishman. There are acquaintances of later years, familiars, shipmates, whom I remember less clearly. He marched rapidly towards the east (attended by a hang-dog Swiss guide) with the mien of an ardent and fearless traveller. He was 25 clad in a knickerbocker suit, but as at the same time he wore short socks under his laced boots, for reasons which whether hygienic or conscientious were surely imaginative, his calves exposed to the public gaze and to the tonic air of high altitudes, dazzled the beholder by the splendour of their marble-like condition and their 30 rich tone of young ivory. He was the leader of a small caravan. The light of a headlong, exalted satisfaction with the world of men and the scenery of mountains illumined his clean-cut, very red face, his short, silver-white whiskers, his innocently eager and tri- umphant eyes. In passing he cast a glance of kindly curiosity and 35 a friendly gleam of big, sound, shiny teeth towards the man and the boy sitting like dusty tramps by the roadside, with a modest knapsack lying at their feet. His white calves twinkled sturdily, the uncouth Swiss guide with a surly mouth stalked like an unwilling bear at his elbow; a small train of three mules followed in single 40 file the lead of this inspiring enthusiast. Two ladies rode past one behind the other, but from the way they sat I saw only their calm, uniform backs, and the long ends of blue veils hanging behind far down over their identical hat-brims. His two daughters surely. An industrious luggage-mule, with unstarched ears and guarded by a slouching, sallow driver, brought up the rear. My tutor, after pausing for a look and a faint smile, resumed his earnest argument.

I tell you it was a memorable year! One does not meet such an Englishman twice in a lifetime. Was he in the mystic ordering of common events the ambassador of my future, sent out to turn the scale at a critical moment on the top of an Alpine pass, with the peaks of the Bernese Oberland for mute and solemn witnesses? His glance, his smile, the unextinguishable and comic ardour of his striving-forward appearance helped me to pull myself together. It must be stated that on that day and in the exhilarating atmosphere of that elevated spot I had been feeling utterly crushed. It was the year in which I had first spoken aloud of my desire to go to sea. At first, like those sounds that, ranging outside the scale to which men's ears are attuned remain inaudible to our sense of hearing, this declaration passed unperceived. It was as if it had not been. Later on, by trying various tones I managed to arouse here and there a surprised momentary attention – the "What was that funny noise?" – sort of inquiry. Later on it was – "Did you hear what that boy said? What an extraordinary outbreak!" Presently a wave of scandalised astonishment (it could not have been greater if I had announced the intention of entering a Carthusian monastery) ebbing out of the educational and academical town of Cracow spread itself over several provinces. It spread itself shallow but far-reaching. It stirred up a mass of remonstrance, indignation, pitying wonder, bitter irony and downright chaff. I could hardly breathe under its weight, and certainly had no words for an answer. People wondered what Mr. T. B. would do now with his worrying nephew and, I dare say, hoped kindly that he would make short work of my nonsense.

What he did was to come down all the way from Ukraine to have it out with me and to judge by himself, unprejudiced, impartial and just, taking his stand on the ground of wisdom and affection. As far as is possible for a boy whose power of expression is still unformed I opened the secret of my thoughts to him and he in return allowed me a glimpse into his mind and heart; the first

glimpse of an inexhaustible and noble treasure of clear thought
and warm feeling, which through life was to be mine to draw upon
with a never deceived love and confidence. Practically, after several exhaustive conversations, he concluded that he would not
have me later on reproach him for having spoiled my life by 5
an unconditional opposition. But I must take time for serious
reflection. And I must not only think of myself but of others;
weigh the claims of affection and conscience against my own
sincerity of purpose. "Think well what it all means in the larger
issues, my boy," he exhorted me finally with special friendliness. 10
"And meantime try to get the best place you can at the yearly
examinations."

The scholastic year came to an end. I took a fairly good place at
the exams, which for me (for certain reasons) happened to be a
more difficult task than for other boys. In that respect I could enter 15
with a good conscience upon that holiday which was like a long
visit *pour prendre congé* of the mainland of old Europe I was to see so
little of for the next four and twenty years. Such, however, was not
the avowed purpose of that tour. It was rather, I suspect, planned
in order to distract and occupy my thoughts in other directions. 20
Nothing had been said for months of my going to sea. But my
attachment to my young tutor and his influence over me were so
well known that he must have received a confidential mission to
talk me out of my romantic folly. It was an excellently appropriate
arrangement, as neither he nor I had ever had a single glimpse 25
of the sea in our lives. That was to come by-and-by for both of us
in Venice, from the outer shore of Lido. Meantime he had taken
his mission to heart so well that I began to feel crushed before we
reached Zurich. He argued in railway trains, in lake steamboats,
he had argued away for me the obligatory sunrise on the Rigi, by 30
Jove! Of his devotion to his unworthy pupil there can be no doubt.
He had proved it already by two years of unremitting and arduous
care. I could not hate him. But he had been crushing me slowly,
and when he started to argue on the top of the Furka Pass he was
perhaps nearer a success than either he or I imagined. I listened 35
to him in despairing silence, feeling that ghostly, unrealised and
desired sea of my dreams escape from the unnerved grip of my
will.

The enthusiastic old Englishman had passed – and the argument went on. What reward could I expect from such a life at 40

the end of my years, either in ambition, honour or conscience? An unanswerable question. But I felt no longer crushed. Then our eyes met and a genuine emotion was visible in his as well as in mine. The end came all at once. He picked up the knapsack
5 suddenly and got on to his feet.

"You are an incorrigible, hopeless Don Quixote. That's what you are."

I was surprised. I was only fifteen and did not know what he meant exactly. But I felt vaguely flattered at the name of the immor-
10 tal knight turning up in connection with my own folly, as some people would call it to my face. Alas! I don't think there was anything to be proud of. Mine was not the stuff the protectors of forlorn damsels, the redressers of this world's wrongs are made of; and my tutor was the man to know that best. Therein, in his indignation,
15 he was superior to the barber and the priest when he flung at me an honoured name like a reproach.

I walked behind him for full five minutes; then without looking back he stopped. The shadows of distant peaks were lengthening over the Furka Pass. When I came up to him he turned to me and
20 in full view of the Finster-Aarhorn with his band of giant brothers rearing their monstrous heads against a brilliant sky, put his hand on my shoulder affectionately.

"Well! That's enough. We will have no more of it."

And indeed there was no more question of my mysterious voca-
25 tion between us. There was to be no more question of it at all, nowhere or with any one. We began the descent of the Furka Pass conversing merrily. Eleven years later, month for month, I stood on Tower Hill on the steps of the St. Katherine's Dockhouse, a master in the British Merchant Service. But the man who put his
30 hand on my shoulder at the top of the Furka Pass was no longer living.

That very year of our travels he took his degree of the Philosophical Faculty – and only then his true vocation declared itself. Obedient to the call he entered at once upon the four-year course
35 of the Medical Schools. A day came when, on the deck of a ship moored in Calcutta, I opened a letter telling me of the end of an enviable existence. He had made for himself a practice in some obscure little town of Austrian Galicia. And the letter went on to tell me how all the bereaved poor of the district, Christians and

Jews alike, had mobbed the good doctor's coffin with sobs and lamentations at the very gate of the cemetery.

How short his years and how clear his vision! What greater reward in ambition, honour and conscience could he have hoped to win for himself when, on the top of the Furka Pass, he bade me 5 to look well to the end of my opening life.

III

THE DEVOURING IN A dismal forest of a luckless Lithuanian dog
by my Grand-uncle Nicholas B. in company of two other military
and famished scarecrows, symbolised, to my childish imagination,
the whole horror of the retreat from Moscow and the immorality 5
of a conqueror's ambition. An extreme distaste for that objection-
able episode has tinged the views I hold as to the character and
achievements of Napoleon the Great. I need not say that these are
unfavourable. It was morally reprehensible for that great captain
to induce a simple-minded Polish gentleman to eat dog by raising 10
in his breast a false hope of national independence. It has been
the fate of that credulous nation to starve for upwards of a hundred years on a diet of false hopes and – well – dog. It is, when
one thinks of it, a singularly poisonous regimen. Some pride in
the national constitution which has survived a long course of such 15
dishes is really excusable. But enough of generalising. Returning
to particulars, Mr. Nicholas B. confided to his sister-in-law (my
grandmother) in his misanthropically laconic manner that this
supper in the woods had been nearly "the death of him." This is
not surprising. What surprises me is that the story was ever heard 20
of; for Grand-uncle Nicholas differed in this from the generality
of military men of Napoleon's time (and perhaps of all time) that
he did not like to talk of his campaigns, which began at Friedland
and ended somewhere in the neighbourhood of Bar-le-Duc. His
admiration of the great Emperor was unreserved in everything but 25
expression. Like the religion of earnest men, it was too profound
a sentiment to be displayed before a world of little faith. Apart
from that he seemed as completely devoid of military anecdotes
as though he had hardly ever seen a soldier in his life. Proud of
his decorations earned before he was twenty-five, he refused to 30
wear the ribbons at the buttonhole in the manner practised to
this day in Europe and even was unwilling to display the insignia

on festive occasions as though he wished to conceal them in the
fear of appearing boastful. "It is enough that I have them," he
used to mutter. In the course of thirty years they were seen on
his breast only twice – at an auspicious marriage in the family
and at the funeral of an old friend. That the wedding which was
thus honoured was not the wedding of my mother I learned only
late in life, too late to bear a grudge against Mr. Nicholas B., who
made amends at my birth by a long letter of congratulation containing the following prophecy: "He will see better times." Even
in his embittered heart there lived a hope. But he was not a true
prophet.

He was a man of strange contradictions. Living for many years
in his brother's house, the home of many children, a house full
of life, of animation, noisy with a constant coming and going of
many guests, he kept his habits of solitude and silence. Considered as obstinately secretive in all his purposes, he was in reality the victim of a most painful irresolution in all matters of civil
life. Under his taciturn, phlegmatic behaviour was hidden a faculty of short-lived, passionate anger. I suspect he had no talent
for narrative; but it seemed to afford him sombre satisfaction to
declare that he was the last man to ride over the bridge of the
river Elster after the battle of Leipsic. Lest some construction
favourable to his valour should be put on the fact he condescended
to explain how it came to pass. It seems that shortly after the retreat
began he was sent back to the town where some divisions of the
French Army (and amongst them the Polish corps of Prince Joseph
Poniatowski), jammed hopelessly in the streets, were being simply
exterminated by the troops of the Allied Powers. When asked what
it was like in there Mr. Nicholas B. muttered only the word "Shambles." Having delivered his message to the Prince he hastened
away at once to render an account of his mission to the superior
who had sent him. By that time the advance of the enemy had
enveloped the town, and he was shot at from houses and chased
all the way to the river bank by a disorderly mob of Austrian Dra-
goons and Prussian Hussars. The bridge had been mined early
in the morning and his opinion was that the sight of the horse-
men converging from many sides in the pursuit of his person
alarmed the officer in command of the sappers and caused the
premature firing of the charges. He had not gone more than
200 yards on the other side when he heard the sound of the
fatal explosions. Mr. Nicholas B. concluded his bald narrative with

the word "Imbecile" uttered with the utmost deliberation. It tes-
tified to his indignation at the loss of so many thousands of lives.
But his phlegmatic physiognomy lighted up when he spoke of
his only wound, with something resembling satisfaction. You will
see that there was some reason for it when you learn that he was   5
wounded in the heel. "Like his Majesty the Emperor Napoleon
himself," he reminded his hearers with assumed indifference.
There can be no doubt that the indifference was assumed, if one
thinks what a very distinguished sort of wound it was. In all the
history of warfare there are, I believe, only three warriors pub-   10
licly known to have been wounded in the heel – Achilles and
Napoleon – demi-gods indeed – to whom the familial piety of
an unworthy descendant adds the name of the simple mortal,
Nicholas B.

The Hundred Days found Mr. Nicholas B. staying with a dis-   15
tant relative of ours, owner of a small estate in Galicia. How he
got there across the breadth of an armed Europe and after what
adventures I am afraid will never be known now. All his papers
were destroyed shortly before his death; but if there was amongst
them, as he affirmed, a concise record of his life, then I am pretty   20
sure it did not take up more than a half-sheet of foolscap or so.
This relative of ours happened to be an Austrian officer, who had
left the service after the battle of Austerlitz. Unlike Mr. Nicholas B.,
who concealed his decorations, he liked to display his honourable
discharge in which he was mentioned as *unschreckbar* (fearless)   25
before the enemy. No conjunction could seem more unpromis-
ing, yet it stands in the family tradition that these two got on very
well together in their rural solitude.

When asked whether he had not been sorely tempted during
the Hundred Days to make his way again to France and join the   30
service of his beloved Emperor, Mr. Nicholas B. used to mutter:
"No money. No horse. Too far to walk."

The fall of Napoleon and the ruin of national hopes affected
adversely the character of Mr. Nicholas B. He shrank from returning to his province. But for that there was also another reason. Mr.   35
Nicholas B. and his brother – my maternal grandfather – had lost
their father early, while they were quite children. Their mother,
young still and left very well off, married again a man of great
charm and of an amiable disposition but without a penny. He
turned out an affectionate and careful step-father; it was unfortu-   40
nate though that while directing the boys' education and forming

their character by wise counsel he did his best to get hold of the fortune by buying and selling land in his own name and investing capital in such a manner as to cover up the traces of the real ownership. It seems that such practices can be successful if one
5 is charming enough to dazzle one's own wife permanently and brave enough to defy the vain terrors of public opinion. The critical time came when the elder of the boys on attaining his majority in the year 1811 asked for the accounts and some part at least of the inheritance to begin life upon. It was then that the step-father
10 declared with calm finality that there were no accounts to render and no property to inherit. The whole fortune was his very own. He was very good-natured about the young man's misapprehension of the true state of affairs, but of course felt obliged to maintain his position firmly. Old friends came and went busily,
15 voluntary mediators appeared travelling on most horrible roads from the most distant corners of the three provinces; and the Marshal of the Nobility (*ex-officio* guardian of all well-born orphans) called a meeting of landowners to "ascertain in a friendly way how the misunderstanding between X and his step-sons had arisen and
20 devise proper measures to remove the same." A deputation to that effect visited X, who treated them to excellent wines, but absolutely refused his ear to their remonstrances. As to the proposals for arbitration he simply laughed at them; yet the whole province must have been aware that fourteen years before, when he married the
25 widow, all his visible fortune consisted (apart from his social qualities) in a smart four-horse turn-out with two servants, with whom he went about visiting from house to house; and as to any funds he might have possessed at that time their existence could only be inferred from the fact that he was very punctual in settling his
30 modest losses at cards. But by the magic power of stubborn and constant assertion, there were found presently, here and there, people who mumbled that surely "there must be something in it." However, on his next name-day (which he used to celebrate by a great three-days' shooting-party), of all the invited crowd only
35 two guests turned up, distant neighbours of no importance; one notoriously a fool, and the other a very pious and honest person but such a passionate lover of the gun that on his own confession he could not have refused an invitation to a shooting-party from the devil himself. X met this manifestation of public opinion with
40 the serenity of an unstained conscience. He refused to be crushed.

Yet he must have been a man of deep feeling, because, when his wife took openly the part of her children, he lost his beautiful tranquillity, proclaimed himself heart-broken and drove her out of the house, neglecting in his grief to give her enough time to pack her trunks.

This was the beginning of a lawsuit, an abominable marvel of chicane, which by the use of every legal subterfuge was made to last for many years. It was also the occasion for a display of much kindness and sympathy. All the neighbouring houses flew open for the reception of the homeless. Neither legal aid nor material assistance in the prosecution of the suit was ever wanting. X, on his side, went about shedding tears publicly over his step-children's ingratitude and his wife's blind infatuation; but as at the same time he displayed great cleverness in the art of concealing material documents (he was even suspected of having burnt a lot of historically interesting family papers), this scandalous litigation had to be ended by a compromise lest worse should befall. It was settled finally by a surrender, out of the disputed estate, in full satisfaction of all claims, of two villages with the names of which I do not intend to trouble my readers. After this lame and impotent conclusion neither the wife nor the step-sons had anything to say to the man who had presented the world with such a successful example of self-help based on character, determination and industry; and my great-grandmother, her health completely broken down, died a couple of years later in Carlsbad. Legally secured by a decree in the possession of his plunder, X regained his wonted serenity and went on living in the neighbourhood in a comfortable style and in apparent peace of mind. His big shoots were fairly well attended again. He was never tired of assuring people that he bore no grudge for what was past; he protested loudly of his constant affection for his wife and step-children. It was true he said that they had tried their best to strip him as naked as a Turkish saint in the decline of his days; and because he had defended himself from spoliation, as anybody else in his place would have done, they had abandoned him now to the horrors of a solitary old age. Nevertheless, his love for them survived these cruel blows. And there might have been some truth in his protestations. Very soon he began to make overtures of friendship to his eldest step-son, my maternal grandfather; and when these were peremptorily rejected he went on renewing them again and again with characteristic obstinacy.

For years he persisted in his efforts at reconciliation, promising
my grandfather to execute a will in his favour if he only would be
friends again to the extent of calling now and then (it was fairly
close neighbourhood for these parts, forty miles or so), or even of
5 putting in an appearance for the great shoot on the name-day. My
grandfather was an ardent lover of every sport. His temperament
was as free from hardness and animosity as can be imagined. Pupil
of the liberal-minded Benedictines who directed the only public school of some standing then in the south, he had also read
10 deeply the authors of the eighteenth century. In him Christian
charity was joined to a philosophical indulgence for the failings of
human nature. But the memory of these miserably anxious early
years, his young man's years robbed of all generous illusions by
the cynicism of the sordid lawsuit, stood in the way of forgiveness.
15 He never succumbed to the fascination of the great shoot; and X,
his heart set to the last on reconciliation with the draft of the will
ready for signature kept by his bedside, died intestate. The fortune
thus acquired and augmented by a wise and careful management
passed to some distant relatives whom he had never seen and who
20 even did not bear his name.

Meantime the blessing of general peace descended upon
Europe. Mr. Nicholas B., bidding good-bye to his hospitable relative, the "fearless" Austrian officer, departed from Galicia, and
without going near his native place, where the odious lawsuit was
25 still going on, proceeded straight to Warsaw and entered the army
of the newly constituted Polish kingdom under the sceptre of
Alexander I., Autocrat of all the Russias.

This kingdom, created by the Vienna Congress as an acknowl-
edgment to a nation of its former independent existence, included
30 only the central provinces of the old Polish patrimony. A brother
of the Emperor, the Grand Duke Constantine (Pavlovitch), its
Viceroy and Commander-in-Chief, married, morganatically, to a
Polish lady to whom he was fiercely attached, extended this affection to what he called "My Poles" in a capricious and savage man-
35 ner. Sallow in complexion with a Tartar physiognomy, and fierce
little eyes, he walked with his fists clenched, his body bent forward,
darting suspicious glances from under an enormous cocked hat.
His intelligence was limited and his sanity itself was doubtful. The
hereditary taint expressed itself, in his case, not by mystic leanings
40 as in his two brothers, Alexander and Nicholas (in their various

ways, for one was mystically liberal and the other mystically auto-cratic), but by the fury of an uncontrollable temper which gen-erally broke out in disgusting abuse on the parade ground. He was a passionate militarist and an amazing drill-master. He treated his Polish Army as a spoiled child treats a favourite toy, except that he did not take it to bed with him at night. It was not small enough for that. But he played with it all day and every day, delight-ing in the variety of pretty uniforms and in the fun of incessant drilling. This childish passion, not for war but for mere militarism, achieved a desirable result. The Polish Army, in its equipment, in its armament and in its battle-field efficiency, as then understood, became, by the end of the year 1830, a first-rate tactical instru-ment. Polish peasantry (not serfs) served in the ranks by enlist-ment, and the officers belonged mainly to the smaller nobility. Mr. Nicholas B., with his Napoleonic record, had no difficulty in obtaining a lieutenancy, but the promotion in the Polish Army was slow, because, being a separate organisation, it took no part in the wars of the Russian Empire either against Persia or Turkey. Its first campaign, against Russia itself, was to be its last. In 1831, on the outbreak of the Revolution, Mr. Nicholas B. was senior cap-tain of his regiment. Some time before he had been made head of the remount establishment quartered outside the kingdom in our southern provinces, whence almost all the horses for the Pol-ish cavalry were drawn. For the first time since he went away from home at the age of eighteen to begin his military life by the battle of Friedland, Mr. Nicholas B. breathed the air of the "Border," his native air. Unkind fate was lying in wait for him amongst the scenes of his youth. At the first news of the rising in Warsaw all the remount establishment, officers, vets. and the very troopers, were put promptly under arrest and hurried off in a body beyond the Dnieper to the nearest town in Russia proper. From there they were dispersed to the distant parts of the Empire. On this occa-sion poor Mr. Nicholas B. penetrated into Russia much farther than he ever did in the times of Napoleonic invasion, if much less willingly. Astrakhan was his destination. He remained there three years, allowed to live at large in the town but having to report himself every day at noon to the military commandant, who used to detain him frequently for a pipe and a chat. It is difficult to form a just idea of what a chat with Mr. Nicholas B. could have been like. There must have been much compressed rage under

his taciturnity, for the commandant communicated to him the
news from the theatre of war and this news was such as it could
be, that is, very bad for the Poles. Mr. Nicholas B. received these
communications with outward phlegm, but the Russian showed a
5 warm sympathy for his prisoner. "As a soldier myself I understand
your feelings. You, of course, would like to be in the thick of it.
By heavens! I am fond of you. If it were not for the terms of the
military oath I would let you go on my own responsibility. What
difference could it make to us one more or less of you?"

10 At other times he wondered with simplicity.

"Tell me, Nicholas Stepanovitch" – (my great-grandfather's
name was Stephen and the commandant used the Russian form of
polite address) – "tell me why is it that you Poles are always looking
for trouble? What else could you expect from running up against
15 Russia?"

He was capable, too, of philosophical reflections.

"Look at your Napoleon now. A great man. There is no denying
it that he was a great man as long as he was content to thrash those
Germans and Austrians and all those nations. But no! He must go
20 to Russia looking for trouble, and what's the consequence? Such
as you see me, I have rattled this sabre of mine on the pavements
of Paris."

After his return to Poland Mr. Nicholas B. described him as a
"worthy man but stupid," whenever he could be induced to speak
25 of the conditions of his exile. Declining the option offered him to
enter the Russian Army he was retired with only half the pension
of his rank. His nephew (my uncle and guardian) told me that the
first lasting impression on his memory as a child of four was the
glad excitement reigning in his parents' house on the day when
30 Mr. Nicholas B. arrived home from his detention in Russia.

Every generation has its memories. The first memories of Mr.
Nicholas B. might have been shaped by the events of the last partition of Poland, and he lived long enough to suffer from the last
armed rising in 1863, an event which affected the future of all my
35 generation and has coloured my earliest impressions. His brother,
in whose house he had sheltered for some seventeen years his
misanthropical timidity before the commonest problems of life,
having died in the early fifties, Mr. Nicholas B. had to screw his
courage up to the sticking-point and come to some decision as to
40 the future. After a long and agonising hesitation he was persuaded

at last to become the tenant of some fifteen hundred acres out of the estate of a friend in the neighbourhood. The terms of the lease were very advantageous, but the retired situation of the village and a plain comfortable house in good repair were, I fancy, the greatest inducements. He lived there quietly for about ten years, 5 seeing very few people and taking no part in the public life of the province, such as it could be under an arbitrary bureaucratic tyranny. His character and his patriotism were above suspicion; but the organisers of the rising in their frequent journeys up and down the province scrupulously avoided coming near his house. 10 It was generally felt that the repose of the old man's last years ought not to be disturbed. Even such intimates as my paternal grandfather, a comrade-in-arms during Napoleon's Moscow campaign and later on a fellow officer in the Polish Army, refrained from visiting his crony as the date of the outbreak approached. 15 My paternal grandfather's two sons and his only daughter were all deeply involved in the revolutionary work; he himself was of that type of Polish squire whose only ideal of patriotic action was to "get into the saddle and drive them out." But even he agreed that "dear Nicholas must not be worried." All this considerate caution 20 on the part of friends, both conspirators and others, did not prevent Mr. Nicholas B. being made to feel the misfortunes of that ill-omened year.

Less than forty-eight hours after the beginning of the rebellion in that part of the country, a squadron of scouting Cossacks passed 25 through the village and invaded the homestead. Most of them remained formed between the house and the stables, while several, dismounting, ransacked the various out-buildings. The officer in command, accompanied by two men, walked up to the front door. All the blinds on that side were down. The officer told the 30 servant who received him that he wanted to see his master. He was answered that the master was away from home, which was perfectly true.

I follow here the tale as told afterwards by the servant to my grand-uncle's friends and relatives, and as I have heard it repeated. 35

On receiving this answer the Cossack officer, who had been standing in the porch, stepped into the house.

"Where is the master gone then?"

"Our master went to J –" (the government town some fifty miles off) "the day before yesterday." 40

"There are only two horses in the stables. Where are the others?"

"Our master always travels with his own horses" (meaning: not by post). "He will be away a week or more. He was pleased to mention to me that he had to attend to some business in the Civil
5   Court."

While the servant was speaking the officer looked about the hall. There was a door facing him, a door to the right and a door to the left. The officer chose to enter the room on the left and ordered the blinds to be pulled up. It was Mr. Nicholas B.'s study
10   with a couple of tall bookcases, some pictures on the walls and so on. Besides the big centre table, with books and papers, there was a quite small writing-table with several drawers, standing between the door and the window in a good light; and at this table my grand-uncle usually sat either to read or write.

15   On pulling up the blind the servant was startled by the discovery that the whole male population of the village was massed in front, trampling down the flower-beds. There were also a few women amongst them. He was glad to observe the village priest (of the Orthodox Church) coming up the drive. The good man in his
20   haste had tucked up his cassock as high as the top of his boots.

The officer had been looking at the backs of the books in the bookcases. Then he perched himself on the edge of the centre table and remarked easily:

"Your master did not take you to town with him, then."

25   "I am the head servant and he leaves me in charge of the house. It's a strong, young chap that travels with our master. If – God forbid – there was some accident on the road he would be of much more use than I."

Glancing through the window he saw the priest arguing vehe-
30   mently in the thick of the crowd, which seemed subdued by his interference. Three or four men, however, were talking with the Cossacks at the door.

"And you don't think your master has gone to join the rebels maybe – eh?" asked the officer.

35   "Our master would be too old for that surely. He's well over seventy and he's getting feeble too. It's some years now since he's been on horseback and he can't walk much either now."

The officer sat there swinging his leg, very quiet and indifferent. By that time the peasants who had been talking with the Cossack
40   troopers at the door had been permitted to get into the hall. One

or two more left the crowd and followed them in. They were seven
in all and amongst them the blacksmith, an ex-soldier. The servant
appealed deferentially to the officer.

"Won't your honour be pleased to tell the people to go back to
their homes? What do they want to push themselves into the house   5
like this for? It's not proper for them to behave like this while our
master's away and I am responsible for everything here."

The officer only laughed a little, and after a while inquired:

"Have you any arms in the house?"

"Yes. We have. Some old things."   10

"Bring them all, here, on to this table."

The servant made another attempt to obtain protection.

"Won't your honour tell these chaps. . . ?"

But the officer looked at him in silence in such a way that he
gave it up at once and hurried off to call the pantry-boy to help   15
him collect the arms. Meantime the officer walked slowly through
all the rooms in the house, examining them attentively but touching nothing. The peasants in the hall fell back and took off their
caps when he passed through. He said nothing whatever to them.
When he came back to the study all the arms to be found in the   20
house were lying on the table. There was a pair of big flint-lock hol-
ster pistols from Napoleonic times, two cavalry swords, one of the
French the other of the Polish Army pattern, with a fowling-piece
or two.

The officer, opening the window, flung out pistols, swords and   25
guns, one after another, and his troopers ran to pick them up.
The peasants in the hall, encouraged by his manner, had stolen
after him into the study. He gave not the slightest sign of being
conscious of their existence and, his business being apparently
concluded, strode out of the house without a word. Directly he   30
left, the peasants in the study put on their caps and began to smile
at each other.

The Cossacks rode away, passing through the yards of the home
farm straight into the fields. The priest, still arguing with the peasants, moved gradually down the drive and his earnest eloquence   35
was drawing the silent mob after him, away from the house. This
justice must be rendered to the parish priests of the Greek Church
that, strangers to the country as they were (being all drawn from
the interior of Russia), the majority of them used such influence as
they had over their flocks in the cause of peace and humanity. True 40

to the spirit of their calling, they tried to soothe the passions of
the excited peasantry and opposed rapine and violence whenever
they could, with all their might. And this conduct they pursued
against the express wishes of the authorities. Later on some of
5   them were made to suffer for this disobedience by being removed
abruptly to the far north or sent away to Siberian parishes.

The servant was anxious to get rid of the few peasants who had
got into the house. What sort of conduct was that, he asked them,
towards a man who was only a tenant, had been invariably good and
10 considerate to the villagers for years; and only the other day had
agreed to give up two meadows for the use of the village herd? He
reminded them, too, of Mr. Nicholas B's. devotion to the sick in the
time of cholera. Every word of this was true and so far effective that
the fellows began to scratch their heads and look irresolute. The
15 speaker then pointed at the window, exclaiming. "Look! there's
all your crowd going away quietly and you silly chaps had better
go after them and pray God to forgive you your evil thoughts."

This appeal was an unlucky inspiration. In crowding clumsily to
the window to see whether he was speaking the truth, the fellows
20 overturned the little writing-table. As it fell over a chink of loose
coin was heard. "There's money in that thing," cried the blacksmith. In a moment the top of the delicate piece of furniture was
smashed and there lay exposed in a drawer eight hundred half-
imperials. Gold coin was a rare sight in Russia even at that time;
25 it put the peasants beside themselves. "There must be more of
that in the house and we shall have it," yelled the ex-soldier blacksmith. "This is war time." The others were already shouting out of
the window urging the crowd to come back and help. The priest,
abandoned suddenly at the gate, flung his arms up and hurried
30 away so as not to see what was going to happen.

In their search for money that bucolic mob smashed everything
in the house, ripping with knives, splitting with hatchets, so that,
as the servant said, there were not two pieces of wood holding
together left in the whole house. They broke some very fine mir-
35 rors, all the windows and every piece of glass and china. They threw
the books and papers out on the lawn and set fire to the heap for
the mere fun of the thing apparently. Absolutely the only one solitary thing which they left whole was a small ivory crucifix, which
remained hanging on the wall in the wrecked bedroom above a
40 wild heap of rags, broken mahogany and splintered boards which

had been Mr. Nicholas B.'s bedstead. Detecting the servant in the act of stealing away with a japanned tin box, they tore it from him, and because he resisted they threw him out of the dining-room window. The house was on one floor but raised well above the ground, and the fall was so serious that the man remained lying stunned till the cook and a stable-boy ventured forth at dusk from their hiding-places and picked him up. By that time the mob had departed carrying off the tin box, which they supposed to be full of paper money. Some distance from the house in the middle of a field they broke it open. They found inside documents engrossed on parchment and the two crosses of the Legion of Honour and For Valour. At the sight of these objects which, the blacksmith explained, were marks of honour given only by the Tsar, they became extremely frightened at what they had done. They threw the whole lot away into a ditch and dispersed hastily.

On learning of this particular loss Mr. Nicholas B. broke down completely. The mere sacking of his house did not seem to affect him much. While he was still in bed from the shock the two crosses were found and returned to him. It helped somewhat his slow convalescence, but the tin box and the parchments, though searched for in all the ditches around, never turned up again. He could not get over the loss of his Legion of Honour Patent, whose preamble, setting forth his services, he knew by heart to the very letter, and after this blow volunteered sometimes to recite, tears standing in his eyes the while. Its terms haunted him apparently during the last two years of his life to such an extent that he used to repeat them to himself. This is confirmed by the remark made more than once by his old servant to the more intimate friends. "What makes my heart heavy is to hear our master in his room at night walking up and down and praying aloud in the French language."

It must have been somewhat over a year afterwards that I saw Mr. Nicholas B., or, more correctly, that he saw me, for the last time. It was, as I have already said, at the time when my mother had a three months' leave from exile, which she was spending in the house of her brother, and friends and relations were coming from far and near to do her honour. It is inconceivable that Mr. Nicholas B. should not have been of the number. The little child a few months old he had taken up in his arms on the day of his home-coming after years of war and exile was confessing her faith in national salvation by suffering exile in her turn. I do not know whether

he was present on the very day of our departure. I have already admitted that for me he is more especially the man who in his youth had eaten roast dog in the depths of a gloomy forest of snow-loaded pines. My memory cannot place him in any remembered scene.
5 A hooked nose, some sleek white hair, an unrelated evanescent impression of a slight, rigid, bowed figure militarily buttoned up to the throat is all that now exists on earth of Mr. Nicholas B.; only this vague shadow pursued by the memory of his grand-nephew, the last surviving human being I suppose of all those he had seen
10 in the course of his taciturn life.

But I remember well the day of our departure back to exile. The elongated, bizarre, shabby travelling-carriage with four post-horses, standing before the long front of the house with its eight columns, four on each side of the broad flight of stairs. On the
15 steps, groups of servants, a few relations, one or two friends from the nearest neighbourhood, a perfect silence, on all the faces an air of sober concentration; my grandmother all in black gazing stoically, my uncle giving his arm to my mother down to the carriage in which I had been placed already; at the top of the flight
20 my little cousin in a short skirt of a tartan pattern with a deal of red in it, and like a small princess attended by the women of her own household: the head *gouvernante*, our dear, corpulent Francesca (who had been for thirty years in the service of the B. family), the former nurse, now outdoor attendant, a handsome
25 peasant face wearing a compassionate expression, and the good, ugly Mlle. Durand, the governess, with her black eyebrows meeting over a short thick nose and a complexion like pale brown paper. Of all the eyes turned towards the carriage, her good-natured eyes only were dropping tears, and it was her sobbing voice alone that
30 broke the silence with an appeal to me: "*N'oublie pas ton français, mon chéri.*" In three months, simply by playing with us, she had taught me not only to speak French but to read it as well. She was indeed an excellent playmate. In the distance, half-way down to the great gates, a light, open trap, harnessed with three horses
35 in Russian fashion, stood drawn up on one side with the police-captain of the district sitting in it, the vizor of his flat cap with a red band pulled down over his eyes.

It seems strange that he should have been there to watch our going so carefully. Without wishing to treat with levity the just
40 timidities of Imperialists all the world over, I may allow myself the

reflection that a woman, practically condemned by the doctors, and a small boy not quite six years old could not be regarded as seriously dangerous even for the largest of conceivable empires saddled with the most sacred of responsibilities. And this good man I believe did not think so either. 5

I learned afterwards why he was present on that day. I don't remember any outward signs, but it seems that, about a month before, my mother became so unwell that there was a doubt whether she could be made fit to travel in the time. In this uncertainty the Governor-General in Kiev was petitioned to grant her 10 a fortnight's extension of stay in her brother's house. No answer whatever was returned to this prayer, but one day at dusk the police-captain of the district drove up to the house and told my uncle's valet, who ran out to meet him, that he wanted to speak with the master in private, at once. Very much impressed (he thought it 15 was going to be an arrest) the servant, "more dead than alive with fright," as he related afterwards, smuggled him through the big drawing-room, which was dark (that room was not lighted every evening), on tiptoe, so as not to attract the attention of the ladies in the house, and led him by way of the orangery to my uncle's 20 private apartments.

The policeman, without any preliminaries, thrust a paper into my uncle's hands.

"There. Pray read this. I have no business to show this paper to you. It is wrong of me. But I can't either eat or sleep with such a 25 job hanging over me."

That police-captain, a native of Great Russia, had been for many years serving in the district.

My uncle unfolded and read the document. It was a service order issued from the Governor-General's secretariat, dealing with the 30 matter of the petition and directing the police-captain to disregard all remonstrances and explanations in regard to that illness either from medical men or others, "and if she has not left her brother's house" – it went on to say – "on the morning of the day specified on her permit, you are to despatch her at once under escort, 35 direct" (underlined) "to the prison-hospital in Kiev, where she will be treated as her case demands."

"For God's sake, Mr. B., see that your sister goes away punctually on that day. Don't give me this work to do with a woman – and with one of your family too. I simply cannot bear to think of it." 40

He was absolutely wringing his hands. My uncle looked at him in silence.

"Thank you for this warning. I assure you that even if she were dying she would be carried out to the carriage."

5   "Yes – indeed – and what difference would it make – travel to Kiev or back to her husband. For she would have to go – death or no death. And mind, Mr. B., I will be here on the day, not that I doubt your promise but because I must. I have got to. Duty. All the same my trade is not fit for a dog since some of you Poles will

10   persist in rebelling and all of you have got to suffer for it."

This is the reason why he was there in an open three-horse trap pulled up between the house and the great gates. I regret not being able to give up his name to the scorn of all believers in the rights of conquest for a reprehensibly sensitive guardian

15   of Imperial greatness. On the other hand, I am in a position to state the name of the Governor-General who signed the order with the marginal note "to be carried out to the letter" in his own handwriting. The gentleman's name was Bezak. A high dignitary, an energetic official, the idol for a time of the Russian Patriotic

20   Press.

Each generation has its memories.

IV

IT MUST NOT BE supposed that in setting forth the memories of this half-hour between the moment my uncle left my room till we met again at dinner, I am losing sight of "Almayer's Folly." Having confessed that my first novel was begun in idleness – a holiday task – I think I have also given the impression that it was a much-delayed book. It was never dismissed from my mind, even when the hope of ever finishing it was very faint. Many things came in its way: daily duties, new impressions, old memories. It was not the outcome of a need – the famous need of self-expression which artists find in their search for motives. The necessity which impelled me was a hidden, obscure necessity, a completely masked and unaccountable phenomenon. Or perhaps some idle and frivolous magician (there must be magicians in London) had cast a spell over me through his parlour window as I explored the maze of streets east and west in solitary leisurely walks without chart and compass. Till I began to write that novel I had written nothing but letters and not very many of these. I never made a note of a fact, of an impression or of an anecdote in my life. The conception of a planned book was entirely outside my mental range when I sat down to write; the ambition of being an author had never turned up amongst these gracious imaginary existences one creates fondly for oneself at times in the stillness and immobility of a day-dream: yet it stands clear as the sun at noonday that from the moment I had done blackening over the first manuscript page of "Almayer's Folly" (it contained about two hundred words and this proportion of words to a page has remained with me through the fifteen years of my writing life), from the moment I had, in the simplicity of my heart and the amazing ignorance of my mind, written that page the die was cast. Never had Rubicon been more blindly forded, without invocation to the gods, without fear of men.

That morning I got up from my breakfast, pushing the chair back, and rang the bell violently, or perhaps I should say resolutely, or perhaps I should say eagerly, I do not know. But manifestly it must have been a special ring of the bell, a common sound
5 made impressive, like the ringing of a bell for the raising of the curtain upon a new scene. It was an unusual thing for me to do. Generally, I dawdled over my breakfast and I seldom took the trouble to ring the bell for the table to be cleared away; but on that morning for some reason hidden in the general mysteriousness
10 of the event I did not dawdle. And yet I was not in a hurry. I pulled the cord casually and while the faint tinkling somewhere down in the basement went on, I charged my pipe in the usual way and I looked for the matchbox with glances distraught indeed but exhibiting, I am ready to swear, no signs of a fine frenzy. I was
15 composed enough to perceive after some considerable time the matchbox lying there on the mantelpiece right under my nose. And all this was beautifully and safely usual. Before I had thrown down the match my landlady's daughter appeared, with her calm, pale face and an inquisitive look, in the doorway. Of late it was the
20 landlady's daughter who answered my bell. I mention this little fact with pride, because it proves that during the thirty or forty days of my tenancy I had produced a favourable impression. For a fortnight past I had been spared the unattractive sight of the domestic slave. The girls in that Bessborough Gardens house were
25 often changed, but whether short or long, fair or dark, they were always untidy and particularly bedraggled as if in a sordid version of the fairy tale the ashbin cat had been changed into a maid. I was infinitely sensible of the privilege of being waited on by my landlady's daughter. She was neat if anæmic.

30 "Will you please clear away all this at once?" I addressed her in convulsive accents, being at the same time engaged in getting my pipe to draw. This, I admit, was an unusual request. Generally on getting up from breakfast I would sit down in the window with a book and let them clear the table when they liked; but if you think
35 that on that morning I was in the least impatient, you are mistaken. I remember that I was perfectly calm. As a matter of fact I was not at all certain that I wanted to write, or that I meant to write, or that I had anything to write about. No, I was not impatient. I lounged between the mantelpiece and the window, not even consciously

waiting for the table to be cleared. It was ten to one that before my landlady's daughter was done I would pick up a book and sit down with it all the morning in a spirit of enjoyable indolence. I affirm it with assurance and I don't even know now what were the books then lying about the room. Whatever they were they were not the works of great masters, where the secret of clear thought and exact expression can be found. Since the age of five I have been a great reader, as is not perhaps wonderful in a child who was never aware of learning to read. At ten years of age I had read much of Victor Hugo and other romantics. I had read in early boyhood in Polish and in French, history, voyages, novels; I knew "Gil Blas" and "Don Quixote" in abridged editions; I had read Polish poets and some French poets, but I cannot say what I read on the evening before I began to write myself. I believe it was a novel and it is quite possible that it was one of Anthony Trollope's novels. It is very likely. My acquaintance with him was then very recent. He is one of the English novelists whose works I read for the first time in English. With men of European reputation, with Dickens and Walter Scott and Thackeray, it was otherwise. My first introduction to English imaginative literature was "Nicholas Nickleby." It is extraordinary how well Mrs. Nickleby could chatter disconnectedly in Polish and the sinister Ralph rage in that language. As to the Crummles family and the family of the learned Squeers it seemed as natural to them as their native speech. It was, I have no doubt, an excellent translation. This must have been in the year '70. But I really believe that I am wrong. That book was not my first introduction to English literature. My first acquaintance was (or were) the "Two Gentlemen of Verona," and that in the very MS. of my father's translation. It was during our exile in Russia, and it must have been less than a year after my mother's death, because I remember myself in the black blouse with a white border of my heavy mourning. We were living together, quite alone, in a small house on the outskirts of the town of T—. That afternoon, instead of going out to play in the large yard which we shared with our landlord, I had lingered in the room in which my father generally wrote. What emboldened me to clamber into his chair I am sure I don't know, but a couple of hours afterwards he discovered me kneeling in it with my elbows on the table and my head held in both hands over the MS. of loose pages. I was greatly confused, expecting to get into trouble. He stood in the doorway looking at me with some surprise, but the only thing he said after a moment of silence was:

"Read the page aloud."

5   Luckily the page lying before me was not overblotted with erasures and corrections, and my father's handwriting was otherwise extremely legible. When I got to the end he nodded and I flew out of doors thinking myself lucky to have escaped reproof for that piece of impulsive audacity. I have tried to discover since the
10 reason of this mildness, and I imagine that all unknown to myself I had earned, in my father's mind, the right to some latitude in my relations with his writing-table. It was only a month before, or perhaps it was only a week before, that I had read to him aloud from beginning to end, and to his perfect satisfaction, as he lay
15 on his bed, not being very well at the time, the proofs of his translation of Victor Hugo's "Toilers of the Sea." Such was my title to consideration, I believe, and also my first introduction to the sea in literature. If I do not remember where, how and when I learned to read, I am not likely to forget the process of being trained in the
20 art of reading aloud. My poor father, an admirable reader himself, was the most exacting of masters. I reflect proudly that I must have read that page of "Two Gentlemen of Verona" tolerably well at the age of eight. The next time I met them was in a 5s one-volume edition of the dramatic works of William Shakespeare, read in Fal-
25 mouth, at odd moments of the day, to the noisy accompaniment of caulkers' mallets driving oakum into the deck-seams of a ship in dry dock. We had run in, in a sinking condition and with the crew refusing duty after a month of weary battling with the gales of the North Atlantic. Books are an integral part of one's life and my
30 Shakespearean associations are with that first year of our bereavement, the last I spent with my father in exile (he sent me away to Poland to my mother's brother directly he could brace himself up for the separation), and with the year of hard gales, the year in which I came nearest to death at sea, first by water and then by
35 fire.

Those things I remember, but what I was reading the day before my writing life began I have forgotten. I have only a vague notion that it might have been one of Trollope's political novels. And I remember, too, the character of the day. It was an autumn day
40 with an opaline atmosphere, a veiled, semi-opaque, lustrous day,

with fiery points and flashes of red sunlight on the roofs and windows opposite, while the trees of the square with all their leaves gone were like tracings of Indian ink on a sheet of tissue paper. It was one of those London days that have the charm of mysterious amenity, of fascinating softness. The effect of opaline mist was often repeated at Bessborough Gardens on account of the nearness to the river.

There is no reason why I should remember that effect more on that day than on any other day, except that I stood for a long time looking out of the window after the landlady's daughter was gone with her spoil of cups and saucers. I heard her put the tray down in the passage and finally shut the door; and still I remained smoking with my back to the room. It is very clear that I was in no haste to take the plunge into my writing life, if as plunge this first attempt may be described. My whole being was steeped deep in the indolence of a sailor away from the sea, the scene of never-ending labour and of unceasing duty. For utter surrender to indolence you cannot beat a sailor ashore when that mood is on him, the mood of absolute irresponsibility tasted to the full. It seems to me that I thought of nothing whatever, but that is an impression which is hardly to be believed at this distance of years. What I am certain of is, that I was very far from thinking of writing a story, though it is possible and even likely that I was thinking of the man Almayer.

I had seen him for the first time some four years before from the bridge of a steamer moored to a rickety little wharf forty miles up, more or less, a Bornean river. It was very early morning and a slight mist, an opaline mist as in Bessborough Gardens only without the fiery flicks on roof and chimney-pot from the rays of the red London sun, promised to turn presently into a woolly fog. Barring a small dug-out canoe on the river there was nothing moving within sight. I had just come up yawning from my cabin. The serang and the Malay crew were overhauling the cargo chains and trying the winches; their voices sounded subdued on the deck below and their movements were languid. That tropical daybreak was chilly. The Malay quartermaster, coming up to get something from the lockers on the bridge, shivered visibly. The forests above and below and on the opposite bank looked black and dank; wet dripped from the rigging upon the tightly stretched deck awnings, and it was in the middle of a shuddering yawn that I caught sight of Almayer. He was moving across a patch of burnt grass, a blurred

shadowy shape with the blurred bulk of a house behind him, a low
house of mats, bamboos and palm-leaves with a high-pitched roof
of grass.

He stepped up on the jetty. He was clad simply in flapping pyja-
5   mas of cretonne pattern (enormous flowers with yellow petals on
a disagreeable blue ground) and a thin cotton singlet with short
sleeves. His arms, bare to the elbow, were crossed on his chest. His
black hair looked as if it had not been cut for a very long time and
a curly wisp of it strayed across his forehead. I had heard of him
10 at Singapore; I had heard of him on board; I had heard of him
early in the morning and late at night; I had heard of him at tiffin
and at dinner; I had heard of him in a place called Pulo Laut from
a half-caste gentleman there, who described himself as the man-
ager of a coal-mine, which sounded civilised and progressive till
15 you heard that the mine could not be worked at present because it
was haunted by some particularly atrocious ghosts; I had heard of
him in a place called Donggala, in the Island of Celebes, when the
Rajah of that little-known seaport (you can get no anchorage there
in less than fifteen fathom, which is extremely inconvenient) came
20 on board in a friendly way with only two attendants and drank bottle after bottle of soda-water on the after-skylight with my good
friend and commander, Captain C—. At least I heard his name
distinctly pronounced several times in a lot of talk in Malay language. Oh yes, I heard it quite distinctly – Almayer, Almayer – and
25 saw Captain C— smile while the fat dingy Rajah laughed audibly.
To hear a Malay Rajah laugh outright is a rare experience I can
assure you. And I overheard more of Almayer's name amongst
our deck passengers (mostly wandering traders of good repute)
as they sat all over the ship – each man fenced round with bun-
30 dles and boxes – on mats, on pillows, on quilts, on billets of wood,
conversing of Island affairs. Upon my word, I heard the mutter of
Almayer's name faintly at midnight, while making my way aft from
the bridge to look at the patent taffrail log tinkling its quarter-
miles in the great silence of the sea. I don't mean to say that our
35 passengers dreamed aloud of Almayer, but it is indubitable that
two of them at least, who could not sleep apparently and were
trying to charm away the trouble of insomnia by a little whispered
talk at that ghostly hour, were referring in some way or other to
Almayer. It was really impossible on board that ship to get away
40 definitely from Almayer; and a very small pony tied up forward

and whisking its tail inside the galley, to the great embarrassment
of our Chinaman cook, was destined for Almayer. What he wanted
with a pony goodness only knows, since I am perfectly certain he
could not ride it; but here you have the man, ambitious, aiming at
the grandiose, importing a pony, whereas in the whole settlement 5
at which he used to shake daily his impotent fist there was only one
path that was practicable for a pony; a quarter of a mile at most
hedged in by hundreds of square leagues of virgin forest. But who
knows? The importation of that Bali pony might have been part
of some deep scheme, of some diplomatic plan, of some hopeful 10
intrigue. With Almayer one could never tell. He governed his conduct by considerations removed from the obvious, by incredible
assumptions which rendered his logic impenetrable to any reasonable person. I learned all this later. That morning seeing the
figure in pyjamas moving in the mist I said to myself: "That's the 15
man."

He came quite close to the ship's side and raised a harassed
countenance, round and flat, with that curl of black hair over the
forehead and a heavy, pained glance.

"Good-morning." 20

"Good-morning."

He looked hard at me: I was a new face, having just replaced the
chief mate he was accustomed to see; and I think that this novelty
inspired him, as things generally did, with deep-seated mistrust.

"Didn't expect you in till this evening," he remarked suspi- 25
ciously.

I don't know why he should have been aggrieved, but he seemed
to be. I took pains to explain to him that having picked up the
beacon at the mouth of the river just before dark and the tide
serving, Captain C— was enabled to cross the bar and there was 30
nothing to prevent him going up the river at night.

"Captain C— knows this river like his own pocket," I concluded
discursively, trying to get on terms.

"Better," said Almayer.

Leaning over the rail of the bridge I looked at Almayer, who 35
looked down at the wharf in aggrieved thought. He shuffled his
feet a little; he wore straw slippers with thick soles. The morning
fog had thickened considerably. Everything round us dripped –
the derricks, the rails, every single rope in the ship – as if a fit of
crying had come upon the universe. 40

Almayer again raised his head and in the accents of a man accustomed to the buffets of evil fortune asked hardly audibly:

"I suppose you haven't got such a thing as a pony on board?"

I told him almost in a whisper, for he attuned my communica-
5 tions to his minor key, that we had such a thing as a pony, and
I hinted, as gently as I could, that he was confoundedly in the
way too. I was very anxious to have him landed before I began to
handle the cargo. Almayer remained looking up at me for a long
while with incredulous and melancholy eyes as though it were not
10 a safe thing to believe my statement. This pathetic mistrust in the
favourable issue in any sort of affair touched me deeply, and I
added:

"He doesn't seem a bit the worse for the passage. He's a nice
pony, too."

15 Almayer was not to be cheered up; for all answer he cleared his
throat and looked down again at his feet. I tried to close with him
on another tack.

"By Jove!" I said. "Aren't you afraid of catching pneumonia or
bronchitis or something walking about in a singlet in such a wet
20 fog?"

He was not to be propitiated by a show of interest in his health.
His answer was a sinister "No fear," as much as to say that even that
way of escape from an inclement fortune was closed to him.

"I just came down . . ." he mumbled after a while.

25 "Well then, now you're here I will land that pony for you at once
and you can lead him home. I really don't want him on deck. He's
in the way."

Almayer seemed doubtful. I insisted:

"Why, I will just swing him out and land him on the wharf right
30 in front of you. I'd much rather do it before the hatches are off.
The little devil may jump down the hold or do some other deadly
thing."

"There's a halter?" postulated Almayer.

"Yes, of course there's a halter." And without waiting any more
35 I leaned over the bridge rail.

"Serang, land Tuan Almayer's pony."

The cook hastened to shut the door of the galley and a moment
later a great scuffle began on deck. The pony kicked with extreme
energy, the kalashes skipped out of the way, the serang issued many
40 orders in a cracked voice. Suddenly the pony leaped upon the

fore-hatch. His little hoofs thundered tremendously; he plunged and reared. He had tossed his mane and his forelock into a state of amazing wildness, he dilated his nostrils, bits of foam flecked his broad little chest, his eyes blazed. He was something under eleven hands; he was fierce, terrible, angry, warlike, he said ha! ha! distinctly, he raged and thumped – and sixteen able-bodied kalashes stood round him like disconcerted nurses round a spoilt and passionate child. He whisked his tail incessantly; he arched his pretty neck; he was perfectly delightful; he was charmingly naughty. There was not an atom of vice in that performance; no savage baring of teeth and laying back of ears. On the contrary, he pricked them forward in a comically aggressive manner. He was totally unmoral and lovable; I would have liked to give him bread, sugar, carrots. But life is a stern thing and the sense of duty the only safe guide. So I steeled my heart and from my elevated position on the bridge I ordered the men to fling themselves upon him in a body.

The elderly serang, emitting a strange inarticulate cry, gave the example. He was an excellent petty officer – very competent indeed and a moderate opium smoker. The rest of them in one great rush smothered that pony. They hung on to his ears, to his mane, to his tail; they lay in piles across his back, seventeen in all. The carpenter, seizing the hook of the cargo-chain, flung himself on the top of them. A very satisfactory petty officer, too, but he stuttered. Have you ever heard a light yellow, lean, sad, earnest Chinaman stutter in pidgin-English? It's very weird indeed. He made the eighteenth. I could not see the pony at all; but from the swaying and heaving of that heap of men I knew that there was something alive inside.

From the wharf Almayer hailed in quavering tones:

"Oh, I say!"

Where he stood he could not see what was going on on deck unless perhaps the tops of the men's heads; he could only hear the scuffle, the mighty thuds, as if the ship were being knocked to pieces. I looked over: "What is it?"

"Don't let them break his legs," he entreated me plaintively.

"Oh, nonsense! He's all right now. He can't move."

By that time the cargo-chain had been hooked to the broad canvas belt round the pony's body, the kalashes sprang off simultaneously in all directions, rolling over each other, and the worthy serang, making a dash behind the winch, turned the steam on.

"Steady!" I yelled, in great apprehension of seeing the animal snatched up to the very head of the derrick.

5   On the wharf Almayer shuffled his straw slippers uneasily. The rattle of the winch stopped, and in a tense, impressive silence that pony began to swing across the deck.

How limp he was! Directly he felt himself in the air he relaxed every muscle in a most wonderful manner. His four hoofs

10   knocked together in a bunch, his head hung down and his tail remained pendent in a nerveless and absolute immobility. He reminded me vividly of the pathetic little sheep which hangs on the collar of the Order of the Golden Fleece. I had no idea that anything in the shape of a horse could be so limp as that, either

15   living or dead. His wild mane hung down lumpily, a mere mass of inanimate horsehair; his aggressive ears had collapsed, but as he went swaying slowly across the front of the bridge I noticed an astute gleam in his dreamy, half-closed eye. A trustworthy quartermaster, his glance anxious and his mouth on the broad grin,

20   was easing over the derrick watchfully. I superintended, greatly interested.

"So! That will do."

The derrick-head stopped. The kalashes lined the rail. The rope of the halter hung perpendicular and motionless like a bell-pull

25   in front of Almayer. Everything was very still. I suggested amicably that he should catch hold of the rope and mind what he was about. He extended a provokingly casual and superior hand.

"Look out then! Lower away!"

Almayer gathered in the rope intelligently enough, but when

30   the pony's hoofs touched the wharf he gave way all at once to a most foolish optimism. Without pausing, without thinking, almost without looking he disengaged the hook suddenly from the sling and the cargo-chain, after hitting the pony's quarters, swung back against the ship's side with a noisy, rattling slap. I suppose I must

35   have blinked. I know I missed something, because the next thing I saw was Almayer lying flat on his back on the jetty. He was alone.

Astonishment deprived me of speech long enough to give Almayer time to pick himself up in a leisurely and painful manner. The kalashes lining the rail had all their mouths open. The mist flew in the light breeze and it had come over quite thick enough to hide the shore completely.

"How on earth did you manage to let him get away?" I asked scandalised.

Almayer looked into the smarting palm of his right hand, but did not answer my inquiry.

"Where do you think he will get to?" I cried. "Are there any fences anywhere in this fog? Can he bolt into the forest? What's to be done now?"

Almayer shrugged his shoulders.

"Some of my men are sure to be about. They will get hold of him sooner or later."

"Sooner or later! That's all very fine, but what about my canvas sling – he's carried it off. I want it now, at once, to land two Celebes cows."

Since Donggala we had on board a pair of the pretty little island cattle in addition to the pony. Tied up on the other side of the fore deck they had been whisking their tails into the other door of the galley. These cows were not for Almayer, however; they were invoiced to Abdullah bin Selim, his enemy. Almayer's disregard of my requirements was complete.

"If I were you I would try to find out where he's gone," I insisted. "Hadn't you better call your men together or something? He will throw himself down and cut his knees. He may even break a leg – you know."

But Almayer, plunged in abstracted thought, did not seem to want that pony any more. Amazed at this sudden indifference I turned all hands out on shore to hunt for him on my own account, or, at any rate, to hunt for the canvas sling which he had round his body. The whole crew of the steamer, with the exception of firemen and engineers, rushed up the jetty past the thoughtful Almayer and vanished from my sight. The white fog swallowed them up; and again there was a deep silence that seemed to extend for miles up and down the stream. Still taciturn, Almayer started to climb on board, and I went down from the bridge to meet him on the after-deck.

"Would you mind telling the captain that I want to see him very particularly?" he asked me in a low tone, letting his eyes stray all over the place.

"Very well. I will go and see."

With the door of his cabin wide open Captain C—, just back from the bathroom, big and broad-chested, was brushing his thick, damp, iron-grey hair with two large brushes.

5   "Mr. Almayer's on board, sir. He told me he wanted to see you very particularly, sir."

Saying these words I smiled. I don't know why I smiled except that it seemed absolutely impossible to mention Almayer's name without a smile of a sort. It had not to be necessarily a mirthful

10   smile. Turning his head towards me Captain C— smiled too, rather joylessly.

"The pony got away from him – eh?"

"Yes sir. He did."

"Where is he?"

15   "Goodness only knows."

"No. I mean Almayer. Let him come along."

The captain's stateroom opening straight on deck under the bridge, I had only to beckon from the doorway to Almayer, who had remained aft, with downcast eyes, on the very spot where I

20   had left him. He strolled up moodily, shook hands and at once asked permission to shut the cabin door.

"I have a pretty story to tell you," were the last words I heard. The bitterness of tone was remarkable.

I went away from the door, of course. For the moment I had

25   no crew on board; only the Chinaman carpenter, with a canvas bag hung round his neck and a hammer in his hand, roamed about the empty decks knocking out the wedges of the hatches and dropping them into the bag conscientiously. Having nothing to do I joined our two engineers at the door of the engine-room.

30   It was near breakfast time.

"He's turned up early, hasn't he?" commented the second engineer, and smiled indifferently. He was an abstemious man with a good digestion and a placid, reasonable view of life even when hungry.

35   "Yes," I said. "Shut up with the old man. Some very particular business."

"He will spin him a damned endless yarn," observed the chief engineer.

He smiled rather sourly. He was dyspeptic and suffered from

40   gnawing hunger in the morning. The second smiled broadly, a

smile that made two vertical folds on his shaven cheeks. And I smiled too, but I was not exactly amused. In that man, whose name apparently could not be uttered anywhere in the Malay Archipelago without a smile, there was nothing amusing whatever. That morning he breakfasted with us silently, looking mostly into 5 his cup. I informed him that my men came upon his pony capering in the fog on the very brink of the eight-foot deep well in which he kept his store of guttah. The cover was off with no one near-by, and the whole of my crew just missed going heels over head into that beastly hole. Jurumudi Itam, our best quartermaster, deft at fine 10 needlework, he who mended the ship's flags and sewed buttons on our coats, was disabled by a kick on the shoulder.

Both remorse and gratitude seemed foreign to Almayer's character. He mumbled:

"Do you mean that pirate fellow?" 15

"What pirate fellow? The man has been in the ship eleven years," I said indignantly.

"It's his looks," Almayer muttered for all apology.

The sun had eaten up the fog. From where we sat under the after awning we could see in the distance the pony tied up in front 20 of Almayer's house, to a post of the verandah. We were silent for a long time. All at once Almayer, alluding evidently to the subject of his conversation in the captain's cabin, exclaimed anxiously across the table:

"I really don't know what I can do now!" 25

Captain C— only raised his eyebrows at him, and got up from his chair. We dispersed to our duties, but Almayer, half-dressed as he was in his cretonne pyjamas and the thin cotton singlet, remained on board, lingering near the gangway as though he could not make up his mind whether to go home or stay with us for good. 30 Our Chinamen boys gave him side glances as they went to and fro; and Ah Sing, our young chief steward, the handsomest and most sympathetic of Chinamen, catching my eye, nodded knowingly at his burly back. In the course of the morning I approached him for a moment. 35

"Well, Mr. Almayer," I addressed him easily, "you haven't started on your letters yet."

We had brought him his mail and he had held the bundle in his hand ever since we got up from breakfast. He glanced at it when I spoke and, for a moment, it looked as if he were on the point 40

of opening his fingers and letting the whole lot fall overboard.
I believe he was tempted to do so. I shall never forget that man
afraid of his letters.

"Have you been long out from Europe?" he asked me.

5 "Not very. Not quite eight months," I told him. "I left a ship
in Samarang with a hurt back and have been in the hospital in
Singapore some weeks."

He sighed.

"Trade is very bad here."

10 "Indeed!"

"Hopeless! . . . See these geese?"

With the hand holding the letters he pointed out to me what
resembled a patch of snow creeping and swaying across the distant
part of his compound. It disappeared behind some bushes.

15 "The only geese on the East Coast," Almayer informed me in a
perfunctory mutter without a spark of faith, hope or pride. There-
upon, with the same absence of any sort of sustaining spirit he
declared his intention to select a fat bird and send him on board
for us not later than next day.

20 I had heard of these largesses before. He conferred a goose as
if it were a sort of Court decoration given only to the tried friends
of the house. I had expected more pomp in the ceremony. The
gift had surely its special quality, multiple and rare. From the only
flock on the East Coast! He did not make half enough of it. That
25 man did not understand his opportunities. However, I thanked
him at some length.

"You see," he interrupted abruptly in a very peculiar tone, "the
worst of this country is that one is not able to realise . . . it's impossible to realise. . . ." His voice sank into a languid mutter. "And
30 when one has very large interests . . . very important interests . . ."
he finished faintly . . . "up the river."

We looked at each other. He astonished me by giving a start and
making a very queer grimace.

"Well, I must be off," he burst out hurried. "So long!"

35 At the moment of stepping over the gangway he checked himself
though, to give me a mumbled invitation to dine at his house that
evening with my captain, an invitation which I accepted. I don't
think it could have been possible for me to refuse.

I like the worthy folk that will talk to you of the exercise of free-
40 will "at any rate for practical purposes." Free, is it? For practical

purposes! Bosh! How could I have refused to dine with that man? I did not refuse simply because I could not refuse. Curiosity, a healthy desire for a change of cooking, common civility, the talk and the smiles of the previous twenty days, every condition of my existence at that moment and place made irresistibly for acceptance; and crowning all that there was the ignorance, the ignorance, I say, the fatal want of fore-knowledge to counterbalance these imperative conditions of the problem. A refusal would have appeared perverse and insane. Nobody unless a surly lunatic would have refused. But if I had not got to know Almayer pretty well it is almost certain there would never have been a line of mine in print.

I accepted then – and I am paying yet the price of my sanity. The possessor of the only flock of geese on the East Coast is responsible for the existence of some fourteen volumes, so far. The number of geese he had called into being under adverse climatic conditions was considerably more than fourteen. The tale of volumes will never overtake the counting of heads, I am safe to say; but my ambitions point not exactly that way, and whatever the pangs the toil of writing has cost me I have always thought kindly of Almayer.

I wonder, had he known anything of it, what his attitude would have been? This is something not to be discovered in this world. But if we ever meet in the Elysian Fields – where I cannot depict him to myself otherwise than attended in the distance by his flock of geese (birds sacred to Jupiter) – and he addresses me in the stillness of that passionless region, neither light nor darkness, neither sound nor silence, and heaving endlessly with billowy mists from the impalpable multitudes of the swarming dead, I think I know what answer to make.

I would say, after listening courteously to the unvibrating tone of his measured remonstrances, which should not disturb, of course, the solemn eternity of stillness in the least – I would say something like this:

"It is true, Almayer, that, in the world below, I have converted your name to my own uses. But that is a very small larceny. What's in a name, O Shade? If so much of your old mortal weakness clings to you yet as to make you feel aggrieved (it was the note of your earthly voice, Almayer) then I entreat you, seek speech without delay with our sublime fellow Shade – with him who, in his transient existence as a poet, commented upon the smell of

the rose. He will comfort you. You came to me stripped of all prestige by men's queer smiles and the disrespectful chatter of every vagrant trader in the Islands. Your name was the common property of the winds: it, as it were, floated naked over the waters
5 about the Equator. I wrapped round its unhonoured form the royal mantle of the tropics and have essayed to put into the hollow sound the very anguish of paternity – feats which you did not demand from me – but remember that all the toil and all the pain were mine. In your earthly life you haunted me Almayer.
10 Consider that this was taking a great liberty. Since you were always complaining of being lost to the world, you should remember that if I had not believed enough in your existence to let you haunt my rooms in Bessborough Gardens, you would have been much more lost. You affirm that had I been capable of looking
15 at you with a more perfect detachment and a greater simplicity, I might have perceived better the inward marvellousness which, you insist, attended your career upon that tiny pinpoint of light, hardly visible far, far below us, where both our graves lie. No doubt! But reflect, O complaining Shade! that this was not so much my fault
20 as your crowning misfortune. I believed in you in the only way it was possible for me to believe. It was not worthy of your merits? So be it. But you were always an unlucky man, Almayer. Nothing was ever quite worthy of you. What made you so real to me was that you held this lofty theory with some force of conviction and with
25 an admirable consistency."

It is with some such words translated into the proper shadowy expressions that I am prepared to placate Almayer in the Elysian Abode of Shades, since it has come to pass that having parted many years ago, we are never to meet again in this world.

V

IN THE CAREER OF the most unliterary of writers, in the sense that literary ambition had never entered the world of his imagination, the coming into existence of the first book is quite an inexplicable event. In my own case I cannot trace it back to any mental or psychological cause which one could point out and hold to. The greatest of my gifts being a consummate capacity for doing nothing, I cannot even point to boredom as a rational stimulus for taking up a pen. The pen at any rate was there, and there is nothing wonderful in that. Everybody keeps a pen (the cold steel of our days) in his rooms in this enlightened age of penny stamps and halfpenny postcards. In fact, this was the epoch when by means of postcard and pen Mr. Gladstone had made the reputation of a novel or two. And I too had a pen rolling about somewhere – the seldom-used, the reluctantly-taken-up pen of a sailor ashore, the pen rugged with the dried ink of abandoned attempts, of answers delayed longer than decency permitted, of letters begun with infinite reluctance and put off suddenly till next day – till next week as likely as not! The neglected, uncared-for pen, flung away at the slightest provocation, and under the stress of dire necessity hunted for without enthusiasm, in perfunctory, grumpy worry, in the "Where the devil *is* the beastly thing gone to?" ungracious spirit. Where indeed! It might have been reposing behind the sofa for a day or so. My landlady's anæmic daughter (as Ollendorff would have expressed it), though commendably neat, had a lordly, careless manner of approaching her domestic duties. Or it might even be resting delicately poised on its point by the side of the table-leg, and when picked up show a gaping, inefficient beak which would have discouraged any man of literary instincts. But not me! "Never mind. This will do."

O days without guile! If anybody had told me then that a devoted household, having a generally exaggerated idea of my talents and importance, were to be put into a state of tremor and flurry by the fuss I would make because of a suspicion that somebody had touched my sacrosanct pen of authorship, I would have never deigned as much as the contemptuous smile of unbelief. There are imaginings too unlikely for any kind of notice, too wild for indulgence itself, too absurd for a smile. Perhaps, had that seer of the future been a friend, I should have been secretly saddened. "Alas!" I would have thought, looking at him with an unmoved face, "the poor fellow is going mad."

I would have been, without doubt, saddened; for in this world where the journalists read the signs of the sky, and the wind of heaven itself, blowing where it listeth, does so under the prophetical management of the Meteorological Office, but where the secret of human hearts cannot be captured either by prying or praying, it was infinitely more likely that the sanest of my friends should nurse the germ of incipient madness than that I should turn into a writer of tales.

To survey with wonder the changes of one's own self is a fascinating pursuit for idle hours. The field is so wide, the surprises so varied, the subject so full of unprofitable but curious hints as to the work of unseen forces, that one does not weary easily of it. I am not speaking here of megalomaniacs who rest uneasy under the crown of their unbounded conceit – who really never rest in this world, and when out of it go on fretting and fuming on the straitened circumstances of their last habitation, where all men must lie in an obscure equality. Neither am I thinking of those ambitious minds who, always looking forward to some aim of aggrandisement, can spare no time for a detached, impersonal glance upon themselves.

And that's a pity. They are unlucky. These two kinds, together with the much larger band of the totally unimaginative, of those unfortunate beings in whose empty and unseeing gaze (as a great French writer has put it) "the whole universe vanishes into a blank nothingness," miss, perhaps, the true task of us men whose day is short on this earth, the abode of conflicting opinions. The ethical view of the universe involves us at last in so many cruel and absurd contradictions, where the last vestiges of faith, hope, charity and even of reason itself, seem ready to perish, that I have come to suspect that the aim of creation cannot be ethical at all. I would fondly believe that its object is purely spectacular: a spectacle for awe, love, adoration or hate, if you like, but in this view, and in this view alone – never for despair! Those visions, delicious or poignant, are a moral end in themselves. The rest is our affair – the laughter, the tears, the tenderness, the indignation, the high tranquillity of a steeled heart, the detached curiosity of a subtle mind – that's our affair! And the unwearied self-forgetful attention 5 to every phase of the living universe reflected in our consciousness may be our appointed task on this earth. A task in which fate has perhaps engaged nothing of us except our conscience, gifted with a voice in order to bear true testimony to the visible wonder, the haunting terror, the infinite passion and the illimitable serenity; to 10 the supreme law and the abiding mystery of the sublime spectacle.

Chi lo sà? It may be true. In this view there is room for every religion except for the inverted creed of impiety, the mask and cloak of arid despair; for every joy and every sorrow, for every fair dream, for every charitable hope. The great aim is to remain true 15 to the emotions called out of the deep encircled by the firmament of stars, whose infinite numbers and awful distances may move us to laughter or tears (was it the Walrus or the Carpenter, in the poem, who "wept to see such quantities of sand"?), or, again, to a properly steeled heart, may matter nothing at all. 20

The casual quotation which had suggested itself out of a poem full of merit leads me to remark that in the conception of the purely spectacular universe, where inspiration of every sort has a rational existence, the artist of every kind finds a natural place; and amongst them the poet as the seer *par excellence.* Even the writer 25 of prose, who, in his less noble and more toilsome task, should be a man with the steeled heart, is worthy of a place, providing he looks on with undimmed eyes and keeps laughter out of his voice, let who will laugh or cry. Yes! Even he, the artist of prose fiction, which after all is but truth often dragged out of a well, and clothed 30 in the painted robe of imaged phrases – even he has his place amongst kings, demagogues, priests, charlatans, dukes, giraffes, Cabinet Ministers, Fabians, bricklayers, apostles, ants, scientists, Kaffirs, soldiers, sailors, elephants, lawyers, dandies, microbes and constellations of a universe whose amazing spectacle is a moral 35 end in itself.

Here I perceive (speaking without offence) the reader assuming a subtle expression, as if the cat were out of the bag. I take the novelist's freedom to observe the reader's mind formulating the exclamation, "That's it! The fellow talks *pro domo.*" 40

Indeed it was not the intention! When I shouldered the bag I was not aware of the cat inside. But, after all, why not? The fair courtyards of the House of Art are thronged by many humble retainers. And there is no retainer so devoted as he who is allowed
5 to sit on the doorstep. The fellows who have got inside are apt to think too much of themselves. This last remark, I beg to state, is not malicious within the definition of the law of libel. It's fair comment on a matter of public interest. But never mind. *Pro domo.* So be it. For his house *tant que vous voudrez.* And yet in truth I was by
10 no means anxious to justify my existence. The attempt would have been not only needless and absurd, but almost inconceivable, in a purely spectacular universe, where no such disagreeable necessity can possibly arise. It is sufficient for me to say (and I am saying it at some length in these pages): *J'ai vécu.* I have existed, obscure
15 amongst the wonders and terrors of my time, as the Abbé Sieyès, the original utterer of the quoted words, had managed to exist through the violences and the enthusiasms of the French Revolution. *J'ai vécu,* as I apprehend most of us manage to exist, missing all along the varied forms of destruction by a hair's-breadth, saving
20 my body, that's clear, and perhaps my soul also, but not without some damage here and there to the fine edge of my conscience, that heirloom of the ages, of the race, of the group, of the family, colourable and plastic, fashioned by the words, the looks, the acts and even by the silences and abstentions surrounding one's
25 childhood, tinged in a complete scheme of delicate shades and crude colours by the inherited traditions, beliefs or prejudices – unaccountable, despotic, persuasive, and often, in its texture, romantic.

And often romantic! . . . The matter in hand, however, is to
30 keep these reminiscences from turning into confessions, a form of literary activity discredited by Jean-Jacques Rousseau on account of the extreme thoroughness he brought to the work of justifying his own existence; for that such was his purpose is palpably, even grossly, visible to an unprejudiced eye. But then, you see, the man
35 was not a writer of fiction. He was an artless moralist, as is clearly demonstrated by his anniversaries being celebrated with marked emphasis by the heirs of the French Revolution, which was not a political movement at all, but a great outburst of morality. He had no imagination, as the most casual perusal of "Émile" will prove.
40 He was no novelist, whose first virtue is the exact understanding

of the limits traced by the reality of his time to the play of his invention. Inspiration comes from the earth, which has a past, a history, a future, not from the cold and immutable heaven. A writer of imaginative prose (even more than any other sort of artist) stands confessed in his works. His conscience, his deeper sense of things, lawful and unlawful, gives him his attitude before the world. Indeed, every one who puts pen to paper for the reading of strangers (unless a moralist, who, generally speaking, has no conscience except the one he is at pains to produce for the use of others) can speak of nothing else. It is M. Anatole France, the most eloquent and just of French prose-writers, who says that we must recognise at last that, "failing the resolution to hold our peace, we can only talk of ourselves."

This remark, if I remember rightly, was made in the course of a sparring match with the late Ferdinand Brunetière over the principles and rules of literary criticism. As was fitting for a man to whom we owe the memorable saying, "The good critic is he who relates the adventures of his soul amongst masterpieces," M. Anatole France maintained that there were no rules and no principles. And that may be very true. Rules, principles and standards die and vanish every day. Perhaps they are all dead and vanished by this time. These, if ever, are the brave, free days of destroyed landmarks, while the ingenious minds are busy inventing the forms of the new beacons which, it is consoling to think, will be set up presently in the old places. But what is interesting to a writer is the possession of an inward certitude that literary criticism will never die, for man (so variously defined) is before everything else a critical animal. And, as long as distinguished minds are ready to treat it in the spirit of high adventure, literary criticism will appeal to us with all the charm and wisdom of a well-told tale of personal experience.

For Englishmen especially, of all the races of the earth, a task, any task, undertaken in an adventurous spirit acquires the merit of romance. But the critics as a rule exhibit but little of an adventurous spirit. They take risks, of course – one can hardly live without that. The daily bread is served out to us (however sparingly) with a pinch of salt. Otherwise one would get sick of the diet one prays for, and that would be not only improper, but impious. From impiety of that or any other kind – save us! An ideal of reserved manner, adhered to from a sense of proprieties, from shyness, perhaps, or

caution or simply from weariness, induces, I suspect, some writers
of criticism to conceal the adventurous side of their calling, and
then the criticism becomes a mere "notice," as it were the relation
of a journey where nothing but the distances and the geology of
5 a new country should be set down, the glimpses of strange beasts,
the dangers of flood and field, the hair's-breadth escapes and the
sufferings (oh, the sufferings too! I have no doubt of the sufferings) of the traveller being carefully kept out, no shady spot, no
fruitful plant being ever mentioned either, so that the whole per-
10 formance looks like a mere feat of agility on the part of a trained
pen running in a desert. A cruel spectacle – a most deplorable
adventure. "Life," in the words of an immortal thinker of, I should
say, bucolic origin, but whose perishable name is lost to the worship of posterity – "life is not all beer and skittles." Neither is the
15 writing of novels. It isn't really. *Je vous donne ma parole d'honneur*
that it – is – not. Not *all.* I am thus emphatic because some years
ago, I remember, the daughter of a general . . .

Sudden revelations of the profane world must have come now
and then to hermits in their cells, to the cloistered monks of Mid-
20 dle Ages, to lonely sages, men of science, reformers, the revelations
of a world's superficial judgment, shocking to the souls concentrated upon their own bitter labour in the cause of sanctity, or of
knowledge, or of temperance, let us say, or of art, if only the art of
cracking jokes or playing the flute. And thus this general's daugh-
25 ter came to me – or I should say one of the general's daughters
did. There were three of these bachelor ladies, of nicely graduated
ages, who held a neighbouring farmhouse in a united and more
or less military occupation. The eldest warred against the decay
of manners in the village children, and executed frontal attacks
30 upon the village mothers for the conquest of curtseys. It sounds
futile, but it was really a war for an idea. The second skirmished
and scouted all over the country; and it was that one who pushed
a reconnaissance right to my very table – I mean the one who wore
stand-up collars. She was really calling upon my wife, in the soft
35 spirit of afternoon friendliness, but with her usual martial determination. She marched into my room swinging her stick . . . but no –
I mustn't exaggerate. It is not my speciality. I am not a humouristic
writer. In all soberness, then, all I am certain of is that she had a
stick to swing.

No ditch or wall encompassed my abode. The window was open; the door too stood open to that best friend of my work, the warm, still sunshine of the wide fields. They lay around me infinitely helpful, but truth to say I had not known for weeks whether the sun shone upon the earth and whether the stars above still moved on their appointed courses. I was just then giving up some days of my allotted span to the last chapters of the novel "Nostromo," a tale of an imaginary (but true) seaboard, which is still mentioned now and again, and indeed kindly, sometimes in connection with the word "failure" and sometimes in conjunction with the word "astonishing." I have no opinion on this discrepancy. It's the sort of difference that can never be settled. All I know is that, for twenty months, neglecting the common joys of life that fall to the lot of the humblest on this earth, I had, like the prophet of old, "wrestled with the Lord" for my creation, for the headlands of the coast, for the darkness of the Placid Gulf, the light on the snows, the clouds on the sky and for the breath of life that had to be blown into the shapes of men and women, of Latin and Saxon, of Jew and Gentile. These are, perhaps, strong words, but it is difficult to characterise otherwise the intimacy and the strain of a creative effort in which mind and will and conscience are engaged to the full, hour after hour, day after day, away from the world and to the exclusion of all that makes life really lovable and gentle – something for which a material parallel can only be found in the everlasting sombre stress of the westward winter passage round Cape Horn. For that too is the wrestling of men with the might of their Creator, in a great isolation from the world, without the amenities and consolations of life, a lonely struggle under a sense of overmatched littleness, for no reward that could be adequate, but for the mere winning of a longitude. Yet a certain longitude, once won, cannot be disputed. The sun and the stars and the shape of your earth are the witnesses of your gain; whereas a handful of pages, no matter how much you have made them your own, are at best but an obscure and questionable spoil. Here they are. "Failure" – "Astonishing": take your choice; or perhaps both, or neither – a mere rustle and flutter of pieces of paper settling down in the night, and undistinguishable, like the snowflakes of a great drift destined to melt away in sunshine.

"How do you do?"

It was the greeting of the general's daughter. I had heard nothing – no rustle, no footsteps. I had felt only a moment before a
sort of premonition of evil; I had the sense of an inauspicious
presence – just that much warning and no more; and then came
5　the sound of the voice and the jar as of a terrible fall from a great
height – a fall, let us say, from the highest of the clouds floating in
gentle procession over the fields in the faint westerly air of that July
afternoon. I picked myself up quickly, of course; in other words,
I jumped up from my chair stunned and dazed, every nerve quiv-
10　ering with the pain of being uprooted out of one world and flung
down into another – perfectly civil.

"Oh! How do you do? Won't you sit down?"

That's what I said. This horrible but, I assure you, perfectly true
reminiscence tells you more than a whole volume of confessions *à*
15　*la* Jean-Jacques Rousseau would do. Observe! I didn't howl at her,
or start upsetting furniture, or throw myself on the floor and kick
or allow myself to hint in any other way at the appalling magnitude
of the disaster. The whole world of Costaguana (the country, you
may remember, of my seaboard tale), men, women, headlands,
20　houses, mountains, town, *campo* (there was not a single brick, stone
or grain of sand of its soil I had not placed in position with my own
hands); all the history, geography, politics, finance; the wealth of
Charles Gould's silver-mine, and the splendour of the magnificent
Capataz de Cargadores, whose name, cried out in the night (Dr.
25　Monygham heard it pass over his head – in Linda Viola's voice),
dominated even after death the dark gulf containing his conquests
of treasure and love – all that had come down crashing about my
ears. I felt I could never pick up the pieces – and in that very
moment I was saying, "Won't you sit down?"

30　The sea is strong medicine. Behold what the quarter-deck training even in a merchant ship will do! This episode should give you
a new view of the English and Scots seamen (a much-caricatured
folk) who had the last say in the formation of my character. One
is nothing if not modest, but in this disaster I think I have done
35　some honour to their simple teaching. "Won't you sit down?" Very
fair; very fair indeed. She sat down. Her amused glance strayed
all over the room. There were pages of MS. on the table, and
under the table, a batch of typed copy on a chair, single leaves had
fluttered away into distant corners; there were there living pages,
40　pages scored and wounded, dead pages that would be burned at

the end of the day – the litter of a cruel battlefield, of a long, long and desperate fray. Long! I suppose I went to bed sometimes, and got up the same number of times. Yes, I suppose I slept, and ate the food put before me, and talked connectedly to my household on suitable occasions. But I had never been aware of the even flow 5 of daily life, made easy and noiseless for me by a silent, watchful, tireless affection. Indeed, it seemed to me that I had been sitting at that table surrounded by the litter of a desperate fray for days and nights on end. It seemed so, because of the intense weariness of which that interruption had made me aware – the 10 awful disenchantment of a mind realising suddenly the futility of an enormous task, joined to a bodily fatigue such as no ordinary amount of fairly heavy physical labour could ever account for. I have carried bags of wheat on my back, bent almost double under a ship's deck-beams, from six in the morning till six in the evening 15 (with an hour and a half off for meals), so I ought to know.

And I love letters. I am jealous of their honour and concerned for the dignity and comeliness of their service. I was, most likely, the only writer that neat lady had ever caught in the exercise of his craft, and it distressed me not to be able to remember when 20 it was that I dressed myself last, and how. No doubt that would be all right in essentials. The fortune of the house included a pair of grey-blue watchful eyes that would see to that. But I felt somehow as grimy as a Costaguana *lepero* after a day's fighting in the streets, rumpled all over and dishevelled down to my very heels. And I 25 am afraid I blinked stupidly. All this was bad for the honour of letters and the dignity of their service. Seen indistinctly through the dust of my collapsed universe, the good lady glanced about the room with a slightly amused serenity. And she was smiling. What on earth was she smiling at? She remarked casually: 30

"I am afraid I interrupted you."

"Not at all."

She accepted the denial in perfect good faith. And it was strictly true. Interrupted – indeed! She had robbed me of at least twenty lives, each infinitely more poignant and real than her own, because 35 informed with passion, possessed of convictions, involved in great affairs created out of my own substance for an anxiously meditated end.

She remained silent for a while, then said with a last glance all round at the litter of the fray: 40

"And you sit like this here writing your – your . . ."

"I – what? Oh, yes! I sit here all day."

"It must be perfectly delightful."

I suppose that, being no longer very young, I might have been
5   on the verge of having a stroke; but she had left her dog in the
porch, and my boy's dog, patrolling the field in front, had espied
him from afar. He came on straight and swift like a cannon-ball,
and the noise of the fight, which burst suddenly upon our ears,
was more than enough to scare away a fit of apoplexy. We went out
10 hastily and separated the gallant animals. Afterwards I told the lady
where she would find my wife – just round the corner, under the
trees. She nodded and went off with her dog, leaving me appalled
before the death and devastation she had lightly made – and with
the awfully instructive sound of the word "delightful" lingering in
15 my ears.

Nevertheless, later on, I duly escorted her to the field gate. I
wanted to be civil, of course (what are twenty lives in a mere novel
that one should be rude to a lady on their account?), but mainly,
to adopt the good sound Ollendorffian style, because I did not
20 want the dog of the general's daughter to fight again (*encore*) with
the faithful dog of my infant son (*mon petit garçon*). – Was I afraid
that the dog of the general's daughter would be able to overcome
(*vaincre*) the dog of my child? – No, I was not afraid. . . . But away
with the Ollendorff method. However appropriate and seemingly
25 unavoidable when I touch upon anything appertaining to the lady,
it is most unsuitable to the origin, character and history of the
dog; for the dog was the gift to the child from a man for whom
words had anything but an Ollendorffian value, a man almost
childlike in the impulsive movements of his untutored genius,
30 the most single-minded of verbal impressionists, using his great
gifts of straight feeling and right expression with a fine sincerity
and a strong if, perhaps, not fully conscious conviction. His art
did not obtain, I fear, all the credit its unsophisticated inspiration
deserved. I am alluding to the late Stephen Crane, the author of
35 "The Red Badge of Courage," a work of imagination which found
its short moment of celebrity in the last decade of the departed
century. Other books followed. Not many. He had not the time.
It was an individual and complete talent, which obtained but a
grudging, somewhat supercilious recognition from the world at
40 large. For himself one hesitates to regret his early death. Like

one of the men in his "Open Boat," one felt that he was of those
whom fate seldom allows to make a safe landing after much toil
and bitterness at the oar. I confess to an abiding affection for that
energetic, slight, fragile, intensely living and transient figure. He
liked me even before we met on the strength of a page or two of   5
my writing, and after we met I am glad to think he liked me still.
He used to point out to me with great earnestness, and even with
some severity, that "a boy *ought* to have a dog." I suspect that he
was shocked at my neglect of parental duties. Ultimately it was he
who provided the dog. Shortly afterwards, one day, after playing   10
with the child on the rug for an hour or so with the most intense
absorption, he raised his head and declared firmly: "I shall teach
your boy to ride." That was not to be. He was not given the time.

But here is the dog – an old dog now. Broad and low on his
bandy paws, with a black head on a white body and a ridiculous   15
black spot at the other end of him, he provokes, when he walks
abroad, smiles not altogether unkind. Grotesque and engaging
in the whole of his appearance, his usual attitudes are meek, but
his temperament discloses itself unexpectedly pugnacious in the
presence of his kind. As he lies in the firelight, his head well up, 20
and a fixed, far-away gaze directed at the shadows of the room, he
achieves a striking nobility of pose in the calm consciousness of an
unstained life. He has brought up one baby, and now, after seeing
his first charge off to school, he is bringing up another with the
same conscientious devotion, but with a more deliberate gravity   25
of manner, the sign of greater wisdom and riper experience, but
also of rheumatism, I fear. From the morning bath to the evening
ceremonies of the cot you attend, old friend, the little two-legged
creature of your adoption, being yourself treated in the exercise of
your duties with every possible regard, with infinite consideration, 30
by every person in the house – even as I myself am treated; only
you deserve it more. The general's daughter would tell you that it
must be "perfectly delightful."

Aha! old dog. She has never heard you yelp with acute pain (it's
that poor left ear) while, with incredible self-command, you pre-   35
serve a rigid immobility for fear of overturning the little two-legged
creature. She has never seen your resigned smile while the little
two-legged creature, interrogated sternly, "What are you doing to
the good dog?" answers with a wide, innocent stare: "Nothing.
Only loving him, mama dear!"   40

The general's daughter does not know the secret terms of self-imposed tasks, good dog, the pain that may lurk in the very rewards of rigid self-command. But we have lived together many years. We have grown older, too; and though our work is not quite done yet we may indulge now and then in a little introspection before the fire – meditate on the art of bringing up babies and on the perfect delight of writing tales where so many lives come and go at the cost of one which slips imperceptibly away.

VI

IN THE RETROSPECT OF a life which had, besides its preliminary
stage of childhood and early youth, two distinct developments,
and even two distinct elements, such as earth and water, for its
successive scenes, a certain amount of naïveness is unavoidable. I   5
am conscious of it in these pages. This remark is put forward in
no apologetic spirit.

As years go by and the number of pages grows steadily, the feeling grows upon one too that one can write only for friends. Then
why should one put them to the necessity of protesting (as a friend   10
would do) that no apology is necessary, or put, perchance, into
their heads the doubt of one's discretion? So much as to the care
due to those friends whom a word here, a line there, a fortunate
page of just feeling in the right place, some happy simplicity or
even some lucky subtlety, has drawn from the great multitude of   15
fellow beings even as a fish is drawn from the depths of the sea.
Fishing is notoriously (I am talking now of the deep sea) a matter
of luck. As to one's enemies, those will take care of themselves.

There is a gentleman, for instance, who, metaphorically speaking, jumps upon me with both feet. This image has no grace, but   20
it is exceedingly apt to the occasion – to the several occasions. I
don't know precisely how long he had been indulging in that inter-
mittent exercise, whose seasons are ruled by the custom of the
publishing trade. Somebody pointed him out (in printed shape,
of course) to my attention some time ago, and straightway I expe-   25
rienced a sort of reluctant affection for that robust man. He leaves
not a shred of my substance untrodden: for the writer's substance
is his writing; the rest of him is but a vain shadow, cherished or
hated on uncritical grounds. Not a shred! Yet the sentiment owned
to is not a freak of affectation or perversity. It has a deeper, and,   30
I venture to think, a more estimable origin than the caprice of
emotional lawlessness. It is, indeed, lawful, in so much that it is

given (reluctantly) for a consideration, for several considerations. There is that robustness, for instance, so often the sign of good moral balance. That's a consideration. It is not, indeed, pleasant to be stamped upon, but the very thoroughness of the operation,

5 implying not only a careful reading, but some real insight into work where qualities and defects, whatever they may be, are not so much on the surface, is something to be thankful for in view of the fact that it may happen to one's work to be condemned without being read at all. This is the most fatuous adventure that can well

10 happen to a writer venturing his soul amongst criticisms. It can do one no harm, of course, but it is disagreeable. It is disagreeable in the same way as discovering a three-card-trick man amongst a decent lot of folk in a third-class compartment. The open impudence of the whole transaction, appealing insidiously to the folly

15 and credulity of mankind, the brazen, shameless patter, proclaiming the fraud openly while insisting on the fairness of the game, give one a feeling of sickening disgust. The honest violence of a plain man playing a fair game fairly – even if he means to knock you over – may appear shocking, but it remains within the pale of

20 decency. Damaging as it may be, it is in no sense offensive. One may well feel some regard for honesty, even if practised upon one's own vile body. But it is very obvious that an enemy of that sort will not be stayed by explanations or placated by apologies. Were I to advance the plea of youth in excuse of the naïveness to be found

25 in these pages, he would be likely to say "Bosh!" in a column and a half of fierce print. Yet a writer is no older than his first published book, and, notwithstanding the vain appearances of decay which attend us in this transitory life, I stand here with the wreath of only fifteen short summers on my brow.

30   With the remark, then, that at such tender age some naïveness of feeling and expression is excusable, I will proceed to admit that upon the whole my previous state of existence was not a good equipment for a literary life. Perhaps I should not have used the word literary. That word presupposes an intimacy of acquaintance

35 with letters, a turn of mind and a manner of feeling to which I dare lay no claim. I only love letters; but the love of letters does not make a literary man, any more than the love of the sea makes a seaman. And it is very possible, too, that I love the letters in the same way a literary man may love the sea he looks at from

40 the shore – a scene of great endeavour and of great achievements

changing the face of the world, the great open way to all sorts of
undiscovered countries. No, perhaps I had better say that the life
at sea – and I don't mean a mere taste of it, but a good broad span
of years, something that really counts as real service – is not, upon
the whole, a good equipment for a writing life.   5

God forbid, though, that I should be thought of as denying
my masters of the quarter-deck. I am not capable of that sort of
apostasy. I have confessed my attitude of piety towards their shades
in three or four tales, and if any man on earth more than another
needs to be true to himself as he hopes to be saved, it is certainly   10
the writer of fiction.

What I meant to say, simply, is that the quarter-deck training does
not prepare one sufficiently for the reception of literary criticism.
Only that, and no more. Yet this defect is not without gravity. If
it be permissible to twist, invert, adapt (and spoil) M. Anatole   15
France's definition of a good critic, then let us say that the good
author is he who contemplates without marked joy or excessive
sorrow the adventures of his soul amongst criticisms. Far be from
me the intention to mislead an attentive public into the belief
that there is no criticism at sea. That would be dishonest, and   20
even impolite. Everything can be found at sea, according to the
spirit of your quest – strife, peace, romance, naturalism of the
most pronounced kind, ideals, boredom, disgust, inspiration –
and every conceivable opportunity, including the opportunity to
make a fool of yourself – exactly as in the pursuit of literature.   25
But the quarter-deck criticism is somewhat different from literary
criticism. This much they have in common, that before the one
and the other the answering back, as a general rule, does not pay.

Yes, you find criticism at sea, and even appreciation – I tell
you everything is to be found on salt water – criticism generally   30
impromptu, and always *vivâ voce*, which is the outward, obvious
difference from the literary operation of that kind, with conse-
quent freshness and vigour which may be lacking in the printed
word. With appreciation, which comes at the end, when the critic
and the criticised are about to part, it is otherwise. The sea appre- 35
ciation of one's humble talents has the permanency of the written word, seldom the charm of variety, is formal in its phrasing.
There the literary master has the superiority, though he, too, can
in effect but say – and often says it in the very phrase – "I can
highly recommend." Only usually he uses the word "We," there   40

being some occult virtue in the first person plural, which makes it specially fit for critical and royal declarations. I have a small handful of these sea appreciations, signed by various masters, yellowing slowly in my writing-table's left-hand drawer, rustling under my
5   reverent touch, like a handful of dry leaves plucked for a tender memento from the tree of knowledge. Strange! It seems that it is for these few bits of paper, headed by the names of a few ships and signed by the names of a few Scotch and English shipmasters, that I have faced the astonished indignations, the mockeries and the
10 reproaches of a sort hard to bear for a boy of fifteen, that I have been charged with the want of patriotism, the want of sense and the want of heart too, that I went through agonies of self-conflict and shed secret tears not a few, and had the beauties of the Furka Pass spoiled for me, and have been called an "incorrigible Don
15 Quixote," in allusion to the book-born madness of the knight. For that spoil! They rustle, those bits of paper – some dozen of them in all. In that faint, ghostly sound there live the memories of twenty years, the voices of rough men now no more, the strong voice of the everlasting winds and the whisper of a mysterious spell, the
20 murmur of the great sea, which must have somehow reached my inland cradle and entered my unconscious ear, like that formula of Mohammedan faith the Mussulman father whispers into the ear of his new-born infant, making him one of the faithful almost with his first breath. I do not know whether I have been a good
25 seaman, but I know I have been a very faithful one. And after all there is that handful of "characters" from various ships to prove that all these years have not been altogether a dream. There they are, brief, and monotonous in tone, but as suggestive bits of writing to me as any inspired page to be found in literature. But then,
30 you see, I have been called romantic. Well, that can't be helped. But stay. I seem to remember that I have been called a realist also. And as that charge too can be made out, let us try to live up to it, at whatever cost, for a change. With this end in view, I will confide to you coyly, and only because there is no one about to see my
35 blushes by the light of the midnight lamp, that these suggestive bits of quarter-deck appreciation one and all contain the words "strictly sober."

Did I overhear a civil murmur, "That's very gratifying, to be sure"? Well, yes, it is gratifying – thank you. It is at least as gratify-
40 ing to be certified sober as to be certified romantic, though such

certificates would not qualify one for a secretaryship of a temperance association or for the post of official troubadour to some lordly democratic institution such as the London County Council, for instance. The above prosaic reflection is put down here only in order to prove the general sobriety of my judgment in mundane 5
affairs. I make a point of it because a couple of years ago, a certain short story of mine being published in a French translation, a Parisian critic – I am almost certain it was M. Gustave Kahn in the *Gil-Blas* – giving me a short notice, summed up his rapid impression of the writer's quality in the words *un puissant rêveur*. So be 10
it! Who would cavil at the words of a friendly reader? Yet perhaps not such an unconditional dreamer as all that. I will make bold to say that neither at sea nor ashore have I ever lost the sense of responsibility. There is more than one sort of intoxication. Even before the most seductive reveries I have remained mindful of 15
that sobriety of interior life, that asceticism of sentiment, in which alone the naked form of truth, such as one conceives it, such as one feels it, can be rendered without shame. It is but a maudlin and indecent verity that comes out through the strength of wine. I have tried to be a sober worker all my life – all my two lives. I 20
did so from taste, no doubt having an instinctive horror of losing my sense of full self-possession, but also from artistic conviction. Yet there are so many pitfalls on each side of the true path that, having gone some way, and feeling a little battered and weary, as a middle-aged traveller will, from the mere daily difficulties of the 25
march, I ask myself whether I have kept always, always faithful to that sobriety wherein there is power and truth and peace.

As to my sea-sobriety, that is quite properly certified under the sign-manual of several trustworthy shipmasters of some standing in their time. I seem to hear your polite murmur that "Surely this 30
might have been taken for granted." Well, no. It might not have been. That august academical body the Marine Department of the Board of Trade takes nothing for granted in the granting of its learned degrees. By its regulations issued under the first Merchant Shipping Act the very word S O B E R must be written, or a whole 35
sackful, a ton, a mountain of the most enthusiastic appreciation will avail you nothing. The door of the examination rooms shall remain closed to your tears and entreaties. The most fanatical advocate of temperance could not be more pitilessly fierce in his rectitude than the Marine Department of the Board of Trade. As I 40

have been face to face at various times with all the examiners of the
Port of London, in my generation, there can be no doubt as to the
force and the continuity of my abstemiousness. Three of them were
examiners in seamanship, and it was my fate to be delivered into
the hands of each of them at proper intervals of sea service. The
first of all, tall, spare, with a perfectly white head and moustache,
a quiet, kindly manner and an air of benign intelligence, must,
I am forced to conclude, have been unfavourably impressed by
something in my appearance. His old thin hands loosely clasped
resting on his crossed legs, he began by an elementary question
in a mild voice, and went on, went on. . . . It lasted for hours,
for hours. Had I been a strange microbe with potentialities of
deadly mischief to the Merchant Service I could not have been
submitted to a more microscopic examination. Greatly reassured
by his apparent benevolence, I had been at first very alert in my
answers. But at length the feeling of my brain getting addled crept
upon me. And still the passionless process went on, with a sense
of untold ages having been spent already on mere preliminaries.
Then I got frightened. I was not frightened of being plucked;
that eventuality did not even present itself to my mind. It was
something much more serious, and weird. "This ancient person,"
I said to myself, terrified, "is so near his grave that he must have
lost all notion of time. He is considering this examination in terms
of eternity. It is all very well for him. His race is run. But I may find
myself coming out of this room into the world of men a stranger,
friendless, forgotten by my very landlady, even were I able after
this endless experience to remember the way to my hired home."
This statement is not so much of a verbal exaggeration as may
be supposed. Some very queer thoughts passed through my head
while I was considering my answers; thoughts which had nothing
to do with seamanship, nor yet with anything reasonable known to
this earth. I verily believe that at times I was light-headed in a sort
of languid way. At last there fell a silence, and that, too, seemed to
last for ages, while, bending over his desk, the examiner wrote out
my pass-slip slowly with a noiseless pen. He extended the scrap of
paper to me without a word, inclined his white head gravely to my
parting bow. . . .

When I got out of the room I felt limply flat, like a squeezed
lemon, and the doorkeeper in his glass cage, where I stopped to
get my hat and tip him a shilling, said:

"Well! I thought you were never coming out."

"How long have I been in there?" I asked faintly.

He pulled out his watch.

"He kept you, sir, just under three hours. I don't think this ever happened with any of the gentlemen before."

It was only when I got out of the building that I began to walk on air. And the human animal being averse from change and timid before the unknown, I said to myself that I would not mind really being examined by the same man on a future occasion. But when the time of ordeal came round again the doorkeeper let me into another room, with the now familiar paraphernalia of models of ships and tackle, a board for signals on the wall, a big long table covered with official forms, and having an unrigged mast fixed to the edge. The solitary tenant was unknown to me by sight, though not by reputation, which was simply execrable. Short and sturdy as far as I could judge, clad in an old brown morning-suit, he sat leaning on his elbow, his hand shading his eyes, and half averted from the chair I was to occupy on the other side of the table. He was motionless, mysterious, remote, enigmatical, with something mournful too in the pose, like that statue of Giuliano (I think) de Medici shading his face on the tomb by Michael Angelo, though, of course, he was far, far from being beautiful. He began by trying to make me talk nonsense. But I had been warned of that fiendish trait, and contradicted him with great assurance. After a while he left off. So far good. But his immobility, the thick elbow on the table, the abrupt, unhappy voice, the shaded and averted face grew more and more impressive. He kept inscrutably silent for a moment, and then, placing me in a ship of a certain size, at sea, under certain conditions of weather, season, locality, &c. &c. – all very clear and precise – ordered me to execute a certain manœuvre. Before I was half through with it he did some material damage to the ship. Directly I had grappled with the difficulty he caused another to present itself, and when that too was met he stuck another ship before me, creating a very dangerous situation. I felt slightly outraged by this ingenuity in piling up trouble upon a man.

"I wouldn't have got into that mess," I suggested mildly. "I could have seen that ship before."

He never stirred the least bit.

"No, you couldn't. The weather's thick."

"Oh! I didn't know," I apologised blankly.

I suppose that after all I managed to stave off the smash with suffi-cient approach to verisimilitude, and the ghastly business went on. You must understand that the scheme of the test he was applying to me was, I gathered, a homeward passage – the sort of passage I would not wish to my bitterest enemy. That imaginary ship seemed to labour under a most comprehensive curse. It's no use enlarg-ing on these never-ending misfortunes; suffice it to say that long before the end I would have welcomed with gratitude an oppor-tunity to exchange into the *Flying Dutchman*. Finally he shoved me into the North Sea (I suppose), and provided me with a lee-shore with outlying sandbanks – the Dutch coast, presumably. Distance, eight miles. The evidence of such implacable animosity deprived me of speech for quite half a minute.

"Well," he said – for our pace had been very smart indeed till then.

"I will have to think a little, sir."

"Doesn't look as if there were much time to think," he muttered sardonically from under his hand.

"No, sir," I said with some warmth. "Not on board a ship I could see. But so many accidents have happened that I really can't remember what there's left for me to work with."

Still half averted, and with his eyes concealed, he made unex-pectedly a grunting remark.

"You've done very well."

"Have I the two anchors at the bow, sir?" I asked.

"Yes."

I prepared myself then, as a last hope for the ship, to let them both go in the most effectual manner, when his infernal system of testing resourcefulness came into play again.

"But there's only one cable. You've lost the other."

It was exasperating.

"Then I would back them, if I could, and tail the heaviest hawser on board on the end of the chain before letting go, and if she parted from that, which is quite likely, I would just do nothing. She would have to go."

"Nothing more to do, eh?"

"No, sir. I could do no more."

He gave a bitter half-laugh.

"You could always say your prayers."

He got up, stretched himself and yawned slightly. It was a sallow, strong, unamiable face. He put me in a surly, bored fashion through the usual questions as to lights and signals, and I escaped from the room thankfully – passed! Forty minutes! And again I walked on air along Tower Hill, where so many good men had lost 5
their heads, because, I suppose, they were not resourceful enough to save them. And in my heart of hearts I had no objection to meeting that examiner once more when the third and last ordeal became due in another year or so. I even hoped I should. I knew the worst of him now, and forty minutes is not an unreasonable 10
time. Yes, I distinctly hoped . . .

But not a bit of it. When I presented myself to be examined for Master the examiner who received me was short, plump, with a round, soft face in grey, fluffy whiskers and fresh, loquacious lips. 15

He commenced operations with an easy-going "Let's see. H'm. Suppose you tell me all you know of charter-parties." He kept it up in that style all through, wandering off in the shape of comment into bits out of his own life, then pulling himself up short and returning to the business in hand. It was very interesting. "What's 20
your idea of a jury-rudder now?" he queried suddenly, at the end of an instructive anecdote bearing upon a point of stowage.

I warned him that I had no experience of a lost rudder at sea, and gave him two classical examples of makeshifts out of a text-book. In exchange he described to me a jury-rudder he had invented 25
himself years before, when in command of a 3000-ton steamer. It was, I declare, the cleverest contrivance imaginable. "May be of use to you some day," he concluded. "You will go into steam presently. Everybody goes into steam."

There he was wrong. I never went into steam – not really. If 30
I only live long enough I shall become a bizarre relic of a dead barbarism, a sort of monstrous antiquity, the only seaman of the dark ages who had never gone into steam – not really.

Before the examination was over he imparted to me a few interesting details of the transport service in the time of the Crimean 35
War.

"The use of wire rigging became general about that time too," he observed. "I was a very young master then. That was before you were born."

"Yes, sir. I am of the year 1857." 40

"The Mutiny year," he commented, as if to himself, adding in
a louder tone that his ship happened then to be in the Gulf of
Bengal, employed under a Government charter.

Clearly the transport service had been the making of this exam-
5 iner, who so unexpectedly had given me an insight into his existence, awakening in me the sense of the continuity of that sea-life
into which I had stepped from outside, giving a touch of human
intimacy to the machinery of official relations. I felt adopted.
His experience was for me, too, as though he had been an
10 ancestor.

Writing my long name (it has twelve letters) with laborious care
on the slip of blue paper, he remarked:

"You are of Polish extraction."

"Born there, sir."

15 He laid down the pen and leaned back to look at me as it were
for the first time.

"Not many of your nationality in our service, I should think. I
never remember meeting one either before or after I left the sea.
Don't remember ever hearing of one. An inland people, aren't
20 you?"

I said yes – very much so. We were remote from the sea not only
by situation, but also from a complete absence of indirect association, not being a commercial nation at all, but purely agricultural.
He made then the quaint reflection that it was "a long way for me
25 to come out to begin a sea-life"; as if sea-life were not precisely a
life in which one goes a long way from home.

I told him, smiling, that no doubt I could have found a ship
much nearer my native place, but I had thought to myself that if I
was to be a seaman then I would be a British seaman and no other.
30 It was a matter of deliberate choice.

He nodded slightly at that; and as he kept on looking at me
interrogatively, I enlarged a little, confessing that I had spent a little
time on the way in the Mediterranean and in the West Indies. I did
not want to present myself to the British Merchant Service in an
35 altogether green state. It was no use telling him that my mysterious
vocation was so strong that my very wild oats had to be sown at
sea. It was the exact truth, but he would not have understood the
somewhat exceptional psychology of my sea-going, I fear.

"I suppose you've never come across one of your countrymen
40 at sea. Have you now?"

I admitted I never had. The examiner had given himself up to
the spirit of gossiping idleness. For myself, I was in no haste to leave
that room. Not in the least. The era of examinations was over. I
would never again see that friendly man who was a professional
ancestor, a sort of grandfather in the craft. Moreover, I had to wait 5
till he dismissed me, and of that there was no sign. As he remained
silent, looking at me, I added:

"But I have heard of one, some years ago. He seems to have
been a boy serving his time on board a Liverpool ship, if I am not
mistaken." 10

"What was his name?"

I told him.

"How did you say that?" he asked, puckering up his eyes at the
uncouth sound.

I repeated the name very distinctly. 15

"How do you spell it?"

I told him. He moved his head at the impracticable nature of
that name, and observed:

"It's quite as long as your own – isn't it?"

There was no hurry. I had passed for Master, and I had all the 20
rest of my life before me to make the best of it. That seemed a long
time. I went leisurely through a small mental calculation, and said:

"Not quite. Shorter by two letters, sir."

"Is it?" The examiner pushed the signed blue slip across the
table to me, and rose from his chair. Somehow this seemed a very 25
abrupt ending of our relations, and I felt almost sorry to part from
that excellent man, who was master of a ship before the whisper
of the sea had reached my cradle. He offered me his hand and
wished me well. He even made a few steps towards the door with
me, and ended with good-natured advice. 30

"I don't know what may be your plans but you ought to go into
steam. When a man has got his master's certificate it's the proper
time. If I were you I would go into steam."

I thanked him, and shut the door behind me definitely on the
era of examinations. But that time I did not walk on air, as on the 35
first two occasions. I walked across the Hill of many beheadings
with measured steps. It was a fact, I said to myself, that I was now
a British master mariner beyond a doubt. It was not that I had an
exaggerated sense of that very modest achievement, with which,
however, luck, opportunity or any extraneous influence could have 40

had nothing to do. That fact, satisfactory and obscure in itself, had
for me a certain ideal significance. It was an answer to certain out-
spoken scepticism, and even to some not very kind aspersions. I
had vindicated myself from what had been cried upon as a stupid
obstinacy or a fantastic caprice. I don't mean to say that a whole
country had been convulsed by my desire to go to sea. But for a boy
between fifteen and sixteen, sensitive enough in all conscience,
the commotion of his little world had seemed a very considerable
thing indeed. So considerable that, absurdly enough, the echoes
of it linger to this day. I catch myself in hours of solitude and retrospect meeting arguments and charges made thirty-five years ago
by voices now for ever still; finding things to say that an assailed
boy could not have found, simply because of the mysteriousness
of his impulses to himself. I understood no more than the people
who called upon me to explain myself. There was no precedent.
I verily believe mine was the only case of a boy of my nationality
and antecedents taking a, so to speak, standing jump out of his
racial surroundings and associations. For you must understand
that there was no idea of any sort of "career" in my call. Of Russia or Germany there could be no question. The nationality, the
antecedents, made it impossible. The feeling against the Austrian
service was not so strong, and I daresay there would have been no
difficulty in finding my way into the Naval School of Pola. It would
have meant six months' extra grinding at German, perhaps, but I
was not past the age of admission, and in other respects I was well
qualified. This expedient to palliate my folly was thought of –
but not by me. I must admit that in that respect my negative
was accepted at once. That order of feeling was comprehensible
enough to the most inimical of my critics. I was not called upon
to offer explanations; the truth is that what I had in view was not a
naval career. There seemed no way open to it but through France.
I had the language at any rate, and of all the countries in Europe it
is with France that Poland has most connection. There were some
facilities for having me a little looked after at first. Letters were
being written, answers were being received, arrangements were
being made for my departure for Marseilles, where an excellent
fellow called Solary, got at in a roundabout fashion through various French channels, had promised good-naturedly to put *le jeune
homme* in the way of getting a decent ship for his first start if he
really wanted a taste of *ce métier de chien*.

I watched all these preparations gratefully, and kept my own counsel. But what I told the last of my examiners was perfectly true. Already the determined resolve, that "if a seaman, then an English seaman," was formulated in my head though, of course, in the Polish language. I did not know six words of English, and I was astute enough to understand that it was much better to say nothing of my purpose. As it was I was already looked upon as partly insane at least by the more distant acquaintances. The principal thing was to get away. I put my trust in the good-natured Solary's very civil letter to my uncle, though I was shocked a little by the phrase about the *métier de chien.*

This Solary (Baptistin), when I beheld him in the flesh, turned out quite a young man, very good-looking, with a black, fine short beard, a fresh complexion and soft, merry black eyes. He was as jovial and good-natured as any boy could desire. I was still asleep in my room in a modest hotel near the quays of the old port, after the fatigues of the journey *via* Vienna, Zurich, Lyons, when he burst in, flinging the shutters open to the sun of Provence and chiding me boisterously for lying abed. How pleasantly he startled me by his noisy objurgations to be up and off instantly for a "three years' campaign in the South Seas." O magic words! "*Une campagne de trois ans dans les mers du sud*" – that is the French for a three years' deep-water voyage.

He gave me a delightful waking, and his friendliness was unwearied; but I fear he did not enter upon the quest for a ship for me in a very solemn spirit. He had been at sea himself, but had left off at the age of twenty-five, finding he could earn his living on shore in a much more agreeable manner. He was related to an incredible number of Marseilles well-to-do families of a certain class. One of his uncles was a ship-broker of good standing, with a large connection amongst English ships; other relatives of his dealt in ships' stores, owned sail-lofts, sold chains and anchors, were masters, stevedores, caulkers, shipwrights. His grandfather (I think) was a dignitary of a kind, the Syndic of the Pilots. I made acquaintances amongst these people, but mainly amongst the pilots. The very first whole day I ever spent on salt water was by invitation, in a big half-decked pilot-boat, cruising under close reefs on the look-out, in misty, blowing weather, for the sails of ships and the smoke of steamers rising out there beyond the slim and tall Planier lighthouse, cutting the line of the wind-swept horizon with a white

perpendicular stroke. They were hospitable souls, these sturdy
Provençal seamen. Under the general designation of *le petit ami
de Baptistin* I was made the guest of the corporation of pilots, and
had the freedom of their boats night or day. And many a day and
5 a night too did I spend cruising with these rough, kindly men,
under whose auspices my intimacy with the sea began. Many a
time "the little friend of Baptistin" had the hooded cloak of the
Mediterranean sailor thrown over him by their honest hands while
dodging at night under the lee of Château d'If on the watch for
10 the lights of ships. Their sea-tanned faces, whiskered or shaved,
lean or full, with the intent wrinkled sea-eyes of the pilot-breed,
and here and there a thin gold hoop at the lobe of a hairy ear,
bent over my sea-infancy. The first operation of seamanship I had
an opportunity of observing was the boarding of ships at sea, at all
15 times, in all states of the weather. They gave it to me to the full.
And I have been invited to sit in more than one tall, dark house of
the old town at their hospitable board, had the *bouillabaisse* ladled
out into a thick plate by their high-voiced, broad-browed wives,
talked to their daughters – thick-set girls, with pure profiles, glori-
20 ous masses of black hair arranged with complicated art, dark eyes
and dazzlingly white teeth.

I had also other acquaintances of quite a different sort. One of
them, Madame Delestang, an imperious, handsome lady in a stat-
uesque style, would carry me off now and then on the front seat of
25 her carriage to the Prado, at the hour of fashionable airing. She
belonged to one of the old aristocratic families in the south. In
her haughty weariness she used to make me think of Lady Dedlock in Dickens's "Bleak House," a work of the master for which I
have such an admiration, or rather such an intense and unreason-
30 ing affection, dating from the days of my childhood, that its very
weaknesses are more precious to me than the strength of other
men's work. I have read it innumerable times, both in Polish and
in English; I have read it only the other day, and, by a not very
surprising inversion, the Lady Dedlock of the book reminded me
35 strongly of the "belle Madame Delestang."

Her husband (as I sat facing them both), with his thin bony nose,
and a perfectly bloodless, narrow physiognomy, clamped together
as it were by short formal side-whiskers, had nothing of Sir Leices-
ter Dedlock's "grand air" and courtly solemnity. He belonged to

the *haute bourgeoisie* only, and was a banker, with whom a modest
credit had been opened for my needs. He was such an ardent –
no, such a frozen-up, mummified Royalist that he used in current
conversation turns of speech contemporary, I should say, with the
good Henri Quatre, and when talking of money matters reckoned   5
not in francs, like the common, godless herd of post-Revolutionary
Frenchmen, but in obsolete and forgotten écus – écus of all money
units in the world! – as though Louis Quatorze were still prome-
nading in royal splendour the gardens of Versailles, and Monsieur
de Colbert busy with the direction of maritime affairs. You must   10
admit that in a banker of the nineteenth century it was a quaint
idiosyncrasy. Luckily in the counting-house (it occupied part of
the ground floor of the Delestang town residence, in a silent,
shady street) the accounts were kept in modern money, so that
I never had any difficulty in making my wants known to the grave,   15
low-voiced, decorous, Legitimist (I suppose) clerks, sitting in the
perpetual gloom of heavily barred windows behind the sombre,
ancient counters, beneath lofty ceilings with heavily moulded cor-
nices. I always felt on going out as though I had been in a temple
of some very dignified but completely temporal religion. And it   20
was generally on these occasions that under the great carriage
gateway Lady Ded – I mean Madame Delestang, catching sight of
my raised hat, would beckon me with an amiable imperiousness
to the side of the carriage, and suggest with an air of amused non-
chalance, "*Venez donc faire un tour avec nous*," to which the husband   25
would add an encouraging "*C'est ça. Allons, montez, jeune homme.*"
He questioned me sometimes, significantly but with perfect tact
and delicacy as to the way I employed my time, and never failed to
express the hope that I wrote regularly to my "honoured uncle." I
made no secret of the way I employed my time, and I rather fancy   30
that my artless tales of the pilots and so on entertained Madame
Delestang, so far as that ineffable woman could be entertained by
the prattle of a youngster very full of his new experience amongst
strange men and strange sensations. She expressed no opinions,
and talked to me very little; yet her portrait hangs in the gallery of   35
my intimate memories, fixed there by a short and fleeting episode.
One day, after putting me down at the corner of a street, she
offered me her hand, and detained me by a slight pressure, for a
moment. While the husband sat motionless and looking straight

before him, she leaned forward in the carriage to say, with just a shade of warning in her leisurely tone: "*Il faut, cependant, faire attention à ne pas gâter sa vie.*" I had never seen her face so close to mine before. She made my heart beat, and caused me to remain thoughtful for a whole evening. Certainly one must, after all, take care not to spoil one's life. But she did not know – nobody could know – how impossible that danger seemed to me.

VII

CAN THE TRANSPORTS OF first love be calmed, checked, turned to
a cold suspicion of the future by a grave quotation from a work on
Political Economy? I ask – is it conceivable? Is it possible? Would it
be right? With my feet on the very shores of the sea and about to   5
embrace my blue-eyed dream, what could a good-natured warning
as to spoiling one's life mean to my youthful passion? It was the
most unexpected and the last too of the many warnings I had
received. It sounded to me very bizarre – and, uttered as it was
in the very presence of my enchantress, like the voice of folly,   10
the voice of ignorance. But I was not so callous or so stupid as
not to recognise there also the voice of kindness. And then the
vagueness of the warning – because what can be the meaning of
the phrase: to spoil one's life? – arrested one's attention by its air
of wise profundity. At any rate, as I have said before, the words of la   15
belle Madame Delestang made me thoughtful for a whole evening.
I tried to understand and tried in vain, not having any notion of
life as an enterprise that could be mismanaged. But I left off being
thoughtful shortly before midnight, at which hour, haunted by no
ghosts of the past and by no visions of the future, I walked down   20
the quay of the Vieux Port to join the pilot boat of my friends. I
knew where she would be waiting for her crew, in the little bit of a
canal behind the Fort at the entrance of the harbour. The deserted
quays looked very white and dry in the moonlight and as if frost-
bound in the sharp air of that December night. A prowler or two   25
slunk by noiselessly; a custom-house guard, soldier-like, a sword by
his side, paced close under the bowsprits of the long row of ships
moored bows on opposite the long, slightly curved, continuous flat
wall of the tall houses that seemed to be one immense abandoned
building with innumerable windows shuttered closely. Only here   30
and there a small dingy *café* for sailors cast a yellow gleam on
the bluish sheen of the flagstones. Passing by, one heard a deep

murmur of voices inside – nothing more. How quiet everything
was at the end of the quays on the last night on which I went
out for a service cruise as a guest of the Marseilles pilots! Not a
footstep, except my own, not a sigh, not a whispering echo of the
5 usual revelry going on in the narrow unspeakable lanes of the Old
Town reached my ear – and suddenly, with a terrific jingling rattle
of iron and glass, the omnibus of the Joliette on its last journey
swung round the corner of the dead wall which faces across the
paved road the characteristic angular mass of the Fort St. Jean.
10 Three horses trotted abreast with the clatter of hoofs on the granite
setts, and the yellow, uproarious machine jolted violently behind
them, fantastic, lighted up, perfectly empty and with the driver
apparently asleep on his swaying perch above that amazing racket.
I flattened myself against the wall and gasped. It was a stunning
15 experience. Then after staggering on a few paces in the shadow of
the Fort, casting a darkness more intense than that of a clouded
night upon the canal, I saw the tiny light of a lantern standing on
the quay, and became aware of muffled figures making towards it
from various directions. Pilots of the Third Company hastening to
20 embark. Too sleepy to be talkative they step on board in silence.
But a few low grunts and an enormous yawn are heard. Somebody
even ejaculates: "*Ah! Coquin de sort!*" and sighs wearily at his hard
fate.

The *patron* of the Third Company (there were five companies
25 of pilots at that time, I believe) is the brother-in-law of my friend
Solary (Baptistin), a broad-shouldered, deep-chested man of forty,
with a keen, frank glance which always seeks your eyes. He greets
me by a low, hearty "*Hé, l'ami. Comment va?*" With his clipped moustache and massive open face, energetic and at the same time placid
30 in expression, he is a fine specimen of the southerner of the calm
type. For there is such a type in which the volatile southern passion
is transmuted into solid force. He is fair, but no one could mistake
him for a man of the north even by the dim gleam of the lantern
standing on the quay. He is worth a dozen of your ordinary Nor-
35 mans or Bretons, but then, in the whole immense sweep of the
Mediterranean shores, you could not find half a dozen men of his
stamp.

Standing by the tiller, he pulls out his watch from under a thick
jacket and bends his head over it in the light cast into the boat.
40 Time's up. His pleasant voice commands in a quiet undertone

"*Larguez.*" A suddenly projected arm snatches the lantern off the quay – and, warped along by a line at first, then with the regular tug of four heavy sweeps in the bow, the big half-decked boat full of men glides out of the black breathless shadow of the Fort. The open water of the *avant-port* glitters under the moon as if sown over with millions of sequins, and the long white breakwater shines like a thick bar of solid silver. With a quick rattle of blocks and one single silky swish, the sail is filled by a little breeze keen enough to have come straight down from the frozen moon, and the boat, after the clatter of the hauled-in sweeps, seems to stand at rest, surrounded by a mysterious whispering so faint and unearthly that it may be the rustling of the brilliant, over-powering moon rays, breaking like a rain-shower upon the hard, smooth, shadowless sea.

I may well remember that last night spent with the pilots of the Third Company. I have known the spell of moonlight since, on various seas and coasts – coasts of forests, of rocks, of sand dunes – but no magic so perfect in its revelation of unsuspected character, as though one were allowed to look upon the mystic nature of material things. For hours I suppose no word was spoken in that boat. The pilots seated in two rows facing each other dozed with their arms folded and their chins resting upon their breasts. They displayed a great variety of caps: cloth, wool, leather, peaks, ear-flaps, tassels, with a picturesque round *béret* or two pulled down over the brows; and one grandfather, with a shaved, bony face and a great beak of a nose, had a cloak with a hood which made him look in our midst like a cowled monk being carried off goodness knows where by that silent company of seamen – quiet enough to be dead.

My fingers itched for the tiller and in due course my friend, the *patron*, surrendered it to me in the same spirit in which the family coachman lets a boy hold the reins on an easy bit of road. There was a great solitude around us; the islets ahead, Monte Cristo and the Château d'If in full light, seemed to float towards us – so steady, so imperceptible was the progress of our boat. "Keep her in the furrow of the moon," the *patron* directed me in a quiet murmur, sitting down ponderously in the stern-sheets and reaching for his pipe.

The pilot station in weather like this was only a mile or two to the westward of the islets; and presently, as we approached the spot,

the boat we were going to relieve swam into our view suddenly, on her way home, cutting black and sinister into the wake of the moon under a sable wing, while to them our sail must have been a vision of white and dazzling radiance. Without altering the course
5 a hair's-breadth we slipped by each other within an oar's-length. A drawling sardonic hail came out of her. Instantly, as if by magic, our dozing pilots got on their feet in a body. An incredible babel of bantering shouts burst out, a jocular, passionate, voluble chatter, which lasted till the boats were stern to stern, theirs all bright
10 now and with a shining sail to our eyes, we turned all black to their vision, and drawing away from them under a sable wing. That extraordinary uproar died away almost as suddenly as it had begun; first one had enough of it and sat down, then another, then three or four together, and when all had left off with mutters
15 and growling half-laughs the sound of hearty chuckling became audible, persistent, unnoticed. The cowled grandfather was very much entertained somewhere within his hood.

He had not joined in the shouting of jokes, neither had he moved the least bit. He had remained quietly in his place against
20 the foot of the mast. I had been given to understand long before that he had the rating of a second-class able seaman (*matelot léger*) in the fleet which sailed from Toulon for the conquest of Algeria in the year of grace 1830. And, indeed, I had seen and examined one of the buttons of his old brown patched coat, the only brass button
25 of the miscellaneous lot, flat and thin, with the words *Équipages de ligne* engraved on it. That sort of button, I believe, went out with the last of the French Bourbons. "I preserved it from the time of my Navy Service," he explained, nodding rapidly his frail, vulture-like head. It was not very likely that he had picked up that relic in the
30 street. He looked certainly old enough to have fought at Trafalgar – or at any rate to have played his little part there as a powder-monkey. Shortly after we had been introduced he had informed me in a Franco-Provençal jargon, mumbling tremulously with his toothless jaws, that when he was a "shaver no higher than that" he
35 had seen the Emperor Napoleon returning from Elba. It was at night, he narrated vaguely, without animation, at a spot between Fréjus and Antibes in the open country. A big fire had been lit at the side of the cross-roads. The population from several villages had collected there, old and young – down to the very children
40 in arms, because the women had refused to stay at home. Tall

soldiers wearing high, hairy caps, stood in a circle facing the people silently, and their stern eyes and big moustaches were enough
to make everybody keep at a distance. He, "being an impudent
little shaver," wriggled out of the crowd, creeping on his hands
and knees as near as he dared to the grenadiers' legs, and peep- 5
ing through discovered standing perfectly still in the light of the
fire "a little fat fellow in a three-cornered hat, buttoned up in a
long straight coat, with a big pale face, inclined on one shoulder,
looking something like a priest. His hands were clasped behind
his back. . . . It appears that this was the Emperor," the Ancient 10
commented with a faint sigh. He was staring from the ground with
all his might, when "my poor father," who had been searching for
his boy frantically everywhere, pounced upon him and hauled him
away by the ear.

   The tale seems an authentic recollection. He related it to me 15
many times, using the very same words. The grandfather honoured me by a special and somewhat embarrassing predilection.
Extremes touch. He was the oldest member by a long way in
that Company, and I was, if I may say so, its temporarily adopted
baby. He had been a pilot longer than any man in the boat could 20
remember; thirty – forty years. He did not seem certain himself,
but it could be found out, he suggested, in the archives of the Pilot-
office. He had been pensioned off years before, but he went out
from force of habit; and, as my friend the *patron* of the Company
once confided to me in a whisper, "the old chap did no harm. He 25
was not in the way." They treated him with rough deference. One
and another would address some insignificant remark to him now
and again, but nobody really took any notice of what he had to say.
He had survived his strength, his usefulness, his very wisdom. He
wore long, green, worsted stockings, pulled up above the knee, 30
over his trousers, a sort of woollen nightcap on his hairless cra-
nium and wooden clogs on his feet. Without his hooded cloak he
looked like a peasant. Half a dozen hands would be extended to
help him on board, but afterwards he was left pretty much to his
own thoughts. Of course he never did any work, except, perhaps, 35
to cast off some rope when hailed: "*Hé, l'Ancien!* let go the halyards
there, at your hand" – or some such request of an easy kind.

   No one took notice in any way of the chuckling within the
shadow of the hood. He kept it up for a long time with intense
enjoyment. Obviously he had preserved intact the innocence of 40

mind which is easily amused. But when his hilarity had exhausted itself, he made a professional remark in a self-assertive but quavering voice:

"Can't expect much work on a night like this."

5 No one took it up. It was a mere truism. Nothing under canvas could be expected to make a port on such an idle night of dreamy splendour and spiritual stillness. We would have to glide idly to and fro, keeping our station within the appointed bearings, and, unless a fresh breeze sprang up with the dawn, we would land
10 before sunrise on a small islet that, within two miles of us, shone like a lump of frozen moonlight, to "break a crust and take a pull at the wine bottle." I was familiar with the procedure. The stout boat emptied of her crowd would nestle her buoyant, capable side against the very rock – such is the perfectly smooth amenity of
15 the classic sea when in a gentle mood. The crust broken, and the mouthful of wine swallowed – it was literally no more than that with this abstemious race – the pilots would pass the time stamping their feet on the slabs of sea-salted stone and blowing into their nipped fingers. One or two misanthropists would sit apart perched
20 on boulders like man-like sea-fowl of solitary habits; the sociably disposed would gossip scandalously in little gesticulating knots; and there would be perpetually one or another of my hosts taking aim at the empty horizon with the long, brass tube of the telescope, a heavy, murderous-looking piece of collective property, everlast-
25 ingly changing hands with brandishing and levelling movements. Then about noon (it was a short turn of duty – the long turn lasted twenty-four hours) another boatful of pilots would relieve us – and we should steer for the old Phœnician port, dominated, watched over from the ridge of a dust-grey arid hill by the red-and-white
30 striped pile of the Notre Dame de la Garde.

All this came to pass as I had foreseen in the fulness of my very recent experience. But also something not foreseen by me did happen, something which causes me to remember my last outing with the pilots. It was on this occasion that my hand touched, for
35 the first time, the side of an English ship.

No fresh breeze had come with the dawn, only the steady little draught got a more keen edge on it as the eastern sky became bright and glassy with a clean, colourless light. It was while we were all ashore on the islet that a steamer was picked up by the
40 telescope, a black speck like an insect posed on the hard edge of

the offing. She emerged rapidly to her water-line and came on
steadily, a slim hull with a long streak of smoke slanting away from
the rising sun. We embarked in a hurry, and headed the boat out
for our prey, but we hardly moved three miles an hour.

She was a big, high-class cargo-steamer of a type that is to be met   5
on the sea no more, black hull, with low, white superstructures,
powerfully rigged with three masts and a lot of yards on the fore;
two hands at her enormous wheel – steam steering-gear was not a
matter of course in these days – and with them on the bridge three
others, bulky in thick blue jackets, ruddy faced, muffled up, with   10
peaked caps – I suppose all her officers. There are ships I have
met more than once and known well by sight, whose names I have
forgotten, but the name of that ship seen once so many years ago
in the clear flush of a cold pale sun rise I have not forgotten. How
could I – the first English ship on whose side I ever laid my hand!   15
The name – I read it letter by letter on the bow – was *James Westoll.*
Not very romantic you will say. The name of a very considerable,
well-known and universally respected North-country shipowner, I
believe. James Westoll! What better name could an honourable
hard-working ship have. To me the very grouping of the letters is   20
alive with the romantic feeling of her reality as I saw her floating
motionless, and borrowing an ideal grace from the austere purity
of the light.

We were then very near her and, on a sudden impulse, I volunteered to pull bow in the dinghy which shoved off at once to put   25
the pilot on board while our boat, fanned by the faint air which had
attended us all through the night, went on gliding gently past the
black glistening length of the ship. A few strokes brought us alongside, and it was then that, for the very first time in my life, I heard
myself addressed in English – the speech of my secret choice, of my   30
future, of long friendships, of the deepest affections, of hours of
toil and hours of ease, and of solitary hours too, of books read, of
thoughts pursued, of remembered emotions – of my very dreams!
And if (after being thus fashioned by it in that part of me which
cannot decay) I dare not claim it aloud as my own, then, at any rate   35
the speech of my children. Thus small events grow memorable by
the passage of time. As to the quality of the address itself I cannot
say it was very striking. Too short for eloquence and devoid of all
charm of tone, it consisted precisely of the three words "Look out
there!" growled out huskily above my head.   40

It proceeded from a big fat fellow (he had an obtrusive, hairy
double chin) in a blue woollen shirt and roomy breeches pulled
up very high, even to the level of his breast-bone, by a pair of
braces quite exposed to public view. As where he stood there was
5 no bulwark but only a rail and stanchions I was able to take in at a
glance the whole of his voluminous person from his feet to the high
crown of his soft black hat, which sat like an absurd flanged cone on
his big head. The grotesque and massive aspect of that deck hand
(I suppose he was that – very likely the lamp-trimmer) surprised
10 me very much. My course of reading, of dreaming and longing for
the sea had not prepared me for a sea-brother of that sort. I never
met again a figure in the least like his except in the illustrations to
Mr. W. W. Jacobs' most entertaining tales of barges and coasters;
but the inspired talent of Mr. Jacobs for poking endless fun at
15 poor, innocent sailors in a prose which, however extravagant in
its felicitous invention, is always artistically adjusted to observed
truth, was not yet. Perhaps Mr. Jacobs himself was not yet. I fancy
that, at most, if he had made his nurse laugh it was about all he
had achieved at that early date.

20   Therefore, I repeat, other disabilities apart, I could not have
been prepared for the sight of that husky old porpoise. The object
of his concise address was to call my attention to a rope which he
incontinently flung down for me to catch. I caught it, though it
was not really necessary, the ship having no way on her by that
25 time. Then everything went on very swiftly. The dinghy came with
a slight bump against the steamer's side; the pilot, grabbing the
rope ladder, had scrambled half-way up before I knew that our
task of boarding was done; the harsh, muffled, clanging of the
engine-room telegraph struck my ear, through the iron plate; my
30 companion in the dinghy was urging me to "shove off – push hard";
and when I bore against the smooth flank of the first English ship
I ever touched in my life, I felt it already throbbing under my open
palm.

Her head swung a little to the west, pointing towards the minia-
35 ture lighthouse of the Jolliette breakwater, far away there, hardly
distinguishable against the land. The dinghy danced a squashy,
splashy jig in the wash of the wake and turning in my seat I followed the *James Westoll* with my eyes. Before she had gone in a
quarter of a mile she hoisted her flag as the harbour regulations
40 prescribe for arriving and departing ships. I saw it suddenly flicker

and stream out on the flagstaff. The Red Ensign! In the pellucid, colourless atmosphere bathing the drab and grey masses of that southern land, the livid islets, the sea of pale glassy blue under the pale glassy sky of that cold sunrise, it was as far as the eye could reach the only spot of ardent colour – flame-like, intense 5 and presently as minute as the tiny red spark the concentrated reflection of a great fire kindles in the clear heart of a globe of crystal. The Red Ensign – the symbolic, protecting warm bit of bunting flung wide upon the seas, and destined for so many years to be the only roof over my head. 10

[1] Sole surviving manuscript leaf of *A Personal Record*,
Chapter 6

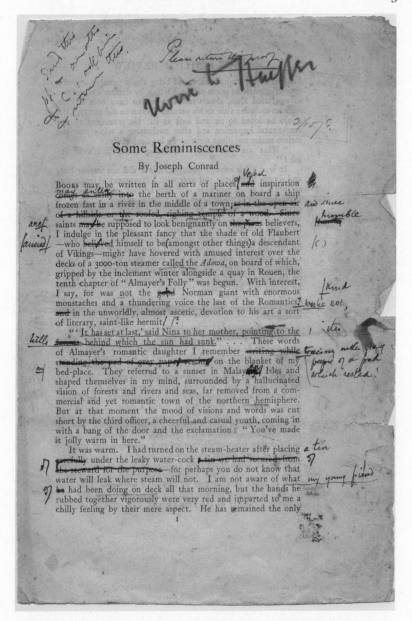

Some Reminiscences

By Joseph Conrad

Books may be written in all sorts of places, and inspiration may enter into the berth of a mariner on board a ship frozen fast in a river in the middle of a town; as in the open air of a hillside or the roofed, sighing temple of a wood. Since saints may be supposed to look benignantly on the pious believers, I indulge in the pleasant fancy that the shade of old Flaubert —who believed himself to be (amongst other things) a descendant of Vikings—might have hovered with amused interest over the decks of a 3000-ton steamer called the *Adowa*, on board of which, gripped by the inclement winter alongside a quay in Rouen, the tenth chapter of "Almayer's Folly" was begun. With interest, I say, for was not the good Norman giant with enormous moustaches and a thundering voice the last of the Romantics? and in the unworldly, almost ascetic, devotion to his art a sort of literary, saint-like hermit / ?

"'It has set at last,' said Nina to her mother, pointing to the hills behind which the sun had sunk." ... These words of Almayer's romantic daughter I remember writing while standing, the pad of grey paper resting on the blanket of my bed-place. They referred to a sunset in Malayan Isles and shaped themselves in my mind, surrounded by a hallucinated vision of forests and rivers and seas, far removed from a commercial and yet romantic town of the northern hemisphere. But at that moment the mood of visions and words was cut short by the third officer, a cheerful and casual youth, coming in with a bang of the door and the exclamation : " You've made it jolly warm in here."

It was warm. I had turned on the steam-heater after placing carefully under the leaky water-cock a tin we had secured from the steward for the purpose—for perhaps you do not know that water will leak where steam will not. I am not aware of what he had been doing on deck all that morning, but the hands he rubbed together vigorously were very red and imparted to me a chilly feeling by their mere aspect. He has remained the only

I

Some Reminiscences

By Joseph Conrad

PART II.

I.

In the career of the most unliterary of writers, in the sense
that literary ambition had never entered the world of his imagination, the coming into existence of the first book is quite an
inexplicable event. In my own case I cannot trace it back to
any mental or psychological cause which one could point out
and hold to. The greatest of my gifts being a consummate
capacity for doing nothing, I cannot even point to boredom as
a rational stimulus for taking up a pen. The pen at any rate
was there, and there is nothing wonderful in that. Everybody
keeps a pen (the cold steel of our days) in his rooms in this
enlightened age of penny stamps and halfpenny postcards. In
fact, this was the epoch when by means of postcard and pen
Mr. Gladstone had made the reputation of a novel or two.
And I too had a pen rolling about somewhere—the seldom-
used, the reluctantly-taken-up pen of a sailor ashore, the pen
rugged with the dried ink of abandoned attempts, of answers
delayed longer than decency permitted, of letters begun with
infinite reluctance and put off suddenly till next day—till
next week as likely as not! The neglected, uncared-for pen,
flung away at the slightest provocation, and under the stress
of dire necessity hunted for without enthusiasm, in a sort of
perfunctory, grumpy worry, in the " Where the devil *is* the
beastly thing gone to ?" ungracious spirit. Where indeed!
It might have been reposing behind the sofa for a day or
so. My landlady's anæmic daughter (as Ollendorff would
have expressed it), though commendably neat, had a lordly,
careless manner of approaching her domestic duties. Or it
might even be resting delicately poised on its point by the
side of the table-leg, and when picked up show a gaping,
inefficient beak which would have discouraged any man of

59

[3] Page 59 of 'Some Reminiscences' in the *English Review*, April 1909

3   (Written in 1911)
        to my Reminiscences

Preface

As a general rule we do not want
much encouragement to talk about
ourselves; yet this paper little book is
the result of a friendly suggestion adopted
reluctantly and even of a little friendly
pressure. I defended myself with
some spirit; but, with characteristic tenacity, the friendly voice insisted.

— "You know, you must."

You perceive the force of that word. If
you want to persuade but your trust not the
in the right argument but in the right word.
The power of sound has been always
greater than the power of sense. I don't
say this in a spirit of disparagement.
It is better for mankind to be impressionable
than reflective. Nothing humanely great
—great in the sense of affecting a whole
mass of lives — has come from reflection.

[4] Page 1 of the manuscript of 'A Familiar Preface'

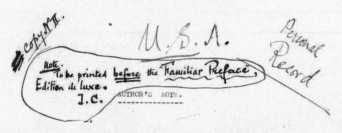

The re-issue of this book in a new form does not
strictly speaking require a Preface. But since this is
distinctly a place for personal remarks I take the opportunity to refer in this Author's Note to two points arising
from certain statements about myself I have noticed of late in
the press.

One of them bears upon the question of language.
I have always felt myself looked upon somewhat in the light
of a phenomenon, a position which outside the circus world
cannot be regarded as desirable.   It needs a special temperament for one to derive much gratification from the fact of
being able to do freakish things intentionally, and, as it
were, from mere vanity.

The fact of my not writing in my native language
has been of course commented upon frequently in reviews and
notices of my various works and in the more extended critical
articles.   I suppose that was unavoidable; and indeed those
comments were of the most flattering kind to one's vanity.
But in that matter I have no vanity that could be flattered.

[5] Page 1 of the original typescript of the 'Author's Note'

THE TEXTS
AN ESSAY

THE BOOK PUBLISHED in 1912 as *Some Reminiscences* in England and as *A Personal Record* in America, and after that as the latter everywhere, first appeared in seven consecutive issues of the *English Review*. The series ran in the magazine's inaugural number of December 1908 through its June 1909 issue. During this period Conrad was also at times writing 'Razumov', later titled *Under Western Eyes*. Warming to a project about which he initially had doubts and which his literary agent, J. B. Pinker, feared would impede work on the novel, Conrad apparently wrote his memoirs fluently, with little time elapsing between writing, revision, and publication. Composition of the final three instalments during the spring of 1909 was, however, clouded by increasingly troubled relations with the monthly's editor, Conrad's friend and sometime collaborator, Ford Madox Ford. As Conrad experienced problems with his mental and physical health, his mood shifted. Writing to a deadline, never his strong suit, had become onerous, and pressures to get on with 'Razumov' continued to mount. Various factors led him to such a breaking-point that he peremptorily and somewhat angrily discontinued the series of recollections, simultaneously putting an end, for some time, to his relationship with Ford.

Deeply in debt to his agent and with his finances in disarray, Conrad had at first welcomed the prospect of additional income from his arrangement with Ford. Moreover, Ford's offer to take down the text from dictation was a further attraction – although one perhaps made as much to reassure Pinker that composition would not hold up 'Razumov' as to encourage Conrad himself. Whatever the reasons, the plan to dictate his memoirs to Ford was quickly jettisoned, and Conrad dictated most of the text to a secretary and possibly some of it to his wife. He wrote out at least part of the second series, published from April to June 1909, in longhand, though precisely how much cannot now be known.

In contrast to the rapid writing and uninterrupted serial publication of these recollections, the volume was slow to come together and did not appear until January 1912, first in America under the imprint of Harper & Brothers and, about a fortnight later, in England with Eveleigh Nash. There were several reasons for this delay. The need to finish 'Razumov' was pressing; Conrad was experiencing intense emotional difficulties (which led to a complete breakdown in 1910); he contemplated expanding the memoirs beyond the seven instalments that had appeared in the *English Review*; and his quarrel with his agent involved Conrad himself in finding a publisher. Even when the book was ready, its publication was delayed in order to allow reviewers to give full play to *Under Western Eyes* (October 1911).

Despite Conrad's forcefully put, even somewhat heated, statement to Ford that the work was 'finished' as he had left it, book publication deserved and, indeed, would require, further attention. Conrad was obviously of two minds about how 'finished' this project was, at one point even contemplating two volumes of memoirs (*Letters*, IV, 189). In time he laid these ambitions aside, seemingly with some reluctance. Precisely when he did so is not known, but he set about composing 'A Familiar Preface', the introductory essay that justifies the book and explains its origins, in the late summer and early autumn of 1911. In October, Conrad revised his reminiscences, first in serial tear-sheets and then in book proofs. In September 1919, he provided a preface ('Author's Note') for a new edition (Dent, 1919).

The publication history of *A Personal Record* consists of several stages, each having its own character and responding to specific market and production pressures. Compared to many of Conrad's works, however, its textual history is relatively straightforward. Nonetheless Conrad's free hand in making publishing arrangements – an exception to the general practice after Pinker undertook to represent him in 1900 – complicates the story. Between January 1912, when the book was first published, and summer 1921, when it appeared in the collected editions published by Doubleday in America and by Heinemann in England, three separate editions made their way into print: Nelson republished the book in October 1916, Doubleday in 1917, and Dent in November 1919.

From 1919 onwards, *A Personal Record* contained not only the reminiscences and 'A Familiar Preface' but also the 'Author's Note', each with individual though related textual histories. Hardly any preprint documents survive for the reminiscences themselves – a single holograph sheet in Conrad's hand (Syracuse) and corrected proofs of the first serial instalment (HRHRC). The writing and revision of 'A Familiar Preface' is witnessed in the manuscript itself (Berg). For the

'Author's Note', the original typescript (Princeton) and two other
typescripts (Berg and Princeton) survive. As each of the later editions
was typeset from its predecessor, the reminiscences ultimately derive
through Nash's edition from the instalments in the *English Review*, 'A
Familiar Preface' from Nash's edition, and the 'Author's Note' from
Dent's 1919 edition. For the present edition, the serial text of the reminiscences provides the copy-text except where earlier preprint forms
survive; the revised manuscript serves as the copy-text for 'A Familiar Preface', and the revised and corrected original typescript for the
'Author's Note'.

The textual history of the serial and book forms of the reminiscences
is followed by a textual history of 'A Familar Preface' and then by
a discussion of the selection and emendation of the copy-texts for
the present edition. A discussion of the 'Author's Note' closes the
essay.

A Personal Record

SERIALIZATION

THE FIRST INSTALMENT of 'Some Reminiscences' appeared in
the December 1908 issue of the *English Review*,[1] an inaugural number that also included Conrad's review of Anatole France's recent
novel *L'Île des Pingouins* (later collected in *Notes on Life and Letters*).
Conrad's appearance in this issue placed him in good company: the
issue also contained contributions by Thomas Hardy, Henry James,
John Galsworthy, W. H. Hudson, R. B. Cunninghame Graham, and
H. G. Wells, as well as a translation of a Tolstoy story by Constance
Garnett.[2]

Six further instalments of Conrad's recollections were published
monthly, the last in the June 1909 issue.[3] The first four instalments

---

[1] For a history of composition, see 'Introduction', pp. xxvi–xxxi.

[2] Despite the distinguished list of contributors, circulation was small: the first two issues
together had a circulation of about 2,000 (Miss Thomas to H. G. Wells, 31 March 1909,
Illinois).

[3] The instalments appeared as follows: December 1908, 36–51; January 1909, 234–47; February 1909, 432–46; March 1909, 650–64; April 1909, 59–69; May 1909, 231–45; and June
1909, 500–7. Printed by Duckworth, these issues appeared on the 25th of the month prior
to that named on their covers (Paul R. Reynolds to J. B. Pinker, 23 November 1908, Berg).
Stephen Reynolds' correspondence with Pinker indicates that the second issue was to go to
press on 17 December and suggests a final due date for copy of at least some days before
(see Christopher Scoble, *Fisherman's Friend: A Life of Stephen Reynolds* (2000), p. 200).

were introduced by roman numerals under the series title and a by-line; the three instalments of April, May, and June 1909 were prefaced by the heading 'Part II' and then by roman numerals beginning with I. The April and May instalments appeared along with Conrad and Ford's collaborative work *The Nature of a Crime*, published under the pseudonym Baron Ignatz Aschendrof. (The fictional surname includes both of theirs.)

The surviving preprint material for the series of reminiscences consists of a single holograph leaf of Chapter 6 (Syracuse)[1] and a set of corrected and revised page proofs for the first instalment of the *English Review* typesetting (HRHRC).[2] The holograph leaf establishes that Conrad wrote out at least part of his recollections by hand and suggests that he may have drafted all of Chapter 6 in this way. The surviving leaf is labelled '*ER* | VI 18' and, as revised, contains 148 words. Assuming that deletions were made in the manuscript and that a leaf contained approximately 130 words on average, its place as leaf 18 accords fairly well with the sixth instalment's length.

Comprising sixteen pages, the extant proofs are dated '2 / 10 / 8' in an unknown hand. Conrad's revisions throughout are in black ink. Pages 1 and 9 bear the printers' proof-stamp and the handwritten direction 'Please return this proof'.[3] On page 1 in Ford's hand, in black ink, is the note 'Send this pg. & another to C.: ask him to return this' and in Conrad's hand in pencil 'revise to Hueffer'. Page 9 is also dated and stamped and requests return of the proofs. This may suggest that it and page 1 were handled separately; they both underwent somewhat

---

[1] Conrad sent this leaf to an admirer on 6 May 1909 (*Letters*, IV, 231). See Fig. 1, p. 122.

[2] These are preserved with an envelope addressed to 'Miss Garnett | Orchard End, | East Hendred, | Berks' and postmarked 'OXFORD | PAID 1^D | 29 SEP 1924'; the extant proofs made their way into Edward Garnett's hands, whose note 'Proof of Joseph Conrad's with his own corrections. G.' appears on the envelope. On Garnett's having seen proofs, see Conrad to Pinker, 17 December 1908 (*Letters*, IV, 169). The description of Lot 155 in the Hodgson & Company sale of 13 March 1925 is as follows: 'Proof Sheets of "Some Reminiscences," being the first serial instalment in the "English Review," for December 1908, comprising section 1 (pp. 25–59), of the edition in book form, 1912, 16 pp., 8vo., with numerous alterations and corrections, differing from the 1912 edition, entirely in the Author's hand' (*A Catalogue of Books, Manuscripts and Corrected Typescripts from the Library of the late Joseph Conrad*, 1925). The set sold for £9 (see the annotated catalogue indicating buyers and prices, BL Add. MS. 54590). Since the extant proofs were Garnett's, the set Hodgson sold must have been a duplicate (which remains unlocated) or, for reasons unclear, this item was sold along with materials belonging to Mrs Conrad and to Richard Curle.

[3] The proof-stamps read as follows: BALLANTYNE & C^O. | THE BALLANTYNE PRESS | TAVISTOCK ST. LONDON | FINAL PROOF.

heavy revision, and page 9 has an editor's query to which Conrad replied.

Conrad worked on the proofs between 2 and 4 October, sending them revised to Pinker on the 4th, and indicating that retyping from 'this scored proof' might be necessary for circulating the piece for sale in America (*Letters*, IV, 135). It seems unlikely, however, that such typing occurred, with Pinker simply waiting for a corrected set of proofs to forward to Paul R. Reynolds, the New York literary agent through whom he regularly placed his clients' work in America. The extant set may have been a duplicate kept for checking against final revises.[1]

The text of the proofs was impeccably set, with only a single instance of misaligned type and a single misprint – 'unassuring', which Conrad corrected to 'unassuming' (28.22).[2] A proofreader – Ford's assistant, Douglas Goldring, or some other person[3] – queried the repetition of 'that day . . . that day' in the same sentence (21.3–5), the spelling of Champel (27.22), and the Gallicism 'the groom affected specially to' (33.37–38).[4] A 'Q' in the margin in the first instance and the abbreviation 'Qy' in the latter two were used to pose the queries. Whether the proofs came to Conrad directly from Duckworth's, the publisher then printing the *English Review*, or through Ford is unknown. In any case, the notes on the first page establish that communications between writer and editor relied on Pinker and on Ford's assistant as intermediaries.

Conrad provided copy well in advance of publication for the first four instalments, having in hand the writing of the fourth – the last of the series as originally planned – before the first made its way into print. The production of the three later instalments appears to have been more pressured as a combination of illness, the need to make headway

---

[1] Similar procedures may have been followed for the third instalment, the corrected proofs of which were put up for sale for £42 in Maggs Catalogue 487 (1927), item 583 (along with Conrad's letter to Ford of Tuesday [29 September or 6 October 1908]). Resold by Swann in 1943, the proofs remain unlocated. A facsimile of the concluding page appears in Violet Hunt's biography *The Flurried Years* (1926), facing p. 32. (The volume appeared in New York in 1926 under the title *I Have This to Say*.)

[2] Citations of the page and line numbers of this edition refer throughout to its critical text and, where variation in the early texts occurs, particularly to entries in the 'Apparatus'. Lower-case letters immediately following page–line numbers (e.g., 1.2a, 1.2b) distinguish entries that have readings in the same line. When the 'Notes' discuss readings, an '*n*' appended to a page–line citation refers to this part of the volume as well.

[3] Ford's involvement can be discounted: the queries are not in his handwriting.

[4] In response, Conrad eliminated the repetition, confirmed the spelling, and altered 'affected' to 'attached'.

with 'Razumov', and a growing frustration with Ford's management of the *English Review* and of his personal life took their toll. These factors collaborated to bring the reminiscences to an abrupt end in the June 1909 issue, a conclusion that Conrad justified in a sharply worded letter as 'an excellent terminal, a perfect pause carrying out the spirit of the work'.[1] The disintegration of Conrad's friendship with Ford and the necessity of finishing 'Razumov' served to redirect Conrad's energies. Pinker's attitude may also have played a role: he thought little of the venture,[2] and was presumably sceptical about its marketability in book form.

On the other hand, Conrad seems to have persuaded himself that financial gains were to flow from writing that he initially viewed as not overly demanding. From an early stage of his work, he hoped to sell serial rights in America, telling his agent on 4 October 1908: 'Go in for the Yanks with it'.[3] They, however, proved highly resistant despite an energetic sales campaign by Reynolds. Even before the series began to appear in England, Reynolds was circulating the first two instalments, only, however, to receive a discouraging response.[4] The somewhat unusual character of the reminiscences, with subjects and themes remote from an American audience, apparently had little appeal at a time when Conrad, though respected and admired, did not enjoy the wide readership that he would secure with *Chance* in 1913. After receiving the third instalment, Reynolds reported to Pinker that an editor to whom he had showed it 'found there too much about life in Poland and about Mr. Conrad's uncle, and very little about himself and about how he came to write, which is really what people would be interested in'.[5]

Reynolds nonetheless followed up Pinker's directive about safeguarding Conrad's rights in the American market by copyrighting the first instalment.[6] As Ford explained in December 1936 to the American collector George T. Keating, who had queried him about this

---

[1] Conrad to Ford, 31 July 1909 (*Letters*, IV, 264). For a fuller discussion, see 'Introduction', pp. xxx–xxxi.
[2] Conrad to Pinker, 15 April 1909; see also Conrad to John Galsworthy, 30 April 1909 (*Letters*, IV, 216, 224).
[3] Conrad to Pinker, Sunday [4 October 1908] (*Letters*, IV, 135).
[4] By 12 November, McClure, *Harper's Magazine*, the *Saturday Evening Post*, Putnam, the *Bookman*, *Outlook*, and the *American* had refused serialization; Reynolds later added *Forum* and *Collier's Weekly* to this list (Paul R. Reynolds to Pinker, 12 November and 23 November 1908, Berg).
[5] Reynolds to Pinker, 23 November 1908 (Berg). The uncle in question is Mikołaj Bobrowski.
[6] Certificate of Registration of Copyright A223510, issued on 27 November 1908.

printing's authenticity when a copy of it turned up in a sales catalogue, copyright in the first instalment in effect protected the whole
series, since its opening would be unavailable to potential pirates.[1]
Ford's recollection that a typescript he produced 'must have formed
the original script' for this printing is faulty:[2] bound in yellow wrap-
pers and with a title-page, Reynolds' 'issue' is the *English Review* typesetting. The number of copies so bound has been estimated as 'probably
six'.[3]

Reynolds' efforts to secure serialization having proved unsuccessful in November 1908, Conrad himself later hawked the serial to the
North American Review, edited by Colonel George M. Harvey, Harpers'
president, who was on a business trip in England in the spring of
1909.[4] Although Conrad had Harpers in mind as a venue as early as
December 1908[5] and was still courting them in late October 1909 –
when he reminded the firm that he had offered serialization for £80 in
July – they declined.[6] In the event of their refusal, Conrad planned to
offer the series to the Canadian poet Bliss Carman, then in New York
editing *Gentleman's Journal*.[7] Despite Conrad's efforts, the work was
never serialized in America. His persistence with Harpers did eventually pay off, however, with the firm, which was to publish *Under Western
Eyes* in book form, taking up book publication.

Various myths have circulated about the preparation of copy for
the serial.[8] When, in October 1908, Conrad elaborated his plans for
the project, he stated forcefully to his agent: 'It must all be dictated
and then revised. *No other* method will do.'[9] In time, this approach
was modified, as were his plans for covering certain topics. With the
composition of the first four instalments behind him, Conrad told

[1] Ludwig, pp. 267–8.   [2] Ludwig, p. 268.

[3] James T. Babb, comp., 'A Check List of Additions to *A Conrad Memorial Library*, 1929–1938',
Yale University Library Gazette, 13 (July 1938), 35–7. Babb gives no authority for this number.
It is, however, credible, given the issue's purpose. Only the two Library of Congress deposit
copies and Keating's copy at Yale are known.

[4] If Conrad's later memory served, he did not see Harvey on this occasion. He claimed to
have met him only once 'years ago' (*Letters*, v, 257); see also *Letters*, iii, 32.

[5] Conrad to Pinker, Wednesday [9 December 1908] (*Letters*, iv, 159). The firm had published
the first American editions of *Nostromo*, *The Mirror of the Sea*, and *The Secret Agent*. On Conrad and Harper's, see S. W. Reid, 'American Markets, Serials, and Conrad's Career', *The
Conradian*, 28.1 (2003), 57–99.

[6] Conrad to Harpers, 31 October 1909 (*Letters*, iv, 284).   [7] Ibid.

[8] Accounts of Ford's involvement rely on his two retrospective statements cited here. For a
summary of the received view, see Saunders, i, 243–4, 549–50.

[9] Conrad to Pinker, [7] October 1908 (*Letters*, iv, 139).

Pinker that the memoirs were indebted to 'the insistence together
with actual help' of Ford,[1] but what this 'help' constituted needs close
investigation.

Ford himself twice claimed a role in creating *A Personal Record*. In
his memoirs he stated:

The Mirror of the Sea and *A Personal Record* were mostly written by my hand from
Conrad's dictation. Whilst he was dictating them, I would recall incidents to him –
I mean incidents of his past life which he had told me but which did not come
freely back to his mind because at the time he was mentally ill, in desperate need of
money, and, above, all, sceptical as to the merits of the reminiscential form which
I had suggested to him. The fact is I could make Conrad write at periods when his
despair and fatigue were such that in no other way would it have been possible to
him. He would be lying on the sofa or pacing the room, railing at life and literature
as practised in England, and I would get a writing pad and pencil and, whilst he
was still raving, would interject ... and gradually there would come *Landfalls and
Departures* ... And equally gradually there would come the beginnings of *A Personal
Record*.   (*Return to Yesterday* (1931), p. 190)

At the close of 1936, at a date even more distant from the pur-
ported events, Ford, adding details, repeated this account to George
T. Keating:

he would begin to talk about the Ukraine of his uncle's day and Palmerston's
Emissary with a sledgefull of gold or about Venice when he was a boy or about his
exile in Siberia or, of course, if I suggested that he should talk about the Ukraine
or Venice or Siberia, he would insist on telling anecdotes about the "*Tremolino*" or
his Transvaal mine. In any case, once he was started, he would go on for a long time
and as I wrote shorthand very fast, I could take him down without much trouble.

The trouble really came when I had to transcribe my notes by means of an
appallingly primitive typewriter, called the Blickensderfer which had a little cylin-
der the types of which struck the paper exactly as if it were a hammer, and indeed
you had to hit the keys almost as hard as if you were knocking in tenpenny nails.
This pain was increased when you had to make a carbon copy and it was still worse,
as I can well remember, when you had to make two.[2]

Both these accounts are unreliable, at odds with the known facts and
with the evidence that can be pieced together. Ford took down very
little – not most – of *A Personal Record*; he is likely to have typed up
hardly any of it; and, Conrad, although under emotional strain in the
autumn of 1908, was not 'mentally ill'. The letter to Keating confuses
A Personal Record with *The Mirror of the Sea*: Conrad's experiences in

[1] Conrad to Pinker, 17 December 1908 (*Letters*, IV, 167).
[2] Ford to George T. Keating, [December 1936], Ludwig, pp. 267–8.

Venice and of exile, in fact, receive only passing mention in the earlier work.

Whatever the appeal of working together again as friends and fellow writers, practical factors – proximity, incompatible schedules, the pressure of other commitments – quickly led to abandoning what at the outset seemed to be an efficient way of producing Conrad's memoirs – if, indeed, the plan to dictate to Ford was anything more than a reassurance to Pinker that this new venture would not delay work on 'Razumov'. The whereabouts of Ford and Conrad limited possibilities for collaboration after Conrad worked up the first instalment while visiting Ford at Aldington in September 1908.[1] On a visit to Someries in early October, Ford did take down dictation from Conrad, but, as Conrad later told Ford, he 'made a fresh start' and omitted the dictated words from his final text.[2]

The extant set of revised proofs shows that Conrad conscientiously revised at this stage, taking full advantage of this opportunity to refine his ideas and improve phrasing and displaying his usual concern about the text's correctness. The proofs also demonstrate that Ford played only a small role as an editor. Although Conrad revised on every page, he made no major additions or deletions: the alterations aim at concision as well as greater stylistic nuance and descriptive precision.[3] At some cost of vividness, he simplified his opening sentence 'Inspiration comes as easily into the berth of a mariner ... as in the open air of a hillside or the roofed, sighing temple of a wood' to 'Verbal inspiration may enter the berth of a mariner' (19.3–4). Likewise refined is a central statement about the art of writing (27.39–28.4). The awkwardly formulated sentence – which had eluded his revision in typescript – was typeset as follows:

What is it that Novalis says: "It is certain that the conviction gains in strength as soon as another soul can be found to share it," and what is a novel if not a conviction in the reality of our fellow men's existence, strong enough to take upon itself a form of imagined life stronger than reality and the exciting vividness of a dream dreamed to the very end in its illogical and deeply moving sequence, whose accumulated verisimilitude of detail puts to shame the futile logic of authentic history.

[1] See Introduction, p. xxx. The Conrads returned to Someries on 21 September 1908 and resided there until they moved to Aldington on 14 February (*Letters*, IV, 114, 127). Ford was nearer after this move but spent much time in London and, as his marriage unravelled, was increasingly away throughout the spring.

[2] Conrad to Ford, [12 October 1908] (*Letters*, IV, 144).

[3] He deleted only two sentences (23.18) and (24.38). See 'Emendation and Variation' for the proof's rejected readings.

Conrad thus reshaped it:

What is it that Novalis says: "It is certain my conviction gains infinitely, the moment another soul will believe in it," and what is a novel if not a conviction of our fellow men's existence, strong enough to take upon itself a form of imagined life clearer than reality and whose accumulated verisimilitude of selected episodes puts to shame the pride of documentary history.

Small-scale alterations of meaning and style are more typical than such wholesale revision. Conrad changed 'light music setting' to 'setting of light music' (21.1–2) and 'artfully intertwined' to 'artfully tangled up' (21.24–25); he tightened 'there existed' to 'he had' (22.11) and 'being ashamed, or rather remorseful' to the more vivid 'blushing with shame' (25.36). And he typically strove for verbal precision, revising 'a house' to 'furnished apartments' (23.24), 'the river' to 'the Congo rapids' (28.5), and 'horses' to 'bays' (32.13). Opinions of individuals became more considered: Captain Froud, originally 'a distinguished master', became 'a very excellent master' (22.13–14); Mr Paramor, first described as 'an excellent fellow', became 'a most excellent fellow' (26.1); and 'a delightful little girl' was, on second thoughts, 'a delightful quick tempered little girl' (34.26–7).

A handful of variants separates the revised proof and serial texts. To avoid repetition in proximity it was apparently Conrad who changed 'on board' (21.30) to 'aboard' and 'matter' to 'it' (24.20). However, the modification of 'has prompted' to 'prompted' (24.8b) suggests a typical editorial tidying of verb forms, an aspect of English with which Conrad sometimes had problems. This intervention implies that similar alterations were made in later instalments, but, if characteristic, the paucity of such change suggests that the editorial hand at work was relatively light.

As Conrad revised, casual and imprecise phrasing that had survived in the setting-copy typescript disappeared, but several such phrasings remain, and a number escaped his notice when he later revised the book proofs. Idiomatic lapses of various degrees of seriousness occur, including 'pointing a chair to me' (a direct translation of the Polish *wskazując mi krzesło*), which he altered to 'motioning me to a chair' (22.39) in book proofs. His multiple linguistic heritages are also evident in 'achieve the crossing' (24.35) and 'achieve even a single passage' (25.3), derived from the French *achever*; 'my satanic suggestion' (26.11) (from the Polish *szatańska sugestia*); 'arrested them short' (26.18), again from French (*arrêter*); and 'clear' used for 'bright' (32.15, 33.2), from the Polish *jasne* or the French *clair*.

Characteristic problems with articles occurred,[1] and a general tendency to place adverbs after verbs, an influence of Polish syntax, led to occasional awkwardness.[2] Some of the writing is ragged and flabby, as, for example, the sentence 'These words of Almayer's romantic daughter I remember tracing on the grey paper of a pad which rested on the blanket of my bed-place' (19.16–18). This almost certainly betrays dictation (as well as imperfect revision).[3] Although removing a few Gallicisms, perhaps in the normal course of tightening his work, Conrad failed to identify a number of weaknesses as he revised.[4] The problems highlight the general awkwardness – and even the occasional outright crudeness – of the first instalment's prose.

This evidence sheds light on Ford's services as an amanuensis and editor. Ford slavishly recorded wordings and sentences that, at times, were manifestly defective or highly, even grossly, unidiomatic.[5] Moreover, he resisted the temptation to correct, smooth out, or otherwise improve Conrad's writing not only during dictation but also while typing up the text, which he claims to have done. The text of the unrevised proofs, the closest to the lost setting-copy typescript and thus the nearest to any in which Ford could have been directly involved as an amanuensis, shows scant input from a conscientious and skilled editor, himself a master prose stylist.

[1] Articles are superfluous, for example, in 'unlike the roses' (21.21), 'from the eastern waters' (23.22), 'the Victoria Dock' (24.39–40), and 'in a handwriting like mine' (28.12).
[2] E.g., 'I resembled sufficiently a man' (23.13), 'we were impressed favourably' (24.22), 'as if already the story-teller' (29.25), 'I saw again the sun setting' (33.1), 'may serve worthily' (35.10). The Polish syntactical feature of post-positional adverbs is no less pronounced in later instalments. For a detailed discussion of this aspect of Conrad's prose, see Mary Morzinski, *Linguistic Influence of Polish on Joseph Conrad's Style* (1994), pp. 61–7, 115–17.
[3] Other awkward phrasing includes ' "I have had in here a shipmaster" ' (22.38), 'It became at last unreasonable' (27.35), and the sentence 'That which . . . derived' (35.1–6). The phrase 'subjects under heaven' (31.12–13) misconstrues the idiom 'topics under the sun'.
[4] 'Range' (for 'line' or 'row', from *rangée* or *rang*) in 'As a background a range of grimy houses' was revised to 'The background of grimy houses' (20.29) (see also 'A range of gabled houses,' *The Secret Agent*, ed. Bruce Harkness and S. W. Reid (1990), p. 127.22), and 'a sort of colonnade', from *une espèce de*, was altered to 'a colonnade' (35.35). At the book proof stage, presumably Conrad rather than an editor altered 'This last' (from *ce dernier*) to 'He' (32.14a).
[5] That Ford took down Conrad exactly is supported by the fact that he did so when taking down dictation for *Nostromo*; see Xavier Brice, 'Ford Madox Ford and the Composition of *Nostromo*', in *Nostromo: Centennial Essays* (2004), ed. Allan H. Simmons and J. H. Stape, pp. 75–95.

Ford's 'actual help', then, amounted to taking down verbatim the first instalment at Aldington and a brief session of dictation at Someries in October 1908.[1] He may have typed the ancestor of the text found in the unrevised proofs of the first chapter of 'Some Reminiscences', but his recollections about typing mainly bear on his work on *The Mirror of the Sea*. Since the published serial text suggests little editorial supervision of correctness, phrasing, or idiom, his editorial function appears mainly to have been acting as go-between for Conrad and the printers. That Ford's role was not larger is unsurprising. Conrad was but one of several contributors, even if a signally important one, to an ambitious new venture that variously consumed Ford's time and energies as he was learning how to manage and put together a literary monthly.

Since documents are lacking, the production processes involved in the subsequent six instalments of 'Some Reminiscences' cannot be followed in close detail. It seems safe to assume that the practices established during preparation of the first instalment for print were generally applied to the later ones. Conrad revised in typescripts matter that he had dictated (or had written out). This was followed by further polishing in first proofs and – assuming deadlines permitted – in revise proofs. Little involved in changing or improving the text, Ford or his assistant ensured that copy was produced in a timely fashion and that the typesetting was free from misprints and other technical errors.

With only the first instalment behind him,[2] Conrad was already writing to his agent about his intention to dictate his reminiscences to his secretary, L. M. Hallowes, then engaged in typing up his novel.[3] He followed through on these, dictating the second, third, and fourth instalments to her.[4] Whether he dictated the instalments composed

---

[1] Conrad to Ford, Monday [12 October 1908] (*Letters*, IV, 144). See 'Introduction', p. xxvii.

[2] Laurence Davies has suggested that material withheld from *A Personal Record* became 'Prince Roman' (*Letters*, IV, 159, n. 1).

[3] Conrad to Pinker, 30 September and 13 October 1908 (*Letters*, IV, 133, 145). Saunders' conclusion that Miss Hallowes 'probably took down some of the reminiscences' (I, 550) underestimates Conrad's reliance on her. (It might be noted in passing that Tekla's recollections of her dictation sessions with Peter Ivanovich in Part Second, Chapter IV of *Under Western Eyes* have a possible self-caricatural element.)

[4] Miss Hallowes' comings and goings at Someries assist dating composition: she was there from 29 September to 17 October; she arrived again *ca.* 31 October 'for a week'; and she departed on 23 November, with Conrad reporting on the 20th that he was 'getting on better with R[azumov]', this stint having possibly been for a week or more (*Letters*, IV, 132, 145, 156). She was again back at Someries on 4 December, staying until the 10th or 11th (*Letters*, IV, 158–9). Given that Conrad posted twenty-five typed pages to Pinker on 7 and

between late February and April 1909 to Miss Hallowes is not shown
in the extant letters, and Jessie Conrad – actively involved in typing
sections of 'Razumov' in the autumn,[1] and, moreover, not needing to
be paid – may have filled in. No evidence survives about the compositional methods relied on for instalments 5 and 7, the latter the shortest
of the series.

Conrad's statement in 1911 to the wealthy American lawyer John
Quinn, who was eagerly amassing a collection of Conrad holographs
and typescripts and had enquired about the originals of 'Some Reminiscences', that 'All the text almost was dictated and then worked
upon in typed copy'[2] suggests that Conrad heavily revised first typescripts. Fair-copy typescripts would have been made from these by
his secretary or possibly through Pinker, with Conrad typically making
further changes before sending them to the printers. It should also be
recalled that at the time, although he had relied upon dictation for
The Mirror of the Sea, it was not yet the favoured compositional method
that it would later become, and both its advantages and restrictions
likely urged on his extensive revision in a typescript or perhaps several
typescripts.

The other issue that requires attention is the intertwined writing of
Some Reminiscences and 'Razumov'. In his detailed study of the composition of *Under Western Eyes*, Keith Carabine argues that 'progress with
Razumov ... was severely affected, as Pinker feared, by his [Conrad's]
volatile re-involvement with Ford on *The English Review* and by his dictation and preparation of his "Reminiscences". Between September and
December 1908 Conrad, as co-editor, saw Ford regularly and partici-
pated enthusiastically in all the activities connected with the *Review*.'[3]
True as this general statement is, elements of it require qualification:
Ford was paying ready money against copy and paying well at a time
when Conrad was deeply in debt to Pinker and could ill afford to
ask him for further advances; at this time Conrad was writing at a
respectable rate, although making little headway on 'Razumov'; and
fretting about his finances could have either inhibited or goaded on
the composition of the novel.

---

9 December, the time-frame for composition in early December seems too short, and Chapter 4 was probably mostly finished prior to 23 November, with finishing touches and revisions
being made in early December.

[1] See Carabine, pp. 37–8, 40.

[2] Conrad to Quinn, 30 September [= November] 1911 (*Letters*, IV, 514–15).

[3] Carabine, pp. 36–7.

The work that Conrad completed from September to December 1908 suggests neither writer's block nor sloth but implies that 'Razumov' was stalled and that Conrad eagerly seized the opportunity offered by Ford to see him through a creative lull. By his own estimate, typically rosy, his reminiscences by December 1908 amounted to 32,000 words (*Letters*, IV, 159). The actual word count is closer to just over 27,000. To these can be added 'Prince Roman', about 8,000 words presumably drafted during October–November and initially intended to form part of *Some Reminiscences*,[1] and a 1,000-word review of Anatole France's *L'Île des Pingouins*, written in late November at the last minute for the *English Review*'s first issue. The rough tally, if 'Prince Roman' indeed amounted to as many as 8,000 words at that time, is 36,000 words for the period, to which can be added about 6,500 words of 'Razumov'[2] (some of Part Second, Chapter IV of the final version).

This evidence requires a readjustment of perspective. Rather than 'hampering' 'Razumov', 'Some Reminiscences' displaced it, becoming Conrad's main project during the autumn of 1908. The new project offered respite from the writing and revision of a highly complex, slowly evolving work that demanded intense psychological investment and sustained concentration, and the 'Recollections' also proved easier to 'write' as Conrad cobbled sections of the second and third instalments more or less directly from the memoirs of his uncle Tadeusz Bobrowski.[3] As the editor to whom Reynolds showed the later instalment observed, these instalments bore little on Conrad's personal experience. Opting for a more modest presentation of selected memories – gathered secondhand – of his great-uncle Mikołaj's life, Conrad had already abandoned his original, more ambitious plans 'to make Polish life enter English literature' (*Letters*, IV, 138). Not only had the work's emotional pitch significantly dropped as he deflected attention from himself, but in shifting his energies from 'Razumov' Conrad was also resorting to a pattern witnessed during other periods of his career. Unable to get on with *The Sisters*, he had begun 'The Rescuer'. He then put it aside as *Lord Jim* took over his energies, and in the interstices of

---

[1] The completion of 'Prince Roman' is assumed from Conrad's statement to Pinker (*Letters*, IV, 159) that he had laid aside 8,000 words, a word count closely corresponding to the story's as published.

[2] The figure for 'Razumov' is from Carabine, p. 255.   [3] See 'Appendix'.

Lord Jim he had composed 'Heart of Darkness'. Like other projects, including apparently *The Secret Agent*, 'Razumov' itself apparently displaced *Chance*, and at a later stage during the writing of the former Conrad paused to write 'The Secret Sharer'.[1] Juggling projects was, it seems, a habitual way of dealing with the demands of his creative urge as well as a way of coping with earning a living. This strategy was perhaps especially needed when working on 'Razumov', which, it seems, presented so many psychological difficulties.

With the turn of the year, progress on the novel picked up considerably, with Conrad grinding out approximately 22,000 words between January and mid-May 1909.[2] Meanwhile, he began composing the second series of his recollections in late February, and on finishing the June instalment by mid-May, had added some 15,500 words to his reminiscences. Although the novel grew steadily if slowly, Conrad, in fact, wrote fewer words during the eighteen weeks from January to mid-May 1909 than during the thirteen weeks from September to early December 1908.

During the first half of 1909, the general pattern of his activity also reversed itself, with the memoirs now bogging down. The fifth instalment, as he reported to John Galsworthy, was written against the grain: 'I had the greatest difficulty to finish my paper for the *ER*. It's done at last! Very silly. I am sick of everything I write.'[3] Whatever the statement's self-dramatizing aspect, its force is real: the seventh instalment of 'Some Reminiscences' adds up to a mere 3,500 words, half the first instalment's length. A project that Conrad had begun with mixed feelings and then quickly warmed to expired prematurely as a number of factors came into play: emotionally harrowing ructions with Ford; the *English Review*'s chronic financial problems, which presaged a change of ownership; the onset of gout and depression with the attendant threat of creative fallowness; and the do-or-die necessity of finishing 'Razumov'.

When Conrad faltered over writing the July instalment, giving up after a page or two,[4] he must have felt relief. However much he might

---

[1] On the writing of the story, see '*Twixt Land and Sea* (2007), ed. J. A. Berthoud, Laura L. Davis, and S. W. Reid, pp. 205–08.

[2] This constitutes Part Second, the remainder of Chapter IV and all of Chapter V, and Part Third, Chapters I and II; see Carabine, p. 255.

[3] Conrad to Galsworthy, 6 March 1909 (*Letters*, IV, 198).

[4] Conrad to Galsworthy, 13 July 1909 (*Letters*, IV, 254).

have regretted losing a source of income, writing to a deadline had never been congenial and, unlike the first series of 'Reminiscences', the second was concurrently written and published and thus done under a very different time pressure. Nonetheless, he did not lack for material, being optimistic about adding chapters for the eventual book and even foreseeing a second volume.[1] By late June, not long after the crisis-point he had reached in writing for Ford, he was dangling a possible 'autobiographical sea-paper' before Bliss Carman for the *Gentlemen's Journal*, possibly 'The Secret Sharer'.[2] However he might exploit his life for fiction, at this point Conrad laid aside his attempt at straightforward autobiography – as it turned out, for once and all.

BOOK EDITIONS

IN LATE DECEMBER 1909, Conrad's interest in seeing 'Some Reminiscences' published in book form was qualified by a desire to add 30,000 words to what he had written – the equivalent, given the serial form's length, of five chapters, of, then, a planned dozen.[3] He predicted that publication would be at least a year off. As events were to prove, he was optimistic on both counts. He added only 'A Familiar Preface' to what he had written, and some two years were to elapse between serialization and book publication.

The contractual arrangements with Ford left Conrad free to place his material as he wished after its first appearance.[4] Several factors, however, conspired against immediate book publication. Pre-eminent among these was the desire to add to what had been written. But he was also constrained by the pressing need to complete 'Razumov'. Becoming estranged from Pinker, with whom he had quarrelled in late January 1910, Conrad experienced a mental collapse on finishing his novel. When he recovered, his finances remained shaky, and the specific reason he adduced for publishing the volume as he had left it in 1908 was that he required ready money to pay for his son Borys' education in the training-ship *Worcester*. Mentioning this to Edward

---

[1] Conrad to E. V. Lucas, 23 June 1909 (*Letters*, IV, 247). See 'Introduction', pp. xxx–xxxi.

[2] Conrad to Bliss Carman, 29 June 1909 (*Letters*, IV, 250). See '*Twixt Land and Sea*, p. 214.

[3] Conrad to H.-D. Davray and to Robert d'Humières, 23 December 1909 (*Letters*, IV, 307, 309–10).

[4] The verso of an *English Review* cheque for £25 (Berg), signed by Ford and dated 9 March 1909 (paid out on the 15th), specifies that payment was for 'SINGLE SERIAL RIGHTS'. This cheque may represent payment for *The Nature of a Crime*, but, if so, arrangements for 'Some Reminiscences' were probably identical.

Garnett, Conrad also aired an uneasiness about the unconventional character of his reminiscences:

For a long time I hesitated as to letting them go out in book form – and if it had not been that I wanted the sixty pounds Nash has advanced me for them ... they should have remained unprinted yet. Still I felt that what was there formed a whole in itself. And since I see that you seem to think so I feel much comforted and cheered.[1]

Conrad took the first steps towards book publication in late spring 1911. On 17 May, he told T. Fisher Unwin, his first publisher, that he was contemplating a 'small vol. of reminiscences' (*Letters*, IV, 441) with an introduction – the eventual 'A Familiar Preface'. Mentioning that he was then involved in negotiations, Conrad nonetheless dangled the book before Unwin, perhaps as a backup should the said negotiations fall through. Given Conrad's long-standing grievance over the rights to *Almayer's Folly*, coming to an arrangement with Unwin would likely have been a last resort. It has been speculated that Dent and Macmillan – both interested in bringing out *Under Western Eyes* – may have cast longing glances at *Some Reminiscences*.[2] However this may be, the contract for the book was not signed until the end of July, and the negotiations Conrad mentioned to Unwin were apparently with Eveleigh Nash.[3]

Nash's account of publishing the book might explain the prolonged negotiations: he had received the book from Conrad along with a letter suggesting terms but had forgotten to acknowledge the book's receipt before leaving on holiday.[4] Returning to London, he found a note from Conrad enquiring whether the book had been received; in reply, he telegraphed acceptance and sent off an advance on royalties before reading the text. Conrad's reputation and Nash's long-standing acquaintance with him figured in this, but Nash's series of autobiographies certainly influenced the firm's interest. How well Conrad's memoirs suited a list made up of the recollections of aristocrats, officers, and

---

[1] Conrad to Garnett, 27 January 1912; see also Conrad to Pinker, 13 September 1911 (*Letters*, V, 12, and IV, 477–8).

[2] *Letters*, IV, 442n.

[3] The firm had previously been involved in reprinting 'An Outpost of Progress' in a collection titled *The Ladysmith's Treasury* (1900) and *Almayer's Folly* in 1904. Much later, in the early 1920s, and then Eveleigh Nash & Grayson, it issued reprints of Unwin's titles – *Almayer's Folly*, *An Outcast of the Islands*, *Tales of Unrest*, and *The Arrow of Gold* – in Nash's Great Novel Library and Nash's Famous Fiction Library.

[4] Eveleigh Nash, *I Liked the Life I Lived* (1941), pp. 171–3.

sportsmen is, perhaps, a moot point,[1] but he signed a memorandum of agreement with Nash on 27 July 1911.[2]

The book fell outside Conrad's general arrangements with Pinker, with Conrad arranging for publication off his own bat.[3] (This exempted him from paying Pinker his usual 10 per cent fee, but required him to devote his energies to landing a publisher.) He informed his agent of his successful dealings with Nash only in mid-September 1911,[4] repeating terms that he had reported to John Galsworthy – a £60 advance and a 20 per cent royalty – almost six weeks previously.[5] Shortly after conveying this information to Pinker, Conrad announced that the volume would appear sometime in October, about a fortnight after *Under Western Eyes*.[6] Conrad was at work on Nash proofs early that month, but a fortnight later stated that he did not know when the book would appear.[7] Some ten days later, however, a publication date in early January had been settled on,[8] a delay probably engineered to ensure that the appearance of *Under Western Eyes* would not completely overshadow *Some Reminiscences*.[9]

Conrad's first bout of revision – conscientious though not heavy – in early October 1911 must have been in serial tear-sheets, doubtless the form in which he had submitted the book to Nash. A cursory review of the text in book proofs came later in the month. In addition to typically polishing his style and tightening his wording, Conrad reconsidered factual details (26.29, 34.11, 119.6), clarified meaning (32.2, 55.29), and made a few cuts,[10] notably softening a virulent *ad*

---

[1] The end-pages of Nash's edition of *Some Reminiscences* advertise among 'Autobiographies Published by Mr. Eveleigh Nash': Princess Caroline Murat's *My Memoirs*, Colonel the Hon. Fred Wellesley's *Recollections of a Military Attaché*, and W. R. Woodgate's *Reminiscences of an Old Sportsman*.

[2] The memorandum of agreement is at Indiana.

[3] Directions on the extant serial proofs establish that Pinker was actively involved as an intermediary with Ford or his assistant, and correspondence establishes his efforts to market the serial in America. The two-year break with Pinker led to different arrangements from usual for the sale of book rights, and Nash's account as well as the surviving correspondence confirm that Pinker was not involved in these.

[4] Conrad to Pinker, 13 September 1911 (*Letters*, IV, 477).

[5] Conrad to Galsworthy, [1 or 8 August 1911] (*Letters*, IV, 467).

[6] Conrad to Galsworthy, 23 September 1911, and to Quinn, 25 September 1911 (*Letters*, IV, 480, 481).

[7] Conrad to Galsworthy, 15 October 1911 (*Letters*, IV, 487).

[8] Conrad to Placci, 26 October 1911 (*Letters*, IV, 494). See also Conrad to Quinn, 3 November 1911, and Conrad to Pinker, [4 November] 1911 (*Letters*, IV, 499, 500).

[9] Conrad's concern that *The Rescue* and *The Arrow of Gold* 'not get into each other's way' (to Pinker, 4 December 1918; *Letters*, VI, 319–20) suggests a typical marketing strategy.

[10] E.g., 20.21a, 24.38, 38.13, 84.18, 89.38.

hominem attack on Rousseau (89.38). On occasion he added emphasis by making declarative statements exclamatory.[1]

Editorial intrusion was light, amounting to a score or so of verbal changes, most involving the tidying of verbs and articles[2] – aspects of usage that Conrad typically found challenging – or mandating preferred forms, such as, for example, 'Scots' for 'Scotch' (100.8) and 'burnt' for 'burned' (92.40). The first gathering of proofs evidences a heavier hand at work than the later ones. Prepositions and wording were regularized, and 'will' was changed to 'shall' and 'that' to 'which'.[3] Punctuation was liberally altered throughout, and commas were systematically added to separate independent clauses. At times such changes have a marked impact on Conrad's rhythms. Nash's compositors, or possibly Conrad himself, caught misprints in the serial text (e.g., 'particuarly', 'fainly'), but Nash's edition was not itself flawlessly proofread. Ligatures disappeared, and the cedilla was dropped from 'Provençal'. French words were italicized, sometimes fussily as in the case of 'écus'. Misimpression resulted in the book having 'spoi' for 'spoil' (112.6).

More significantly, a few typesetting errors wreaked havoc with Conrad's sense. The serial's 'stepped up on the jetty' was mis-set as 'stepped upon the jetty' (74.4), and 'masters, stevedores', originally set as 'masters-stevedores', was 'corrected' to 'master-stevedores' (109.32–3). The adjustment of compound words was intrusive, hyphens being added, for instance, to 'refreshment room' (30.36), 'fellow officer' (61.14), and 'ruddy faced' (119.10), but removed from 'free-will' (82.39–40) and 'prose-writers' (89.11). At the same time 'majordomo' (31.25) and 'sheepskin' (31.32–3) were hyphenated.

Two sets of uncorrected revise proofs, stamped by Nash's printers, Ballantyne and Co., Ltd, and having the handwritten date '24 / 10 / 11' within the printers' stamp, are extant: the set Conrad gave to Wise in October 1921 (BL Ashley 469)[4] and that which he presented to Curle

[1] See 78.8, 87.1, 87.5.
[2] For verb changes, see, for example, 82.2, 86.1, 95.6, 98.31; for articles, 76.23, 86.26, 86.32, 87.22–3.
[3] See 'Emendation and Variation' for the comprehensive list.
[4] Conrad to Thomas J. Wise, 4 October 1921 (*Letters*, VII, 348). Touted as a private 'limited edition' to enhance their market value, the proofs are described in *The Ashley Library: A Catalogue of Printed Books, Manuscripts and Autographs Collected by Thomas James Wise* (1922), I, 238. Collations for the present edition confirm Eveleigh Nash's statements in letters to George T. Keating of 14 February and 16 May 1927 (Yale) that these were simply proofs, not a separate edition.

(Colgate). The latter was sold at auction in April 1927 as a privately printed or trial edition.[1] According to Wise, Conrad made a few final alterations in yet another set that was sent to the printers and pulped after use.[2] Collations for the present edition bear out Wise's statement.

An unrevised set of proofs, pulled before those now extant, provided Harpers' setting copy,[3] and thus Conrad's late alterations appear only in Nash's edition and the editions derived from it. Harpers produced a thoroughly Americanized text. Spelling was systematically altered with -*our*, -*ise*, and -*re* forms becoming, respectively, -*or*, -*ize*, and -*er* ones. 'Towards', 'amongst', and 'afterwards' were systematically changed to 'toward', 'among', and 'afterward', and forms such as 'spoilt' were modified to 'spoiled', and double -*ll* spellings were changed to single -*l* ones. Harpers' text was somewhat more heavily punctuated than Nash's, and an editor with an eye to detail tidied grammar and phrasing. For example, 'these' became 'those' (58.12), 'either against' was changed to 'against either' (59.18), and 'not only think' was altered to 'think not only' (49.7). Faulty verb forms were noticed (116.11), and attention was given to idiom (69.22a, 72.10) and proper usage – 'Indian ink' (73.3b), for instance, being corrected to 'India ink'.[4]

Publication by Harpers in the United States (A1), under the title *A Personal Record*, was apparently on 3 January,[5] thus before English publication. The title was later adopted, at Conrad's direction, for all subsequent editions. The book sold for $1.25. Harpers, which had published *The Mirror of the Sea* in America, gave Conrad a 10 per cent

---

[1] See *The Richard Curle Conrad Collection* (1927), Item 68. The description was concocted on the advice of Wise, whose own set increased in value by virtue of the price that Henry A. Colgate paid for Curle's set. On Curle's set, see Frederick M. Hopkins, 'Curle Sale of Conradiana', *Publishers' Weekly*, 4 June 1927, pp. 2186–88. Nash objected to Wise's description as follows: 'As the only person qualified to make a definite statement on the subject, I repeat that the copy of *Some Reminiscences* by Joseph Conrad, listed as item 68 in the catalogue of the Richard Curle Conrad Collection (sold April 28th, 1927) is nothing but a paper bound set of proofs, and that it is not a copy of a privately printed or trial edition of the work in this country' (Eveleigh Nash to George T. Keating, 16 May 1927 (Yale)).

[2] Letter from Thomas J. Wise to Arthur Swann, Director of the Department of Books, Prints and Autographs, American Art Association, cited in Hopkins, p. 2187.

[3] For the pattern of variants, see 'Apparatus'.

[4] Conrad's 'Indian ink' also slipped through the editor's skein in *Under Western Eyes*, Part Third, ch. III.

[5] The Registration of a Claim to Copyright A305426, United States Copyright Office, gives *ca.* 19 January, but Harpers' stock ledger for 1912–22 (Columbia) gives 3 January three times and 13 January once (the last presumably a copying error for '3').

royalty and no advance.[1] The initial print run was 2,500 copies; the first 1,000 sold well, and an additional 500 copies were bound in April to meet demand.[2] Further printings of 300 copies and of 400 copies were ordered in December 1918 and April 1921, respectively.[3]

The first English edition (E1), published by Eveleigh Nash under the title *Some Reminiscences*, appeared on or about 22 January 1912, selling for five shillings.[4] The volume sold sufficiently well for Nash to issue a second impression by early March.[5] The firm also released a small colonial issue bound by George Bell & Sons, with Bell's blind-stamped device on the spine and lacking the domestic advertisement leaf.

Nash's rights to the volume were strictly limited: were a reprint not to be issued at the author's request within six months of the book's going out of print, rights reverted to the author.[6] Conrad was thus free to sign a contract with the large and long established Edinburgh firm of Thomas Nelson & Sons for a second English edition in late December 1915.[7] Nelson's enquiry to Pinker at the beginning of November asking if any Conrad novels were available for inclusion in their Continental or Sevenpenny Library series probably led to their issuing *A Personal Record*.[8] It appeared under Nelson's imprint in October 1916 (E2), selling for one shilling and threepence.[9] The British Museum's deposit copy is date-stamped 24 NOV 16.

The title's next appearance in England, under the imprint of J. M. Dent & Sons, is connected with complex, sometimes fraught, negotiations with T. Fisher Unwin[10] and witnesses Dent's desire to strengthen

[1] Conrad to Alfred A. Knopf, 20 July 1913, and to Harpers, 27 October 1912 (*Letters*, v, 259, 120).

[2] See William R. Cagle and Robert W. Trogdon, *A Bibliography of Joseph Conrad*, forthcoming.

[3] Ibid.

[4] The dust-jacket featured a 1904 photograph of Conrad by C. G. Beresford, emphasizing the book's autobiographical character. Another photograph by Beresford served as the frontispiece to Nelson's 1916 edition (see frontispiece).

[5] Conrad to Captain David Wilson Barker, 7 March 1912 (*Letters*, v, 28).

[6] Memorandum of Agreement (Indiana).

[7] Conrad to Pinker, 23 December 1915 (*Letters*, v, 542).

[8] Thomas Nelson & Sons (signed J. Buchan) to J. B. Pinker, 1 November 1915 (Berg).

[9] *The English Catalogue of Books* records the month of publication.

[10] Dent, which had brought out '*Twixt Land and Sea* in 1912, had signed a contract with Conrad in 1913 for three books. Under its terms *Within the Tides* (1915) and *The Shadow-Line* (1917) had appeared. On Unwin's renewed interest, see Conrad to Pinker, 21 March 1919 (*Letters*, vi, 393).

their Conrad list by adding earlier titles to it. In 1917, the firm published new editions of *Lord Jim* and *Youth: A Narrative and Two Other Stories*, and in 1918 brought out a new edition of *Nostromo*, all with specially commissioned prefaces.[1] Conrad's query to his agent in the spring of 1918 whether 'a copy of Rems. out of Nash's stock can be obtained from J. M. Dent, or from some bookseller'[2] suggests that Dent may already have had an active interest in bringing out a new edition of *A Personal Record*. Pinker's negotiations with Dent during March 1919[3] concluded in a contract that was finalized on 11 April.[4] Its terms stipulated a generous 25 per cent royalty but no advance, a five-year limit on copyright, and freedom to include the volume in the collected editions being planned by Doubleday and Heinemann. Before this was settled, however, Dent broached expanding the text, since Nelson still retained rights over a shilling edition; Conrad rejected the idea on the grounds of the volume's artistic integrity.[5] Surprisingly, in reply to a letter from Pinker of 26 May, well after the agreement with Dent had been concluded, Nelson indicated only in mid-June that they had no plans to reprint the title and would not 'stand in the way of your making arrangements for the publication of this book elsewhere'.[6]

Dent set up their text (E3) from a copy of E1. The compositors or a copy-editor introduced changes, mostly relating to punctuation, but 'will' was changed to 'shall' (26.34, 32.19a) and 'that' to 'which' (27.17a, 33.5a), and 'proper' usage was imposed, with, for instance, 'saw only' being changed to 'only saw' (48.2). There was also a medley of substitutions,[7] some apparently inadvertent and some intentional,

---

[1] Dent's rights in these titles were non-exclusive. For example, their new five-shilling edition of *Lord Jim* went on sale at the end of June 1917, whilst Blackwood issued a one-shilling reprint in October (William Blackwood & Sons to J. B. Pinker, 14 July 1920, Berg).

[2] Conrad to Pinker, 9 May 1918, and Conrad to Pinker, [3 May 1918] (*Letters*, VI, 213). The copy was intended for presentation to Edmund Gosse, himself a distinguished autobiographer (*Letters*, VI, 209).

[3] See J. M. Dent to Conrad, 19 March 1919 (TS copy Berg); Conrad to Dent, 20 March 1919 (*Letters*, VI, 390); Dent to Conrad, 21 March 1919 (TS copy Berg).

[4] Conrad dispatched the signed contract to Pinker on 21 March 1919 (*Letters*, VI, 393). The account of Conrad's dealings with publishers records two dates concerning the contract: 21 March and 'Signed. Ap: 11th 1919', the latter possibly confirming Dent's acceptance of terms; see Lilian M. Hallowes' 'Note Book of Joseph Conrad', ed. Allan H. Simmons and J. H. Stape, in *Conrad between the Lines: Documents in a Life*, ed. Gene M. Moore, Allan H. Simmons, and J. H. Stape (2000), p. 210.

[5] J. M. Dent to Conrad, [28 March 1919] (TS copy Berg); Conrad to Dent, 29 March 1919 (*Letters*, VI, 396–7); Dent to Conrad, 31 March 1919 (TS copy Berg).

[6] Thomas Nelson & Sons to J. B. Pinker, 13 June 1919 (Berg).

[7] E.g., 30.37, 34.1, 34.35a.

such as, for example, the tightening of 'than on any other spot' to 'than any other spot' (26.30) or the replacement of the subjunctive by the indicative mood (28.37). Conrad's desire to oversee the edition – 'I don't wish to revise the Rems in any sense but of course Dent must send me proofs, so that his edition may establish the correct text'[1] – suggests that at an early stage he planned to have misprints hunted down. Whether this was done, a task likely to have been delegated to Miss Hallowes, is uncertain, as the final volume has only a few errors and was possibly proofread only in house.

Dent's volume, featuring the first appearance of the 'Author's Note', was printed by Butler and Tanner of London and Frome.[2] Published in November 1919, it sold for six shillings. The British Museum's deposit copy is date-stamped 31 OCT 19. The firm issued a reprint in 1920.

In America, Doubleday had sought to purchase the title as early as July 1913 and was still attempting to secure it from Harpers in November 1914.[3] Despite Conrad's view that the book was 'just wasted' in Harpers' hands,[4] nothing came of these efforts, with Doubleday eventually publishing the second American edition of *A Personal Record* in its 1917 'Deep Sea' edition (A2), setting copy being A1.[5] By this time Harpers' rights, probably for five years, had lapsed.[6]

The work next appeared in the collected editions published by Doubleday and Heinemann in 1920–21. The contracts for these, signed in late February 1920,[7] stipulated that Conrad was to provide a preface to each volume, correct proofs, and sign the first volume of each set, 735 sets to be printed by Doubleday and 780 by Heinemann.[8] *A Personal Record* appeared in Doubleday's collected 'Sun-Dial Edition'

---

[1] Conrad to Pinker, 21 March 1919 (*Letters*, VI, 394).

[2] For full bibliographical details of this and subsequent editions, see Cagle and Trogdon, *Bibliography*.

[3] Conrad to Alfred A. Knopf, 20 July 1913 (*Letters*, V, 259–60); F. N. Doubleday to Conrad, 4 November 1914 (Berg).

[4] Conrad to Pinker, 20 July 1913 (*Letters*, V, 259).

[5] See 'Apparatus' for evidence that A2 was set from A1 as well as for evidence that Doubleday's second edition (A3), which shares unique variants with E3 and E4, derives from E4, probably in the form of Heinemann proofs.

[6] When discussing Doubleday's interest in wresting the book from Harpers, Conrad proposed to forgo royalties on it for three years (Conrad to Alfred A. Knopf, 20 July 1913, *Letters*, V, 259).

[7] Conrad to Pinker, 27 February 1920, and Conrad to John Quinn, 2 March 1920 (*Letters*, VII, 36–7, 37–8).

[8] On the arrangements for the collected editions, see *The Secret Agent*, ed. Bruce Harkness and S. W. Reid (1990), pp. 283–88.

(A3) and in Heinemann's collected edition (E4) in 1921, being paired with *The Mirror of the Sea* in both editions. The British Museum's deposit copy of E4 is date-stamped 23 AUG 21. After publication, type for the Heinemann collected edition was distributed, and no later printings derive from it.[1] Some of its unique readings, however, passed into Doubleday's 1923 'Concord Edition' and later Doubleday printings.

For the collected editions it was originally planned that Doubleday should set up a volume and then send proofs to Conrad for revision and correction. Doubleday was to use these and forward them to Heinemann to set up their edition. As it turned out, this plan, which required multiple transatlantic exchanges, quickly proved impractical and was abandoned, although *A Personal Record* proved in this respect an exception to the general rule.

Conrad instructed Pinker to send Dent's edition of *A Personal Record* directly to Heinemann, that is, without any intervention on his part.[2] A copy of E3 was used by Heinemann's printers, Morrison & Gibb of Edinburgh, to set up E4.[3] In the copy, an editor made a few alterations, and spelling and paragraphing were changed in proofs.[4] An exception to the general practice of Heinemann's collected edition, intervention in this volume was remarkably light, due possibly to production pressures on the edition or an especially busy in-house schedule at the time the volume was making its way through press.

The subsequent publication history of *A Personal Record* in both England and America is straightforward. In America, Doubleday sold the book throughout the 1920s in variously named sets made from the plates manufactured for their 1921 'Sun-Dial' issue.[5] Conrad was

---

[1] The text was revived in Mara Kalnins' 1996 edition in Penguin's Twentieth-Century Classics series, as it uses the Heinemann collected edition as copy-text.

[2] 'I have sent Mr Pawling the Authors Notes he asked for & also the American proof of "Romance". We have not had the American proofs of "Western Eyes" and "Personal Record"; so Mr Conrad asks if you will kindly ask Dent & Methuen to send a copy direct to Heinemanns': L. M. Hallowes to J. B. Pinker, 14 December 1920 (Berg).

[3] The disbound copy is preserved in the Rare Books and Manuscripts Division, Hofstra University Library.

[4] In the disbound copy an editor corrected 'Cuninghame' to 'Cunninghame' (3.28), changed 'Sclavonism' to 'Slavonism' (5.37), 'Scotch' to 'Scottish' (51.4), and altered 'Leipsic' to 'Leipzig' (58.22). Punctuation was untouched. The copy has galley numbers and indicates lines that were reflowed. In E4 proofs 'Carlsbad' was altered to 'Karlsbad' (61.25).

[5] The book appeared in 1923 in the 'Concord Edition'; in 1924 in the 'Complete' and 'Canterbury' issues; in 1925 in the 'Kent', 'Memorial', 'Personal', and 'Inclusive' issues; and in 1928 in the 'Deep Sea', 'Malay', and 'Special' issues.

consulted about bindings for some of these 'editions' – in fact, merely issues of A3 – and supplied photographs for the frontispieces of the 1923 'Concord Edition', but he made no alterations to the texts.[1] In them *A Personal Record* was most often accompanied by *The Mirror of the Sea*; in the 'Malay Edition' it was paired with *The Shadow-Line*, perhaps stressing the latter's autobiographical character.

In England, preliminary negotiations for a popularly priced collected edition to be published by Dent got under way in September 1922[2] and continued sporadically throughout the next year. Not at first interested in using Doubleday's plates,[3] Dent in the end made arrangements with the American firm, printing their 'Uniform Edition' from Doubleday's 'Sun-Dial' plates in 1924. The same plates, leased from Dent, were used to produce the 'Medallion Edition' issued by Grant of Edinburgh in 1925. Dent again used the plates to reissue the 'Uniform Edition' during the late 1940s and early 1950s, renaming it 'Dent's Collected Edition'. *A Personal Record* was published in this set, again paired with *A Mirror of the Sea*, in 1946. A cosmetically corrected photographic reprint, with an introduction and notes by Zdzisław Najder, was issued in the Oxford World's Classics series in 1988. Although Dent's preliminaries are their own, their 1924 and 1946 issues of *A Personal Record* constitute printings of A3, itself derived, as pointed out above, from their own 1917 edition and thus from E1.

A FAMILIAR PREFACE

ONCE CONRAD ABANDONED his plans to add to his reminiscences, the next stage in the work's development became the writing of an introduction for initial book publication. Originally simply titled 'Preface', the piece later named 'A Familiar Preface' served to justify Conrad's method. It also gave ballast to what remains a relatively slim volume. Conrad was proud of this introduction, accepting the verdict that it was 'the best piece of purely abstract English' he had written.[4]

---

[1] For a discussion of the relationship of the 'Concord' alterations to the Heinemann collected edition, see *The Secret Agent*, pp. 290–93.

[2] Conrad to Eric Pinker, 6 September 1922, and to J. M. Dent & Sons, 12 September 1922 (*Letters*, VII, 516, 518–19).

[3] Conrad to Eric Pinker, 6 September 1922 (*Letters*, VII, 516).

[4] See Conrad to John Quinn, 11 December 1913, and Conrad to Pinker, 28 December 1913 (*Letters*, V, 313, 321).

The 25-leaf holograph manuscript (MS) survives in the Berg Collection.[1] Written in black ink on fine quality lined paper removed from a writing-tablet, the leaves, which measure 10 × 8 inches, are consecutively numbered after the first unnumbered leaf. Interlinear deletions and revisions are not especially heavy, but marginal doodles suggest that Conrad experienced short-lived bouts of writer's block. The revised MS serves as the copy-text for the present edition; it is emended by reference to E1 to incorporate the authorial revisions made in documents now lost.

An introduction to the volume was obviously needed, and Conrad mentioned his intention to write one when he dangled the book before T. Unwin Fisher in mid-May 1911 (*Letters*, IV, 441). The sole reference to actual composition in the extant correspondence occurs in a letter Conrad wrote towards the end of that September about work he had completed during the previous seven weeks.[2] This suggests that drafting and initial revision occurred sometime during August and September, at a time when he was also making last-minute changes to the proofs of *Under Western Eyes*, which was published on 5 October.

Conrad normally did not have an opportunity to see American proofs of his work, and *A Personal Record* proves no exception. The following changes, all touching on grammar, can confidently be attributed to a Harpers' editor and as a matter of course are excluded from the critical text: 'either amongst' (12.27) was changed to 'among either', 'either of' (14.33) to 'of either', 'one's own breast' (15.18) to 'one's breast', and 'you can' (16.16b) to 'can you'. Harpers' editor also provided commas in series and added a question mark after 'unmoved' (12.6). A compositor's mis-setting of E1's 'anger' (17.25) as 'danger' altered meaning.

'A Familiar Preface' was published, along with the volume's 'Author's Note', in *Notes on My Books* (C), a collection of Conrad's

---

[1] Purchased by John Quinn in 1913 (*Letters*, V, 313), the manuscript sold for $700 in the Quinn sale of 14 November 1923 (Item 1874); see *Complete Catalogue of the Library of John Quinn* (1924). At the Kern sale of 7–10 January 1929, it fetched $600 (Item 291); see *The Library of Jerome Kern, New York City: Part One, A–J* (1929). The slipcase preserving the manuscript has W. T. H. Howe's bookplate.

[2] Conrad to John Galsworthy, 28 September 1911 (*Letters*, IV, 482). On the basis of a letter to Pinker (*Letters*, IV, 441), Carabine places writing in 'early summer' (p. 103). Jean M. Szczypien states that the preface 'must have been composed shortly after 13 September 1911, for in his letter to Pinker of that date Conrad states that he had not yet started to write it': 'The Manuscript of Conrad's "A Familiar Preface": An Encoded Proclamation of Triumph', *Conradiana*, 27.3 (1995), 165. Conrad, in fact, moots *A Personal Note* as a possible book title (see *Letters*, IV, 477–8).

prefaces issued by Doubleday in America on 4 March 1921 and by Heinemann in England on 19 May. This was a limited edition, type being distributed after printing. The publication history of this volume is complex,[1] but, in short, most of the setting was completed and plated by Doubleday's printers by 22 December 1920. To accommodate Conrad's preferences about format, the entire book was reset, with the result that it was not printed until February 1921. The typesetting of the American and English issues is identical, Heinemann merely issuing the book with its own preliminaries and binding. The preface was set either from A1 or from A2, the lack of variants making it impossible to establish which. Thus even the English issue of *Notes on My Books* inherits A1's Americanizations and editorial changes as well as the erroneous 'danger'. It has a unique setting error, 'taking' (16.15) being omitted.

The collected edition texts vary little. Published in the summer of 1921, Heinemann's text (E4) derived from the extant disbound copy of E3. Doubleday's 'Sun-Dial' (A3) text, likely published at about the same time as Heinemann's, shares with *Notes on My Books* the wording 'of either' (14.33), found in A1 and A2, as well as the American spellings introduced into A1.

COPY-TEXTS

THE SCARCITY OF preprint materials for *A Personal Record* makes the choice of copy-text axiomatic: the serial text published in the *English Review* (S), with some exceptions noted below, serves as copy-text. It requires emendation to eliminate typesetting errors and to incorporate the revisions that Conrad made when he read proofs for the first English edition in October 1911. The manuscript serves as copy-text for 'A Familiar Preface'.[2]

All the book editions after E1, including A1 (based on E1 proofs), lack independent textual authority, and even E1, although it contains isolated revisions introduced by Conrad into the body of his text, derives largely from S in its wording and wholly so in its accidentals. None of these can rival S as a source for the accidentals, S being closer to the pointing and other forms of the lost originals than any later printing.

---

[1] For a history of its production, see *The Secret Agent* (1990), pp. 317–18.
[2] The 'Author's Note' is dealt with separately below.

The reliability of S's forms is, however, very much a relative matter. Based mostly on dictated documents, S's text inevitably contains the preferences of the typists who prepared the typescripts. Conrad is unlikely to have interrupted the flow of his thoughts to dictate punctuation or spelling, and, in this sense, the typescripts from which S derived were, to a degree more than usual with him, collaborative texts. S was, moreover, subject to compositorial intervention and underwent some house-styling by Ford or his assistant editor, Douglas Goldring. The evidence of the marked proofs for the first serial instalment suggests, however, that this editorial intrusion was light.

While the manuscript of 'A Familiar Preface' offers unimpeachable evidence for Conrad's preferences, the lack of preprinting documents for the 'Reminiscences' themselves determines by default the adoption of a copy-text that surely does not embody all of Conrad's decisions with respect to punctuation, spelling, and word-division. The use of the text's first printed state guarantees, at least, that later editorial and compositorial interventions – few as these may have been compared to some in other Conrad texts – are not perpetuated in the present edition.

The revised proofs for Chapter 1, which received Conrad's careful supervision, are free from later intervention, however much they incorporate the typist's and compositor's preferences. As a matter of course, they provide the copy-text for that chapter. Only a small section of the authorially revised proofs of Chapter 3 is available in a facsimile page published in Violet Hunt's autobiography *The Flurried Years* (1926). The revised state of this text has greater authority than any later version. Comparison of this proof with the serial as published reveals no variant wordings; the serial, however, does have a single change of punctuation. Since the source for this change cannot be established, the proof text, which bears the mark of Conrad's hand, provides the more reliable copy-text.

The adoption of the single holograph leaf for the text of a section of Chapter 6, though its wordings are identical with those in S, restores Conrad's sense and rhythm where compositorially altered punctuation damaged both. MS has 'I did so from taste, no doubt – having an instinctive horror of losing my sense of full self-possession', whereas S reads 'I did so from taste, no doubt having an instinctive horror of losing my sense of full self-possession' (101.20–22).

Such a change serves notice that the expression of Conrad's ideas can depend upon small, subtle effects that may be dulled or lost in an editor's or compositor's drive to impose a standard style. This effect is likewise witnessed later when S's 'The Red Ensign, the symbolic, protecting warm bit of bunting' (125.8–9) became in E1 'The Red Ensign — the symbolic, protecting, warm bit of bunting'. Two hands were probably at work here. Conrad likely effected the rhetorically charged delay by changing his original comma after 'Ensign' to an em-dash since this involves tonal nuance and is not a mere convention, but Nash's proofreader is more likely to have fussily installed the grammatically correct comma after 'protecting'. Cumulatively, changes like the latter flatten and standardize Conrad's text; they do so particularly in the prose of a conscientious stylist whose acute sense of cadence and rhythm found shape in painstakingly won effects.

The adoption of S and of the few preprint documents that survive helps to restore to Conrad's prose the rhythms he himself presumably gave to it. For example, the effect of measured deliberation in S's 'In his attractive, reserved manner, and in a veiled, sympathetic voice, he asked' relies on punctuation that is absent from E1: 'In his attractive reserved manner and in a veiled sympathetic voice he asked' (28.25–27). This later rapid-fire version, whether the work of a hurried compositor or a fastidious editor, softens the sentence. The revisions in the serial proofs of chapter 1 show that this kind of change is atypical of Conrad himself, and it can, with some confidence, be assigned to one of the agents responsible for seeing his work into print. Similarly, E1's pace-slowing comma after 'promise' in S's 'not that I doubt your promise but because I must' (68.7–8) is, on balance, an intrusive change.

Even if S's punctuation is not in every instance of many thousands unimpeachably Conrad's, the selection of it as copy-text restores to his autobiographical writing many of his preferences and disposes of the accumulating intrusions, whether deleterious or merely indifferent, of later printed forms.

The manuscript of 'A Familiar Preface', although its light punctuation requires some adjustment for print, guarantees a final text much closer to the one Conrad created than does that in any printed version. Conrad's verbal revisions made in the now-lost typescripts and proofs and present in E1, as well as his rhetorical and emphatic styling (which would normally fall outside the province of magazine and book editors) are adopted here. The present edition repairs four errors traceable to faulty inscription. Unnoticed as the text underwent revision, these errors have appeared in all later printings.[1]

---

[1] See 12.29n, 14.13n, 14.16n, and 15.23n.

The adoption of MS also restores Conrad's spellings and styling that typists or editors regularized and smoothed out. For example, in addition to reinstating 'can not' (12.37),[1] 'sea-books' (13.36), 'sea-stories' (13.37), 'judgements' (17.11), and his apparently preferred form 'reflexion' (which he seems, at least sometimes, to have used to distinguish between mental activity and the play of light)[2] the present edition adopts his capitalization of 'Merchant Service' (13.34). E1's editorial changes are rejected, and the text published here does not carry over the semi-colons imposed by that edition on matter that Conrad added in the typescript. Where punctuation, however, forms an integral part of a revision, it has been adopted. The texts that Conrad polished in the late summer and early autumn of 1911 appear here in a form that more faithfully represents his own wording, spellings, word-division, and rhythms than do the first printed versions and later ones based on them.

EMENDATION

THE VARIED SITUATIONS under which *A Personal Record* was created and printed necessitate emendation of the selected copy-texts. Problems unique to one of the work's parts are susceptible to discrete resolution; others involve the work as a whole and demand the application of a coherent emendation policy. The copy-texts have been emended as the surviving historical evidence warrants as well as to eliminate outright errors, whether of inscription or of transmission, and to incorporate Conrad's later revisions of wording and, where identifiable, of accidentals. Compositorial interference that damages Conrad's sense and intrudes on his practice has also been rejected.

Although the general aim of the present edition is to preserve Conrad's own work and to expunge changes made to it by other persons and without his approval, the lack of preprint documents as well as the fact that most of the text was dictated prevents determination of all of Conrad's preferences with respect to punctuation, spelling, and

---

[1] His 'cannot' (13.8) confirms that his spelling of this word varied. Other manuscripts – *Lord Jim*, for instance – establish an inconsistent practice.

[2] Conrad's spelling varied. In the manuscript of *Under Western Eyes*, a text close in time to this, twelve instances of 'reflexion' and four of 'reflection' occur. The *OED* indicates that the 'x' form, from French, is the earlier of the two.

word-division. The dictated texts – in a limited sense, a product of invited collaboration – received only passive authorial sanction at best, and the preferences of Conrad's typists inevitably appear in those parts of this work that rely upon print material for their copy-texts.

Lapses in grammar, tense, and idiom occurred throughout Conrad's career, even in its late stages when he had lived in England for many years, and his difficulties with standard English tended to encourage his typists and editors to standardize usage, give wording a 'proper' cast, and smooth out awkwardness. For example, he typically had problems with 'shall' and 'will', which editors tended to adjust (26.34, 32.19a, 89.29). Articles, which are not a feature of Polish grammar, likewise proved troublesome and provoked editorial intervention.[1] Conrad also did not systematically distinguish between 'that' and 'this' and 'these' and 'those', his practice again being influenced by Polish and, possibly, French. Given his general habits, then, E1's 'These were good reasons' and 'this is an impression', for example, are rejected in favour of the earlier 'Those were good reasons' (18.8) and 'that is an impression' (73.20). There was, moreover, a tendency to alter Conrad's prose for the sake of 'correctness', as witnessed by E1's alteration of 'a hotel' to 'an hotel' (46.1) and the alteration by various editors of 'Scotch' to 'Scottish' and 'Scots' (47.4, 100.8).[2]

In the absence of the serial tear-sheets, in which Conrad revised for book publication, and the book proofs, the readings introduced in later forms are a mixture of authorial revision and editorial change that require sifting. Simply because a reading appears for the first time in the book texts does not guarantee that Conrad himself was responsible for it. For example, a copy-editor clearly changed 'a historian', appearing in S as well as in the proof of E1 (E1p), to 'an historian' (16.33a, 16.33b) in revise proofs. The variants in the first English and American editions and Dent's 1919 edition likewise indicate that editors adjusted Conrad's prose to suit then-current notions of correct usage. Harpers, for instance, changed 'Mathematics command' to 'Mathematics commands' (11.25) and tidied 'either of' to 'of either' (14.33). Cumulatively, such gentrifying alterations produced an image of Conrad as a more 'correct' and idiomatic writer of English than he, in fact, was.

[1] E.g., 59.20, 76.23, 86.25, 86.32, 87.22.
[2] Conrad's use of 'Scotch' was also 'corrected' by *Blackwood's Magazine*.

Conrad's punctuation – generally light in MS, and in dictated texts probably first added by the typist and then by Conrad in revision – is a vexed area, with magazines tending to impose a heavier punctuation system on somewhat loosely punctuated texts. Fortunately, the *English Review* seems generally to have dealt with a light editorial hand in this respect, particularly compared to some of the editing and heavy house-styling that Conrad's earlier work underwent as it passed through the hands of the editors and compositors.[1] The clearest evidence of house-styling in the *English Review* occurs with commas in series, which Conrad used only occasionally. Their use is erratic in the issues in which 'Some Reminiscences' appeared. Such commas do not appear in the December 1908 and the March and May 1909 issues; they appear in the January 1909 issue; and simultaneously they appear and do not appear in the February, April, and June 1909 issues. Given Conrad's general – though varying – practice, final commas in series have thus been removed where the *English Review* supplies the copy-text.

Where required punctuation is absent from the copy-texts (e.g., a full stop at the end of a sentence, closing inverted commas around quoted matter, a comma after the *inquit* in dialogue, such as, for example, 'he said'), it has been silently supplied. On this basis, a full stop has, for instance, been furnished to Conrad's handwritten addition of 'M^r' (26.6) since the proofs in which he was working have 'Mr.' and 'Mrs.' throughout. Where the copy-text's lack of punctuation might cause confusion or disruption or is manifestly defective, it has been provided, and a report duly made in the Apparatus.

In a critical edition rather than a diplomatic transcription of a historical text, the retention of obviously faulty or merely eccentric typing or typesetting would be a pointless distraction. Thus, for instance, the variable placement of punctuation both within and outside inverted commas by typists – an indifferent matter with respect to meaning – is standardized here throughout so that the punctuation is placed within inverted commas. Similarly, the single inverted commas used for dialogue and titles in S's fourth instalment, anomalous in styling for the series, have been regularized to the double inverted commas of the other instalments. Such changes are made without notice in the Apparatus. Where altered styling and punctuation almost certainly represent Conradian revision, it has been adopted. For instance, E1's

---

[1] On this topic, see Owen Knowles and J. H. Stape, 'The Rationale of Punctuation in Conrad's *Blackwood's* Fictions', *The Conradian*, 30.1 (2005), 1–45.

'Glory ... or Pity' (11.16–17), 'alas!' (29.31), and 'Look out there!' (119.39–40) replace the lower case and unemphatic forms of earlier states. Such changes are unrepresentative of the kind usually made by editors and compositors, and betray an authorial presence. On the other hand, this can be a subtle matter, and S's 'What better name could an honourable hard-working ship have' (119.19–20) is unemended, E1's question mark being, arguably, an editorial intrusion rather than a revision.

This edition, as do the other volumes of the Cambridge Edition, declines to regularize spelling. This not surprisingly varies in texts which were composed in 1908–9, 1911, and 1919, each of which had discrete origins and distinct status as projects. The critical texts therefore retain orthographic inconsistencies that derive from their inscription and printing histories (e.g., 'cannot' and 'can not').

The spelling of proper names, where wrong, and where neither anglicization nor a possible effect is at issue, has been corrected to the form accepted at the time of writing. Thus, 'Rigi', 'Furka', 'Donggala', and 'Joliette' replace S's incorrect 'Righi', 'Furca', 'Dongala', and 'Jolliette'. On the other hand, 'Carlsbad' and 'Pulo' remain unchanged; the former is an acceptable Anglicized form, widely used during the late nineteenth and early twentieth centuries, and the latter reflects usage at the time of writing.

As a corollary, the spelling of foreign words and names is adjusted to the conventions of the language in question. Hence, the correct 'Jean-Jacques' (88.31, 92.15) replaces the copy-text's unhyphenated form, and E1's correction of 'Giugliano' to 'Giuliano' (103.20) is accepted. Accents have been provided where they are missing and altered when incorrect. The italicization of certain words was almost certainly a matter of house-styling or compositorial preference, and thus, for example, S's italicized '*bizarre*' (66.12, 113.9) and '*Vieux Port*' (113:21) are not retained.

Word-division proves no less problematic a matter in that it often, like spelling, reflects a typist's or a compositor's preference.[1] Hyphenation tends to be light in manuscript, with Conrad adding hyphens when revising a typed transcription. When he refused to bow to convention, the individuals who saw his work into print liberally intervened

---

[1] See 'End-of-line Word-Division' in the Apparatus for decisions on word-division. For this edition, this element has been established as a discrete step in the editorial process through on-site examination of the documents by more than one editor and by reference to Conrad's general as well as particular practices.

to hyphenate compound words and adjectives that he had left as two words and also occasionally rejected what appeared, to their lights, to be unorthodox forms. On balance, however, the relatively light editorial hand evident in the surviving proofs of the first instalment may suggest that many of Conrad's preferences about this matter largely survived into S. The adoption of MS for the copy-text of 'A Familiar Preface' restores 'down wind' (12.5) and 'open eyed' (16.40), and the adoption of the earliest surviving states of the texts for copy-texts likewise reinstates, for example, 'refreshment room' (30.36), 'mapped out' (47.12), and 'light yellow' (77.25), all with hyphens in E1 and the texts descending from it.

The policy of the present edition is not to preserve mere idiosyncrasies or anomalies, or genuine errors, spawned during production. S and E1p's 'middle ages' (90.18–19), which appears in upper case in E1, is suggestive. The lower case is the work of a typist attempting to keep pace with dictation, and Conrad, possibly influenced by the Polish *sredniowiecze* or the French *moyen âge*, overlooked this form during proofreading. Similarly, both double and single inverted commas appear on the same page of the 'Author's Note' – around 'crystallized' and 'rectification' (4.29, 4.36), and the two systems, elsewhere in the preface, are here edited to double inverted commas, in any case a matter not involving sense. Tidying for the sake of mere consistency is also not an aim of the present edition, and thus in Chapter 1 commas in series have not been regularized even when their use is erratic, as in the authorially revised proofs that serve as copy-text.

The source of an emendation to a copy-text is duly recorded in the 'Emendation and Variation' and 'Emendations of Accidentals' lists in the Apparatus. These lists do not, however, report the correction of obvious misspellings (for example, 'posession' [13.11] and 'strenght' [13.26]), straightforward typing or typesetting errors (for example, 'the the drawing-room' [8.7]), faults caused by misimpression, or, unless meaning is potentially at issue, spelling variants. As in other volumes in the Cambridge Edition, the Apparatus does not report Conrad's original rejected wordings in the manuscript of 'A Familiar Preface' or in the dictated typescript of the 'Author's Note' but only those of their final revised states. The Apparatus also does not report matter which properly forms no part of the texts but which is present in the documents containing them. These features fall outside the general concern of the Cambridge Edition to present critical texts of Conrad's writings rather than diplomatic transcriptions of the documents in which they are located.

THE 'AUTHOR'S NOTE'

IN EARLY SEPTEMBER 1919, Conrad began and completed the 'Author's Note' for the new edition of *A Personal Record* for which he had signed a contract with J. M. Dent & Sons in March.[1] First published in November by Dent (E3), the preface was written with an eye to Doubleday's and Heinemann's collected editions, in which the volume would appear in the summer of 1921. To publicize Dent's new edition, a brief extract from the preface appeared in *Book Monthly* in December 1919.[2]

Three preprint documents survive:

(1) a ten-page ribbon-copy typescript (TS1) at Princeton, measuring 10 × 8 inches, watermark '1169 | UNDERWRITER | BOND'. This is labelled 'Original' in Conrad's hand, has his autograph corrections and revisions, and contains an authenticating note similar to those on other dictated typescripts he sold to T. J. Wise.[3]

(2) an eleven-page ribbon-copy typescript (TS2) in the Berg collection, measuring 10 × 8 inches, watermark '1299'. This is labelled 'Personal Record | 1st copy' in Conrad's hand in the upper-left corner of page 1. It incorporates the changes he made in TS2c transcribed by his secretary, Lilian M. Hallowes, as well as a few verbal alterations and printers' marks.

(3) an eleven-page black ink carbon-copy typescript (TS2c) at Princeton. This has the same measurements and watermark as TS2. It is labelled 'Copy N° II' and 'U.S.A.' in Conrad's hand, and has a few revisions by him.

The final revised text of TS1 (Princeton) provides the copy-text for the present edition.

---

[1] On this contract, see above p. 148.

[2] 'My English', *Book Monthly*, 14 (December 1919), p. 928.

[3] The last page of TS1 bears the following note, signed and dated '25 Sept 1919': 'This is an additional note to a new English edition planned for 1919 (Dent & Sons) of *Some Reminiscences* under the proper title *A Personal Record*. The reasons for writing it, apart from D & Sons express request, are stated in the text.' A further initialled note states: 'A copy has been sent to US to be printed in the de luxe Am Ed^{on} pub^{d} by Messrs: Doubleday Page & Co.'

Although no statement survives to the effect, Conrad almost certainly dictated this preface, as he did in the case of much of his writing at this time.[1] He forwarded this document to Pinker on 8 September 1919, requesting that two copies be made – one for Dent and one for Doubleday – but indicating his intention to revise further.[2] He also instructed Pinker to return his original, doubtless having in mind its sale to Wise, to whom he offered it for £10 at the end of September 1919.[3] Conrad's offer to Wise illuminates the processes involved in preparing the 'Author's Note' for print:

They all contain as much pen-and-ink writing, nearly, as type and are the original first drafts with all the corrections and alterations, except such as may have been made in proof. Of each no more than two clean copies have been made for the printers in England and America, and these when sent back to me with the first proofs have been invariably destroyed by myself.[4]

On 25 September, copies of the preface were sent to Dent and to Doubleday, the date on which Conrad completed his essay 'Stephen Crane: A Note without Dates'.[5] Conrad himself forwarded TS2 to Dent, with the following instructions: 'I am sending you here the *Author's Note* to the *Personal Record*. It is to be printed first, after the preliminary pages, before the *Familiar Preface*. Pray send me a proof'.[6] Dent acknowledged receipt of the typescript (TS2) on 29 September, characterizing the preface as 'of extreme interest' and stating that he was 'quite sure' it would 'call attention to the book'.[7] Dent's setting copy, the typescript, bears printers' directions in pencil – 'Set in same type as book', '19 ems | 9 1/4 Set.', '58' within a circle – and what are apparently tracking marks on pages 5 and 9.[8] It survives by Dent's special

[1] On Conrad's use of dictation in his late career, see Frederick R. Karl, *Joseph Conrad: The Three Lives* (1979), pp. 839–41.

[2] Conrad to Pinker, 6 September 1919, and [8 September 1919] (*Letters*, VI, 484, 485).

[3] Conrad to Pinker, [8 September 1919], and Conrad to Wise, 30 September 1919 (*Letters*, VI, 485, 500). Wise's purchase of the typescript is confirmed in Hallowes, 'Note Book of Joseph Conrad', p. 219. The slipcase in which the typescript is preserved has the bookplate of Nelson Doubleday, who presumably bought it from Wise.

[4] Conrad to Wise, 30 September 1919 (*Letters*, VI, 500).

[5] Conrad to Dent, 25 September 1919 (*Letters*, VI, 494), and L. M. Hallowes to Pinker, 25 September 1919 (Berg). For the composition of the essay on Crane, see *Notes on Life and Letters* (2004), pp. 251–2.

[6] Conrad to Dent, 25 September 1919 (*Letters*, VI, 494).

[7] Dent to Conrad, 29 September 1919 (TS copy Berg).

[8] The numbers 2, 3, and 4 also appear in pencil in its left-hand margins towards the bottom of pages 2, 4 and 6. Illegible in page 1's upper right-hand corner are possibly compositors' initials or font names.

request or was returned with proofs; if the latter is the case, then contrary to what Conrad claimed was his invariable practice, it escaped destruction. On 9 October, Dent thanked Conrad for the corrected proof, received on that date.[1]

Conrad kept his promise to send Doubleday a 'clean copy of the new *Author's Note* for the *Personal Record*' for their collected edition,[2] having his secretary post it to Pinker for forwarding to Doubleday.[3] In addition to the indication 'U.S.A.' on its first page, this carbon-copy typescript (TS2c), which is labelled '*copy* N⁰II.' in Conrad's hand, bears his initialled direction: '*Note*. To be printed <u>before</u> the "*Familiar Preface*", | Edition de luxe'. The pages are numbered 26–36 in the bottom left-hand corner.[4] As discussed below, this typescript did not in the end serve as setting copy for Doubleday's 'Sun-Dial' Edition.

The relationship of the three typescripts is complex, and the history of revision and publication is tangled despite the brevity of the preface. For the sake of clarity, if at a risk of slight repetition, the general outline is as follows: as Conrad indicated to his agent, he revised his text after he dictated TS1; he himself altered the typewritten text of TS2c to accommodate these revisions; his secretary then copied these alterations (not flawlessly) into TS2. The book texts, including Doubleday's, ultimately trace their text to TS2. The arguments for this scenario are developed below.

After dictation, Conrad, as he usually did when readying a dictated piece for print, polished wording and added punctuation. For instance, he changed 'burst into laughter' to 'burst out laughing' (4.13–14) and 'tired' to 'weary' (7.10). He also deleted an emotionally charged sentence about his father.[5] Shared variants in TS2 and TS2c establish that he tinkered with the text after his initial revision. TS2c's tidy condition and the impeccable handwriting in it suggest that actual revision may have occurred in a now lost typescript, Conrad merely copying his alterations into the surviving one and making a few

[1] Dent to Conrad, 9 October 1919 (TS copy Berg).
[2] Conrad to F. N. Doubleday, 13 September 1919 (*Letters*, VI, 487).
[3] 'I am enclosing typed copy of "Author's Note", for "A Personal Record", for the de luxe Edition (and no other) in America. The "Note" for Dent has gone direct today': L. M. Hallowes to J. B. Pinker, 25 September 1919 (Berg).
[4] Page 4 was counted as 29 in this scheme but lacks a number.
[5] The deleted sentence, which follows 'To . . . enemy' (7.12–13), reads: 'The bitterest thought in my after life was that it was not to death that he was surrendering.'

further changes on the fly.[1] The addition of his initials and the year 1919 – styling for print – on the last pages of TS2 and TS2c are not present in TS1; these could have been added on direct instructions to the typist or may be accounted for by a lost typescript.

TS2 and TS2c are copies of TS1's revised state.[2] The revised document was on the whole carefully transcribed, with the typist sensibly correcting 'right' to 'rights' (6.6a) and omitting a stray and incorrect 'its' (8.11). On the other hand, she mistyped 'Those' as 'These' (6.21) or intentionally altered the word, omitted several commas (which Conrad reinstated in TS2c), and added others, and, somewhat surprisingly, maintained the erratic system of double and single inverted commas that occurs in TS1.

The fact that typewritten texts of TS2 and TS2c contain matter deleted in TS1 prompted Jean M. Szczypien to hypothesize that Conrad made 'additional handwritten corrections' (that is, revisions) in TS2c and copied these back, although imperfectly, into TS1.[3] This attractive and even necessary hypothesis requires qualification on two points: whether Conrad actually *revised* in TS2c itself is uncertain, and he almost certainly entered his changes into his original typescript not, as Szczypien speculates, to boost its price – 'the more corrections in the author's hand that a typed document had the more money it commanded' – but to sell a document incorporating his latest revisions.[4]

In TS2 and TS2c, TS1's 'Cuninghame Graham' to 'Cunninghame Graham' (3.28) and 'The Outpost of Progress' to 'An Outpost of Progress' (3.29) are corrected in hand and 'Impossible' placed in upper case (5.22, 5.23). In TS2c, Conrad inserted what appears to be a marking for a new paragraph at 'All I can claim' (5.25a), an

---

[1] For example, he altered 'received' to 'had received' (6.1), 'myself, and' to 'myself; and' (6.40), and 'too, for' to 'too; for' (7.33). Copied into TS2, these changes descend to the printed texts.

[2] The text on p. 2 of TS2 and TS2c is identical, but TS2's page has twenty-four lines whereas TS2c's has twenty-five. Why TS2's second page required retyping is unclear: TS1 is not heavily revised at this point and is quite legible. Perhaps physical damage to the page explains its replacement.

[3] 'Untyrannical Copy-texts for the Prefatory Essays to Joseph Conrad's *A Personal Record*', *The Conradian*, 11.1 (1986), 18.

[4] At the end of September 1919, Conrad sold a six-page typescript of 'Stephen Crane: A Note without Dates' to Wise for the same amount as this ten-page preface. For details, see *Notes on Life and Letters* (2004), pp. 251–2. (The typescript noted as unlocated in that discussion was sold at Sotheby's, New York, on 23 April 1999 for $11,000 to a private collector.)

alteration not appearing in any printed text because that typescript was laid aside.

TS2 has several unique readings in a hand other than Conrad's: 'aware of that. I had' appears as 'aware of this. I have' (4.8b), 'that' was changed to 'nothing else' (4.22), and 'all the remembered anguish' to 'the accumulated anguish' (5.25–6). Missing from the printed texts, these represent stylistic polishing evidently originating with Conrad himself, either by his verbal direction or effected in a now lost document. Three further variants in TS2 represent the defective transcription of TS2c or offer more evidence for a lost working-copy typescript: lacking are 'new' in 'my new friend' (4.17a) as well as an exclamation mark Conrad had added after 'for ever' (5.16) in TS2c. TS2 also has the reading 'more inapplicable', which he had altered to 'less applicable' (6.16–17) in both TS1 and TS2c.

The publication history of the preface is more straightforward than the story of its revision. Conrad made a handful of changes in Dent's proofs but also overlooked a few errors: Dent's final text has the misspelling 'Cuninghame' (corrected in TS2), gives 'The Outpost' rather than 'An Outpost' (similarly corrected in TS2), and also has 'aware of this. I had', that is, only part of the change that Conrad had made by hand in TS2c and transcribed into TS2. E3's text contains two typical editorial alterations: 'those' (3.16a), was changed to 'these' and the awkward 'two first friends' (3.27) was smoothed out to 'first two friends'.

Subsequent printings of the 'Author's Note' during Conrad's lifetime derive from E3. The note next appeared in the spring of 1921 in *Notes on My Books* (C), along with 'A Familiar Preface'. This text has the correct title 'An Outpost of Progress', spells 'Cuninghame' correctly, and has 'have' rather than 'had' (4.8b). These departures from E3, even the last, could have been made independently by an alert editor. A strict grammarian added punctuation at a few points, and spellings were partly Americanized, with *-ise-* forms becoming *-ize-* forms, although 'splendour' and 'honourable' were allowed to stand. The text also has a compositorial (or editorial) change, 'mentioned' replacing 'mention' (8.20).

The essay next appeared in Doubleday and Heinemann's collected editions published in the summer of 1921. TS2c, contrary to the indication on its first page that it was for Doubleday's 'Edition de luxe', the 'Sun-Dial' Edition (A3), did not provide setting copy for that edition's 'Author's Note'. The numerous variants between A3 and TS2c establish that it was laid aside,[1] as its very survival also suggests (setting copy normally being discarded after use). Time and convenience were probable contributing factors in this since Doubleday began typesetting their collected edition of *A Personal Record* some year and a half after receiving the typescript. Dent's edition provided the basis for Heinemann's collected edition (E4) of the volume.[2] A3 retains British spellings in the preface, including *-ise-* verb forms, an indication that Doubleday probably set up its text from Heinemann proofs. A3 and E4 also share two variants (7.9a, 8.18) found in no other edition.

Despite the complicated interrelationships of the extant typescripts, the selection of copy-text is axiomatic: TS1 contains Conrad's final text and has thus been adopted for the present edition. TS2c and TS2, which descend from TS1, contain a few last-minute revisions but are not reworked states of the preface. Conrad's revisions of both wording and punctuation in TS2c as well as his changes for E3 provide emendations. The unique wordings in TS2 are sufficiently compelling to suggest authorial sanction and also provide emendations to the copy-text. E3's editorial changes of wording are rejected as a matter of course, and the use of inverted commas has been regularized to double inverted commas, a matter Conrad would have expected to see in print, and making this piece fall into line with the practice of the book. Located in no preprint document, some wordings and emphases which were deemed to be Conrad's appear in the present edition for the first time.

THE CAMBRIDGE TEXTS

THE CAMBRIDGE EDITION presents deliberately eclectic texts of *A Personal Record* and its two prefaces, 'A Familiar Preface' and the 'Author's Note', based on the original documents or, where these are no longer extant, on the printed forms closest to the lost originals.

The copy-text for Conrad's reminiscences is the serial printing, with the following exceptions: revised serial page proofs provide Chapter 1's copy-text; revised serial page proofs recoverable in a published facsimile serve as the copy-text for Chapter 3's concluding paragraphs; and the sole surviving holograph leaf supplies the copy-text for a brief passage in Chapter 6. The copy-text for 'A Familiar Preface' is the manuscript, and that for the 'Author's Note' the original typescript as

---

[1] See 'Emendation and Variation'.
[2] On Heinemann's use of a disbound copy of Dent's edition as setting copy, see the discussion above, p. 150.

revised and corrected by Conrad himself.[1] Conrad's revisions, made at several stages, supply emendations to the selected copy-texts. The Cambridge texts also incorporate both editorial corrections and readings found in other documents when an analysis of the history of composition, revision, transmission, and publication indicate that these would more faithfully represent Conrad's work.

This new Cambridge text of *A Personal Record* removes from the received texts non-authorial intervention affecting wording and 'accidentals' – punctuation, spelling, and word-division. Such alterations, whether inadvertent or intentional, by the typists, compositors, and editors who first saw Conrad's texts into print and by later copy-editors and compositors who 'corrected', 'improved', and house-styled his writings have been removed to the extent that the surviving documents and historical evidence allow.

Given that this volume consists largely of dictated texts subject from their inception to intervention by amanuenses, Conrad's wordings, pointing, and orthography have been restored to his most extended autobiographical statement and to the two introductions that preface it to the degree that it has been possible. Wordings and emphases present in no previously printed text of 'A Familiar Preface' and the 'Author's Note' appear here for the first time, and the reminiscences themselves are published in a form more authoritative than any in which they have hitherto appeared in print.

---

[1] The physical properties and typography of these documents, as distinguished from their texts, are not preserved here. Aside from typographical styling of display capitals and indentation, for example, new lineation has created new syllabication, but only the hyphens at the ends of certain lines (7.7, 20.36, 21.16, 31.17, 31.32, 42.13, 45.11, 45.39, 46.38, 64.23, 65.3, 66.12, 66.35, 67.12, 74.33, 82.39, 96.1, 113.22, 115.23, 116.31, 117.22) are intended to signify word-division in the critical text itself.

APPARATUS

EMENDATION AND VARIATION

This list records the present edition's emendations of substantive readings together with the variants in substantive readings amongst the texts collated. Each note provides the full history of the readings in these texts. The reading of the Cambridge text appears immediately after the page–line citation. It is followed by a bracket, then by a siglum (or sigla) identifying the text(s) in which it occurs, and then by the variant reading(s) of the remaining texts and their sigla. A substantive variant shared by more than one text appears here in the form (the 'accidentals') that it takes in the copy-text or, otherwise, in the earliest one recorded. A separate list (below) records emendations of accidentals.

Formal conventions and appurtenances of the documents – such as Conrad's signatures, serial bylines, editorial headings, and instalment statements – are ignored unless they bear upon variants otherwise being reported, as are differences in typography and styling (see the 'Preface', p. xii). Excluded in the same way, and with the same proviso, are impossible word forms created by mere typographical errors as well as those containing unreadable or uncertain characters (usually an original typewritten text that has been blotted during revision). Also not reported as such are legitimate variants in word forms, including abbreviations.

Reports on major variation, usually in the preprinting or serial texts, employ two special symbols. First, the abbreviation OM appears when one or more texts lacks the entire passage in which occur those words that are the subject of the note. Second, when such a passage is present in a text, but in a version different from that in the other texts reported (owing, for instance, to general revision or recasting), the abbreviation VAR shows that the context for that reading is variant.

Emendations are recorded in entries headed by page–line citations in bold-face. Lower-case letters immediately follow page–line citations when lemmas occur in the same line. The paragraph symbol (¶) indicates the beginning of a new paragraph. Three unspaced dots (...) mean the note omits one or more words in a series, whereas spaced dots (. . .) represent those that actually appear in the text(s). An asterisk (*) represents an unreadable character in an early text. A vertical stroke (|) marks the break between lines. The en-rule appears between sigla when three or more texts in sequence agree in a given reading; when all subsequent texts agree, no siglum follows the en-rule (e.g., TSr–). The symbol ED identifies readings adopted for the first time in this edition – that is, not present in the texts collated. Cross-references to entries in the 'Notes' that discuss an instance of variation appear in italic (i.e., *n*), as do editorial statements, which are enclosed in square brackets.

Listed in sequence below their headings are the sigla used for the prefaces and for the chapters of *A Personal Record* as well as the collated texts they represent. Those for the following are not repeated, because throughout they are uniform:

E1   first English edition (Nash, 1912)
  E1ᴾ   unrevised page proofs of **E1** typesetting, October 1911 (BL Ashley 469 and Colgate)
A1   first American edition (Harper, 1912)
E2   second English edition (Nelson, 1916)
A2   second American edition (Doubleday 'Deep Sea', 1917)
E3   third English edition (Dent, 1919)
A3   third American edition (Doubleday collected, Sun-Dial, 1921)
  A3a   first state of **A3**, American Sun-Dial and all British issues (1923–)
  A3b   second state of **A3**, Concord and subsequent American issues (1923–)
E4   fourth English edition (Heinemann collected, 1921)

Author's Note

TS1   ribbon-copy typescript (Princeton), final text: copy-text
TS2   ribbon-copy typescript (Berg), transcription of TS1 as revised, with additional corrections and revisions from **TS2c** copied in by Lilian M. Hallowes
  TS2ct carbon-copy typescript (Princeton), transcription of TS1 as revised, typewritten text
  TS2cr carbon-copy typescript (Princeton), transcription of TS1 as revised, with additional corrections and revisions in Conrad's hand
C   *Notes on My Books* (Doubleday, 1921; Heinemann, 1921), pp. 87–99

3.2   a new form] **TS1 TS2 TS2cr**– this edition **TS2ct**
3.3   another] **E3**– a **TS1–TS2cr**
3.5   statements about] **TS1 TS2 TS2cr**– references to **TS2ct**
3.14 commented upon] **TS1 TS2 TS2cr**– brought out **TS2ct**
3.16a those] **TS1–TS2cr** these **E3**–
3.16b comments] **TS1 TS2 TS2cr**– references **TS2ct**
3.27 two first] **TS1–TS2cr** first two **E3**–
3.28 Cunninghame] **TS2ct C**– Cuninghame **TS1 TS2 TS2cr E3**
3.29 An] **TS2 C A3 E4** The **TS1 TS2ct TS2cr E3**
3.33 delighted] **E3**– very delighted **TS1–TS2cr**
4.6   truths even] **TS1 TS2 TS2cr**– truths **TS2ct**
4.8a this] **TS2 E3**– that **TS1 TS2ct TS2cr**
4.8b have] **TS2 C A3** had **TS1 TS2ct–E3 E4**

4.9   and I] **TS2**– and I I **TS1**
4.16a was] **E3**– being **TS1–TS2cr**
4.16b them] **E3**– the topics **TS1–TS2cr**
4.17a my new] **TS1 TS2cr** my **TS2**–
4.17b away with him] **TS1 TS2 TS2cr**– away **TS2ct**
4.22 nothing else] **TS2 E3**– that **TS1 TS2ct TS2cr**
4.25 meant to say] **TS1 TS2 TS2cr**– said **TS2ct**
4.29a This] ED – this **TS1** was **TS2ct** This, **TS2 TS2cr**–
4.29b was] **TS1 TS2 TS2cr**– OM **TS2ct**
4.30 told] **E3**– had to tell **TS1–TS2cr**
4.34 as well] **TS2 E3**– so well **TS1 TS2ct TS2cr**
4.36 writer] **TS2 E3**– writer whom **TS1 TS2ct TS2cr**
4.37 and] **TS1 TS2 TS2cr**– a d **TS2ct**
5.2   inherent] **TS1 TS2 TS2cr**– a*e***e **TS2ct**

5.9–10   too mysterious] **TS1 TS2**
           TS2cr– very difficult **TS2ct**

5.10   The task] **TS1 TS2 TS2cr**–
           I have an idea that it **TS2ct**

5.12   exulting] **TS1 TS2 TS2cr**–
           mysterious **TS2ct**

5.13   emotional] **TS1 TS2**
           TS2cr– mental **TS2ct**

5.15a   dreadful] **TS1 TS2 TS2cr**–
           OM **TS2ct**

5.15b   falls] **TS1 TS2 TS2cr**– lies
           TS2ct

5.15c   the very flame of our] **TS1**
           TS2 TS2cr– our **TS2ct**

5.17   discovery] **TS1 TS2 TS2cr**–
           gift **TS2ct**

5.19   life-long] **TS2cr TS2 E3** life
           long **TS1** sort of anxious
           TS2ct lifelong **C A3 E4**

5.25   All I can claim] **TS1 TS2**
           TS2cr– Yet **TS2ct**

5.25–6 the accumulated] **TS2 E3**–
           all the remembered **TS1**
           TS2ct TS2cr

5.27a   is] **TS1 TS2 TS2cr**– I think
           I may claim **TS2ct**

5.27b   say] **TS1 TS2 TS2cr**–^ay
           TS2ct

5.33   was receiving] **E3**– received
           TS1–TS2cr

5.34–35   their ... has] **TS1 TS2**
           TS2cr– in their interest
           and sympathy which I may
           truly call unfailing much
           has been **TS2ct**

5.35   much] **TS1 TS2 TS2cr**– OM
           TS2ct

5.37   Sclavonism] **TS1–A3**
           Slavonism **E4**

5.39   restraints] **TS1 TS2 TS2cr**–
           obligations **TS2ct**

6.1   had received] **TS2 TS2cr**–
           received **TS1 TS2ct**

6.2a   historically,] **TS1 TS2ct**
           historically, had **TS2**
           TS2cr–

6.2b   always remained] **TS2**–
           remained always **TS1**

6.6a   rights] **TS2**– right **TS1**

6.6b   the unprivileged] **TS1 TS2**
           TS2cr– he unprivileged
           TS2ct

6.7a   grounds] **TS1–TS2cr E3**
           ground **C**–

6.7b   grounds] **TS1–E3** ground
           C–

6.7c   simple fellowship] **TS1 TS2**
           TS2cr– a simple solidarity
           TS2ct

6.8   reciprocity of services] **TS1**
           TS2 TS2cr– obligation
           TS2ct

6.11   removed as far] **TS1 TS2**
           TS2cr– as far removed
           TS2ct

6.12   crazy] **TS1 TS2 TS2cr**–
           weak **TS2ct**

6.14   tried] **TS1 TS2 TS2cr**–
           trying **TS2ct**

6.15   by] **TS1 TS2 TS2cr**–
           ascribed them possibly to
           TS2ct

6.15–16   in his own words,] **TS1 TS2**
           TS2cr– OM **TS2ct**

6.16–17   less applicable] **TS1 TS2cr**
           more inapplicable **TS2**
           TS2ct E3–

6.18   indifferent to the] **TS1 TS2**
           TS2cr– much above all
           TS2ct

6.21   Those] **TS1** These **TS2ct**–

6.24   concerned] **TS1 TS2**
           TS2cr– active **TS2ct**

6.26–27   subversion] **TS1 TS2**
           TS2cr– success **TS2ct**

6.27   scheme] **TS1 TS2 TS2cr**–
           theory **TS2ct**

6.29   could not] **TS2 TS2cr**–
           cannot **TS1 TS2ct**

6.31   of my past] **E3**– OM
           TS1–TS2cr

6.32   father's] **TS2**– fathers **TS1**

6.40   nothing ... knowledge] **TS1**
           TS2 TS2cr– that feeling
           TS2ct

7.8   My father] **TS2 TS2cr**– He
           TS1 TS2ct

7.9a   is] **TS1–C** was **A3 E4**

7.9b	him] **TS2 TS2cr**– my father **TS1 TS2ct**
7.10a	so much] **TS2 TS2cr**– OM **TS1 TS2ct**
7.10b	as] **TS2 TS2cr**– but **TS1 TS2ct**
7.11	affected] **TS1 TS2 TS2cr**– struck **TS2ct**
7.17a	the existence of] **E3**– that the library had **TS1–TS2cr**
7.17b	especially of] **E3**– especially **TS1–TS2cr**
7.31	an eloquent] **TS1 TS2 TS2cr**– a magnificent **TS2ct**
7.33a	The political] **TS1 TS2 TS2cr**– And another **TS2ct**
7.33b	was] **TS2 TS2cr**– he was **TS1** *** **TS2ct**
8.1	Memoirs] **TS1 TS2 TS2cr**– Memoirs of a certain distinguished man **TS2ct**
8.4	on] **TS1 TS2 TS2cr**– OM **TS2ct**
8.6a	is] **TS2**– OM **TS1**
8.6b	one room] **TS1 TS2 TS2cr**– a room i^ **TS2ct**
8.7a	drawing-room] **TS2**– the drawing-room **TS1**
8.7b	its] **TS2 TS2cr**– the **TS1 TS2ct**
8.11	it] **TS2**– it its **TS1**
8.18	thirty yet] **TS1–C** yet thirty **A3 E4**
8.20	mention] **TS1–E3 A3 E4** mentioned **C**
8.23	deadly] **E3**– mortal **TS1–TS2cr**
8.26	and] **TS1 TS2 TS2cr**– OM **TS2ct**
8.29–30	J. C.	1919] **TS2–TS2cr E4** OM **TS1** world. 1919.	J. C. **E3–A3**

A Familiar Preface

MS holograph manuscript (Berg), final text: copy-text
C *Notes on My Books* (Doubleday, 1921; Heinemann, 1921), pp. 100–16

11.1	A Familiar] **E1**– OM **MS**
11.7	really] **E1**– OM **MS**
11.7–8	It … must! …] **E1**– OM **MS**
11.9a	a word] **E1**– that word **MS**
11.9b	He who wants] **E1**– If you want **MS**
11.10	should put his] **E1**– put your **MS**
11.11	been always] **MS** always been **E1**–
11.12	by way] **E1**– in a spirit **MS**
11.14a	I mean, as] **E1**– in the sense of **MS**
11.14b	had] **MS** has **E1**–
11.15	On … see] **E1**– But only look at **MS**
11.17a	more] **E1**– others **MS**
11.17b	They … seek.] **E1**– OM **MS**
11.18	two] **E1**– two alone **MS**
11.19	sound alone] **E1**– very sound **MS**
11.20	dry … fabric] **E1**– very ground of our social existence **MS**
11.21	course] **E1**– course there is **MS**
11.21–22	must be attended to] **E1**– too **MS**
11.23	the tender] **E1**– tender **MS**
11.24	an absent-minded] **E1**– a dreamy **MS**
11.25–26	Mathematics command … but] **E1 E2 E3 A3a E4** and besides **MS** Mathematics commands … but **A1 A2 C A3b**
11.26a	no use for] **E1**– a distaste for all **MS**
11.26b	Give] **E1**– But give **MS**
11.31	poured out aloud] **E1**– uttered **MS**

11.33	good] **E1**– use **MS**		13.7–8	never wrote] **E1**– has never written **MS**
11.33–	I believe there are men]		13.8	for print] **E1**– OM **MS**
12.1	**E1**– Men there are **MS**		13.11	regrets, and] **E1**– regrets **MS**
12.2a	For myself,] **E1**– But **MS**			
12.2b	such] **E1**– much **MS**		13.12	hands] **E1**– craft **MS**
12.3	who is] **E1**– who's **MS**		13.15–16	have never ...
12.5	to be heard] **E1**– OM **MS**			recommended] **E1 E2 E3 E4** haven't even understood them very well **MS** have never ... recommend **A1 A2 C A3**
12.7	He] **E1**– for he **MS**			
12.8	on ivory tablets] **E1**– OM **MS**			
12.10a	sayings] **E1**– utterances **MS**			
12.10b	I remember] **E1**– he left us **MS**		13.17a	its men] **E1**– men **MS**
			13.17b	remain] **E1**– am **MS**
12.13	jot down] **E1**– give **MS**		13.18–19	shape ... shades] **E1**– form **MS**
12.14–15	not heroic:] **E1**– OM **MS**			
12.20	for my self-esteem,] **E1**– it is for me **MS**		13.19	a question] **E1**– question **MS**
12.23	praiseworthy] **E1**– OM **MS**		13.21	but] **E1**– and if so **MS**
12.27	either amongst] **MS E1 E2** among [amongst = **E3 E4**] either **A1 A2**–		13.22	the surroundings] **E1**– these surroundings **MS**
			13.23	towards] **MS E1 E2 E3 C E4** toward **A1 A2 A3**
12.29	Almost all] ED Most | almost all my **MS** Most, almost all, **E1**–		13.25	elation] **E1**– delight **MS**
			13.26	the call] **E1**– a call **MS**
12.32–33	happenings] **E1**– events **MS**		13.31	from them by the] **E1**– by the to them **MS**
12.33	people.] **E1**– people. They live with his own authentic life and with no other. **MS**		13.33	through] **E1**– by **MS**
			13.34	to be] **E1**– OM **MS**
			13.40	also] **E1**– OM **MS**
12.34	But] **E1**– Yet **MS**		14.1	creatures] **E1**– creations **MS**
12.35	veil] **E1**– veil | the veil woven from the stuff of his own imagination, **MS**			
			14.5a	one's] **E1**– ones **MS**
12.37a	In] **E1**– But in **MS**		14.5b	only] **E1**– OM **MS**
12.37b	veil.] **E1**– veil. The figure stands forth—disclosed. **MS**		14.8	prepared] **E1**– prepared in consequence **MS**
			14.10a	not] **E1**– not naturaly [*sic*] **MS**
12.38a	a passage] **E1**– that passage **MS**			
12.38b	"Imitation of Christ"] **E1**– Imitation **MS**		14.10b	some] **E1**– one **MS**
			14.10c	other] **E1**– another **MS**
13.1–2	is the danger incurred by] **E1**– certainly is a danger for **MS**		14.11	spectator] **E1**– spectators **MS**
			14.12	onwards] **MS E1 E2 E3** onward **A1 A2 C A3**
13.4	While] **E1**– Already while **MS**			
			14.13	of a little insight] ED a | of so much | little **MS** of so much insight as can be **E1**–
13.5	such writing] **E1**– it **MS**			
13.6	volumes] **E1**– work **MS**			
13.7	Indeed,] **E1**– I did not see the force of that objection | And indeed **MS**		14.14	a voice] **E1**– terms **MS**
			14.15	It seems to me that] **E1**– Yet **MS**

14.15–16 criticism] **E1**– criticims
[*sic*] it seems to me that **MS**

14.16 unemotional] **ED**
unemotional grim **MS**
unemotional, grim **E1**–

14.17a of what] **E1**– what **MS**

14.17b Fifteen] **E1**– Sixteen **MS**

14.19 that] **E1**– the **MS**

14.22a in the] **E1**– on the **MS**

14.22b public] **E1**– OM **MS**

14.23–24 it amounted to a charge at
all] **E1**– there is a charge
MS

14.24–25 terms, in a tone of regret]
E1– and almost friendly
terms **MS**

14.26 My answer is] **E1**– I can
answer **MS**

14.33 either of] **MS E1 E2 E4** of
either **A1 A2 C A3**

14.34 should] **E1**– when **MS**

14.35a be] **E1**– is **MS**

14.35b should] **E1**– when **MS**

14.35c fail] **E1**– fails **MS**

14.36 then it must perish
unavoidably in] **E1**– men it
runs unavoidably against
MS

14.37 a] **E1**– such a **MS**

14.38 dare] **E1 A1 E2 A2 C A3a**
can **MS** dare to **E3** dares to
E4 dares **A3b**

15.4 it is] **E1**– it **MS**

15.7 weaknesses] **E1**– the
weaknesses **MS**

15.9 other] **E1**– other
antagonistic yet united **MS**

15.10 mysterious] **E1**– vast **MS**

15.11 ocean] **E1**– sea **MS**

15.11–12 supreme hopes] **E1**– hope
MS

15.12a and still] **E1**– OM **MS**

15.12b distant] **E1**– very **MS**

15.12c the] **E1**– an **MS**

15.14a I] **E1**– no doubt I **MS**

15.14b giving] **E1**– giving me **MS**

15.18 own] **MS E1 E2 E3 E4** OM
A1 A2 C A3

15.21 anything of the sort] **E1**–
this **MS**

15.22 lay claim] **E1**– pretend **MS**

15.22–23 because ... distrust] **E1**–**A2**
C A3 in my dislike and
distrust **MS** and distrust **E3**
E4

15.23 a transaction] **ED**
transaction **MS**
transactions **E1**–

15.24 thing] **E1**– thing that is **MS**

15.26a that full] **E1**– the full **MS**

15.26b myself which] **E1**– myself.
This **MS**

15.28 existence.] **E1**– existence.
Yes! **MS**

15.29 word] **E1**– word of
imaginative literature for
MS

15.30 over] **E1**– OM **MS**

15.32 act] **E1**– OM **MS**

15.32–33 imperfect in the eyes of
the] **E1**– suspect to the
whole **MS**

15.34–35 wins friends for himself]
E1– endears himself to his
friends **MS**

15.36 never] **E1**– neither **MS**

15.37a or] **E1**– nor yet **MS**

15.37b for] **E1**– to **MS**

15.40a consider] **E1**– look at **MS**

15.40b tranquil mind] **E1**– more
tranquil eye **MS**

15.40c proceed] **E1**– will proceed
MS

16.1a declare] **E1**– say **MS**

16.1b I have always suspected in]
E1– it had always seemed
to me that **MS**

16.2 the debasing] **E1**– can not
succed [*sic*] without a little
MS

16.3 deliberately] **E1**– OM **MS**

16.4 normal] **E1**– OM **MS**

16.6 raises] **E1**– must raise **MS**

16.8a lies in] **E1**– is that **MS**

16.8b becoming] **E1**– may
become **MS**

16.9 losing] **E1**– lose **MS**

16.10 coming] **E1**– come **MS**

16.11a good] **E1**– true **MS**

16.11b insistent] **E1**– facile **MS**

16.14–15 you can't in sound morals] E1– in sound morals you can't **MS**

16.15 for taking] **MS** E1 A1 E2 A2 E3 A3 E4 taking **C**

16.16a his clear] E1– a clear **MS**

16.16b you can] **MS** E1 E2 E3 E4 can you A1 A2 **C** A3

16.20–21 within bounds] E1– straight **MS**

16.21 then] E1– om **MS**

16.23 besides – this, remember,] E1– then – this **MS**

16.25a that] **MS** which E1–

16.25b upwards] **MS** E1 E2 E3 E4 upward A1 A2 **C** A3

16.30 such a mad presumption] E1– so very mad **MS**

16.32 this ... appeal] E1–A2 A3 it in **MS** this ... appeals E3 E4

16.33 A historian] **MS** E1ᴾ A1 A2 An historian E1 E2 E3–

16.33–4 a historian] **MS** E1ᴾ A1 A2 an historian E1 E2 E3–

16.34 further] E1– deeper **MS**

16.35 to reach] E1– om **MS**

16.36 deserves] E1– provokes **MS**

16.38 and of] E1– and **MS**

16.39 a grin] E1– mockery **MS**

17.5 being certain] E1– knowing **MS**

17.12 is] E1– is expressed or at least **MS**

17.14 my conviction] E1– that I believe **MS**

17.15 a few very] E1– very few **MS**

17.16a It] E1– I **MS**

17.16b amongst [among = A1 A2 **C** A3] others] E1– om **MS**

17.19 writings.] E1– writing. I haven't got the spirit. **MS**

17.24 claim to] E1– pretence of **MS**

17.25 anger from] E1 E2 E3 A3 E4 suspicion of **MS** danger from A1 A2 **C**

17.27 trying to] E1– trying **MS**

17.30 the days] E1– om **MS**

17.32 them] E1– it **MS**

17.34 They, too,] E1– While appearing serially they themselves **MS**

17.39 Could I] E1– was I to **MS**

18.1 have robbed the statement] E1– rob it **MS**

18.4a fatuous] E1– unkind **MS**

18.4b scandalous] E1– even only scandalous **MS**

18.5 This] E1– It **MS**

18.6a it] E1– om **MS**

18.6b put forward] E1– state **MS**

18.8 Those] **MS** These E1–

18.9–10 he said] E1– om **MS**

18.11 admit] E1– admitted **MS**

18.12–13 But ... these] E1– Yet those **MS**

18.14–15 conventions have not been] E1– formulas were not **MS**

18.15 system and purpose] E1– intention **MS**

18.16 reading] E1– text **MS**

18.17a there may emerge] E1– more consecutive indeed than they may appear there will **MS**

18.17b the vision] E1– disengage itself a vision **MS**

18.18 fundamentally] E1– om **MS**

18.20 This] E1– That **MS**

18.21a closely associated] E1– insolubly connected **MS**

18.21b is to] E1– was to **MS**

18.22a personal memories by] E1– humble personal experience in **MS**

18.22b the feelings] E1– my feelings **MS**

18.23 the writing of] E1– om **MS**

18.24 with my] E1– my **MS**

18.25–26 In ... accord.] E1– om **MS**

18.27 J. C. K.] E1–E3 E4 J. C. **C** A3 om **MS**

A Personal Record

MS   holograph manuscript, single leaf of Chapter 6, 1909 (Syracuse):
copy-text for 101.12–23

S   serialization, *English Review* (Duckworth), December 1908 – June 1909:
copy-text for Chapters 2–7 (with exceptions as noted for **MS** and **S^Pr3**)

S^Pu1   unrevised proofs of Chapter 1, **S** typesetting, 1908 (HRHRC)

S^Pr1   revised proofs of Chapter 1, **S** typesetting, 1908 (HRHRC): copy-text for
Chapter 1

S^Pu3   unrevised proofs of Chapter 3, **S** typesetting, 1908, facsimile in Violet
Hunt, *The Flurried Years* (1926), p. 32

S^Pr3   revised proofs of Chapter 3, **S** typesetting, 1908, facsimile in Hunt, *The
Flurried Years*, p. 32: copy-text for 67.35–68.21

19.3	Verbal] **S^Pr1**– and **S^Pu1**	19.28	water-cock] **S^Pr1**–
19.4	may enter] **S^Pr1**– comes as easily into **S^Pu1**		water-cock a tin we had secured from the steward for the purpose **S^Pu1**
19.5a	and since] **S^Pr1**– as in the open air of a hillside or the roofed, sighing temple of a wood. Since **S^Pu1**	19.28–30	my young friend] **S^Pr1**– he **S^Pu1**
		20.5	a while] **S^Pu1–A3** awhile **E4**
19.5b	are] **S^Pr1**– may be **S^Pu1**	20.6	scrutiny] **S^Pr1**– scrutiny he **S^Pu1**
19.6	humble] **S^Pr1**– the pious **S^Pu1**	20.12	words] **S^Pr1**– ominous words **S^Pu1**
19.7	imagined] **E1**– believed **S^Pu1** fancied **S^Pr1 S**	20.12–13	the ominous oncoming] **S^Pr1**– their setting **S^Pu1**
19.8	amongst] **S^Pu1–E1 E2 E3**– among **A1 A2**	20.13	night] **S^Pr1**– vision **S^Pu1**
19.9a	decks] **S^Pu1**– docks **A1 A2**	20.17	impatience] **S^Pr1**– impatience with time **S^Pu1**
19.9b	2000-ton] **E1**– 3000-ton **S^Pu1–S**	**20.21a**	positions] **E1**– positions of second and third officer of a steamer **S^Pu1–S**
19.12	kind] **S^Pr1**– good **S^Pu1**		
19.14a	Was he not, in his] **S^Pr1**– and in the **S^Pu1**	20.21b	entitled to] **S^Pr1**– entitled **S^Pu1**
19.14b	his unworldly] **S**– the unworldly **S^Pu1 S^Pr1**	20.22a	He] **S^Pr1**– And as he **S^Pu1**
19.16	*hills*] **S^Pr1**– *forests* **S^Pu1**	20.22b	banjo and] **S^Pr1**– banjo **S^Pu1**
19.18	tracing on the] **S**– writing while standing the pad of **S^Pu1** tracing under **S^Pr1**	**20.29**	The background] **E1**– As a background a range **S^Pu1** A background **S^Pr1 S**
19.18–19	of a pad which rested] **S^Pr1**– resting **S^Pu1**	**20.31**	The] **E1**– Their **S^Pu1–S**
19.20a	Malayan] **S^Pr1**– Malay*an **S^Pu1**	20.37–38	best in the town] **S^Pr1**– very café **S^Pu1**
19.20b	in a] **E1**– surrounded by a **S^Pu1–S**	20.38	and the very one where] **S^Pr1**– where **S^Pu1**
19.20–21	a hallucinated] **S^Pu1–A3** an hallucinated **E4**	20.39	his] **S^Pr1**– his miserably tragic **S^Pu1**
19.27–28	a tin] **S^Pr1**– carefully **S^Pu1**		

21.1a was] **E1**– from descriptive
evidence, I conclude
must have been **SPu1–S**

21.1b in a] **E1**– in its **SPu1–S**

21.1–2 setting of light music]
SPr1– light music setting
SPu1

21.3 recall no more] **E1**– no
more that day recall **SPu1**
no more recall **SPr1 S**

21.4 again. The] **SPr1**– again,
and the **SPu1**

21.24 all white] **SPr1**– white
SPu1

21.25 tangled up] **SPr1**–
intertwined **SPu1**

21.30 aboard] **S**– on board
SPu1 SPr1

21.33 last employment in my
calling] **SPr1**–
employment at sea **SPu1**

21.36 London Shipmasters']
SPr1– Shipmasters' **SPu1**

21.36–37 with ... Street] **SPr1**– OM
SPu1

21.39–40 can hardly] **SPr1**– cannot
SPu1

21.40 Froud] **SPr1**– Froude
SPu1

22.11 he had] **SPr1**– there
existed **SPu1**

22.13–14 very excellent] **SPr1**–
distinguished **SPu1**

22.15 Froud] **SPr1**– Froude
SPu1

22.17 interests] **S**– interest
SPu1 SPr1

22.20 union spirit] **SPr1**– union
SPu1

22.24 In] **SPr1**– And in **SPu1**

22.30 on any] **SPu1–A2** any
E3–

22.32 Froud] **SPr1**– Froude
SPu1

22.35 a crooked] **SPr1**– that
crooked **SPu1**

22.36 is] **SPr1**– are **SPu1**

22.39 motioning ... chair] **E1**–
pointing a chair to me
SPu1–S

23.1 steamship] **E1**– steamer
SPu1–S

23.1–2 more than to be asked]
SPr1– more **SPu1**

23.2 way ...] **SPr1**– way to get
him what he wants **SPu1**

23.6 the captain of that ship] **E1**–
that Captain Patten **SPu1**
the captain of that steamer
SPr1 S

23.9 care] **E1**– care perhaps
SPu1–S

23.11 It] **E1**– I **SPu1–S**

23.14a could] **E1**– would **SPu1–S**

23.14b officer for] **SPr1**– mate of
SPu1

23.15 sign] **E1**– signs **SPu1–S**

23.18 features.] **SPr1**– features.
Use had done it. **SPu1**

23.24 furnished apartments]
SPr1– a house **SPu1**

23.37 these beings seen] **SPr1**–
mankind seem **SPu1**

23.38 demand] **SPr1**– to demand
SPu1

24.5 decayed] **SPr1**– slightly
decayed **SPu1**

24.7 slowly] **E1**– laboriously
SPu1–S

24.8a piety] **SPu1–E1 E2 E3**– pity
A1 A2

24.8b has prompted] **SPu1 SPr1**
prompted **S**–

24.11 Froud] **SPr1**– Froude **SPu1**

24.18 said gravely] **SPr1**– said
SPu1

24.20 it] **S**– the matter **SPu1**
SPr1

24.23 mate] **E1**– mate, Mr.
Paramor, **SPu1–S**

24.24 give me] **SPr1**– give **SPu1**

24.25 second officer] **SPr1**–
second **SPu1**

24.38 cases.] **E1**– cases. These
words seem strictly to apply
to the traffic between
English and Channel ports
and the U. S. seaboard to
the north of Savannah.
SPu1–S

25.2 cause] S^Pr1– reason or cause S^Pu1

25.12 deck-beams] E1– beams S^Pu1–S

25.16 expression] S^Pr1– expression and S^Pu1

25.18a filed] E1– filed, bowed to by me, S^Pu1–S

25.18b monition] S^Pr1– conviction S^Pu1

25.23 towards] S^Pu1–S E1 E2 E3– toward A1 A2

25.36 blushing with shame] S^Pr1– being ashamed, or rather remorseful S^Pu1

26.1 a most] S^Pr1– an S^Pu1

26.4–5 cables up] S^Pr1– cables S^Pu1

26.6 Mr.] S– OM S^Pu1 Mr S^Pr1

26.14 may] S^Pr1– would S^Pu1

26.15 favoured] S^Pr1– would have favoured S^Pu1

26.18 that fateful] S^Pr1– the S^Pu1

26.22–23 Abdullah's (his enemy)] S^Pr1– his enemy, and Abdullah's S^Pu1

26.24 closes] S^Pr1– close S^Pu1

26.29 nine] E1– ten S^Pu1–S

26.33 which are] S– which is S^Pu1 which ** S^Pr1

26.34 will] S^Pu1–S shall E1–

26.37 were] S^Pu1–E2 A2 was E3–

26.40 as] S^Pu1–S as if E1–

27.3 more] S^Pr1– much more S^Pu1

27.7 had] S^Pr1– has S^Pu1

27.8 failed in being] S^Pr1– might have been S^Pu1

27.13 more or less alive] S^Pr1– all right S^Pu1

27.16a where] S^Pr1– where certainly S^Pu1

27.16b departure] S^Pr1– arrival S^Pu1

27.17a that] S^Pu1–S which E1–

27.17b was] S^Pr1– was going S^Pu1

27.25a of] S^Pu1 S^Pr1 of the S–

27.25b a waterside] S^Pr1– the waterside S^Pu1

27.28 end.] S^Pr1– end, for S^Pu1

27.29 nothing] S^Pr1– nothing then S^Pu1

27.30 like] E1– as if it were S^Pu1–S

27.39 my] S^Pr1– that the S^Pu1

27.40a infinitely the moment] S^Pr1– in strength as soon as S^Pu1

27.40b will believe in it] S^Pr1– can be found to share it S^Pu1

28.1 conviction] S^Pr1– conviction in the reality S^Pu1

28.2 clearer] S^Pr1– stronger S^Pu1

28.3a and] S^Pr1– and the exciting vividness of a dream dreamed to the very end in its illogical and deeply moving sequence, S^Pu1

28.3b selected episodes] S^Pr1– detail S^Pu1

28.4 pride of documentary] S^Pr1– futile logic of authentic S^Pu1

28.5 Congo rapids] S^Pr1– river S^Pu1

28.12a reading] S^Pu1–E1 E2 E3– in reading A1 A2

28.12b had asked] S^Pu1–S asked E1–

28.14 Gibbon's "History."] E1– the famous chapter xiii. of Gibbon's History. S^Pu1–S

28.22 unassuming] S^Pr1– unassuring S^Pu1

28.24 undistinguished] S^Pr1– commonplace S^Pu1

28.28 tale] S^Pr1– story S^Pu1

28.36 subdued] S^Pr1– still subdued S^Pu1

28.39 farthest] S^Pu1–S A1 A2 furthest E1 E2 E3–

29.4 silence. He] E1– silence and he S^Pu1–S

29.8 I turned] S^Pr1– This done I turned S^Pu1

29.12a his] E1– a S^Pu1–S

29.12b veiled] E1– slightly veiled S^Pu1–S

29.17　on] S^{Pu1}–S upon E1–

29.18　as] S^{Pr1}–E1 E2 E3– as if S^{Pu1} A1 A2

29.20　40] S^{Pu1}–E3 A3a 40° A3b E4

29.29　Aha] S^{Pr1}– Ah S^{Pu1}

29.30　blow coming on] S^{Pr1}– gale S^{Pu1}

29.33　quite] E1– perfectly S^{Pu1}–S

29.40　whilst] S^{Pu1}–E1 E2 E3– while A1 A2

30.1　arrived in] S^{Pu1}–E2 A2 arrived at E3 A3 E4

30.2　suddenly] S^{Pr1}– unexpectedly S^{Pu1}

30.16　had been] S^{Pu1}–S was E1–

30.17　each other] S^{Pu1}–E1 E2 E3– one another A1 A2

30.19　One – one] S^{Pr1}– one S^{Pu1}

30.25　wash-tub] S^{Pr1}– tub S^{Pu1}

30.29　consent to write without] S^{Pr1}– be content to work with less than S^{Pu1}

30.35a　to Ukraine] S^{Pu1}–A2 Ukraine E3–

30.35b　On] S^{Pr1}– It was S^{Pu1}

30.35c　morning] S^{Pr1}– morning when S^{Pu1}

30.36　in a hurry] S^{Pr1}– and in a hurry S^{Pu1}

30.37a　rescued] S^{Pr1}– reserved S^{Pu1}

30.37b　Yet] S^{Pr1}– But S^{Pu1}

31.2　once to] E1– to the S^{Pu1}–S

31.3　a chair] S^{Pu1}–E1 E2 E3– the chair A1 A2

31.5　paternal acres] S^{Pr1}– a large scale S^{Pu1}

31.8　might] S^{Pr1}– may S^{Pu1}

31.18　towards] S^{Pu1}–E1 E2 E3– toward A1 A2

31.21　were always written] S^{Pr1}– always S^{Pu1}

31.22　received from that house] S^{Pu1}–S from that house received E1–

31.23　inn] S^{Pr1}– hotel S^{Pu1}

31.24　servant,] S^{Pr1}– Uhlan S^{Pu1}

31.32　travelling costume of] S^{Pr1} S a travelling costume of E1– OM S^{Pu1}

31.33　coat] S^{Pr1}– fur coat S^{Pu1}

31.35　moustachioed] S^{Pu1}–E1 E2 E3– mustached A1 A2

31.37　shade] S^{Pr1}– measure S^{Pu1}

32.2　He ... language.] E1– OM S^{Pu1}–S

32.6　our Master's nephew] S^{Pr1}– Captain Kurzaniosk S^{Pu1}

32.8a　age yet] S^{Pu1}–S age E1 A1

32.8b　had] S^{Pr1}– had indeed S^{Pu1}

32.8c　delightful boyish] S^{Pr1}– boyish S^{Pu1}

32.11a　side] S^{Pr1}– side in the sledge S^{Pu1}

32.11b　The sledge] S^{Pr1}– It S^{Pu1}

32.13　big bays] E1– horses S^{Pu1} bays S^{Pr1} S

32.14a　He] E1– This last S^{Pu1}–S

32.14b　with] S^{Pr1}– with a fair moustache and S^{Pu1}

32.16　level with the top of] S^{Pr1}– well above S^{Pu1}

32.19a　will] S^{Pu1}–S shall E1–

32.19b　manage] S^{Pr1}– arrange S^{Pu1}

32.19c　His] S^{Pr1}– The S^{Pu1}

32.20　providing] S^{Pr1}– providing if S^{Pu1}

32.24　amongst] S^{Pu1} S^{Pr1}– among A1 A2

32.25　the horses] E3– his horses S^{Pu1}–A2

32.26　suppose] S^{Pu1}–E3 E4 supposed A3

32.36　epidemic] S^{Pu1}–E1 E2 E3– epidemic that A1 A2

32.39　reposing in] S^{Pr1}– in S^{Pu1}

33.5a　that fell] S^{Pu1}–S which fell E1–

33.5b　till] E1– till suddenly S^{Pu1}–S

33.8　interminable] E1– park S^{Pu1} garden S^{Pr1} S

33.13–14　affectedly] S^{Pu1}–E1 E2 E3– affectionately A1 A2

33.14　awaiting] E1– waiting for S^{Pu1}–S

33.17	won't have] **E1**– will have not **S^{P}u1–S**
33.18–19	borrowed ... peasants] **S^{P}r1**– OM **S^{P}u1**
33.20	in a] **E1**– of a **S^{P}u1**
33.23	other. I invaded] **S^{P}r1**– other, I into **S^{P}u1**
33.26	many] **S^{P}r1**– innumerable **S^{P}u1**
33.27	families] **S^{P}r1**– stock **S^{P}u1**
33.28	1860] **S^{P}r1**– 1862 **S^{P}u1**
33.30	One or two] **S^{P}r1**– Some of them, of course, **S^{P}u1**
33.33–34	general] **S^{P}r1**– a general **S^{P}u1**
33.35	colonnade] **S^{P}r1**– sort of colonnade **S^{P}u1**
33.37	attached] **S^{P}r1**– affected **S^{P}u1**
34.8	left] **S^{P}r1**– left behind **S^{P}u1**
34.9	great world] **S^{P}r1**– world **S^{P}u1**
34.11	three months'] **E1 E2 E3**– six-months' **S^{P}u1** four-months' **S^{P}r1–E1^P A1 A2**
34.15	commanding] **S^{P}r1**– severe **S^{P}u1**
34.16	gathering] **S^{P}r1**– concourse **S^{P}u1**
34.18	paying ... in] **S^{P}r1**– filling **S^{P}u1**
34.19	a few] **S^{P}r1**– in a few short **S^{P}u1**
34.26a	period] **S^{P}r1**– six months **S^{P}u1**
34.26b	existence] **S^{P}r1**– life **S^{P}u1**
34.27	delightful quick tempered] **S^{P}r1**– delightful **S^{P}u1**
34.29	fifteenth] **S^{P}r1**– seventeenth **S^{P}u1**
34.30a	many] **S^{P}r1**– most **S^{P}u1**
34.30b	not a few] **S^{P}r1**– many **S^{P}u1**
34.31	oppressive shadow] **S^{P}r1**– shadow **S^{P}u1**
34.33a	new-born national] **S^{P}r1**– national **S^{P}u1**
34.33b	hatred] **S^{P}r1**– hatred that was **S^{P}u1**

34.34	the Poles] **S^{P}r1**– us Poles **S^{P}u1**
34.36	but] **E1**– and yet **S^{P}u1–S**
34.38	egotism] **S^{P}r1**– vanity **S^{P}u1**
34.39a	It] **S^{P}r1**– And perhaps it **S^{P}u1**
34.39b	more] **S^{P}r1**– else **S^{P}u1**
34.40	colours] **S^{P}r1**– mere colours **S^{P}u1**
35.4	unconscious response] **S^{P}r1**– response **S^{P}u1**
35.10	towards] **S^{P}u1–E1 E2 E3**– toward **A1 A2**
35.12	the emotions] **S^{P}r1**– to the emotions **S^{P}u1**
37.19–20	the village] **S–E2 A2** a village **E3**–
37.20	outside the gates] **E1**– at the five-barred gate **S**
37.21	snow-track;] **E1**– snow-track, for out of the great outside silence **S**
37.27	but] **E1**– yet **S**
38.13	yesterday.] **E1**– yesterday. ¶He went away – vanished quickly, seeing that all the unpacking was done. He wore a modest grey livery with heraldic buttons; and this amused me for the moment, because for very many years I had not had anybody about me with heraldic buttons. These buttons were a sort of familiar novelty. And the heraldry was familiar also though I had not seen the emblem for many years too, except as stamped very small and faint at the head of my uncle's letters – of these messages full of wisdom, good humour and affection which had been following me all round this watery globe of ours, salt and bitter as if three-parts submerged in tears. **S**

38.15	dogs in the village] **E1**– raised by the village dogs **S**	**43.10b** 43.24	character] **E1**– manner **S** &c. &c.] **S E1 E2 E3**– etc. **A1 A2**
38.26	our uncle] **S E1 E2 E3**– your uncle **A1 A2**	**44.5**	Thus] **E1**– Thus may **S**
39.27	round] **S E1 E2** around **A1** **A2 E3**–	**44.6** **44.30**	may] **E1**– OM **S** charm] **E1**– secret **S**
39.28	who] **E1**– yet who **S**	**44.39**	Nevertheless] **E1**– But all
40.3a	were] **E1**– spent no less than **S**	45.14	the same **S** afterwards] **S E1 E2 E3**–
40.3b	Both] **E1**– As the hours passed both **S**	**45.37**	afterward **A1 A2** the unexpected] **E1**–
40.6	afterwards] **S E1 E2 E3**– afterward **A1 A2**		presence of that unexpected **S**
40.17	afterwards] **S E1 E2 E3**– afterward **A1 A2**	46.1	a hotel] **S A1 A2** an hotel **E1 E2 E3**–
40.18a	inflammation] **E1 E2 E3**– an inflammation **S E1ᵖ A1** **A2**	46.26	uncurtained] **S E1 E2 E3**– curtained **A1 A2**
40.18b	set in] **E1**– declared itself **S**	**46.27a**	a bunch] **E1**– bunches **S**
40.19	away] **E1**– OM **S**	**46.27b**	above each ear] **E1**– OM **S**
40.29	brusquely] **S E1 E2 E3**– bruskly **A1** briskly **A2**	47.4 47.5	Scotch] **S**–**A3** Scottish **E4** since, both] **S E1 E2 E3**–
41.3	afterwards] **S E1 E2 E3**– afterward **A1 A2**	47.8	OM **A1 A2** reasons] **S E1 E2 E3**–
41.10	seeing] **S**–**A2 A3b E4** seeking **E3 A3a**	**47.13a**	reason **A1 A2** Furka] **ED** Furca **S**–
41.13a	rises] **E1**– falls **S**	**47.13b**	towards] **S E1 E2 E3**–
41.13b	a mist] **S E1 E2 E3**– mist **A1** **A2**	47.17	toward **A1 A2** sat] **E1**– had sat **S**
41.24	his] **E1**– that **S**	47.24	towards] **S E1 E2 E3**–
41.26	compassion] **S**–**E3 E4** companion **A3**	47.36	toward **A1 A2** towards] **S E1 E2 E3**–
41.29– **32**	It ... impressed.] **E1**– I don't know why I should have been so frightfully impressed. It is a good forty years since I first heard the tale, and the effect has not worn off yet. **S**	48.2 48.7 **48.24** **48.26**	toward **A1 A2** saw only] **S**–**A2** only saw **E3**– earnest] **S**–**A3** eager **E4** said] **E1**– says **S** the intention] **E1**– an intention **S**
41.35	fastidious] **E1**– refined **S**	49.7	not only think] **S E1**
42.3	rests] **E1**– is **S**		**E2 E3**– think not only **A1**
42.14	amongst] **S E1 E2 E3**– among **A1 A2**	**49.10**	**A2** my boy] **E1**– brother **S**
43.1	starvation] **E1**– hunger **S**	**49.30**	Rigi] **A3b E4** Righi **S**–**E3**
43.2	revolting] **E1**– dishonouring **S**	**49.34**	**A3a** Furka] **ED** Furca **S**–
43.3	his] **S E1 E2 E3**– the **A1 A2**	50.5	on to] **S E1 E2 E3**– onto **A1**
43.10a	bare patches of] **E1**– in bare patches in **S**	50.13	**A2** wrongs] **S E1 E2 E3**– wrong **A1 A2**

50.19a   Furka] ED Furca S–
50.19b   came] E1– had come S
50.26   Furka] ED Furca S–
50.30   Furka] ED Furca S–
51.5a   on ... me] E1– he bade
          me, on the top of the
          Furca Pass, to S
51.5b   Furka] ED Furca S–
53.4   famished] E1– desolate S
53.9   unfavourable.] E1–
          unfavourable for,
          obviously, S
53.12   upwards] S E1 E2 E3–
          upward A1 A2
54.19   short-lived] E1– OM S
54.22   Leipsic] S–A3 Leipzig E4
54.24   shortly] E1– long S
54.26   amongst] S E1 E2 E3–
          among A1 A2
54.29   only the] A1 A2 the only S
          E1 E2 E3–
54.36   opinion] E1– conviction S
55.7   assumed] E1– affected S
55.8   assumed] E1– affected S
55.12   familial] S–A3 familiar
          E4
55.19   amongst] S E1 E2 E3–
          among A1 A2
55.29–30 during the Hundred
          Days] E1– OM S
57.11   was] E1– were S E1ᴾ
57.25   Carlsbad] S–A3 Karlsbad
          E4
57.32   their best] S E1 E2 E3–
          OM A1 A2
58.12   these] S E1 E2 E3– those
          A1 A2
58.30   the central] E1– a few
          central S
59.18   either against] S E1 E2
          E3– against either A1
          A2
59.20   senior] S the senior E1–
59.27   amongst] S E1 E2 E3–
          among A1 A2
59.35   Astrakhan] E1 E2 E3–
          Astrakan S E1ᴾ A1 A2
60.3–4   these communications]
          E1– them S
60.34   rising] E1– rebellion S

61.1   become the tenant of]
          E1– take on lease S
61.13   a comrade-in-arms] S E1
          E2 E3– comrade-in-arms
          A1 A2
61.34   afterwards] S E1 E2 E3–
          afterward A1 A2
62.18   amongst] S E1 E2 E3–
          among A1 A2
62.38   and] E1– as if S
63.2   amongst] S E1 E2 E3–
          among A1 A2
63.11   on to] S E1 E2 E3– onto
          A1 A2
63.25   window] S–A2 A3 E4
          widow E3
63.27   manner] E1– indifference
          S
64.9   towards] E1 E2 E3– to S
          toward A1 A2
64.12–13 the time] S E1 E2 E3–
          time A1 A2
64.23   eight hundred] ED eight S
          eighty E1–
64.31   their] E1– the S
64.33   not] ED no S–
65.7   By] S E1 E2 E3– But by A1
          A2
65.31   afterwards] S E1 E2 E3–
          afterward A1 A2
66.3   snow-loaded] E1–
          snow-charged S
66.6   slight, rigid] E1– tall,
          bowed S
66.28a   Of all the] E1– In all these
          S
66.28b   towards] S E1 E2 E3–
          toward A1 A2
66.28c   carriage,] E1– carriage, it
          is S
66.29   only] E1– only that S E1ᴾ
67.6   afterwards] S E1 E2 E3–
          afterward A1 A2
67.39   that day] E1– the day
          Sᴾu3–S
68.3   this warning. I] Sᴾr3–
          warning me. Let me Sᴾu3
68.5   travel] Sᴾr3– go Sᴾu3
68.6   back to her husband]
          Sᴾr3– over there Sᴾu3

68.6–7	go – death or no death.] S^{Pr3}– go. Orders S^{Pu3}
68.9a	is] S^{Pr3}– is getting S^{Pu3}
68.9b	Poles] S^{Pr3}– OM S^{Pu3}
68.10a	rebelling] S^{Pu3} S^{Pr3} making trouble S–
68.10b	you] S^{Pr3}– you Poles S^{Pu3}
68.11	there] S^{Pr3}– sitting S^{Pu3}
68.12	gates] S^{Pr3}– gates to wait for our passage S^{Pu3}
68.13	scorn] S^{Pr3}– pitying scorn S^{Pu3}
68.14	conquest for] S^{Pr3} S conquest as S^{Pu3} E_1–
68.18	high] S^{Pr3}– great S^{Pu3}
68.19	official] S^{Pr3}– ruler S^{Pu3}
69.1	IV] S– Chapter Four E_4
69.22a	amongst these] S E_1 E_2 E_3– among those A_1 A_2
69.22b	existences] E_1– existences that S
71.10–11	in early boyhood] E_1– OM S
71.30	than] E_1– then S
71.37a	don't] E_1– do not S
71.37b	afterwards] S E_1 E_2 E_3– afterward A_1 A_2
72.10	of] S E_1 E_2 E_3– for A_1 A_2
72.22	"Two] S– *The Two* E_4
72.23	5s] ED 5s. S–E_2 5s. A_2 five shilling E_3 A_3 five-shilling E_4
73.3a	tracings] S E_1 E_2 E_3– the tracings A_1 A_2
73.3b	Indian] S E_1^P indian E_1 E_2 E_3– India A_1 A_2
73.6	the] E_1– its S
73.8a	is] E_1– was S
73.8b	that effect] E_1– it S
73.20	that] S this E_1–
73.40	burnt] S E_1 E_2 E_3– burned A_1 A_2
74.2–3	a high-pitched roof of grass] E_1– an enormous roof S
74.4	up on] S upon E_1–
74.9	strayed] E_1– hung S
74.12	Pulo Laut] S– Poulo Laut E_4
74.17	Donggala] ED Dongala S Dongola E_1–
74.27	amongst] S E_1 E_2 E_3– among A_1 A_2
74.31	mutter] E_1– sound S
75.13	which] E_1– and this S
75.24	deep-seated] E_1– a certain deep-seated S
75.25	in] S E_1 E_2 E_3– OM A_1 A_2
75.27	don't] S E_1 E_2 E_3– didn't A_1 A_2
75.31	at night] E_1– in the dark S
76.3a	got] E_1– OM S
76.3b	pony] E_1– pony for me S
76.4	he] S–A_2 A_3 I E_3 E_4
76.5	his minor] E_1– a minor S
76.6	hinted] E_1– added S
76.10	believe] S E_1 E_2 E_3– believe in A_1 A_2
76.11	in any] S of any E_1–
76.17	tack] S–A_2 track E_3 A_3 E_4
76.23	an inclement] S inclement E_1–
77.7	spoilt] S E_1 E_2 E_3– spoiled A_1 A_2
77.11	teeth] E_1– the teeth S
77.16	ordered] E_1– shouted to S
77.21	hung on] E_1– hung S
77.26	in pidgin-English] E_1– OM S
77.27	but] E_1– yet S
77.33a	heads;] E_1– heads, but S
77.33b	only] E_1– OM S
77.37	now] E_1– OM S
78.10	knocked together] E_1– hung down S
78.12	which] E_1– that S
78.26	the rope] E_1– it S
78.33	back] E_1– OM S
78.36	flat] E_1– full length S
78.39	had all] S E_1 E_2 E_3 A_{3a} all had A_1 A_2 A_{3b} E_4
79.14	carried it off] E_1– gone with it S
79.16	Donggala] ED Dongala S Dongola E_1–
80.5a	Mr. Almayer's] E_1– Amayer's S
80.5b	on board sir. He told] S Mr. Almayer told E_1

80.6   particularly, sir] **E1–**
particularly **S**

80.10   towards] **S E1 E2 E3–** toward
A1 A2

80.30   near] **E1–** a little past **S**

81.7a   in the fog] **E1–** OM **S**

81.7b   eight-foot deep] **E1ᴾ**
twelve-foot **S** eight-foot-deep
E1–

81.9   just missed going heels over
head] **E1–** nearly fell **S**

81.10   our] **E1–** my **S**

81.12   was] **E1–** got **S**

81.17   I said indignantly] **E1–** OM **S**

81.18   muttered] **E1–** muttered
absently **S**

81.21   verandah] **E1 E2 E3 A3 E4**
verandah, it seemed **S**
veranda **A1 A2**

81.32   young] **S E1 E2 E3–** OM **A1**
A2

82.2   shall] **E1–** can **S**

82.13   resembled] **E1–** seemed **S**

82.18   select] **E1–** look out **S**

82.19   not] **E1–** no **S**

82.34   hurried] **S A1 A2** hurriedly
E1 E2 E3–

82.37   with my captain] **E1–** OM **S**

82.39   that] **S** who **E1–**

83.22   is something] **S E1ᴾ A1–**
something **E1**

83.26   light nor darkness] **E1–**
night nor day **S**

83.38   speech] **E1–** out **S**

83.39a   with] **E1–** OM **S**

83.39b   with] **E1–** OM **S**

84.18   doubt!] **E1–** doubt! We can
only believe and understand
in the terms of our
imperfect credulity and
under the limitations of our
timid intelligence, which is
so often untrue to our
inspiration. **S**

85.19   likely] **S E1 E2 E3–** like **A1**
A2

85.21   in perfunctory] **ED** in a sort
of perfunctory **S** in a
perfunctory **E1–**

86.1   were to] **S** would **E1–**

86.14   either] **S E1 E2 E3–** OM
A1 A2

86.24   straitened] **E1–** unworthy
S

86.26   an obscure] **S** obscure
E1–

86.27   aggrandisement] **E1–**
achieved greatness **S**

86.32   a blank] **S** blank **E1–**

86.35   at last] **E1–** in the last
instance **S**

86.36   where] **E1–** amongst
which **S**

87.10   serenity; to] **E1–** serenity,
S

87.17   distances] **S–A2** distance
E3–

87.22–23   the purely] **S** a purely **E1–**

87.25a   amongst] **S E1 E2 E3–**
among **A1 A2**

87.25b   Even] **E1–** and even **S**

87.27   heart,] **E1–** heart. He **S**

87.29   artist of prose] **ED** prose
artist of **S–**

87.31   imaged] **S E1 E2 E3–**
imagined **A1 A2**

87.32   amongst] **S E1 E2 E3–**
among **A1 A2**

87.37   speaking without] **S E1**
E2 E3– without speaking
A1 A2

87.38   out] **E1–** let out **S**

88.15   amongst] **S E1 E2 E3–**
among **A1 A2**

88.17a   violences] **ED**
high-minded violences,
the upright crimes, **S**
violences, the crimes, **E1–**

88.17b   enthusiasms] **E1–** vain
enthusiasms **S**

88.38   morality.] **E1–** morality.
Moral earnestness in the
absence of imaginative
faculty runs easily into the
terms of murder and
spoliation. The grace of
imagination, which exalts
our feelings, is the only
thing which can soothe

the cruel passion of
conscientious convictions.
The writer hailed as the
Father of the French
Revolution (the husband of
the meek Thérèse was
obviously predestined to
know nothing of his various
children) was not in general
an abundantly blessed
person, and in that respect
he was not blessed at all. **S**

89.18   amongst] **S E1 E2 E3–**
         among **A1 A2**

89.29   will appeal] **S** shall appeal
         E1–

90.21   a world's] **S** the world's **E1–**

90.30   curtseys] **S E1 E2 E3–**
         courtesies **A1 A2**

90.34   wife,] **ED** wife (who does not
         wear stand-up collars), **S**
         wife **E1–**

91.5   whether] **E1–** OM **S**

91.14   humblest] **E1–** humblest
         man **S**

91.17   clouds on] **S E1 E2 E3–**
         clouds in **A1 A2**

91.26   that] **E1–** that last **S**

92.40   burned] **S A1 A2** burnt **E1**
         E2 E3–

94.10   Afterwards] **S E1 E2 E3–**
         Afterward **A1 A2**

94.24   method] **E1–** style **S**

95.6   met] **S** had met **E1–**

95.10   afterwards] **S E1 E2 E3–**
         afterward **A1 A2**

95.28   old friend] **S E1 E2 E3–** OM
         A1 A2

95.34   has never] **S** never **E1–**

95.35   while] **ED** the while **S–**

95.37   while] **S** when **E1–**

97.7   spirit] **E1–** spirit, nor from
         any particular
         stiff-neckedness in the
         writer, but from the
         profound conviction of its
         uselessness **S**

97.18   those] **S E1 E2 E3–** they **A1**
         A2

97.22   had] **S–E2 E3–** has **A2**

98.6   where] **S** whose **E1–**

98.9   This] **E1–** That last **S**

98.10   amongst] **S E1 E2 E3–**
         among **A1 A2**

98.12   amongst] **S E1 E2 E3–**
         among **A1 A2**

98.31   will proceed] **S** proceed
         E1–

99.5   life] **E1–** life, if not of
         literature, then at least of
         fiction **S**

99.8   towards] **S E1 E2 E3–**
         toward **A1 A2**

99.14   Yet] **S** But **E1–**

99.15   M.] **E1 E2 E3–** Mr. **S E1P**
         A1 A2

99.18   amongst] **S E1 E2 E3–**
         among **A1 A2**

100.8   Scotch] **S** Scots **E1–**

100.13   Furka] **ED** Furca **S–**

100.19   and] **E1–** and, as if **S**

101.1   a secretaryship] **S** the
         secretaryship **E1–**

101.13   I have] **S–** have I **MS**

101.18   It is] **S–** It's **MS**

101.32   body] **S–A2** body of **E3–**

103.4a   under] **E1–** about **S**

103.4b   hours.] **E1–** hours. Not
         quite. **S**

103.8   would not mind really] **S**
         E1 E2 E3– really would not
         mind **A1 A2**

103.20   Giuliano] **E1 E3–**
         Giugliano **S E1P A1 A2**
         Giúliano **E2**

103.24a   trait] **E1–** propensity **S**

103.24b   a while] **S–A3** awhile **E4**

103.35   up] **S E1 E2 E3–** OM **A1 A2**

104.36   go] **E1–** go then **S**

105.40   1857] **S–E2 E3–** of 1857
         A2

107.4   again] **E1–** OM **S**

107.29   towards] **S E1 E2 E3–**
         toward **A1 A2**

108.23   of Pola] **S** at Pola **E1–**

108.30   explanations;] **E1 E2 E3–**
         explanations; but **S E1P A1**
         A2

108.30–   not a naval career,] **E1–**
31   nothing **S**

108.38	French] **E1**– Polish and French **S**	113.32a	flagstones] **S–A2** flagstone **E3**–
109.5	and] **E1**– but **S**	**113.32b**	Passing] **E1**– As one passed **S**
109.13a	quite a] **S** a quite **E1**–		
109.13b	black, fine] **S** fine black, **E1**–	**114.7**	Joliette] **ED** Jolliette **S**–
		114.10	hoofs] **E1**– enormous hoofs **S**
109.21	O] **S–A3** Oh **E4**		
109.25a	enter] **E1**– look **S**	114.18	towards] **S E1 E2 E3**– toward **A1 A2**
109.25b	quest] **E1**– looking out **S**		
109.31	amongst] **S E1 E2 E3**– among **A1 A2**	**114.29**	massive] **E1**– wide-browed **S**
109.32	ships'] **E1**– ship's **S**	**115.13**	the hard] **E1**– a hard **S**
109.32–33	masters, stevedores] **S** masters-stevedores **E1**P master-stevedores **E1**–	115.23	peaks] **S–A2** OM **E3**–
		115.30	in due course] **E1**– sure enough **S**
109.35a	amongst] **S E1 E2 E3**– among **A1 A2**	116.10	eyes] **S–A2** eye **E3**–
109.35b	amongst] **S E1 E2 E3**– among **A1 A2**	116.11	drawing] **S E1 E2 E3**– drew **A1 A2**
110.11	of] **S E1 E2 E3**– OM **A1 A2**	**116.19**	the least bit] **E1**– at all **S**
110.12	hoop] **S–A2** loop **E3**–	**116.38**	The] **E1**– All the **S**
110.22–23	One of them] **E1**– OM **S**	**117.13**	him] **E1**– him suddenly **S**
110.23	Delestang] **E1**– Delestang, for instance, **S**	117.34	afterwards] **S E1 E2 E3**– afterward **A1 A2**
110.28	Dickens's] **S–A2** Dickens' **E3**–	**118.10**	before sunrise] **E1**– OM **S**
110.36	thin] **E1**– great **S**	**118.17**	abstemious] **E1**– sober **S**
110.39	solemnity] **E1**– presence **S**	118.24–25	everlastingly] **S**– everlasting **E1**P
111.15	known] **E1**– understood **S**	**119.6**	low] **E1**– high **S**
111.19	a temple] **S** the temple **E1**–	119.11	peaked] **S E1 E2 E3**– peak **A1 A2**
111.23	my raised hat] **E1**– me **S**	**119.13**	so many] **E1**– thirty-three **S**
111.27	significantly but] **E1**– OM **S**	**119.16**	*James Westoll*] **E1**– *James Westall* **S E1**P
111.32	by] **E1**– by what was **S**		
111.33	amongst] **S E1 E2 E3**– among **A1 A2**	119.19	James Westoll] **E1**– James Westall **S E1**P
111.39–112.1	looking straight before him] **E1**– not looking my way at all **S**	**120.11**	never] **E1**– have never **S**
		120.19	had achieved] **E1**– could have managed to achieve **S**
112.1	in the carriage] **E1**– OM **S**	120.24–25	by that time] **E1**– at all **S**
113.9	received] **E1**– OM **S**	120.27	had] **E1**– instantly had **S**
113.29	to be] **E1**– like **S**	120.34	towards] **S E1 E2 E3**– toward **A1 A2**
113.30	innumerable] **E1**– its innumerable **S**	**120.37**	turning in] **E1**– from **S**
		120.38	*James Westoll*] **E1**– *James Westall* **S E1**P
		121.1	the pellucid] **E1**– this pellucid **S**

Emendations of Accidentals

This list records the present edition's emendations of the accidentals of the copy-texts. A separate list (above) records emendations of substantives. Formal conventions of the documents are, as such, ignored: e.g., Conrad's signatures, the serials' bylines, editorial headings, in-text divisions, and instalment statements. Ignored as well are changes in features of typography and styling (see the 'Preface', p. xii), though such elements may occasionally appear in entries noting other alterations. Also not reported here are corrections of impossible word forms and other obvious errors in the preprint texts, as when Conrad wrote 'naturaly' or 'criticims' or when a typist produced 'the the drawing-room'. Unambiguous typographical errors (e.g., 'particuarly', 'fainly') in the serial that serves as copy-text go unreported.

Reports on the manuscript of 'A Familiar Preface' are based on its final readings, as are those on typescripts for the 'Author's Note' for which no earlier text survives. Reports on the typescript text ignore both part-words generated by false starts at the ends of lines (when they do not involve whole words or possible affixes) and characters x-ed out by the typist.

The purpose of this list is not to provide a history of some particular readings in the texts collated, but to report the alterations made by the present editors to the punctuation and word forms of each copy-text and to record the earliest source (whether one of the collated texts or the Cambridge editors) for the emendation. Earlier texts may be assumed to agree, for present purposes, with the copy-text's reading in the absence of a statement to the contrary: if such a text offers a viable alternative to the adopted form, its rejected reading is reported in a separate line together with identifying siglum. Thus the list usually omits recording the readings of the collected editions, and it ordinarily does not record the typewriting errors found in a copy-text typescript and rejected by Conrad while 'correcting' its text.

In each entry the reading of the Cambridge text appears immediately after the page–line citation. It is followed by a bracket, then by a siglum identifying the text in which the emendation first occurs, and then by the rejected reading of the copy-text, which concludes the main statement. When appropriate, reports on alternative readings in intermediate texts follow in the next line. The symbol ED identifies readings adopted for the first time in this edition – that is, not present in the texts collated. The swung dash ($\sim$) represents the same word as appears before the bracket; it occurs in records of variants in punctuation or other accidentals associated with that word, when the word itself is not the variant being noted. The inferior caret ($\wedge$) signals the absence of punctuation. The en-rule and other conventions of notation conform to those followed in the Emendation and Variation list and explained in its headnote.

The list follows these conventions for the 'Author's Note', 'A Familiar Preface', and the chapters of *A Personal Record*. Listed in sequence below their headings for the prefaces and for the work are the collated texts relevant to the emendations adopted as well as the sigla used to represent them; those for the books are not repeated because throughout they are uniform, as follows:

E1   first English edition (Nash, 1912)
   E1^p   unrevised page proofs of E1 typesetting, October 1911 (BL Ashley 469 and Colgate)
A1   first American edition (Harper, 1912)
E2   second English edition (Nelson, 1916)

A2	second American edition (Doubleday 'Deep Sea', 1917)
E3	third English edition (Dent, 1919)
A3	third American edition (Doubleday collected, Sun-Dial, 1921)
A3a	first state of **A3**, American Sun-Dial and all British issues (1923–)
A3b	second state of **A3**, Concord and subsequent American issues (1923–)
E4	fourth English edition (Heinemann collected, 1921)

Author's Note

TS1	ribbon-copy typescript (Princeton), final text: copy-text
TS2	ribbon-copy typescript (Berg), transcription of TS1 as revised, with additional corrections and revisions from **TS2c** copied in by Lilian M. Hallowes
TS2ct	carbon-copy typescript (Princeton), transcription of TS1 as revised, typewritten text
TS2cr	carbon-copy typescript (Princeton), transcription of TS1 as revised, with additional corrections and revisions in Conrad's hand
C	*Notes on My Books* (Doubleday, 1921; Heinemann, 1921), pp. 87–99

3.10	temperament] **TS2ct** ~,		5.19	life-long] **TS2ct** life long
3.26	first,] **TS2** ~		5.22	Impossible] **TS2cr** impossible
3.27	work;] **TS2cr** ~		5.23	Impossible] **TS2cr** impossible
3.28	Cunninghame] **TS2** Cuninghame		6.8	services,] **TS2ct** ~
3.29	Progress."] **E1** ~.~		6.16	words,] **TS2ct** ~
4.20	*North American Review*] **A1** North American Review		6.19–20	"revolutionary"] **ED** '~'
4.29a	"crystallized."] **TS2** ^~" –		6.23	"rebellions" which,] **TS2cr** '~' ~
4.29b	This I believe,] **TS2** –this ~ ~		6.40	myself;] **TS2ct** ~
4.36	"rectification"] **ED** '~'		7.25	later,] **TS2cr** ~
5.16	ever!] **TS2cr** ~.		7.33	too;] **TS2cr** ~,
			8.6	room,] **TS2ct** ~

A Familiar Preface

MS	holograph manuscript (Berg), final text: copy-text
C	*Notes on My Books* (Doubleday, 1921; Heinemann, 1921), pp. 100–16

11.10	disparagement.] **E1** ~		12.32	things,] **E1** ~
11.16	Glory] **E1** glory		12.39	"there] **E1**^~
11.17	Pity] **E1** pity		13.1	them."] **E1** ~.^
11.21	like! . . . Of] **E1** ~ . . . of		13.8	thirty-six] **E1** thirty six
			13.11	regrets,] **E1**^~
11.28	writer! Because] **E1** ~, because		13.13	"The . . . Sea,"] **E1**^~ . . . ~^
			13.14	Memories,] **E1** ~
11.33	invisible,] **E1** ~		13.16	sea,] **E1** ~
12.3	difficulty. For who is] **E1** ~ ~ who's		13.27	conscience.] **E1** ~
			13.36	"The Nigger] **E1**^the "~

13.36–7   "The ... the Sea"] **E1**
           ⌃the ... The ⌄

13.37   "Youth"] **E1**⌃⌄

13.38   "Typhoon"] **E1**⌃⌄

14.6   generally –] **ED** ⌄

14.7   flatterer,] **E1** ⌄

12.17   cœur."] **ED** ⌄⌃

14.34   humiliating! And] **E1** ⌄
           and

15.2   work.] **E1** ⌄

15.8   all.] **E1** ⌄

15.16   Only,] **E1** ⌄

15.27   service. And] **E1** ⌄ and

16.21   Nay] **E1** nay

16.24   talk –] **E1** ⌄.

16.29   be,] **E1** ⌄

16.36   pity; they] **E1** ⌄. They

16.37   too, and] **A1** ⌄. And

16.38   sob,] **E1** ⌄

16.39   mystic,] **E1** ⌄

17.10a   laughter,] **E1** ⌄

17.10b   tears,] **E1** ⌄

17.14   world,] **E1** ⌄

17.15a   world,] **E1** ⌄

17.15b   ideas,] **ED** ⌄

17.20   this,] **E1** ⌄

17.21   hard,] **E1** ⌄

17.24   Philosopher] **E1**
           philosopher

17.28   discursive] **E1** discursive

17.33   discursiveness] **E1**
           discoursiveness

17.35   discursiveness] **E1**
           discoursiveness

17.39a   Alas,] **E1** ⌄

17.39b   mildly.] **E1** ⌄

17.40a   'I] **E1** "⌄

17.40b   place?'|"] **E1** ⌄?"

18.11   world,] **E1** ⌄

18.18–19   "Almayer's Folly"] **E1**⌃⌄ ⌄

18.19   "The Secret Agent"] **E1**
           ⌃the ⌄ ⌄

A Personal Record

MS   holograph manuscript, single leaf of Chapter 6, 1909 (Syracuse):
          copy-text for 101.12–23

S   serialization, *English Review* (Duckworth), December 1908 – June 1909:
          copy-text for Chapters 2–7 (with exceptions as noted for **MS** and **S**ᵖr3)

Sᵖu1 unrevised proofs of Chapter 1, **S** typesetting, 1908 (HRHRC)

Sᵖr1 revised proofs of Chapter 1, **S** typesetting, 1908 (HRHRC): copy-text for
          Chapter 1

Sᵖu3 unrevised proofs of Chapter 3, **S** typesetting, 1908, facsimile in Violet
          Hunt, *The Flurried Years* (1926), p. 32

Sᵖr3 revised proofs of chapter 3, **S** typesetting, 1908, facsimile in Hunt, *The
          Flurried Years*, p. 32: copy-text for 67.35–68.21

19.16   sunk. . . ."] **ED** ⌄." . . .

22.29   men] **ED** ⌄,

26.6   Mr.] **S** ⌄

26.12   again] **ED** ⌄,

27.40   it." And] **S**ᵖu1 ⌄," and

28.4   history?] **S**ᵖu1 ⌄.

28.36   *Torrens*] **ED** ⌄,

28.39   o'clock] **S** o-clock

29.19   gimbals] **ED** ⌄,

29.31   alas!,] **ED** ⌄,

31.23   can] **ED** ⌄,

31.24   servant,] **E1** ⌄

34.18   homage] **S** hommage

37.21   track;] **ED** ⌃,

40.29   sighed⌃] **ED** ⌄,

41.2   Army⌃] **ED** ⌄,

44.25   sheep⌃] **ED** ⌄,

46.22   o'clock.] **A1** ⌄?

59.29   vets.] **ED** ⌄.,

61.40   off)⌃ "the] **E1** ⌄),⌃⌄

62.10   walls⌃] **ED** ⌄,

62.23   easily:] **E1** ⌄.

66.12   bizarre] **E4** *bizarre*

68.6   go – death] **S** ⌄⌄

71.22	language. As] **E1** ~; as		94.26	character^] **ED** ~,
74.21	after-skylight] **E1** after skylight		97.14	simplicity^] **ED** ~,
			99.15	M.] **E1** Mr.
75.12	assumptions^] **ED** ~,		100.11	sense^] **ED** ~,
78.8	was!] **E1** ~.		100.19	winds^] **ED** ~,
78.10	down] **ED** ~,		101.16	sentiment,] **S** ~^
79.36	after-deck] **A1** after deck		101.17	truth,] **S** ~^
84.21	merits?] **E1** ~.		101.18	it,] **S** ~^
84.36	charity^] **ED** ~,		101.21	doubt having] **S** ~ – ~
84.40	adoration^] **ED** ~,		101.22	possession, but] **S** ~ – ~
87.1a	alone –] -**E1** ~,		101.23	that,] **S** ~^
87.1b	despair!] **E1** ~.		102.7	manner] **ED** ~,
87.5	affair! And] -**E1** ~; and		105.1	himself] **ED** ~,
87.7	earth. A] **E1** ~ – a		105.14	whiskers] **ED** ~,
87.10	serenity;] -**E1** ~,		105.28	day,"] **E1** ~^"
88.4	retainers. And] -**E1** ~, and		107.40	opportunity^] **ED** ~,
88.8	*domo*. So] -**E1** ~: so		109.14	complexion^] **ED** ~,
88.24	acts^] **ED** ~,		109.17	*via*] **E1** *viâ*
88.26	beliefs^] **ED** ~,		109.21	"*Une*] **A1** ^~
88.31	Jean-Jacques] -**ED** Jean Jacques		110.20	eyes^] **ED** ~,
90.1	caution^] **ED** ~,		113.9	bizarre] **ED** *bizarre*
90.6	escapes^] **ED** ~,		113.21	Vieux Port] **ED** *Vieux Port*
90.19	monks^] -**E1** ~,		114.3	pilots!] **E1** ~.
90.19–20	Middle Ages] **E1** middle ages		115.12	moon rays] **A1** moonrays
91.17	sky^] **ED** ~,		116.25	*Équipages*] **ED** *Equipages*
91.22	world^] **ED** ~,		117.31–2	cranium^] **ED** ~,
92.15	Jean-Jacques] -**ED** Jean Jacques		119.33	emotions –] **E1** ~,
92.16	kick^] **ED** ~,		119.40	there!] **A1** ~,
92.20	stone^] **ED** ~,		120.26	side;] **A1** ~,
			121.5	intense^] **ED** ~,
			121.8	Ensign –] **E1** ~,

End-of-line Word-Division

This list records editorial decisions on the word-division of divisible compounds that are ambiguously hyphenated in the copy-texts. It contains, in the form of the critical text, each compound hyphenated and divided at the ends of the copy-texts' lines. The list omits words that have hyphens between capitalized elements (e.g., North-American) and those that are clearly mere syllabication (including syllabication of compound words falling elsewhere than at the point of word-division). Each compound is preceded by a reference to the page and line of the present edition.

A Familiar Preface

13.36   sea-books

A Personal Record

23.37	sun-bathed	74.26	outright
29.18	bulkhead	78.18	quar-|termaster
30.33	Friedrichstrasse	81.27	half-dressed
33.3	twenty-three	84.17	pinpoint
46.32	bald-headed	89.18	masterpieces
48.4	hat-brims	90.27	farmhouse
62.22	centre table	91.37	snowflakes
72.26	deck-seams	110.10	sea-tanned
72.40	semi-opaque	119.8	steering-gear

APPENDIX
EXTRACTS FROM TADEUSZ
BOBROWSKI'S *PAMIĘTNIK*

THE FOLLOWING passages from Tadeusz Bobrowski's two-volume *Pamiętnik mojego życia. O sprawach i ludziach mego czasu* [*Memoirs of My Life: On the Affairs and Men of My Time*], edited by J. N. Niewiarowski and published posthumously in Lwów in 1900, are sources for *A Personal Record*, Conrad partly translating and partly summarizing some of this material in his text. The passages are keyed to the text of *A Personal Record* by page–line number. The translations are by Zdzisław Najder.

For a discussion and analysis of Conrad's use of Bobrowski's memoirs, see 'Joseph Conrad and Tadeusz Bobrowski', Najder, 1997, pp. 44–67.

[38.27–39.21]

[Teofila's] outstanding qualities were not so much her education and beauty – in which my elder sister excelled, although she had a pleasant appearance and an adequate education – but her commonsense, sweet disposition, and an adaptability to people and situations. Her death was a great moral loss to us all, for it deprived us of that daily assistance that can be given only by a woman convinced that every occupation in family life is worthwhile as long as it brings satisfaction to someone. I am certain that had she lived she would have brought a blessing to her home as a wife, mother, and mistress of the house, and that she would always have exuded that atmosphere of contentment that she could create under all circumstances.

My elder sister possessed beauty and worldly deportment, her education was above that of contemporary women, her mind very lively and her heart very warm; she was not as complaisant and her demands were more difficult to meet, and at that time she required more attention from others than she was able and prepared to give herself. As she was rather sickly, the conflict between her love for her future husband and the known will of her father, whose memory and opinion she cherished, naturally upset her inner balance; dissatisfied with herself, she could not give others what she herself lacked. Only once united with her beloved could she develop to the full her unusual qualities of intelligence, feeling, mind, and heart. Amidst the greatest hardships of personal life, beset by all possible national and social misfortunes, she always knew how to choose, and with fortitude adhere to, her duties as wife, mother, and citizen, winning the respect of her kin and of strangers, sharing her husband's exile and representing Polish womankind with dignity.   (II, ch. 1)

[39.31–40.16]

My sisters fulfilled their promise and took weekly turns to keep me company at Oratów. On one journey the sledge in which my younger sister was travelling got stuck, and she was forced to get out into the snow; as a result she caught a slight cold and began to cough, but her health being on the whole quite good, no one paid any particular attention. However [. . .] her condition suddenly deteriorated. She developed galloping consumption and died within six weeks.   (II, ch. 1)

[40.18–25]

The years of infancy and childhood did not augur well for my life or health . . . Yet things turned out contrary to human expectations! Among numerous and much stronger siblings I survived four brothers and two sisters as well as many other contemporaries and my wife and daughter. In my family only a brother and nephew are left. Thus, I had to bury prematurely many hopes full of life.   (II, ch. 1)

[53.6–54.5]

By temperament he was melancholic and reclusive, and although outwardly phleg-matic, he was easily roused . . . Throughout his life he worshipped Napoleon without any reserve in the depths of his thoughts, as he did not like to talk about this; also, unlike other Napoleonic soldiers at the time, he never spoke about his exploits although he had been decorated with the Legion of Honour and the Military Cross. Temporarily *officier d'ordonnance* to Marshal Marmont, he was the last to ride over the bridge in Leipzig before it was blown up, he himself carrying the order to do so. He was wounded only once – in the heel like Napoleon the Great himself, a fact he would on occasion mention in moments of good humour. He never wore his decorations, saying that to possess them was enough. Yet I saw him wear his medals twice: in 1837 at the wedding of his friend Konstanty Bernatowicz, and twenty years later at my own.   (II, ch. 2)

[59.19–60.30]

My first childhood memories go back to 1833. I was just over four at the time, and the first event that struck my childish memory and imagination was my uncle's (Mikołaj Bobrowski's) return from exile in Russia. At the time the 1831 Insurrection broke out my uncle, who was responsible for remounting the Second Regiment of Fusiliers of the Polish Army, had been staying in Biłołówka (then Machnów District), the main rallying-point of the Polish Army remounts. There all the offi-cers responsible for remounting had been arrested and deported first to Kozielec (Chernikhov Province) and later to the depths of Russia. In my uncle's case it was first to Vyatka and later to Astrakhan. He returned home in 1833, discharged with only half the pension he qualified for because of his refusal to join the Russian army.   (II, ch. 2)

[61.24–65.27]

While supposedly pursuing insurgents, the peasantry indulged in breaking into and robbing houses, as the following fact, well-known to me, testifies, the victim being my uncle Mikołaj Bobrowski, then aged seventy . . . He was away from home when a Cossack patrol, commanded by an officer, arrived at his manor house in Solotnin, asking for the owner. A servant explained that he had gone to Berdyczów, and to the question if by chance he had gone to join the insurrection answered: 'My master is too old for that – he's over seventy'. 'Do you have any arms in your house?' 'Yes, we do', and he showed an old cutlass and a pair of flintlock pistols, relics of Napoleonic campaigns . . .

The officer gave the command to retreat and left the manor and village, but a mob of peasants, crowding into the courtyard, broke into the house, saying to one another: 'The old fellow has money somewhere'. Someone accidentally overturned a writing-table. The clink of gold was heard, and the table was immediately smashed and its contents removed. They were so excited by their search that they broke all the furniture to pieces, including the mirrors, for the sheer pleasure of destruction. They took away everything that could be moved, and, loading up a few carts with their spoil, drove to the nearby town of Cudnów. They took about 800 half-imperials, 1,200 rubles in silver and banknotes, and over 2,000 rubles in chattels, not counting the broken furniture and the extremely valuable mirrors.

Among the chattels was a box containing the decorations of the Legion of Honour and the Polish military cross; they apparently took fright of this booty, which, as they saw it, could come from no one but the Emperor himself, and secretly returned it in the garden . . . Characteristically, from among his considerable losses my uncle missed most the torn patent of the Legion, which he remembered verbatim and repeated almost with tears in his eyes, never even mentioning the other things. (II, ch. 11)

[67.16–68.12]

[Ewa Korzeniowska's] health was at that time visibly greatly impaired and required a long rest followed by careful treatment, but we could ensure neither as after the lapse of these few months our then overlord, Governor-General Bezak, ordered that she would not be permitted to stay on for any reason whatsoever, and in the event she justified herself by illness that she be taken to the prison hospital in Kiev by the chief of the Skwira police station. The said police officer himself secretly warned me of this in order to ward off that extremity. And thus in the first days of autumn she had to leave for Chernihiv, in the company of her mother. (II, ch.11)

NOTES

Topics sufficiently explained in a standard desk dictionary receive no notice. Place-names and other topographical matters identified by the maps at the end of this volume are glossed only when historical or other information might be useful. Where place-names have changed since the time of writing, the present-day name is given on its first occurrence only.

Whenever possible, the sources cited here are those that Conrad or his first readers could have known. Conrad's family history and his personal experiences in Europe, the Far East, and Africa are glossed briefly below, and biographies provide more information on these matters than can be given here. The genealogical table at the end of this volume summarizes information presented discursively here.

In notes dealing with alternative readings – whether in the early texts or proposed as emendations (adopted here or not) – a bracket follows the reading drawn from the text (the lemma) and a statement of variation precedes the commentary. Conventions of notation conform to those followed in the Emendation and Variation list and explained in its headnote. For sigla used for the texts throughout, see the same list.

Author's Note

3.2 **re-issue of this book** In November 1919, J. M. Dent & Sons published the new edition for which this 'Author's Note' was written. For a detailed discussion of the publication history of the book texts, see 'The Texts', pp. 142–51.

3.6 **noticed . . . press** In his review of *The Arrow of Gold*, published not long before Conrad wrote this preface, David S. Meldrum, Conrad's editor at Blackwood's and himself a writer, recalled that English was not Conrad's native language: see *Book Monthly* (September 1919), pp. 697–700.

3.17 **most flattering kind** From his first novel, *Almayer's Folly* (1895), onwards, Conrad's work met with a generally favourable reception, though some conservative critics found cause for complaint. For a selection of contemporary reviews, see *CH*.

3.24 **article . . . Clifford** 'Mr. Conrad at Home and Abroad', one of the first general assessments of Conrad's writing, in the *Singapore Free Press* of 1 September 1898 by Hugh Charles Clifford (1866–1941; knighted 1909), then British Resident in Pahang, Malaya. Clifford also wrote stories set in the colony. His review was published under a pseudonym.

3.26 **came to see me** Clifford first visited Conrad at Pent Farm in Kent in mid-August 1899 (see *Letters*, II, 194).

3.28–29 **Cunninghame Graham . . . "An Outpost of Progress"** R. B. Cunning-hame Graham (1852–1936), a Scottish aristocrat, writer, traveller, champion of the oppressed, Member of Parliament, and Labour Party supporter, was a good friend of Conrad's despite their divergent political views. Contact was first made when Graham wrote to Conrad to express his enthusiasm for 'An Outpost of Progress', published in *Cosmopolis* in June and July 1897.

3.33 **first volume . . . sketches** *In Court and Kampong* (1897). Conrad reviewed Clifford's second volume of Malay stories, *Studies in Brown Humanity* (1898) in the *Academy* of 23 April 1898. See 'An Observer in Malaya', *Notes on Life and Letters*, ed. J. H. Stape (2004), pp. 50–52.

4.1 **first books . . . stories** That is, the novels *Almayer's Folly* (1895) and *An Outcast of the Islands* (1896) and the stories 'The Lagoon' and 'Karain: A Memory' (both 1897).

4.2 **Malay Archipelago** The archipelago stretches from the west of the Malay Peninsula to a point north of western Australia, embracing the British Straits Set-tlements (present-day Malaysia and Singapore), the British parts of Borneo (Sabah and Sarawak), and the whole of the Dutch East Indies (present-day Indonesia).

4.11–12 **If I . . . sit up** Cf. 'Hugh Clifford and his wife paid me a flying visit. . . . His knowledge is unique. If I only knew one hundre[d]th part of what he knows I would move a mountain or two': Conrad to William Blackwood, 22 August 1899 (*Letters*, II, 194).

4.11–12 **Frank Swettenham** Frank Athelstane Swettenham (1850–1946; knighted 1897), began his career as an administrator in the Malay Archipelago in 1871, rising to become Resident-General of the Federated Malay States and Governor of the Straits Settlements. A specialist on the Malay language, he collaborated with Hugh Clifford on a Malay–English dictionary. At the time of Clifford's visit to Conrad, his *Malay Sketches* (1895) had appeared. His later books include *British Malaya* (1907) and *Also and Perhaps* (1912).

4.20 **study** Cf. 'The fact that he debated within himself seriously as to the choice of the language in which he should elect to write, will be found to be full of significance to any thoughtful student of his work. French at first attracted him more than English . . . Men of British breed, it seemed to him, would perhaps understand the things of which he had to tell as no other men could. In the end, therefore, he decided upon the use of English': 'The Genius of Mr. Joseph Conrad', *North American Review* (June 1904) pp. 847–8. Conrad repeated his position that he 'could not' have hesitated between writing in English or in French in terms similar to those here in a letter to H. L. Mencken of 11 November 1917 (*Letters*, VI, 4–5). On 7 June 1918, belatedly thanking Hugh Walpole for his study *Joseph Conrad* (published in June 1916), Conrad stated that the 'only thing that grieves me and makes me dance with rage is the cropping up of the absurd legend set afloat by Hugh Clifford . . . about my hesitation between English and French as a writing language' (*Letters*, VI, 7).

4.33 **Governor of Nigeria** A post to which Clifford had recently been appointed and which he held from 1919 to 1925.

5.36–6.4 **Nothing . . . European thought** For elaboration of these ideas, see 'Autoc-racy and War' (1905), *Notes on Life and Letters*, pp. 71–93.

5.37 **Sclavonism** Becoming rare at the time Conrad wrote, this spelling is not noted in the *OED*, whereas *Webster's New International Dictionary of the English Language* (Springfield, MA: Merriam, 1913) indicates it as a variant of 'Slavonic'. The spelling is used throughout Edward Creasy's classic *Fifteen Decisive Battles of the World from Marathon to Waterloo* (1851). Cf. also 'Sclavonic Love Song' by Marie Corelli (1855–1924). Conrad vigorously rejected the characterization of his cultural heritage as Slav, as was done by his friend Edward Garnett (see Conrad to Garnett, [8 October 1907], *Letters*, v, 492) and, later and more complexly, in an essay on his work by the American literary and social critic H. L. Mencken in *A Book of Prefaces* (1917), a copy of which Conrad received from Mencken himself (*Letters*, VI, 144–5). In writing to George T. Keating on 14 December 1922 about an article by Mencken, Conrad stated: 'What, however, surprises me is that a personality so genuine in its sensations so independent in judgment, should now and then condescend to mere parrot talk; for his harping on my Sclavonism is only that. I wonder what meaning he attaches to the word. Does he mean by it primitive natures fashioned by [a] byzantine-theological conception of life, with an inclination to perverted mysticism? Then it can not possibly apply to me. Racially I belong to a group which has historically a political past, with a Western Roman culture derived at first from Italy and then from France; and a rather Southern temperament; an outpost of Westernism with a Roman tradition situated between Slavo-Tartar Byzantine barbarism on one side and the German tribes on the other; resisting both influences desperately and still remaining true to itself to this very day' (*Letters*, VII, 615). In 'A Note on the Polish Problem' (1916) and 'The Crime of Partition' (1919), collected in *Notes on Life and Letters*, pp. 108–13, 94–107, Conrad insists on Poland's ideological and political affinities not to Slav autocracy but to Western European aspirations and traditions.

5.39–40 **exaggerated . . . rights** Probably an allusion to the *liberum veto*, which between 1652 and 1791 allowed a single member of the Polish legislative body, the *sejm*, to block a decision and dissolve a session.

6.14–16 **critics . . . Revolutionist** The Polish writer and critic Tadeusz Nalepiński (1885–1918) in *Kurier Warszawski* of 24 March 1912 stated that 'Korzeniowski was born in Poland in 1857 of a revolutionist father'. See 'Introduction', pp. xxxiii–xxxiv.

6.19 **my father** Apollo Korzeniowski (1820–69), poet, translator, and political publicist and organizer, strove for the re-establishment of an independent Poland but shunned terror and violence as means.

6.21 **risings of 1831 and 1863** Polish insurrections against Russian rule of 29 November 1830 and 22 January 1863. In 1772, 1793, and 1795, Poland had been partitioned by Russia, Prussia, and Austria. Conrad's concept of the 'revolutionary' here was doubtless influenced by the then-recent October 1917 Revolution in Russia. Both Polish uprisings were, indeed, wars of national liberation, not internal conflicts, but the suggestion that the insurgents were not interested in changing the existing socio-political order is incorrect: most were democrats and republicans, and all opposed Russian autocratic and monarchic rule.

6.25–26 **father . . . others** Siding with the more radically democratic and egalitarian groups, especially with respect to the status of the peasantry, Korzeniowski took a position that implied systemic change to the socio-economic and political orders.

6.34   **public funeral** On 26 May 1869 in Cracow. Conrad describes his father's death and funeral in 'Poland Revisited' (1915), *Notes on Life and Letters*, pp. 133–7.

7.3–4   **burning of his manuscripts** Several hundred pages of Korzeniowski's manuscripts survive in the Jagiellonian Library, Cracow.

7.15   **July of 1914 the Librarian** Conrad visited the Jagiellonian Library on 30 July (as his signature in its visitors' book witnesses). The librarian Józef Korzeniowski (1863–1921), not a relative, held his post from 1905 to 1919. Until 1939 the library was housed in the Collegium Maius, a building purchased by King Władysław Jagiełło in 1400 and renovated for the university. Conrad also recalls this visit in 'First News' (1918), *Notes on Life and Letters*, p. 139.

7.15–16   **University of Cracow** The Jagiellonian University (founded 1364). Conrad probably altered its name as a concession to his English and American audience.

7.18–19   **most intimate friend** Kazimierz Kaszewski (1825–1910), a classical scholar, translator from Greek, literary critic, and editor, lived in Warsaw. A participant in the Hungarian Insurrection of 1848, he was active in the Polish national underground during 1863–4. For translations of some of Korzeniowski's letters to him, see Najder, *Conrad*.

7.29–30   **translator . . . de Vigny** Korzeniowski's translations (with their publication dates) are as follows: Shakespeare's *The Comedy of Errors* (1866); Victor Hugo's *Hernani* (1862), *Marion Delorme* (1863), and the opening of *La Légende des siècles* (1869); Alfred de Vigny's *Chatterton* (1857).

7.36   **their memoirs** Various accounts and recollections in which Korzeniowski's activities were recalled appeared in 1913 on the occasion of the fiftieth anniversary of the 1863 Insurrection. Conrad is likely to have seen some of these during his visit to Poland in July–October 1914. The source for some of his information about his father's career and political activities, Stefan Buszczyński's *Malo znany poeta, stanowisko jego przed ostatnim powstaniem, wygnanie i śmierć* [A Little-known Poet, His Position before the Last Insurrection, Exile, and Death] had been published in Cracow in 1870. An eminent political writer of liberal-democratic allegiances, Buszczyński (1821–92) was a close friend of Korzeniowski.

8.2   **National Committee** Formed on 17 October 1861, the Committee of the Movement, the kernel of the later underground National Government, had organizational and political as well as moral objectives.

8.5   **our Warsaw house** Nowy Świat, no. 45, where Conrad's parents briefly lived in 1861 prior to their arrest.

8.13–14   **national mourning** Women and children wore mourning to honour the approximately 100 persons killed by Russian troops during a peaceful patriotic demonstration in Warsaw in April 1861.

8.18–19   **not thirty . . . exile** Ewelina, or Ewa, Korzeniowska (née Bobrowska, 1832–65), Conrad's mother, was thirty-three at the time of her death from tuberculosis on 18 April 1865 in Chernihiv, north-east Ukraine (see Map 1).

8.20–21   **brother's house** She visited her brother Tadeusz Bobrowski (see 31.39*n*) in the Ukraine from August to November 1863.

8.24–25   **Shades . . . rest** The image derives from the famous scene in Homer's *Odyssey*, Bk XI, in which Odysseus, at the threshold of the Underworld, calls up the spirits of the dead to question them. In addition to heroes and companions, the spirits evoked include his mother.

A Familiar Preface

11.4   **friendly suggestion** From Ford Madox Ford (né Hueffer, 1873–1939), novelist, critic, editor, and memoirist, who encouraged Conrad to write his recollections. For a full discussion, see 'Introduction', pp. xxiv–xxv.

11.24   **Archimedes' lever** The Greek mathematician and inventor Archimedes is said to have summed up his principle of the lever to Hiero II of Syracuse *ca.* 240 BC as 'Give me a lever long enough and a place to stand, and I will move the earth.'

12.6   **an Emperor** Marcus Aurelius (121–80), Roman emperor (after 161) and Stoic philosopher.

12.11   **Let all . . . truth** Not an exact quotation but a faithful rendering of an idea expressed in Marcus Aurelius' *Meditations*, Bk III.12. Conrad's direct source is possibly George Long's 1891 translation: 'with heroic truth in every word and sound thou utterest' (p. 91).

12.29   **Almost all]** ED Most | almost all MS Most, almost all, E1– Conrad apparently had immediate second thoughts about his initial formulation but neglected to delete 'Most' when revising. His typist or an editor dealt with this eccentric formulation by adding punctuation to an error that Conrad let slip by in proofs, but the received reading conveys a sense of hesitation at odds with the statement's force.

12.38   **"Imitation of Christ"** *De imitatione Christi*, a Christian counterpart of Marcus Aurelius' *Meditations*, was written *ca.* 1425, probably by the German Augustinian monk Thomas à Kempis. The passage is from I.viii.2. Conrad's immediate source is probably Anatole France's essay '*Mensonges*' par M. Paul Bourget', *La Vie littéraire*, 1st series (1888): 'Cette parole de l'ascète se vérifia pour lui: "Il arrive que, sans la connaître, on estime une personne sur sa bonne réputation, et, en se montrant, elle détruit l'opinion qu'on avait d'elle"' [The ascetic's statement turned out to be true in his case: 'It does happen that a person esteemed on the basis of a good reputation loses, on actual acquaintance, the good opinion one had of him'] (Hervouet, p. 144).

13.4   **appearing serially** On the serial publication, see 'Introduction', pp. xxvi–xxxi, and 'The Texts', pp. 129–40.

13.8   **thirty-six** Conrad, who had begun writing *Almayer's Folly* (1895) in autumn 1889, implies that he did not contemplate publication until 1893, his thirty-sixth year. For the writing of the novel, see *Almayer's Folly*, ed. Floyd Eugene Eddleman and David Leon Higdon (1994), pp. xxvi–xli.

13.12   **some three years ago** Published in October 1906, *The Mirror of the Sea* had appeared five years before Conrad drafted 'A Familiar Preface' during August–September 1911.

13.13–14   **volume . . . Memories** An allusion to the volume's subtitle, 'Memories and Impressions'.

14.13   **of a little insight**] ED a | of so much | little MS of so much insight as can be E1– MS evidences Conrad's groping for a phrase, and this influenced the one printed. He revised his first inscription 'the faculty of sympathy and compassion' to 'of so much understanding as is necessary for sympathy and compassion'. This in turn he partly revised, apparently as 'of certain insight in the terms of', before breaking off. MS's final formulation is considerably muddled because Conrad failed to delete 'of so much', whereas his typist repaired impossible phrasing by deleting 'little'. Conrad's revision in typescript or book proofs was conditioned by his typist's response to the confusion in MS and hence occurred on terms he was not aware of.

14.16   **unemotional**] ED unemotional grim MS unemotional, grim E1– Immediately after inscribing 'hard' Conrad replaced it by 'grim' and then proceeded both to revise and to correct his phrasing, adding the necessary article 'a' to the qualifying 'certain' and writing 'unemotional' above 'hard', which he had crossed out. In this series of steps he failed, however, to delete 'grim'. A typist or compositor later supplied punctuation to rationalize redundant phrasing.

14.17   *sécheresse du cœur* Hard heartedness (French); literally, 'dryness of heart'.

14.17   **Fifteen years** *Almayer's Folly* appeared in 1895, seventeen years prior to the writing of this preface. MS has 'sixteen' years, which Conrad must have revised in typescript or proofs.

14.22   **personal note** A possible echo of a once-contemplated title: 'The vol: will be entitled "*A Personal Note*" or something of that kind': Conrad to Pinker, 13 September 1911 (*Letters*, IV, 477).

14.38   **fools run to meet** Cf. 'For *Fools* rush in where *Angels* fear to tread': Alexander Pope, *An Essay on Criticism* (1711), line 625.

15.23   **a transaction**] ED transaction MS transactions E1p– Conrad's failure to supply required articles, an influence from Polish (cf. also 11.23), likely influenced his initial inscription. A typist or editor radically repaired the omission with a plural not required by the sense of the passage.

15.27–30   **I . . . Beautiful** A borrowing from Anatole France's essay 'Maurice Spronck', *La Vie littéraire*, 3rd series (1891): 'M. Maurice Spronck étudie quelques excellents écrivains du XIXe siècle qui ne cherchèrent jamais dans la parole écrite autre chose qu'une forme du beau.' [Mr Maurice Spronck analyzes some excellent nineteenth-century writers who in their writings never seek anything other than a form of the Beautiful] (Hervouet, pp. 143–4).

15.39   **middle . . . way** Cf. the opening words of Dante Alighieri's *La divina commedia* (1307–21): 'Nel mezzo del cammin di nostra vita / mi ritrovai per una selva oscura / ché la diritta via era smarrita' [In the middle of our life's journey, I found myself in a dark wood with the right road lost].

15.40 **tranquil mind** In altering his original 'more tranquil eye' to this phrase, Conrad possibly intended to allude to Shakespeare's famous line from *Othello*: 'Farewell the tranquil mind' (III.iii.395).

15.40–16.1 **proceed in peace** Possibly an echo of the phrase intoned by the priest at the beginning of a solemn procession in the Roman Catholic liturgy: 'Procedamus in pace' [Let us go forth in peace]. The Anglican liturgy has taken over this ritual and its words.

16.29–30 **virtue . . . reward** A commonplace dating to Socrates and drawn on variously by later writers. See, for example, John Dryden's 'To follow Vertue, as its own reward': *Tyrannick Love, or The Royal Martyr* (1669), II.i, 193 or Alexander Pope's 'And conscious Virtue, still its own Reward': 'The First Book of Statius his Thebais' (1712), line 758.

16.36 **The sight . . . pity** A borrowing (Hervouet, p. 144) from Anatole France's essay '*La Terre*', *La Vie littéraire*, 1st series (1888): 'les choses humaines n'inspirent que deux sentiments aux esprits bien faits: l'admiration ou la pitié' [human affairs inspire only two emotions to the well-informed: admiration or pity].

16.38 **tribute of a sigh** Cf. 'Some frail memorial still erected nigh, / With uncouth rhymes and shapeless sculpture decked, / Implores the passing tribute of a sigh': Thomas Gray, *Elegy Written in a Country Church Yard* (1751), lines 78–80. Cf. 'they could still draw from him the tribute of a sigh that rose from the depths of his being': Henry James, 'The Beast in the Jungle' (1903), ch. 2.

17.4–8 **proper wisdom . . . the How** A borrowing (Hervouet, p. 144) from Anatole France's essay 'Édouard Rod', *La Vie littéraire*, 3rd series (1891): 's'il nous est impossible de découvrir un sens quelconque à ce qu'on nomme la vie, il convient de vouloir ce que veulent les dieux, sans savoir ce qu'ils veulent, ni même s'ils veulent, et ce qu'il importe de connaître, puisque enfin il s'agit de vivre, ce n'est pas pourquoi, c'est comment' [if it is impossible to discover any sense in what we call life, it is fitting to want what the gods want, without knowing what they want or even if they have a will; and what really matters with respect to the question of living is in the end not the 'why' but the 'how'].

17.8–9 **Il y a . . . manière** There is always the manner (French). Monod (p. 1429) suggests two possible sources: 'Il n'y a que manière en la plupart des choses du monde' from Cardinal de Retz's *Mémoires* (1717) and the last line, 'Il y a la manière', of Henri Lavedan's satiric drama *Le Prince d'Aurec* (1894).

18.8 **my objector** Two candidates are possible. Conrad's friend Sidney Colvin apparently made some critical remarks regarding the method of the first instalment, to which Conrad responded on 28 December 1908: 'The defect you point out is manifest to myself and as a matter of fact has been considered. Yes. There it is. And in a sense it expresses a reluctance to start that kind of work at all. That sort of discursiveness gives an air of detachment – interprets really a sincere attitude – I am not a personage for an orderly biography either auto or otherwise.' Conrad's agent J. B. Pinker more forcefully complained about the series, Conrad writing to him on 15 April 1909: 'I think I will talk to him [Colonel George Harvey, head of Harpers] of my Rem^ces (so called) of which you don't seem to think much. Nevertheless they will be a quite unique thing in their way.' Conrad summarized this to John Galsworthy on 30 April 1909: 'Pink. . . . gave me to understand that he does not think much of them. I have lived long enough to hear that. However I differ from him on that matter' (*Letters*, IV, 175, 216, 224).

18.17   **at last . . . personality** Cf. 'and, who knows, from the rambling discourse a personality of sorts will yet emerge': Conrad to Sidney Colvin, 28 December 1908 (*Letters*, IV, 175).

18.27   **J. C. K.** That is, Joseph Conrad Korzeniowski, a combination of Conrad's pen-name with his original surname.

A Personal Record

19.7   **Flaubert** Gustave Flaubert (1821–80), French novelist, whose artistic scrupulousness made him both a legend and an example. He lived most of his life in his native Normandy on his family's estate at Croisset, near Rouen.

19.8   **descendant of Vikings** Flaubert's 'fancy' derived not from his family history but from the Viking occupation of Normandy, which began in the early ninth century. Rouen became their administrative base from *ca.* 850, and in 911 a treaty with Charles the Simple formalized de facto occupation.

19.10   *Adowa* The 2,097-ton passenger steamer, in which Conrad served as second mate from 29 November 1893 to 17 January 1894, was to take emigrants from France to Québec. The project roused little interest, the French not participating in the great, late-nineteenth-century waves of emigration from Europe to North America, and she arrived in port on 4 December 1893 merely to sail back to England on 10 January 1894.

19.11   **Rouen** In northern France, the town on the Seine, though seventy-five miles inland, was a major deep-water port.

19.14–15   **unworldly . . . hermit** A possible recollection of Gustave Flaubert's *La Tentation de saint Antoine* (1874) whose title-character devoted his life to asceticism and prayer in the desert, or of 'La Légende de St-Julien l'hospitalier' in Flaubert's *Trois contes* (1872).

19.15–16   *It has . . . sunk* Chapter 10's first words are: '"It has set at last!" – said Nina to her mother pointing towards the hills behind which the sun had sunk': *Almayer's Folly* (1994), 111.2–3. The phrase probably echoes Adam Mickiewicz's poem *Konrad Wallenrod* (1828): '"It has sunk at last", said Alf to Halban, / Pointing at the sun from the window of his loop-hole' (V, 192–3). The lines occur when Alf (also known as Konrad) takes a heroic and supreme farewell.

19.33–20.1   **banjoist . . . son . . . Mr. Kipling** The speaker in Rudyard Kipling's poem 'The Song of the Banjo' in *The Seven Seas* (1896) is an officer. Conrad later refers to his banjoist as 'Young Cole' (25.37). According to *The New Annual Army List* for 1893, the only retired colonel so named was Richard Sweet Cole, a captain who served in the Army Hospital Corps and held the honorary rank of colonel as of August 1875. The 1901 Census lists a Richard Cole, aged twenty-four, as an able-bodied seaman. This young banjo player was possibly recalled in the character Jackson in 'Karain: A Memory' (1897).

20.17–18   **impatience . . . desire** Nina is anxiously awaiting the arrival of her lover, Dain Maroola, with whom she will flee from her unhappy family situation. See *Almayer's Folly*, ch.10, pp. 111–23.

20.20–21 **relative positions** The text of the revised page proofs was precise: 'positions of second and third officer of a steamer' (see 'Emendation and Variation'). Conrad held his Master's certificate, but, as he later explains (24.22–26), the ship already had a chief mate, and he was willing to take a position lower than his rank.

20.27 *capote* Hooded coat (French).

20.36–38 **Opera House . . . town** The Théâtre des Arts on the Quai de la Bourse facing the Seine. The Café Thillard was in the nearby fashionable Cours de Boïeldieu.

20.38–40 **Bovary . . . Père Renault . . . memorable performance** Charles Bovary is the husband of the title-character Emma in Gustave Flaubert's *Madame Bovary* (1857). Her father's name is Rouault. The Théâtre des Arts had been rebuilt after a fire in April 1876. Conrad's reference is to *Madame Bovary*, Bk ii, ch. 15.

21.1 **Lucia di Lammermoor** Based on Sir Walter Scott's novel *The Bride of Lammermoor* (1819), Gaetano Donizetti's opera *Lucia di Lammermoor* was first performed in 1835. Unhappy in love, the title-character, Lucy Ashton (the opera's 'Lucia'), kills her newly wedded husband of a forced marriage, goes mad, and dies.

21.21 **no longer . . . live** An echo of the well-known lines from François de Malherbe's 'Consolations à Monsieur du Périer, gentilhomme d'Aix-en-Provence sur la mort de sa fille' (1598): 'Mais elle était du monde, où les plus belles choses/Ont le pire destin: / Et rose elle a vécu ce que vivent les roses,/L'espace d'un matin' [But she was of this world where the things of greatest beauty have the worst of fates: a rose, she lived as roses live but the space of a morning].

21.31 **Victoria Dock** The Royal Victoria Dock, opened in 1855, was the closest to London of the royal docks.

21.36 **London Shipmasters' Society** An organization devoted to improving the welfare of ships' officers and more informally serving as a social gathering place, its headquarters were at 60 Fenchurch Street, near the docks. Conrad was a member (*Letters*, I, 27–8).

21.40 **Captain Froud** Albert George Froud (*ca.* 1832–1901), a Somerset man by birth, retired to Bristol after his career at sea and involvement in the Shipmaster's Society.

22.5 **St. John ambulance classes** Instruction in first aid and emergency care was offered through the St John Ambulance Association and Brigade (established 1887). The association frequently offered training at the workplace, including the docks, and was instrumental in spreading Western medical knowledge throughout the British empire.

23.6 **captain of that ship** The unrevised serial proofs give the name as 'Patten' (a somewhat unlikely French surname). Conrad's certificate of discharge (dated 17 January 1894 and published in George T. Keating, *A Conrad Memorial Library*, p. 400) is signed 'Fred^k Paton'. The surname is confirmed in *Le Journal de Rouen* of 5 December 1893 and 11 January 1894, [p. 3], and the 1891 Census confirms Frederick Paton as master of the *Adowa*, giving his birthplace as London and his age as 42.

23.22 **return . . . waters** Conrad resigned his command of the *Otago*, in which he made voyages from Bangkok and from Mauritius, on 2 April 1889 and returned to England in mid-May.

23.24–25   **a Pimlico square** Bessborough Gardens, where Conrad lived from May 1889 to May 1890. The west London district, mainly residential at the time, lies between Victoria Station and Vauxhall Bridge.

23.31   **Pantai** The river in north-eastern Borneo (present-day Kalimantan, Indonesia), was also known as the River Berau. Most of the action of *Almayer's Folly* is set on its banks. (It also figures in *An Outcast of the Islands* and provides some of the topographical details for *Lord Jim*'s Patusan.) Conrad knew the area from his four voyages in the *Vidar*, made from August 1887 to January 1888. For a discussion of the actual setting and late-nineteenth-century commerce on the river, see J. N. F. M. à Campo, 'A Profound Debt to the Eastern Seas: Documentary History and Literary Representation of Berau's Maritime Trade in Conrad's Malay Novels', *International Journal of Maritime History*, 12.2 (2000), 85–125. See Map 3.

23.36   **moral character** The word 'moral', used more widely in both Polish and French in this sense, connotes ethics and is sometimes the equivalent of 'spiritual'. Cf. also 'moral loss' (38.34), 'moral balance' (39.12), and 'moral end' (87.2, 87.35–36).

23.39–26.2   **fellowship . . . earth** Cf. 'that feeling of unavoidable solidarity; of the solidarity in mysterious origin, in toil, in joy, in hope, in uncertain fate, which binds men to each other and all mankind to the visible world': 'Preface' to *The Nigger of the 'Narcissus'* (1897).

24.6   **Belgravia** Not a part of Pimlico, but a more elegant and fashionable district adjacent to it.

24.28–29   **Mr. Paramor** William Paramor (1861–1941), who served in the British Merchant Service until 1902, maintained friendly relations with Conrad until at least 1898. On him, see David Gill, 'Joseph Conrad and the S.S. *Adowa*', *Notes and Queries*, 25.4 (1978), 323–4, and 'Joseph Conrad, William Paramor, and the Guano Island: Links to *A Personal Record* and *Lord Jim*', *The Conradian*, 23.2 (1998), 17–26.

24.34   **word on my forehead** A borrowing from a commonplace in Islamic culture, derived from the Koran, that an individual's destiny is written upon his forehead. Conrad also alludes to this tradition in *Lord Jim*, ch. 17: 'As if the initial word of each our destiny were not graven in imperishable characters upon the face of a rock'.

24.35   **achieve** A Gallicism, from 'achever' (to complete or finish). Cf. also 'achieve even a single passage' (25.3).

24.35–36   **Western Ocean** That is, the North Atlantic, which Conrad did eventually cross as a passenger in spring 1923. He had crossed the South Atlantic on the *Duke of Sutherland*'s homeward voyage.

25.7–8   **never . . . humane person** Facilities and accommodations in the emigrant ships of the period were typically modest but could be appalling, the so-called 'cattle boats' cramming emigrants into a space used for cargo on the home voyage. Conrad's short story 'Amy Foster' describes conditions in an emigrant ship.

25.28   **Cook's** A Baptist evangelist, Thomas Cook (1808–92), the father of modern group tourism, began his business of escorted travel and pre-arranged accommodation in 1841. It expanded considerably during the Great Exhibition of 1851, and branched out in the next two decades to the Continent, North America, and Africa, and in the 1880s to the Far East. Mainly serving a middle-class clientele, Cook's also arranged tours for royalty and the aristocracy.

26.11   **satanic suggestion** A possible Polonism ('szatańska sugestia') or Gallicism ('suggestion satanique'), idiomatic English more likely requiring 'devilish'.

26.18   **arrested them short** A Gallicism from 'arrêter', idiomatic English requiring 'stopped short'.

26.25–27   **visit . . . my childhood** Conrad's trip to Poland and Ukraine of August–October 1893.

26.30   **map of Africa** Conrad mentions his childhood desire to travel to Africa in 'Geography and Some Explorers' (*Last Essays*) and the incident here – if it really was one – is recalled in 'Heart of Darkness'. Chris Fletcher suggests a literary source in 'Kurtz, Marlow, Jameson, and the Rearguard: A Few Further Observations', *The Conradian*, 26.1 (2001), 63: 'When quite a small boy, between four and five years old, his grandmother once found him, at a late hour of the night, poring over a map, which strangely enough was the map of Africa. She asked him why he had not gone to bed, as it was some hours past his usual time. "Oh, grandmamma!" he said, "I want to learn all about these strange countries, for I mean to be a big traveller some day" ': James S. Jameson, *Story of the Rear Column of the Emin Pasha Relief Expedition* (1890), p. xxvii. In the Cambridge Edition of *Youth: A Narrative and Two Other Stories* (forthcoming), Owen Knowles notes a somewhat similar passage: 'But I remember that, even at school, Africa had a peculiar fascination for me. A great map of the "Dark Continent" hung on the walls of my class-room; the tentative way in which the geographers of that day had marked down the localities in almost unknown equatorial regions seemed to me delightful and mysterious. There were rivers with great estuaries and territories of whose extent and characteristics, ignorance was openly confessed by unnamed blank spaces': E. J. Glave, *In Savage Africa, or Six Years of Adventure in Congo-Land* (1892), p. 16.

26.38   **did go there** Conrad arrived in the Congo in June 1890 to work in a river steamer for the Société Anonyme Belge pour le Commerce du Haut-Congo [Belgian Limited Company for Trade in the Upper Congo]. Ill with dysentery and tropical fever, disgusted with the ruthless exploitation of the natives, and discovering that as a non-Belgian he lacked prospects of advancement, he resigned after only five months. His African experience provided material for 'An Outpost of Progress' and 'Heart of Darkness'.

27.5–10   **turn of the Congo . . . Kinchassa and Leopoldsville . . . officer** Pointe de Kalina (present-day Pointe de la Gombe and now in central Kinshasa) was named after a young Austrian officer in the Belgian service who drowned there in December 1883. The loss of Conrad's belongings apparently occurred towards the end of October 1890. Kinshasa and Léopoldville, then distinct, have been amalgamated in present-day Kinshasa, the capital of Congo.

27.16   **Boma** Fifty miles upriver from the Congo River estuary, Boma was at the time the capital of the Congo Free State (present-day Congo). Having arrived in Boma in June 1890 at the outset of his African sojourn, Conrad returned there in December.

27.17   **steamer . . . home** The date and route of Conrad's return to Europe are unknown. On 4 December 1890, he was in Matadi, whence he departed some days later for Boma. At the end of January he passed through Brussels en route to England.

27.21–22 **convalescence . . . Champel** Conrad convalesced in the German Hospital, Dalston, London, during February–April 1891, and underwent hydrotherapy at Champel-les-Bains, near Geneva, in May and June. For a detailed discussion of Conrad's illnesses and their treatment, see Martin Bock, *Joseph Conrad and Psychological Medicine* (2002).

27.23–24 **history . . . decline and fall** An echo of the famous title of Gibbon's history of Rome (see 28.14*n*).

27.26 **warehouse . . . city firm** Conrad was briefly employed by Barr, Moering, and Company (in which he had invested) in spring and summer 1889 and in summer 1891. The 'city' is the City of London, the capital's financial district.

27.39–40 **Novalis . . . believe in it** 'Fragment 153' of *Das Allgemeine Brouillon* by the German Romantic poet Friedrich Leopold, Baron von Hardenberg (1772–1801), who wrote under the pen-name Novalis. Conrad uses the sentence as the epigraph to *Lord Jim*. He may have come upon it in Lecture II of Thomas Carlyle's *On Heroes, Hero-Worship, and the Heroic in History* (1841) – '"It is certain", says Novalis, "my Conviction gains infinitely, the moment another soul will believe in it"' – or in Carlyle's *Sartor Resartus* (1838), a volume mentioned in 'Youth' (p. 7).

28.3–4 **accumulated . . . history** The subject of fiction, history, and truth has been debated since antiquity; Conrad's phrasing might, however, be indebted (see Hervouet, p. 141) to a discussion about fiction in Anatole France's novel *Le Lys rouge* (1894), ch. 3: 'C'était une étude, dans laquelle il s'efforçait d'atteindre à cette vérité formée d'une suite de vraisemblances qui, ajoutées les unes aux autres, atteignent à l'évidence. ¶ Par là, dit-il, le roman acquiert une force morale que, dans sa lourde frivolité, n'eut jamais l'histoire' [It was a study in which he laboured to reach that truth made up of a series of likelihoods that, added to one another, became evidence. 'In this way', he said, 'the novel acquires an ethical force that history in its solemn frivolity never had'.]

28.8 **Cambridge man** William Henry Jacques (1869–93) read Classics at Trinity College, Cambridge, from 1888 to 1891, obtaining a first-class degree. He was a passenger in the *Torrens* from London to Adelaide and back in 1892–3.

28.9 *Torrens* A passenger clipper in which Conrad served as first mate for two voyages to Australia, from November 1891 to July 1893. On his service in her, during which he met John Galsworthy and Edward (Ted) Sanderson, see 'The *Torrens*: A Personal Tribute', *Last Essays*. For details, see J. H. Stape and Hans van Marle, '"Pleasant Memories" and "Precious Friendships": Conrad's *Torrens* Connection and Unpublished Letters from the 1890s', *Conradiana*, 27.1 (1995), 21–44.

28.14 **Gibbon's "History"** Edward Gibbon's six-volume *The History of the Decline and Fall of the Roman Empire* (1776–88) covers many centuries of Roman history, from the city's mythical founding in 753 BC to the fall of Constantinople in 1453. In S, the discussion is specified as being about 'the famous chapter xiii' (see 'Emendation and Variation'); this is apparently an error, however, for the highly controversial Chapter 15 (sometimes omitted from early nineteenth-century editions), which deals with the early Church.

28.40 **top-gallant sails** The sails on the third, or top-gallant, mast in a sailing ship.

29.1 **first dog-watch** The first of the two short or half-watches is from 4 p.m. to 6 p.m., the other from 6 p.m. to 8 p.m.

29.18–19 **punkah . . . bulkhead . . . gimbals** Respectively, a large overhead swinging fan, made from cloth or palm fronds, hung from the ceiling and pulled by a rope to ventilate and cool a room; a wall between separate sections of a ship; concentric metal rings holding and keeping an instrument level and in place (a chronometer or compass, for instance).

29.20 **latitude 40 south** That is, south-west of the Cape of Good Hope, in stormy latitudes and with much of the voyage still to be accomplished.

29.29 **Square the yards** An order to lay out the ship's yards (spars to which sails are attached) level and at right angles to the fore-and-aft line of the ship.

30.2 **died rather suddenly** He died in England on 19 November 1893. Conrad later acknowledged his error: 'Yes. Mr Jacques came back with us in the *Torrens*. He was laid up all the passage and I hardly ever saw him. This will partly account for my extraordinary mistake in the Personal Record. Strange lapse of memory! E. L. Sanderson (also a passenger that time) pointed it out to me a long time ago'. Conrad to A. T. Saunders, 26 January 1917 (*Letters*, VI, 18).

30.8 **At last we sailed** The *Torrens* left Adelaide on her return trip on 3 March 1893.

30.26–27 **men . . . railway carriages** A possible allusion to the novelist Anthony Trollope (1815–82), who had a portable writing-desk made to allow him to write during train journeys. His *Autobiography* (1883) recounts regular composition whilst travelling (Monod, p. 1434).

30.33 **ninth chapter** Conrad completed this chapter in the autumn of 1893. For the novel's composition history, see 'The Texts', *Almayer's Folly*, pp. 159–98.

30.35 **Ukraine** The area of the Ukraine in which Conrad's family lived was part of the Polish Commonwealth until the Partition of 1793. Conrad here telescopes two visits to his homeland: one from mid-February to mid-April 1890, prior to his African sojourn, and the other from August to October 1893.

30.36 **Gladstone bag** A light travelling bag, named after William Ewart Gladstone (1809–98), English statesman and prime minister.

30.37 *Kofferträger* Porter (German).

31.1 **spent two days** Conrad arrived in Warsaw on 9 or 10 February 1890, having begun his journey in Brussels and passed through Berlin, as he recounts. He left for Lublin on the 12th to visit relatives, and on 16 February arrived at his uncle's estate (see 33.20*n*), staying with him until 18 April.

31.4–5 **friend . . . Diplomatic Service** The unidentified friend must have served in the Austro-Hungarian diplomatic corps, as Poles could not be employed as Russian diplomats.

31.14 **modernist review** Probably the weekly *Życie* – 'devoted mainly to the sphere of belles lettres' – which was published in Warsaw from 1887 to 1891. Its first editor-in-chief, Zenon Przesmycki, later published a better-known and more ambitious and influential monthly *Chimera* (1901–7). Conrad possibly combines the two periodicals.

31.20 **railway station . . . country house** Kalinówka (Kalinovka) Station, on the Koziatyń (Kazatyn) – Winnica line. The house was Kazimierówka, the family estate of Conrad's uncle and guardian Tadeusz Bobrowski, near Lipowiec (Lipovec).

31.24 **factotum** Man-of-all-work (Latin).

31.30 **a Hebrew** A once common, and sometimes offensive, term used to refer to a Jew.

31.39 **my uncle's** Tadeusz Wilhelm Jerzy Bobrowski (1829–94), Conrad's uncle and guardian, who after the death of Conrad's parents supported him financially until 1886 and remained in regular contact with him until his death. Conrad dedicated *Almayer's Folly* to him. For his letters to Conrad (Conrad's perished during the Bolshevik Revolution of November 1917), see Najder, *Letters*. For a discussion and analysis of their relationship, see 'Joseph Conrad and Tadeusz Bobrowski', Najder, 1997, pp. 44–67.

32.15 **clear blue eyes** The idiomatic phrase 'bright blue eyes' is possibly replaced by a form influenced by the Polish 'jasne' or French 'clair', both translated into English as 'clear' but, unlike English, connoting 'brightness' or 'luminousness'. There is, however, some precedent in English; cf. 'her eyes were so clear and bright that few would wish them darker': Anne Brontë, *Agnes Grey* (1847), ch. 7. Conrad uses 'clear' unidiomatically in *Lord Jim* several times. See also 'the sun . . . set, clear and red' (33.2) and 'her clear dress gave the only festive note' (*Nostromo*, p. 62).

32.26–27 **the Captain remembers** In Polish and several other languages, the polite form of address to a superior requires the third- rather than the second-person singular.

32.27 **late grandmother** Teofila Bobrowska (née Biberstejn-Pilchowska, d. 1875), Conrad's maternal grandmother, with whom he lived in Cracow, after his father's death and after leaving Tadeusz Bobrowski (31.39*n*), from 1869 to the summer of 1873.

32.31–32 **four-in-hand whip** A four-in-hand is a vehicle with four horses driven by one person. Plate 3 in *Letters*, I shows Conrad as a child holding a whip.

33.27 **three southern provinces** Volhynia, Podolia, and the Government of Kiev. See Map 1.

33.39–40 **Cossack trousers** Trousers that fit loosely into half-length riding boots. The Cossacks, a people from Ukraine and southern Russia, were light cavalry in the Russian Imperial Army.

34.1–4 **1864 . . . followed** Ewa Korzeniowska was permitted to leave Chernihiv (see Map 1) for three months, in the summer of 1863, to travel 120 miles (200 km) to her family in Nowochwastów, south-west of Kiev. Like her husband, she had been sentenced to exile.

34.7–8 **eldest brother . . . Guards** Stanisław Bobrowski (1827–59) had been an officer in the hussars of the Tsar's Guard.

34.8 **dying early** The phrasing is probably influenced by the Polish *przedwcześnie*, typically used in this context and meaning 'too early' or 'before time'. The more usual English would be 'dying young' or 'dying prematurely'.

34.17   **grey heads** A direct translation of the Polish 'siwe głowy'.

34.26   **my cousin** Józefa Bobrowska (1858–71), Tadeusz Bobrowski's daughter.

34.33–34   **Moscow school of journalists** Chauvinistic and reactionary views flourished, most notably, in *Moskovskie Viedomosti* and *Russki Viestnik*, both under the editorship of Mikhail Katkov (1818–87).

37.13–14   **maternal grandfather's estate** The Bobrowski family estate at Oratów, about 155 miles (250 km) from Kiev, comprised extensive lands and the manor house Kazimierówka.

38.17   *chibouk* An elongated pipe for smoking tobacco (Turkish).

38.26   **Nicholas B.** Mikołaj Bobrowski (1792–1850), the brother of Conrad's maternal grandfather, served in Napoleon's Grand Army from 1808 to 1814, working his way up through the ranks from sub-lieutenant to captain.

38.27   **aunt** Teofila Bobrowska (1833–51), the sister of Conrad's mother and of Tadeusz Bobrowski.

39.3–4   **her father's death** Her father, Józef Bobrowski (1790–1850), a landowner.

39.6   **the man** That is, Apollo Korzeniowski, Conrad's father, whom Ewa Bobrowska met in 1847, nine years before they married in May 1856.

39.35   **Countess Tekla Potocka** Born Princess Sanguszko (1786–1869), Countess Potocka resided in Daszów (Dashiv), about 25 km from Oratów. She was a distant relative of Prince Roman Stanisław Sanguszko (1800–81), the model for the title-character of Conrad's short story 'Prince Roman' (1911).

40.2–3   **snow . . . thickly** A Polonism from 'geesto', idiomatic English requiring 'heavily'.

40.36   **sixty-two years old** This places the action in 1891.

41.2   *Officier d'Ordonnance* An aide-de-camp, an officer who assists a senior commander in the field.

41.3   **Marmont** Auguste-Frédéric-Louis Viesse de Marmont (1774–1852), Marshal of France, was one of Napoleon's most distinguished commanders. He fought in Italy and Egypt and played a significant defensive role in the Battle of Leipzig (54.22*n*). He was created Duke of Ragusa in 1808 and later Governor of Illyria. His role in Napoleon's first abdication branded him a traitor, and he later went into exile with Charles X. His memoirs attempt to justify his actions.

41.5   **Congress of Vienna** Convened from September 1814 to June 1815 by the Allies victorious over Napoleon, the Congress established spheres of influence in Europe and sanctioned Poland's partition.

41.7   *de visu* By sight (Latin). The phrase was current in French.

41.9   **'64** A minor slip: during the summer of 1863. For details, see Najder, p. 19.

41.20–22   **Knight . . . *Virtuti Militari*** Bobrowski was a *chevalier* in the Légion d'honneur, a French decoration recognizing service to the state which was instituted by Napoleon in 1802. (Bobrowski received patent No. 41847.) Having received the French decoration, Bobrowski was automatically awarded its then

Polish equivalent, 'For military bravery', a practice that applied during 1798–1815. The highest Polish military decoration, the Virtuti Militari was established in 1792 by King Stanisław Poniatowski to recognize and reward military valour beyond the call of duty.

41.24   **resumes** A Gallicism from 'resumer', idiomatic English requiring 'sums up' or 'summarizes'.

42.3   **Man of St. Helena** That is, Napoleon, who was exiled to this remote South Atlantic island after his defeat at Waterloo on 18 June 1815 and his surrender to the British.

42.4–5   **Russian campaign . . . Moscow** Napoleon's attempt to take Russia began on a grand scale and ended in a catastrophic defeat in the winter of 1812. Conrad recalls the French retreat from Moscow in 'The Duel' and 'The Warrior's Soul'.

43.12   **The rest is silence** Hamlet's last words: Shakespeare, *Hamlet*, v.ii.310.

43.19   *la vache enragée* Literally 'furious cow' (French). Eating it means to suffer misery.

43.20   **salt junk . . . trepang** Respectively, salted meat used on long voyages, compared to rope, and a sea slug or sea cucumber of several species of *Holothuria*, an Asian delicacy.

43.23–24   **Polish landed gentry** The *szlachta*, a term covering both the Polish nobility and gentry. There was no legal distinction between the various levels of this class, which, compared with those of England or France, was large, comprising about 10 per cent of ethnic Poland's population. Its members were not necessarily landowners. In the part of Ukraine where the Bobrowskis and Korzeniowskis lived, the *szlachta* comprised about 2 per cent of the Polish population.

43.24   *Chevalier . . . Honneur* See 41.20–22 n.

43.34   **great illusion . . . false beacon** Napoleon exploited the hope for Polish independence to obtain the participation of Poles in his military campaigns. In 1807, he established a Grand Duchy of Warsaw from Polish territory which had been under Prussian and Austrian rule, but after his defeat at Moscow in 1812, most of the Duchy became Russian territory.

43.36–37   *Pro patria . . . decorous* Echoing his phrase 'for the sake of his country' (43.31), Conrad translates and plays on Horace's 'Dulce et decorum est pro patria mori' [It is sweet and fitting to die for one's country] (*Odes*, iii.ii.13).

44.14   **the traced way** A Gallicism from 'tracer' (to mark out).

44.18–19   **Indulgence . . . virtues** Possibly a recollection or transformation of 'Tout comprendre rend très indulgent' [To understand everything makes one very indulgent] from the novel *Corinne* (1807), ch. 5, by the French novelist and critic Madame de Staël (pseudonym of Anne-Louise-Germaine Necker, Baroness de Staël-Holstein), complicated by a sentence from Anatole France's 'Alexandre Dumas fils', *La Vie littéraire*, 2nd series (1890): 'Il est vrai que la clémence est la plus intelligente des vertus et que la philosophie naturelle enseigne le pardon' [It is true that clemency is the most intelligent of virtues and that natural philosophy teaches forgiveness].

44.21–22   **The barber and the priest** From Miguel de Cervantes' *El ingenioso hidalgo Don Quijote de la Mancha* (1605 and 1615), whose chivalric imagination is challenged by the mundane and commonsense values of the barber and the priest who destroy and censor his library and place him in a cage in an attempt to tame his imagination.

44.23–28   **hidalgo ... caballero** Respectively, a nobleman, and a horseman or knight (Spanish).

44.34–36   **giant Brandabarbaran ... city** An imaginary participant in Don Quixote's epic battle with a flock of sheep. Cf. 'the ever-dauntless Brandabarbarán de Boliche, Lord of the Three Arabias, who for armour wears that serpent's skin and for his shield has a gate that, as tradition has it, is from the temple Samson brought to the ground when, by his death, he revenged himself upon his enemies' (*Don Quixote*, pt i, ch. 18).

44.37   **blessed simplicity** From the Latin 'sancta simplicitas'. In context, 'simplicity' denotes innocence, humility, and modesty, rather than lack of guile or an absence of sophistication.

44.39–40   **ingenious hidalgo of La Mancha** See 44.21–22 n.

45.2   **King Louis-Philippe ... exile** The king (1773–1850) accepted the French crown in 1830 after the July rebellion against Charles X, who abdicated. Popular discontent with his rule led to his abdication in 1848; he lived in England thereafter.

45.3   **The people ... fault** Conrad's source is Anatole France's 'M. Charles Morice', *La Vie littéraire*, 2nd series (1890): '"Un peuple n'est jamais coupable", disait le vieux roi Louis-Philippe à Claremont. Voilà une sage parole' ['A people are never at fault', said old King Louis-Philippe to Claremont. *That* is a wise saying] (Monod, p. 1436).

45.6   **knighted at daybreak** A candidate for knighthood passed the evening before being knighted in a solemn vigil of prayer and fasting. For the mock ceremony of Don Quixote's knighthood, see *Don Quixote*, pt i, ch. 3.

45.12   **tutor** Adam Marek Pulman (1846–91) studied at the Jagiellonian University's famed Faculty of Medicine from 1868 to 1875.

45.13–16   **1873 ... school-boy holiday** At the time Conrad was living in Cracow with his grandmother, where, although not enrolled in school, he took regular examinations.

45.17   **other reasons ... that year** The year was one of change: in addition to the May–July holiday with Pulman, Conrad returned only briefly to Cracow, where he had lived since February 1869, and was then sent to Lwów and the care of his cousin Antoni Syroczynski, who ran a boarding-house for boys orphaned by the 1863 Insurrection. The capital of Galicia may have proved an attractive change from Cracow, then somewhat ingrown and provincial.

45.35   **work ... St. Gothard Tunnel** Begun in autumn 1872, construction on the 9¼ mile (14.9 km) tunnel under the Alps linking Switzerland to Italy was completed in March 1880.

47.4–6   **Scotch accent ... second engineer** The ship's papers show that the second engineer was, in fact, Cornish (National Archives BT100/35).

47.6   *Mavis* A 763-ton steamer in which Conrad, probably as an unofficial apprentice, sailed in the spring of 1878 from Marseilles to Lowestoft, where he set foot on English soil for the first time.

47.13   **Furka Pass** The pass in central Switzerland at the eastern end of the Bernese Alps forms the natural border between the Rhone and Reuss Valleys. See Map 2.

48.26   **Carthusian** A monastic order founded in 1084 by St Bruno of Cologne in the Chartreuse Valley of south-eastern France.

48.32   **Mr. T. B.** Tadeusz Bobrowski (see 31.39*n*).

49.14   **certain reasons** Nervous attacks and poor health plagued Conrad's childhood and youth and made his regular attendance at school difficult.

49.17   *pour prendre congé* To take leave of (French).

49.18   **next . . . years** The dating is unclear: between 1874 and 1878, Conrad spent considerably more time ashore in France than at sea; in 1890 and 1893, he travelled on the Continent for several months; in December 1893 to January 1894, he was in Rouen (as Chapter 1 recounts); he spent May 1895 in Geneva; and he honeymooned in Brittany from March to September 1896. See *Chronology*; for details, see Najder.

49.30   **the Rigi** Referred to as the 'Queen of the Mountains' since the fifteenth century, Mount Rigi (1,798 m), situated between Lakes Luzern and Zug, features majestic and famous views of the Alps from its summit. Modern tourism began in earnest in the late-nineteenth century. A railway service operating to a height of 1,600 m opened in 1871, and on 23 June 1873, during Conrad's and Pulman's trip, service began to the summit itself.

50.20   **Finster-Aarhorn** At 14,019 ft (4,273 m), Finsteraarhorn is among the highest peaks of the Alps.

50.27–29   **Eleven years . . . St. Katherine's Dockhouse . . . master** Conrad passed his examination for Ordinary Master in the British Merchant Service on 10 November 1886, more than thirteen years later. St. Katherine's Dock, not dockhouse, was built in 1828.

50.33   **true vocation** Pulman had studied medicine, not philosophy.

50.35–36   **A day came . . . Calcutta** The *Tilkhurst*, in which Conrad served as second officer, docked at Calcutta from 21 November 1885 to 8 January 1886; however, Pulman's death on 30 January 1891 (Lviv Historical Archives) makes the location given here impossible. If, indeed, Conrad learned of this news in a distant seaport, it would have been that at Adelaide where he arrived in the *Torrens* on 28 February 1892 and departed on 10 April. In 1891, after returning from Africa in January, he was, with the exception of a sojourn in Switzerland for a water cure, in London in hospital and then working for Barr, Moering, and Company.

50.38   **obscure little town** Sambor (in Ukrainian, Sambir), a town south-east of Przemyśl in what was then Austrian Poland. See Map 1.

53.23   **Friedland** A town in East Prussia (present-day Pravdinsk, Kaliningrad District, the Russian Federation). The town was the site of a major French victory over the Russians on 14 June 1807.

53.24 **Bar-le-Duc** A town in north-eastern France in the *département* of the Meuse. In January and February 1814, Napoleon's Grand Army, retreating towards Paris, was engaged in several actions there.

53.25 **admiration . . . unreserved** Conrad portrays fanatical allegiance to the person, actions, and ideals of Napoleon in the officer Ferraud in his short story 'The Duel'.

53.27 **little faith** Cf. 'O, ye of little faith' (Matthew vi.30, viii.26, xvi.8, and Luke xii.28) and 'O, thou of little faith' (Matthew xiv.31).

54.6 **not . . . mother** Ewa Bobrowska's marriage to Apollo Korzeniowski was long opposed by her family.

54.22 **battle of Leipsic** The so-called 'Battle of the Nations' of 16–19 October 1813, ending in decisive defeat for Napoleon, whose 185,000 troops faced 320,000 allied Austrian, Prussian, Russian, and Swedish troops.

54.27 **Poniatowski** Prince Józef Poniatowski (1763–1813), Marshal of France, commanded the Polish troops covering Napoleon's retreat. He was killed in the battle.

54.29 **only the] A1–A2** the only **S E1 E2 A3–** The alteration by A1's editor is a reasonable response to an apparent or even obvious typesetting error that Conrad and proof-readers failed to catch.

54.29–30 **Shambles** The word is apparently being used less in its modern sense as simply denoting a chaotic situation than in its older sense of a butcher's slaughterhouse, and, by extension, a scene of carnage.

55.6 **wounded in the heel** Napoleon Bonaparte was so wounded on 23 April 1809, during the taking of Ratisbon.

55.15 **The Hundred Days** The period between Napoleon's escape from exile on Elba on 20 March 1815 and his abdication after the defeat at Waterloo on 22 June 1815. Napoleon's anticipated escape from Elba is an important element in the plot of *Suspense*.

55.15–16 **distant relative** Piotr Pilchowski (1771–1862), the uncle of Tadeusz Bobrowski's mother.

55.23 **battle of Austerlitz** A major battle, also known as the 'Battle of the Three Emperors', on 2 December 1805, in a small Moravian town under Austro-Hungarian rule (present-day Slavkov u Brna, Czech Republic), ending with Napoleon's victory over Austria and Russia.

55.37–38 **mother . . . man** Katarzyna, née Błażowska, wife of Leon Staniszewski. The story is drawn from *Pamiętnik*, 1, 1 (see Appendix).

57.25 **Carlsbad** Better known by its German name Karlsbad, the spa town (present-day Karlovy Vary in the Czech Republic) is famed for its medicinal waters.

57.32 **naked . . . saint** An exact translation of the Polish expression 'goly jak święty turęcki'. Literally, 'completely naked'; metaphorically, 'penniless'.

58.8–9 **public school** In Lubar, Volhynia. Run by Dominicans, it was neither the only nor the most prestigious school of its kind in the province. Conrad departs from Bobrowski's memoirs here.

58.26–27 **Polish kingdom . . . Alexander I** Established by the Congress of Vienna in 1815, the Congress Kingdom of Poland formed part of the Russian Empire but preserved a large degree of legal and administrative autonomy until 1830. Alexander (1777–1825; tsar 1801–25), a ruler of liberal inclinations, held the title King of Poland, but hopes that he would restore Poland to her pre-Partition integrity were quickly dashed.

58.31–33 **Grand Duke . . . Polish lady** Konstantin Pavlovich (1779–1831), the younger brother of Tsar Alexander I, was in effect Poland's ruler during the existence of the Congress Kingdom. He married the Polish noblewoman Joanna Grundzínska (1791–1831) in 1820.

58.40 **Nicholas** Tsar Nicholas I (1796–1855) was an oppressive and reactionary autocrat during his reign from 1825 to 1855.

59.13 **not serfs** Although attached to land and subject to the tenure system, Polish peasants were not, as in Russia, a landowner's personal property.

59.14 **smaller nobility** A literal translation of 'la petite noblesse' (French); see also 43.23–24n.

59.18 **wars . . . Persia or Turkey** Russia fought against Persia in 1828 and against Turkey in 1828–9. Owing to the opposition of Grand Duke Konstantin Pavlovich, the Polish Army did not participate in these wars.

59.19 **In 1831** The insurrection had begun in Warsaw on 29 November 1830, but news of its outbreak reached the Ukraine with some delay.

59.26 **"Border"** In Polish 'Kresy', the Polish Commonwealth's eastern borderlands.

60.11–12 **Stepanovitch . . . Stephen** Conrad's paternal great-grandfather bore the name Stanisław, which, however, was Russified as 'Stepan' (anglicized by Conrad here to 'Stephen'), the name used in Russian documents concerning him. The patronymic Stanislavovitch offered unsurmountable linguistic hurdles and was avoided by this alteration.

60.21–22 **sabre . . . Paris** The Allied armies opposing Napoleon entered Paris on 31 March 1814.

60.32–33 **last partition of Poland** The third and final partition between Russia, Prussia, and Austria occurred in 1795. Conrad treats this subject in 'The Crime of Partition', *Notes on Life and Letters*, pp. 108–13.

60.34 **rising in 1863** Provoked by enforced military conscription (though long brewing as injustices accumulated), the Insurrection broke out on 22 January.

60.35 **His brother** Józef Bobrowski (1790–1850), Tadeusz's father.

60.38–39 **screw . . . sticking-point** An allusion to Lady Macbeth's famous phrase urging her husband to stab King Duncan: 'But screw your courage to the sticking-point / And we'll not fail': Shakespeare, *Macbeth*, i.vii.60–61.

61.3–4 **village** Solotwin, near Kodnia, in the county of Zhytomyr.

61.16 **grandfather's . . . sons . . . daughter** The sons of Teodor Korzeniowski (d. 1863), Robert (killed in the 1863 Insurrection) and Hilary (died in exile in Tomsk in 1878), and Conrad's aunt Emilia, also exiled for her patriotic activities in the 1863 Insurrection. His third son, Conrad's father Apollo, is unmentioned.

61.39 **J–** Jitomir (in Polish 'Żtomierz', in Ukrainian 'Zhytomyr'). See Map 1.

63.37–39 **Greek Church . . . interior of Russia** That is, the Russian Orthodox Church. In 1839, the tsarist government abolished the Ukrainian Catholic Church. Priests who did not convert to Russian Orthodoxy were expelled, and others brought to replace them.

64.23–24 **eight hundred half-imperials**] ED eight half-imperials S eighty half-imperials E1– Conrad's source (see Appendix) gives the figure 800, and 'hundred' was possibly missed out during dictation. If, on the other hand, Conrad erred in adapting his source, then 'y' inadvertently dropped out during S's typesetting. Given that Conrad closely followed and had no apparent reason to alter his source, the correct figure is restored. Half-imperials were gold coins worth five rubles issued by the Imperial Russian government.

64.33 **not**] ED no S– Although the locution of the printed texts is possible, it seems just as likely, if not even more so, that this is a compositorial error that escaped correction.

66.22 *gouvernante* Governess (French).

66.30–31 *N'oublie . . . chéri* Don't forget your French, dear (French).

67.27 **Great Russia** That is, Russia proper, as distinct from Little Russia (Ukraine).

68.18 **Bezak** Aleksandr Pavlovich Bezak (1801–68).

69.18 **letters . . . fact** Conrad may have submitted 'The Black Mate' to a short-story competition for *Tit-Bits* in 1886. The 'Congo Diary' (published in *Last Essays*) and 'Up-river Book', which he kept in 1890, are factual records of his travels in the Congo.

69.30 **die . . . Rubicon** 'To cross the Rubicon' became a proverbial expression for taking a bold and irrevocable decision, announced by Julius Cæsar's words 'The die is cast', pronounced on crossing a small river forming the border between Italy and the province of Cisalpine Gaul. He did so without the permission of the Roman Senate, which was required of military commanders, and thus, in January 49 BC, in effect declared war on Pompey and his supporters in the Senate.

70.21–22 **thirty . . . tenancy** This places the event in June 1889.

70.27 **the fairy tale** A play upon the well-known 'Cinderella; or, The Little Glass Slipper' from Charles Perrault's collection *Stories or Tales from Times Past, with Morals: Tales of Mother Goose* (1697), whose title-character is transformed from a wretched scullery maid into a princess.

71.10 **Victor Hugo** (1802–85), French Romantic poet, dramatist, and novelist. Immensely popular in his day, he is now remembered for *The Hunchback of Notre Dame* (1831) and *Les Misérables* (1862).

71.11–12 **"Gil Blas"** *Les Aventures de Gil Blas de Santillane* (1715), a picaresque novel by the French dramatist and fiction writer Alain-René Le Sage.

71.15 **Anthony Trollope's novels** Trollope's popular novels offered vividly detailed portraits of Victorian society and politics (see 30.26–27*n*). Conrad appears to have

216 NOTES

read both the Barsetshire and Palliser novels in the early 1880s, having begun his acquaintance with the writer with *Phineas Finn* (1869). See Conrad to Allan N. Monkhouse, 8 February 1924 (*Letters*, VIII, 304).

71.18–19 **Dickens . . . Scott . . . Thackeray** The works of these major and popular nineteenth-century novelists were translated into several European languages.

71.20 **"Nicholas Nickleby"** Charles Dickens' novel, serialized in 1837–9, was published in book form in 1839. M. Skotnicki's Polish translation *Nickelby* appeared in 1847.

71.29 **my father's translation** At the time Apollo Korzeniowski was translating *A Comedy of Errors* (published 1866). If he did translate *Two Gentleman of Verona*, his translation was not published, nor does a manuscript survive. Conrad's claim in 1912 that his father had translated 'much of Hugo and Shakespeare' suggests a tendency to overstate the extent of his father's professional work: see 'The Knopf Document: Transcriptions and Commentary', ed. J. H. Stape, in *Conrad Between the Lines: Documents in a Life*, ed. Gene M. Moore, Allan H. Simmons, and J. H. Stape (2000), p. 61.

71.32 **heavy mourning** A Polonism from *ciężka żałoba*, idiomatic English requiring 'deep'.

71.33 **town of T–** Tchernikhov, the French spelling (in Polish 'Czernihow', in Ukrainian 'Chernigiv'). Apollo Korzeniowski resided in the town from 1863 to 1868. See Map 1.

71.39 **confused** A possible Gallicism from *confus* (embarrassed), since disorientation does not seem to be in question.

72.16 **"Toilers of the Sea"** Hugo's *Les Travailleurs de la mer* (1866). No translation by Korzeniowski was published, and no manuscript of it survives. *La Légende des siècles* (1857) is possibly the work at issue (Monod, p. 1439).

72.24–25 **Falmouth** A port in Cornwall where Conrad, as second mate in the *Palestine*, spent January to September 1882 whilst the ship was undergoing repairs.

72.31–32 **to Poland** That is, to Ukraine, pre-Partition Poland.

72.33–35 **gales . . . water . . . fire** The recollections here concern Conrad's service in the 427-ton barque the *Palestine*, which he fictionalized in 'Youth'. The ship set sail for Bangkok on 17 September 1882 from Falmouth after putting in for repairs occasioned by heavy weather (72.24–25n). On 12 March 1883, in Bangka Strait, off Sumatra, her cargo of coal was discovered to be on fire. Attempts to combat the fire proving unsuccessful, the decks blew up on the 14th, and the crew put to sea in open boats. Baptism by fire and water is a trope derived from the words of John the Baptist: 'I indeed baptize you with water unto repentance: but he that cometh after me, is mightier than I . . . he will baptize you with the Holy Ghost, and with fire' (Matthew iii.11).

73.23 **Almayer** The title-character of Conrad's first novel, *Almayer's Folly* (1895), and a major figure in *An Outcast of the Islands* (1896). His prototype was Carel Willem Olmeijer or Ohlmeijer (1842–1900), a Java-born Eurasian living in Berau (see 23.31n). For details, see *CEW*.

73.25–26 **steamer . . . wharf . . . Bornean river** The *Vidar*, a 204-ton coastal steamer plying between Singapore and ports in the Celebes (present-day Sulawesi, Indonesia) and Borneo. Conrad served in her as first mate from August 1887 to January 1888. On the river, see 23.31 n. The wharf was in Tanjong Redeb (or Tanjongredep).

73.32 **serang** Boatswain (Malay), the petty officer in charge of a ship's rigging.

74.11 **tiffin** The mid-day meal (colonial English).

74.12 **Pulo Laut** Sea Island (Malay) present-day Pulau Laut. Off the south-eastern tip of Borneo, the island figures in *Almayer's Folly* (1994), 66.3, and in *Lord Jim*, p. 356.

74.17 **Donggala** A port in north-western Celebes, the Dutch East Indies.

74.22 **Captain C–** James Craig (1854–1929), the *Vidar's* master.

74.33 **taffrail log** A log mounted on the taffrail (the rail around a ship's stern), consisting of a rotator, log line, and recording device to measure the distance travelled.

75.1 **embarrassment** A Gallicism, the meaning in context being an encumbrance, botheration, or nuisance rather than a feeling of mild confusion or shyness.

75.9 **Bali pony** A singularly prized breed of small, high-spirited ponies from the island (then a kingdom) east of Java.

76.36 **Tuan** 'Master', 'sir', or 'Mr' (Malay), a term either of respectful address or of reference to persons of high status, including Europeans. Conrad notably used the word, translating it as 'lord', in *Lord Jim*.

76.39 **kalashes** From Malay 'kelasi', a sailor.

78.13 **Order . . . Fleece** An order of knighthood (recalling the Greek hero Jason) instituted in 1429 by Philip the Good, Duke of Burgundy, and later an order in Spain and Austria, awarded for piety, loyalty, and selfless service. Conrad would have known it as one of the principal decorations of the Austro-Hungarian Empire (Der Orden vom Goldnen-Vlies). Its badge is a golden sheepskin with the head and feet attached.

81.8 **guttah** Gutta-percha, a leathery material obtained from the latex of certain trees in the Malay Archipelago, is used for insulation and in chewing gum.

81.10 **Jurumudi Itam** A nickname: in Malay '*jurumudi*' means 'steersman' and '*hitam*', here elided, means 'black'.

82.5 **eight months** Conrad had sailed from Amsterdam as first mate in the *Highland Forest* on 18 February 1887.

82.5–7 **left ... Singapore** Injured by a falling spar, Conrad left the *Highland Forest* in the central Java port of Semarang on 1 July 1887, arrived in Singapore five days later, and spent a few weeks in hospital in July and August. The incident is recalled in *Lord Jim*, ch. 2; in *The Mirror of the Sea*, ch. 20; and perhaps in the suppressed opening of 'A Smile of Fortune' (see *'Twixt Land and Sea* (2007), ed. J. A. Berthoud, Laura Davis, and S. W. Reid, 13.24–14.12).

82.15 **East Coast** Of Borneo, that is.

83.23–86.28   **meet . . . Shades** Conrad relies on Classical precedents here, perhaps recalling Æneas' famous encounter with Dido in the Underworld. Abandoned by him, she had committed suicide and refuses to speak to him when he tearfully addresses her. See Virgil, *Æneid*, Bk VI.

83.23–25   **Elysian Fields . . . Jupiter** In Greek mythology, the land of the dead. Geese, however, were sacred not to Jupiter, the supreme deity of the Romans, but to his sister–wife Juno.

83.35–84.1   **What's . . . poet . . . rose** An allusion to the famous lines of Shakespeare's *Romeo and Juliet*: 'What's in a name? That which we call a rose / By any other word would smell as sweet' (II.ii.43–4).

85.10   **pen . . . cold steel** The phrase 'cold steel' connotes a sword, and this phrase is possibly an oblique allusion to the tag 'The pen is mightier than the sword' from Edward Bulwer-Lytton's *Richelieu* (II.ii.).

85.13–14   **postcard . . . novel or two** Half-penny postcards were introduced during William Gladstone's first term as prime minster (1868–74). Gladstone's endorsements of the work of the popular novelists Marie Corelli and Mrs Humphry Ward, sometimes on postcards, made welcome copy for publishers' advertisements. Gladstone's political opponent, Benjamin Disraeli, was a novelist.

85.24–25   **Ollendorff** Heinrich Gottfried Ollendorff (1803–65) pioneered a popular technique, 'The Ollendorff Method', to teach languages with quick results. Ollendorff's work focussed on French, German, Italian, and Spanish, but his method was adapted to teaching Latin and even Tamil.

86.11–12   **wind . . . listeth** 'The wind bloweth where it listeth, and thou hearest the sound thereof, but canst not tell whence it cometh, and whither it goeth: so is every one that is born of the Spirit' (John iii.8).

86.20–21   **unprofitable . . . weary** Given this section's allusive character, possibly an echo of Shakespeare's *Hamlet*: 'How weary, stale, flat, and unprofitable / Seem to me all the uses of this world!' (I.ii.137–8).

86.22   **uneasy . . . crown** 'Uneasy lies the head that wears a crown': Shakespeare, *2 Henry IV*, III.i.33.

86.31–32   **great French writer** An allusion to Anatole France's *Le Mannequin d'osier* (1897), ch. 4: 'ces âmes mornes, qui ne reflètent rien, ces êtres en qui l'univers vient s'anéantir' [those blunted souls, dark mirrors that reflect nothing, those beings into which the universe vanishes] (Hervouet, p. 142).

86.36   **faith, hope, charity** In Christian tradition, cardinal virtues. See also 'And now abideth faith, hope, charity, these three; but the greatest of these is charity' (1 Corinthians xiii.13).

87.12   ***Chi lo sà?*** Who knows? (Italian).

87.18   **Walrus or the Carpenter** The characters of Lewis Carroll's poem in *Through the Looking-Glass* (1871): 'The Walrus and the Carpenter / Were walking close at hand / They wept like anything to see / Such quantities of sand'.

87.29   **artist of prose fiction]** ED prose artist of fiction S– Although Conrad's sense of English idiom can occasionally be faulty, S's reading is probably an inadvertent transposition made during typesetting.

87.30   **truth ... well** The notion of truth as something hidden in a well, attributed both to Democritus and Cleanthes, dates to antiquity and is echoed by various writers. Cf. 'truth, which is not a beautiful shape living in a well', 'The Duel' (1907), p. 201; and 'at last the watch came up from the deep pocket like solid truth from a well', *The Shadow-Line* (1917), p. 27.

87.33–34   **Fabians ... Kaffirs** Respectively, members of the Fabian Society (founded 1884), an association of intellectuals sympathetic to socialism, and various South African peoples (the Bantu and Xhosa, for instance), hence by extension the Muslim term for infidels.

87.40   **pro domo** Short for 'pro domo sua' (Latin), that is, 'for his house' (which is translated literally a few lines on) or 'in one's own interest'. Having studied the Classics, Conrad may have known the phrase from Cicero's oration 'Pro domo sua', in which, on his return from exile, Cicero castigates Clodius for confiscating his belongings.

88.9   **tant ... voudrez** As much as you wish (French).

88.14–15   **J'ai vécu ... Abbé Sieyès** 'I survived', a *bon mot* attributed to Emmanuel-Joseph Sieyès (1748–1836), French priest, constitutional theorist, and political pamphleteer, on being asked what he had done during the Reign of Terror (August 1792 – July 1794). The story may be apocryphal.

88.17–18   **violences ... French Revolution** Begun in 1789, the Revolution was initially directed against the monarchy and aristocracy but in time led to bloody infighting amongst its supporters. Conrad's fascination with it and his fundamental rejection of violence as a means to political change are topics in his essay 'Autocracy and War' (1905) and in *The Rover* (1923).

88.30–31   **confessions ... Jean-Jacques Rousseau** Swiss-born French thinker (1712–78) enormously influential for his educational, moral, and political ideas, who justified himself in his lengthy *Confessions* (published posthumously in 1788). With other *philosophes*, he laid the ideological groundwork for the French Revolution. For a discussion of Conrad's negative attitude towards Rousseau, see Najder, 1997, pp. 139–52.

88.36   **anniversaries** A Gallicism, from 'anniversaire' (birthday).

88.39   **"Émile"** Rousseau's famous and popular didactic romance (1762), expounding his theories about the bringing-up of children in accord with so-called principles of nature.

89.10   **Anatole France** The pen-name of Jacques-Anatole-François Thibault (1844–1924), French novelist and essayist known for his ironic wit. Conrad reviewed his collection of short stories *Crainquebille* in 1904 and his novel *L'Île des Pingouins* in 1908 (see *Notes on Life and Letters*, pp. 30–39). On Conrad's interest in France's writings, and borrowings from them, see Hervouet, pp. 149–64.

89.12–15   **failing ... ourselves ... Brunetière** France's 'M. Jules Lemaître', *La Vie littéraire*, 2nd series (1890): 'Nous sommes enfermés dans notre personne comme dans une prison perpétuelle. Ce que nous avons de mieux faire est de reconnaître de bonne grâce cette affreuse condition et d'avouer que nous parlons de nous-mêmes, chaque fois que nous n'avons pas la force de nous taire' [We are shut up in ourselves like someone condemned to prison forever. The best we can do is to recognize this awful condition with good grace and to acknowledge that we speak about ourselves every time we lack the strength to be silent]. France repeats this idea in the preface to the third series of *La Vie littéraire* (1891) in answer to an article in the *Revue des Deux Mondes* of January 1891 by the influential literary critic Ferdinand Brunetière (1849–1906).

89.17–18   **The good critic . . . masterpieces** 'Le bon critique est celui qui raconte les aventures de son âme au milieu des chefs-d'œuvre', Anatole France's Dedicatory Note to *La Vie littéraire*, 1st series (1888); 'M. Jules Lemaître'; and preface to *La Vie littéraire*, 3rd series. Conrad also cites this phrase in 'Henry James: An Appreciation' (1904), *Notes on Life and Letters*, 17.36–7.

89.36   **daily bread** Allusion to the 'Lord's Prayer' (Matthew vi.11 and Luke xi.3).

90.14   **life . . . skittles** A commonplace, the phrase connotes a carefree and pleasant attitude towards life. Skittles or ninepins, the forerunner of ten-pin bowling, had been played for centuries in England's public houses. Although local variations were known, players would generally take turns throwing wooden balls down a lane in an attempt to knock over the wooden skittles at its end.

90.15   **Je . . . d'honneur** On my word of honour (French).

90.17–27   **daughter . . . farmhouse** The incident occurred during Conrad's residence at Pent Farm, in the village of Postling, Kent, where he lived, with periods of absence, from 1898 to 1907. At the time, this part of Kent had numerous military connections and featured barracks. The Conrads' immediate neighbours during the writing of *Nostromo*, according to *Kelly's Directory of Kent, Surrey and Sussex, 1903*, were farmers and graziers. See also 'the writing of novels, as a charming lady who disturbed me cruelly on a certain afternoon said, "is such a delightful occupation" ': Conrad to Arthur Symons, Monday [3, 10, or 17? August 1908] (*Letters*, IV, 100). In a conversation in 1972, Borys Conrad identified this individual as Nazra (or Nazsa) Eden (information from Mario Curreli).

90.34   **my wife** Jessie Emmeline Conrad (née George, 1873–1936), whom Conrad married in March 1896. The second of nine children, she probably met her future husband in 1894 when she was working for a factory making typewriters and living with her widowed mother. She ran the Conrad household and occasionally typed Conrad's work. She later wrote articles, a book on cookery, and two memoirs of her husband.

91.5–6   **stars . . . courses** Cf. 'They fought from heaven; the stars in their courses fought against Sis'era' (Judges v.20).

91.7–8   **"Nostromo" . . . seaboard** Conrad completed the novel, which has the sub-title, 'A Tale of the Seaboard', in August 1904.

91.14   **prophet . . . wrestled** Jacob, not a prophet, wrestled with an angel of the Lord (Genesis xxii.22–32). The phrase is not a quotation from the Bible, though wrestling with the Lord frequently occurs in Anglican hymns and is a Wesleyan hymn tune, 'Wrestling Jacob'.

91.17   **breath of life . . . blown** The metaphor derives from the creation of Adam: 'the Lord God formed man of the dust of the ground and breathed into his nostrils the breath of life; and man became a living soul' (Genesis ii.7).

91.18   **Latin and Saxon . . . Jew** Respectively, Nostromo and the Violas, who are Italian; Charles Gould and Captain Mitchell, who are British; and Hirsch.

91.25–26   **winter passage . . . Cape Horn** Such a passage runs against the prevailing winds and currents. Conrad sailed round the Horn in the summer (that is, the Antarctic winter) of 1879 but was going eastwards.

92.23–27   **magnificent . . . love** Cf. *Nostromo*: 'In that true cry of undying passion that seemed to ring aloud from Punta Mala to Azuera and away to the bright line of the horizon . . . the genius of the magnificent Capataz de Cargadores dominated the dark gulf containing his conquests of treasure and love' (p. 566).

92.30   **quarter-deck** That part of a vessel's upper deck extending between the stern and after-mast and used exclusively by the ship's officers.

93.24   **Costaguana** *lepero* Costaguana is the fictional South American country where the action of *Nostromo* unfolds. A 'lepero' (Spanish), a person of low status, is a member of the local proletariat.

94.27   **gift . . . a man** The dog 'Escamillo', named after the toreador of Georges Bizet's opera *Carmen*, was given to Borys Alfred Conrad (1898–1978), then Conrad's only child, by Stephen Crane (94.34*n*). Conrad also mentions Crane in connection with his son in 'Stephen Crane: A Note without Dates' (1919), *Notes on Life and Letters*, 45.1–3. See also 'Stephen Crane: A Preface', *Last Essays*.

94.34   **Stephen Crane** (1871–1900), American novelist, short-story writer, and journalist, intermittently lived in England for his last three years, becoming a friend of Conrad's. For a discussion of the relationship between the two writers, see Elsa Nettels, 'Conrad and Stephen Crane', *Conradiana*, 10 (1978), 267–83.

94.35   **"The Red Badge of Courage"** Crane's novel about the American Civil War, serialized in 1894, was published in book form in America in September 1895 and brought out in England by Heinemann in November 1895. Conrad discusses it at length in 'His War Book', *Last Essays*.

95.1   **"Open Boat"** The short story 'The Open Boat' (1897) was collected in *The Open Boat and Other Stories*, published in England by Heinemann in April 1898. 'The two stories are excellent. Of course *A Man and Some Others* is the best of the two but the boat thing interested me more'. Conrad to Edward Garnett, 5 December 1897 (*Letters*, I, 416).

95.5–6   **page . . . my writing** Crane, who had read and admired *The Nigger of the 'Narcissus'*, expressed a wish to meet its author.

95.24   **another** John Alexander Conrad (1906–82), the Conrads' second child.

95.35   **while] ED** the while S– Phrasing is sufficiently defective to suggest a typesetting error, 'the' straying in by way of compositorial anticipation or inattention, rather than a lapse in Conrad's idiom.

97.19   **gentleman** Robert Lynd (1879–1949), a critic of conservative tastes, had unfavourably reviewed Conrad's works, going so far in his review of *A Set of Six* of August 1908 as to call him a writer 'without either country or language'. See *CH*, pp. 210–12, and 'Introduction', pp. xxiii–xxiv.

97.28   **a vain shadow** 'For man walketh in a vain shadow, and disquieteth himself in vain': 'The Order for the Burial of the Dead', *Book of Common Prayer* (1853). Conrad was familiar with the service from burials at sea.

98.10   **writer . . . criticisms** See 89.17–18*n.*

98.22   **vile body** 'We look for the Saviour, the Lord Jesus Christ: Who shall change our vile body, that it may be fashioned like unto his glorious body' (Philippians, iii.20–21). Cf. 'We therefore commit his body to the deep, to be turned into corruption, looking for the resurrection of the body . . . through our Lord Jesus Christ; who at his coming shall change our vile body, that it may be like his glorious body': 'At the Burial of the Dead at Sea' from 'Forms of Prayer to Be Used at Sea', *Book of Common Prayer.*

98.29   **fifteen short summers** Conrad gives a round figure to his career, which began with the publication of *Almayer's Folly* in 1895, fourteen years earlier.

99.2   **undiscovered countries** 'But that the dread of something after death, / The undiscover'd country from whose bourn / No traveller returns, puzzles the will'. Shakespeare, *Hamlet*, III.i.78–80.

99.35–36   **sea appreciation** Formally, certificate of discharge from the British Merchant Service. Several of Conrad's are preserved in the Beinecke Rare Book and Manuscript Library, Yale University.

100.16   **some dozen** Given that Conrad as the *Otago*'s master did not testify to his own service, eleven. On his sea career, see *The Mirror of the Sea* and Jerry Allen's *The Sea Years of Joseph Conrad* (1965).

100.22   **Mussulman** Derived from Persian, this form for Moslem or Muslim, now archaic, was already rare at the time of writing.

101.3   **London County Council** Created in 1889 by the Local Government Act of 1888, which made London and its boroughs a separate county, the council was the first city-wide form of general local government in England. It was responsible for the management of roads, bridges, and drains, public safety and education, and, like other county councils, for general business.

101.6–7   **certain short story** 'Karain: A Memory', published in Henry-Durand Davray's translation in the 15 November and 1 December 1906 issues of the *Mercure de France.*

101.8–9   **Gustave Kahn . . . Gil Blas** A French symbolist poet, critic, and editor, Kahn (1859–1936) mentions Conrad in his review of a French translation of George Moore's *Esther Waters*, 'Un réaliste anglais: George Moore', as follows: 'Nous sommes anglophiles littéralement. Kipling et Wells nous sont familiers. Thomas Hardy nous est connu. *Le Mercure de France* révélait, il y a quelques semaines, un puissant visionnaire, Conrad' [We are anglophiles, literally speaking. Kipling and Wells are familiar to us. Thomas Hardy is a known quantity. A few weeks ago, the *Mercure de France* revealed a powerful visionary to us – Conrad] (*Gil Blas*, 24 February 1907, p. 1). Kahn was referring to Davray's translation of 'Karain' (see 101.6–7*n*). A daily, *Gil Blas* (1879–1914) boasted prominent intellectuals and writers among its contributors, including, for instance, Guy de Maupassant. Conrad had come across the comment whilst sojourning in Montpellier; see Conrad to Pinker, 26 February 1907 (*Letters*, III, 413).

101.10 *un puissant rêveur* A powerful dreamer (French). Kahn had, in fact, used the expression 'un puissant visionnaire' [a powerful visionary] (see 101.8–9*n*).

101.19 **verity . . . wine** An allusion to the Latin tag 'In vino veritas' [In wine there is truth].

101.28 **sea-sobriety** Late-Victorian certificates of discharge required a captain to indicate whether a seaman had been of 'sober' character during his service.

101.29 **sign-manual** A technical and legal term for a signature.

101.32–33 **Marine Department . . . Board of Trade** A committee of the Privy Council, the Board functioned as a government department charged with regulating commerce. Its Marine Department oversaw shipping.

101.34–35 **first Merchant Shipping Act** The Merchant Shipping Act, 1854 (17 & 18 Vict. c. 104) formally set out the duties of those engaged in commercial shipping.

101.39 **advocate of temperance** The temperance movement, which championed abstinence from alcoholic drink, had both a religious and secular character, addressing chronic alcoholism particularly among the working-classes. During Conrad's years at sea proselytizing was strong in both the Navy and the Merchant Service, and special efforts were made to get seamen to 'sign the pledge' promising total abstinence. The Naval Temperance Society (Royal as of 1892) was founded as early as 1783.

102.5–6 **The first** Captain James Rankin, who examined Conrad for his certificate as second mate on 28 May 1880. Conrad drew on his examinations for the opening of *Chance*.

102.27 **hired** A Polonism, from 'wynajmowac', idiomatic English requiring 'rented'.

103.10 **ordeal . . . again** Conrad's examination for first mate on 17 November 1884 resulted in failure, but he passed on a second attempt on 3 December 1884. His examiner both times was Captain Peter Thompson (1836–1918). For a detailed discussion of Conrad's examinations and his two failures, unmentioned here, see Hans van Marle, 'Plucked and Passed on Tower Hill: Conrad's Examination Ordeals', *Conradiana*, 8 (1976), 99–109.

103.20–21 **Giuliano . . . de Medici** In fact, the statue of Lorenzo de Medici, Il Magnifico (1440–92), Duke of Urbino, ruler of Florence, and patron of the arts. Lorenzo is portrayed seated, dressed in Roman military garb, and head on hand in a pensive pose. The tomb of his younger brother Giuliano (d. 1478), Duke of Nemours, is opposite his, the figure likewise seated and in Roman military garb, but the hands, reposing on the lap, hold a mace, and the features lack pensive traits. Commissioned by the Medici Pope Leo X in 1520 and constructed 1526–31, Michelangelo's famous tomb is in the Sagrestia Nuova of the Basilica of San Lorenzo, Florence.

103.40 **weather's thick** The phrasing is influenced by the Polish 'geesto' (see 40.2–3*n*), idiomatic English requiring 'heavy weather', though if visibility alone is at issue 'thick' could denote poor visibility, as in the *OED*'s citation of Queen Victoria: 'a very dull, dark, thick morning'.

104.10 **the *Flying Dutchman*** A legendary ship, manned by ghosts and doomed never to cease roaming the seas until her captain finds the love of a faithful woman. The story is perhaps mostly widely known through Richard Wagner's 1843 opera *Der fliegende Holländer*. Captain Frederick Marryat, whom Conrad read, also uses it in *The Phantom Ship* (1838–9).

104.29 **infernal** A euphemism for 'damned'.

105.12–13 **examined for Master** Conrad failed at his first attempt on 28 July 1886, but was successful on his second on 29 October 1886.

105.17 **charter-parties** Deeds made between owners and merchants for hiring ships and delivering cargo.

105.21 **jury-rudder** A makeshift rudder set up to replace one that has been broken or lost.

105.33 **into steam – not really** Conrad served in steam only for brief periods: as first officer in the *Vidar*, as temporary captain of the *Roi des Belges*, and as second mate in the *Adowa*. See 'Chronology'.

105.35–36 **Crimean War** The war, 1854–6, between Russia and Turkey, engaged the latter's allies – England, France, and Sardinia.

105.37 **wire rigging** Wires, instead of ropes, used to support the masts and to manipulate yards and sails.

106.1 **Mutiny year** Begun in 1857, the Sepoy Mutiny against British rule in India was repressed in 1858. Started by Indian troops in the service of the British East India Company, the widespread revolt led to the transfer of government from the Company to the Crown.

106.2–3 **Gulf of Bengal** The sea forming the north-eastern part of the Indian Ocean, now more often referred to as the Bay of Bengal.

106.28–29 **native place . . . British seaman** As a Russian subject and the son of political dissidents who had been sentenced to exile, Conrad's options for a career at sea were problematic (see 108.22–23*n*).

106.33 **Mediterranean . . . West Indies** In the Mediterranean, Conrad sailed in small craft near Marseilles, and possibly in the British steamer *Mavis* in 1878 to the Crimea (see Najder, pp. 54–5). He sailed in French vessels to the French West Indies during 1874–7. For a discussion of the latter, see Hans van Marle, 'Lawful and Lawless: Young Korzeniowski's Adventures in the Caribbean', *L'Époque Conradienne* (1991), 91–113.

107.11 **his name** Andrzej Komorowski. A peasant, he had left the Congress Kingdom of Poland to escape military service in 1880 or 1881. He provided Conrad with the link to Józef Spiridion, with whom he became friendly in Cardiff.

107.36 **Hill of many beheadings** Executions on Tower Hill were public events, but some royal and high-ranking traitors were executed in private. Decapitation by an axe was reserved to the aristocracy and gentry, some 120 persons having so met their deaths in or near the Tower of London during the mediæval and Renaissance periods.

108.22–23 **no difficulty . . . Pola** As a Russian subject until 1886, Conrad would have found admission to the Austro-Hungarian Empire's naval academy difficult at best. The ancient Roman port town on the Adriatic (present-day Pula, Croatia) was the Empire's principal harbour and home to its naval arsenal from 1866 to 1918.

108.37 **Solary** Jean-Baptiste Solari was a friend of Paris-born Viktor-Jean-Adam Chodźko, a sailor of Polish descent living in Toulon, who was charged with looking after the young Conrad in Marseilles.

108.38–40 *le jeune homme . . . ce métier de chien* The young man; that beastly profession (literally, 'a dog's business') (French).

109.39–40 **Planier lighthouse** Constructed in 1829 on the rocky islet of Planier, about 8 miles (12.87 km) south-west of the Vieux Port, the lighthouse was during Conrad's time being replaced by a new one, construction beginning in 1875.

110.2–3 *le petit . . . Baptistin* Baptistin's chum (French). Conrad's translation 'little friend' is, perhaps intentionally, overly literal.

110.9 **Château d'If** A rocky islet, with a castle, at the entrance to the port of Marseilles. The castle, which housed political prisoners, is the scene of Alexandre Dumas' famous swashbuckler *The Count of Monte Cristo* (1845–6).

110.17 *bouillabaisse* A traditional Provençal seafood soup.

110.23 **Madame Delestang** Marguerite-Thérèse (née Solari, b. 1820) wife of César Delestang and a cousin of Baptistin Solari (108.37n). Her husband (b. 1794) and her son, Jean-Baptiste (b. 1848), managed the shipping firm Delestang et Fils (established *ca.* 1850) then located at 3 rue Arcole, near the Vieux Port and close to Conrad's lodgings in rue Sainte (see Map 4). Conrad sailed to the French Antilles for the firm.

110.25 **Prado** That is, the Promenade du Prado, a fashionable and very long tree-lined thoroughfare with elegant houses originating at Place Castellane. See Map 4.

110.27–28 **Lady Dedlock . . . "Bleak House"** The frigidly beautiful Lady Dedlock in Charles Dickens' novel *Bleak House* (1853) has a hidden past in the form of an illegitimate daughter.

110.32 **read . . . in Polish** A Polish translation of *Bleak House* as *Pustkowie* was published in Warsaw in 1856.

110.35 **belle** Beautiful (French).

111.1 *haute bourgeoisie* Upper middle-class (French).

111.3 **Royalist** A supporter of the restoration of the French Bourbons, the Bonaparte dynasty having fallen with Napoleon III's capture at Sedan in 1870. Strong throughout Conrad's Marseilles years, monarchist sentiment continued to enjoy some support in the National Assembly until the beginning of the twentieth century.

111.5 **Henri Quatre** King of France 1589–1610, the first Bourbon monarch, brought peace and prosperity to France after the wars of religion.

111.7 **écus** Silver coins in use during the seventeenth and eighteenth centuries.

111.8 **Louis Quatorze** Louis XIV (1638–1715) was King of France from 1643 to 1715 and her greatest autocratic monarch.

111.10 **Colbert** Jean-Baptiste Colbert (1619–83), Louis XIV's Minister of Finance. A great administrator, he also modernized the French Navy.

111.25 *Venez . . . nous* Come along, then, for a ride with us (French).

111.26 *C'est . . . homme* That's it. Climb up now, young man (French).

112.2–3 *Il faut . . . vie* Conrad translates the sentence a few lines later: 'one must . . . life'.

113.21 **Vieux Port** The oldest part of Marseilles, and its port from the seventh century BC until the mid nineteenth century. See Map 4.

113.23 **the Fort** Part of the extensive military fortifications protecting the entrance by sea, Fort Grasse-Till (or Fort Saint-Jean), built in 1668 by order of Louis XIV, was contiguous to the Bassin de la Joliette and the Vieux Port.

113.25 **December** That of 1874 (see 19.16*n*).

114.7 **Joliette** The Bassin de la Joliette had become the main port of Marseilles in the mid nineteenth century.

114.22 *Coquin de sort* A mild oath particular to the South of France; in context the meaning is 'A damned dog's life, this'.

114.24 *patron* Chief, boss.

114.28 *Hé . . . va?* I say, friend, how are things?

114.31–33 **southern . . . man of the north** Conrad delineates northern and southern French temperaments in 'The Duel'.

115.1 *Larguez* Let go.

115.5 *avant-port* The fore-port.

115.37 **stern-sheets** The area of a boat between the stern and the after rowing seats.

116.22–23 **Toulon . . . Algeria . . . 1830** Toulon had served as France's main naval base for centuries. France's invasion of Algeria, begun in mid-June 1830, was preceded by a three-year naval blockade. Formal annexation as a colony occurred in 1834.

116.25–26 *Équipages de ligne* Naval crew (French). The button also features an anchor.

116.27 **last . . . French Bourbons** The last reigning French Bourbon, Charles X (1757–1836), abdicated in 1830. The French line of the Royal House of Bourbon became extinct in 1883 with the death of Henri V, Count of Chambord, titular King of France and Navarre.

116.30–35 **Trafalgar . . . Elba** The Battle of Trafalgar, won by Great Britain, occurred in October 1805. Napoleon returned from exile on Elba in March 1814 for a period known as the Hundred Days (55.15*n*).

116.37   **Fréjus and Antibes** Ancient port towns on the French Riviera.

117.6   **discovered** In the sense of 'perceived' or 'saw', a Gallicism from 'découvrir'.

117.36   *Hé, l'Ancien* Hey, old fellow (French).

118.11   **break a crust** A literal translation of the French 'casser une croûte' (to break bread).

118.30   **Notre Dame de la Garde** Dominating the city and the Vieux Port, the basilica in Roman-Byzantine style is situated atop La Garde, the steep hill from which it takes its name. Principal construction was in 1853–7, with some work continuing until 1899. See Map 4.

119.16   *James Westoll* The *James Mason*, a steamer that entered Marseilles on 10 December 1874, is the ship's only plausible model. James Westoll, a Scottish shipowner of the mid-1880s, was active after Conrad's time in Marseilles. See Hans van Marle, 'An Ambassador of Conrad's Future: The *James Mason* in Marseilles, 1874', *L'Époque Conradienne*, 14 (1988), 63–7.

120.13   **W. W. Jacobs . . . barges** William Wymark Jacobs (1863–1943), a popular English short-story writer, was known for his sea tales. Conrad read Jacobs to his children. There may be a specific allusion to *Lady of the Barge* (1902). Jacobs was only slightly younger than Conrad himself.

120.35   **lighthouse** The one at the entrance to the modern port, the Bassin de la Joliette; another stood opposite, on the cliffs near military fortifications. See Map 4.

121.1   **Red Ensign** Originally the ensign of the English fleet's senior squadron, the ensign of the British Merchant Service from 1864. It features the Union Jack in its upper left corner against, as its name indicates, a red background.

Joseph Conrad: A Genealogical Table

The Korzeniowski family

Stanisław Korzeniowski m. Helena Choińska

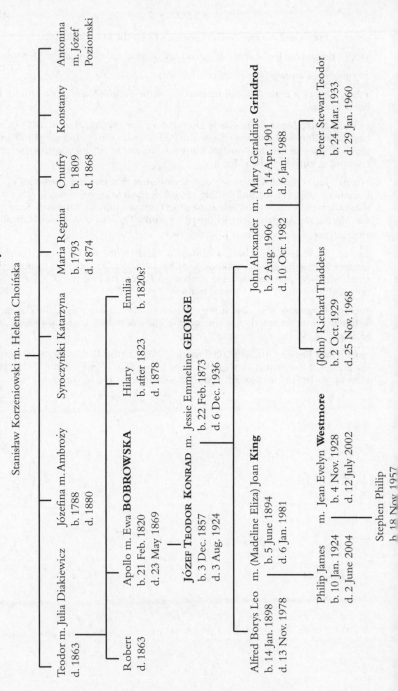

Teodor m. Julia Diakiewicz
d. 1863

Józefina m. Ambroży
b. 1788
d. 1880

Syroczyński Katarzyna

Maria Regina
b. 1793
d. 1874

Onufry
b. 1809
d. 1868

Konstanty

Antonina
m. Józef
Poziomski

Robert
d. 1863

Apollo m. Ewa **BOBROWSKA**
b. 21 Feb. 1820
d. 23 May 1869

Hilary
b. after 1823
d. 1878

Emilia
b. 1820s?

JÓZEF TEODOR KONRAD m. Jessie Emmeline **GEORGE**
b. 3 Dec. 1857   b. 22 Feb. 1873
d. 3 Aug. 1924   d. 6 Dec. 1936

Alfred Borys Leo   m. (Madeline Eliza) Joan **King**
b. 14 Jan. 1898   b. 5 June 1894
d. 13 Nov. 1978   d. 6 Jan. 1981

John Alexander   m.   Mary Geraldine **Grindrod**
b. 2 Aug. 1906   b. 14 Apr. 1901
d. 10 Oct. 1982   d. 6 Jan. 1988

(John) Richard Thaddeus
b. 2 Oct. 1929
d. 25 Nov. 1968

Peter Stewart Teodor
b. 24 Mar. 1933
d. 29 Jan. 1960

Philip James   m. Jean Evelyn **Westmore**
b. 10 Jan. 1924   b. 4 Nov. 1928
d. 2 June 2004   d. 12 July 2002

Stephen Philip
b. 18 Nov. 1957

The Bobrowski family

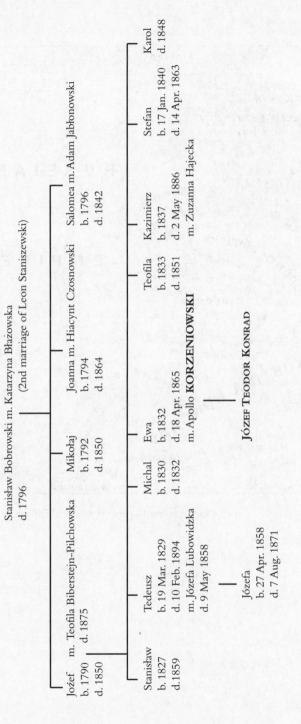

Stanisław Bobrowski m. Katarzyna Błazowska
d. 1796
(2nd marriage of Leon Staniszewski)

Józef   m. Teofila Biberstejn–Pilchowska   Mikołaj   Joanna m. Hiacynt Czosnowski   Salomea m. Adam Jabłonowski
b. 1790   d. 1875   b. 1792   b. 1794   b. 1796
d. 1850   d. 1850   d. 1864   d. 1842

Stanisław   Tedeusz   Michał   Ewa   Teofila   Kazimierz   Stefan   Karol
b. 1827   b. 19 Mar. 1829   b. 1830   b. 1832   b. 1833   b. 1837   b. 17 Jan. 1840   d. 1848
d.1859   d. 10 Feb. 1894   d. 1832   d. 18 Apr. 1865   d. 1851   d. 2 May 1886 d. 14 Apr. 1863
             m. Józefa Lubowidzka   m. Apollo **KORZENIOWSKI**   m. Zuzanna Hajecka
             d. 9 May 1858

             Józefa   **JÓZEF TEODOR KONRAD**
             b. 27 Apr. 1858
             d. 7 Aug. 1871

[1] Late nineteenth-century Eastern Europe

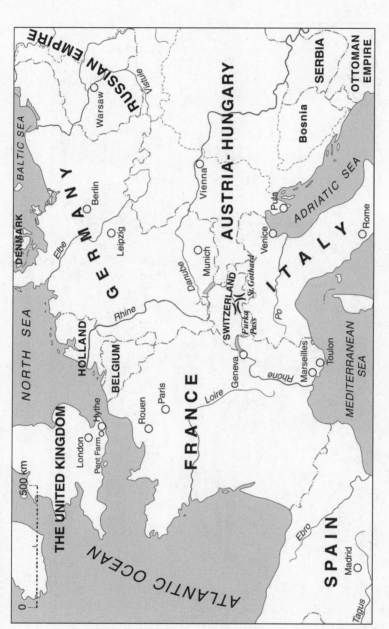

[2] Late nineteenth-century Western Europe

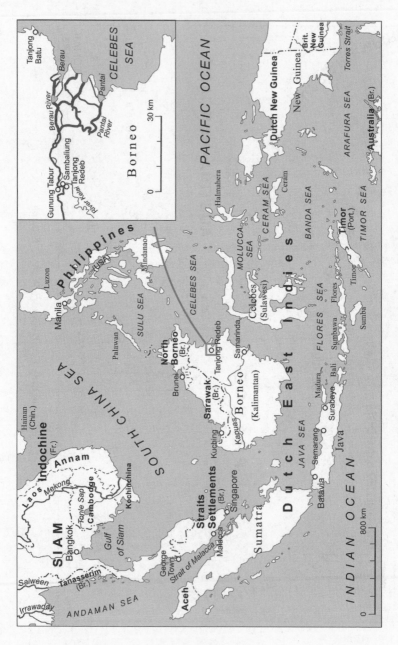

[3] South East Asia and the Berau region in the 1870s

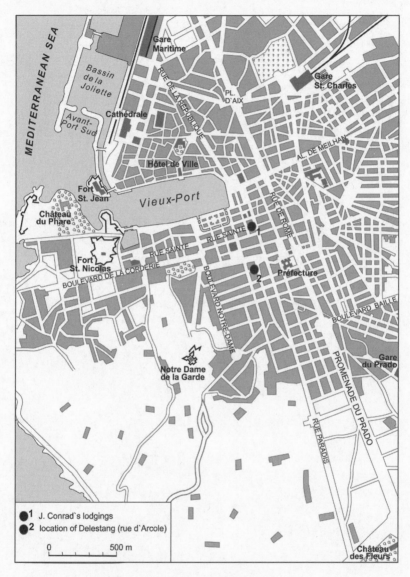

MEDITERRANEAN SEA

Bassin
de la
Joliette

Avant-
Port Sud

Gare
Maritime

RUE DE LA REPUBLIQUE

PL.
D'AIX

Gare
St. Charles

Cathédrale

AL. DE MEILHAN

Hôtel de Ville

Fort
St. Jean

Vieux-Port

Château
du Phare

RUE SAINTE

RUE SAINTE

RUE DE ROME

● 1

Fort
St. Nicolas

BOULEVARD DE LA CORDERIE

BOULEVARD NOTRE-DAME

● 2

Préfecture

BOULEVARD BAILLE

Gare
du Prado

Notre Dame
de la Garde

PROMENADE DU PRADO

RUE PARADIS

●1 J. Conrad's lodgings
●2 location of Delestang (rue d'Arcole)

0   500 m

Château
des Fleurs

[4] Marseilles in the 1870s